BASKETBALL

THE LEGENDS AND THE GAME

BASKETBALL

THE LEGENDS AND THE GAME

VINCENT M. MALLOZZI

FIREFLY BOOKS

A FIREFLY BOOK

First published in Canada in 1998 by
Firefly Books Ltd
3680 Victoria Park Avenue
Willowdale, Ontario, Canada
M2H 3K1

First published in the United States in 1998 by
Firefly Books (U.S.) Inc.
P. O. Box 1338, Ellicott Station
Buffalo, New York, USA
14205

Copyright © 1998 Quintet Publishing Limited.
All rights reserved. No part of this publication may be
reproduced, stored in a retrieval system or transmitted
in any form or by any means, electronic, mechanical,
photocopying, recording or otherwise, without the
permission of the copyright holder.

Cataloguing in Publication Data

Mallozzi, Vincent M
    Basketball : the legends and the game

ISBN 1-55209-247-X

1. Basketball. 2. Basketball players. I Title

GV885.M344 1998   796.323   C98-930265-2

This book was designed and produced by
Quintet Publishing Limited
6 Blundell Street
London N7 9BH

Creative Director: Richard Dewing
Art Director: Silke Braun
Designer: Rod Teasdale
Project Editors: Sally Green, Steve Edgell
Editor: Maggie McCormick

Typeset in Great Britain by
Central Southern Typesetters, Eastbourne
Manufactured in Singapore by Eray Scan Pte Ltd
Printed in China by Leefung-Asco Printers Trading Limited

DEDICATION

This book is dedicated to the people I love, those who make my life a better place each

and every single day: my beautiful wife, Cathy, whose smile grew wider as the hours working on this

book grew longer, who patiently waited as I put our young marriage on hold, writing about

basketball stars she has never heard of; my mom and dad and the rest of the Mallozzi and Ammendolia

clans, who always remind me that family comes first; Dr. Frank Brady, writer, teacher and

friend; all the guys from the old neighborhood, especially those who still think I'm good enough to

hoop with; and last but certainly not least, my friend Larry Elting, who won the game of life,

and is a role model to any kid from a tough corner of the universe who has

ever dribbled a basketball.

ACKNOWLEDGEMENTS

One hundred thousand words in ten weeks.

"I didn't even know you knew one hundred thousand words," said New York Times colleague, Grant Glickson.

"I cheated," was my response. "I used some of the words twice."

That was one of the longer conversations I had while I was writing this book. In fact, visiting the basketball lives of nearly three hundred professional basketball stars from Kareem Abdul-Jabbar to Max Zaslofsky, left little time for me to live my own life. Along the way, phone calls went unanswered, chores went undone, and my lovely wife, Cathy, kept asking over and over again, "are you paying attention to me, or what?" For sure, I had drifted into the basketball zone, but with each passing sentence, each passing day, I was having a ball. After all the research and all the writing, after studying so many stars from different eras, marquee players like Nat Holman, George Gervin and Shaquille O'Neal, I felt as though I had earned a degree in hoopology, and graduated with highest honors.

I'd like to thank a number of people for making this body of work possible. First and foremost, I'd like to thank Elena Gustines, the Most Valuable Player on my research team who always found the time to help out, and often began each day by asking "you need me for anything today?"

In the same breath, I don't known what I would have done without the invaluable material and expert advice I received from NBA Hall-of-Famer Sam Goldaper, a former *New York Times* sportswriter who opened up his basketball vault and let me take a good, long peek inside. *New York Times* copy editor and friend, Richard Goldstein, who gave this book a truly professional read, should also trot out to center-court and take a bow.

Along the way, I got major assists from Ray Corio, who had a joke for every nugget of information he offered, and Joe Brescia, an ABA aficionado who begged me to squeeze Wali Jones between these covers (sorry Joe, sorry Wali.) Thanks also to my brother, Frank Mallozzi, my brother-in-law, Anthony Artuso, Carl Nelson, Kathy Winiarski (my eternal classmate), Stephen Jesselli, Doug Scancarella, Noam Cohen, Bedel Saget, Johnson Stevens, George Bretherton, Orlando Rondon, Kenny Garcia, Jo Colitto, Chuck Slater and Joe Hammond, the greatest basketball player ever to come out of New York City.

Of course, I have the deepest appreciation for Neil Amdur, Sports Editor at *The New York Times*, and Dennis Page, publisher of *Slam* magazine, who always help my star shine a little bit brighter.

Thanks lots,
Vinny

CONTENTS

8
INTRODUCTION

10-349
A–Z DIRECTORY OF THE GREATEST PRO BASKETBALL PLAYERS

SPECIAL FEATURES

16 LONG BEFORE RUSSELL AND BIRD: THE ORIGINAL CELTICS

30 NAT HOLMAN: THE GAME'S FIRST TRUE SUPERSTAR

44 NED IRISH: SALESMAN

58 NEW YORK–TORONTO: THE FIRST GAME

74 TICK, TICK, TICK . . . THE LONGEST GAME EVER PLAYED

88 FATHER TIME: HOW DANNY BIASONE SAVED THE NBA

102 CLASH OF THE TITANS: THE FIRST CHAMBERLAIN-RUSSELL MEETING

118 WILT CHAMBERLAIN'S 100-POINT GAME

132 BEFORE JORDAN, BAYLOR WAS THE STAR OF POST-SEASON THEATER

148 CAZZIE MEETS BILL

162 WILLIS REED: LIMPING INTO HISTORY

178 JUST WIN, BABY: THE LOS ANGELES LAKERS' 33-GAME WINNING STREAK

192 OLYMPIC SHOCK

208 REMEMBERING THE ABA

220 DR J'S LONGEST OPERATION

234 CHAMPIONSHIP HOOPATHON

250 THE NBA'S GREATEST SCORING RACE

264 THE 1980 FINALS: A MAGICAL PERFORMANCE

278 THE ONE AND ONLY DREAM TEAM

292 BULLING THEIR WAY INTO HISTORY

306 STREET MOVES: NEW YORK'S PLAYGROUND LEGENDS

320 SPIDER AND WORM, TO (NICK)NAME JUST A FEW . . .

334 THAT'S ENTERTAINMENT

342 HARDWOOD HONCHOS: PRO BASKETBALL'S GREATEST COACHES

350 THE LANGUAGE OF BASKETBALL

352 THE PLAYERS

INTRODUCTION

On a wintry night in 1891, a young Y.M.C.A. instructor living in Springfield, Massachusetts, tinkered with ideas for an indoor sport.

Before the night was through, Dr. James Naismith nailed two peach baskets to a balcony railing, found a soccer ball, drew up sides—and gave birth to the game of basketball.

More than a century has passed since Dr. Naismith hung his baskets, but the object of the game, putting the round ball in the basket, remains the same. The nature of the game, however, has changed dramatically.

Basketball, a sport now played in over 170 countries and televised around the globe, has grown from humble beginnings to one of the most entertaining and popular pastimes of the twentieth century. Today's players, who benefit from satellite dishes, multimillion dollar contracts and endorsement deals, are much taller in size and stature—but not necessarily more talented—than their roundball ancestors.

From the first professional basketball league, the National League, which sprouted in 1898, to the unification of the National Basketball League and the Basketball Association of America, which merged in 1949 to become the National Basketball Association, to rival leagues like the American Basketball Association, the game has fielded its share of superstars in every era.

Barney Sedran, a 5-4 guard, led the Carbondale, PA, team to 35 consecutive victories and the Tri-County League title in the 1914–15 season; Honey Russell led the Cleveland Rosenblums to an American Basketball League title in the 1925–26 season; Charles "Tarzan" Cooper led the all-black Harlem Rens of New York City in the 1930s; Nat Holman and Joe Lapchick were the stars of the Original Celtics of the 1920s and 1930s, whose fancy ball handling and teamwork took the game to a new level of entertainment; George Mikan, the 6-foot-10-inch giant from Depaul University who was signed by the Chicago Gears before

moving on to great success with the Minneapolis Lakers, was voted the greatest player of the first half century.

The great Boston Celtics playmaker Bob Cousy, and Bob Pettit, a 6-foot-9-inch sharpshooter and rebounder who dazzled for the old Milwaukee Hawks, were among the galaxy of stars that sparkled in the 1950s; Oscar Robertson and Jerry West, a pair of guards who played together on the 1960 U.S. Olympic team, owned the 1960s; Julius Erving, Kareem Abdul-Jabbar, Moses Malone, and Bill Walton were the centers of attention in the 1970s; Magic Johnson, Larry Bird, and Michael Jordan helped the game soar to new heights in the 1980s, setting the stage for superheroes of the 1990s like Shaquille O'Neal, Shawn Kemp, Damon Stoudamire, and Allen Iverson.

In today's electronically connected world, Jordan, who defies gravity like no player in history, stands alone as the most recognizable figure in basketball, and in all of sports. But each and every one of the current twenty-nine NBA franchises has its own star, or two, or three, to cheer for. And in every city where professional basketball was ever played, the memories of great athletes, eye-opening plays, fantastic finishes, and historic moments live on forever.

What follows is a list of two hundred and ninety-two of the best basketball players in history—plus newcomers with star potential—so far up and through the 1996–97 season complete with individual fact files that include statistics and career highlights. The skills and achievements of these players, and many more, will be debated for years in living rooms, classrooms, barrooms, and gymnasiums all over the world.

Vincent M. Mallozzi

BELOW LEFT: ROBERT PARRISH GOES UP FOR A JUMPER AGAINST THE LOS ANGELES LAKERS IN THE 1987 NBA FINALS.

BELOW RIGHT: MICHAEL JORDAN IS THE MOST RECOGNIZABLE FIGURE IN ALL OF SPORTS.

KAREEM ABDUL-JABBAR

FACT FILE

Born: April 16, 1947
Height: 7' 2"
Length of NBA career:
1969–89
Major teams:
Milwaukee Bucks
Los Angeles Lakers
(joined 1975)
Records/Awards:
NBA Rookie of the Year
(1970)
NBA Championships (6)
NBA Most Valuable Player
(6)
NBA All-Star squad (19)
NBA All-Defensive first
team (10)
Hall of Fame (1995)

If greatness was measured in sheer statistics and longevity, then Kareem Abdul-Jabbar is easily the greatest player in the history of the NBA. Kareem, whose signature shot was his sweeping, towering sky hook that left opponents defenseless, racked up 44,149 points during his 20-year career, the most points scored by any player in history.

A product and prodigy of New York City basketball, the 7-foot-2-inch Kareem—then known to the world as Lew Alcindor—went from Power Memorial High School in Manhattan to UCLA in the 1960s, leading the Bruins to three consecutive NCAA championships.

After breaking into the NBA with the Milwaukee Bucks in the 1969–70 season, Kareem won the Rookie of the Year award and began building a legendary career which would include six NBA championships—five with the Los Angeles Lakers in the prime of his career—and a host of records which strongly suggest that he was the most dominant big-man ever to play the game.

A six-time NBA Most Valuable Player, Kareem, who played six seasons with Milwaukee before joining the Lakers in 1975, appeared in 1,815 NBA games, counting regular-season, playoff and All-Star games.

Among Kareem's fondest memories is the night he broke Wilt Chamberlain's career-scoring record of 31,419 points, and the 1985 championship series against the mighty Boston Celtics, which was won by the Lakers.

"The 1985 championship series against the Boston Celtics has to top them all," Kareem once said. "We beat the Celtics easily. You always remember important things like that. The victory brought the entire city of Los Angeles together. Boston had never lost a game in the championship round before on their home court."

In the record 18 seasons that he appeared in the playoffs, Kareem Abdul-Jabbar, who changed his name and converted to Islam in 1971, scored 5,762 points, an average of 24.3 points a game.

For all his offensive fireworks, Kareem was also a solid defensive player. He was an NBA All-Defensive first-team selection five times in his career, leading the league in blocked shots four times during this time. In a storybook professional career which ran from 1969–89, Kareem was selected to the All-Star squad 19 times. He was also selected to the NBA's 35th Anniversary All-Time Team in 1980, and in 1995, was selected to the Basketball Hall of Fame.

RIGHT: KAREEM ABDUL-JABBAR, WHO HAS SCORED MORE POINTS THAN ANY OTHER PLAYER IN NBA HISTORY, ABOUT TO LAUNCH ONE OF HIS LEGENDARY SKY HOOKS.

ALVAN ADAMS

Alvan Adams made a huge splash as a rookie with the Phoenix Suns in the 1975–76 season, helping the Suns scorch a path to the NBA finals, where they lost to the Boston Celtics four games to two. A high-post center with nifty moves around the basket, Adams put up dazzling numbers that season en route to winning the NBA Rookie of the Year award: 1,519 points, 512 rebounds, 450 assists, 121 steals and 116 shots blocked.

While Adams was never able to equal those statistical feats in any of his twelve other NBA seasons—all with Phoenix—he was talented enough to register double-digit scoring totals in all but two of his campaigns and finished with a 14.1 career scoring average.

He kept his scoring totals equally high in the playoffs, averaging double-figures in eight of nine post-seasons, and finishing with a 13.8 career playoff scoring average.

After spending three seasons at the University of Oklahoma in which he averaged 23.4 points in seventy-three games, Adams was not highly-touted when he was chosen by Phoenix as the fourth pick in the first-round of the 1975 draft.

However it wasn't long before he was turning heads on the court and in the seats, and paying handsome dividends to the Suns.

"I never felt that rookie season was an albatross that I carried around my whole career," Adams said upon his retirement in 1988. "But I remember thinking there very likely will never be anything like this again, with this much excitement."

FACT FILE

Born: July 19, 1954
Height: 6' 9"
Length of NBA career:
 1975–88
Major team:
 Phoenix Suns
Records/Awards:
 NBA Rookie of the Year
 (1976)

LEFT: ALVAN ADAMS' ROOKIE SEASON WAS A SMASHING SUCCESS.

MICHAEL ADAMS

FACT FILE

Born: January 19, 1963
Height: 5' 10"
Length of NBA career:
   1985–present
Major teams:
   Sacramento Kings
   Washington Bullets
      (joined 1986)
   Denver Nuggets
      (joined 1987)
   Washington Bullets
      (joined 1991)
   Charlotte Hornets
      (joined 1994)
Records/Awards:
   CBA Rookie of the Year
      (1986)
   NBA All-Star (1)

In NBA parlance, Michael Adams lives downtown. Adams, a 5-foot-10-inch sharp-shooter out of Boston College, seemed to have little chance of making it to the big show when he was drafted by Sacramento in the third round of the 1985 draft.

However, on the strength of his phenomenal three-point accuracy and fearless firing from long distance, the tiny Adams has been able to defy the long odds, and has been shooting down his opponents—and his detractors—for more than 11 seasons.

Adams, who has played for Sacramento, Washington (twice), Denver and most recently Charlotte in his NBA career, ranked as one of the league's all-time leaders in three-point field goals attempted (2,899) and three-point field goals made (972) heading into the 1996–97 season. He also holds the NBA record for the highest number of consecutive contests with at least one three-pointer made, bagging a trifecta in 79 straight games over the 1987–88 and 1988–89 seasons.

After playing just 18 games for Sacramento as a rookie, Adams was cut from the roster, and played the bulk of his freshman campaign with the Bay City Bombers of the Continental Basketball Association. That season, Adams earned CBA Rookie of the Year honors, setting the stage for his triumphant return to the NBA. Adams's finest NBA season was 1990–91, when he averaged 26.5 points per game for the Denver Nuggets.

The following season, the little player with the big heart averaged 18.1 points a game for the Nuggets, and was named an NBA All-Star for the first and only time in his career.

RIGHT: WHAT MICHAEL ADAMS LACKS IN HEIGHT, HE MAKES UP FOR WITH TREMENDOUS SHOOTING RANGE.

MARK AGUIRRE

One of the greatest small forwards in the history of the NBA, Mark Aguirre—a master at backing in against defenders, wheeling, and launching shots over their outstretched fingertips—burned up the cords in Dallas for eight-and-a-half seasons before he was traded to the Detroit Pistons, whom he helped win back-to-back NBA championships in 1989 and 1990.

Aguirre, a standout performer who averaged 24.5 points in three seasons at DePaul University, proved to be one of the missing pieces to Chuck Daly's Bad Boys regime.

While his best scoring seasons took place in Dallas—he averaged 29.5 points in 1983–84 and bagged no less than an average of 22.6 points per game for six straight seasons with the Mavericks—Aguirre's pure shooting skills perfectly complemented a team whose physical tactics not only infuriated and frustrated opponents, but prompted league officials to change some of the defensive rules in order to soften contact between players.

On February 15, 1989, Aguirre was traded by Dallas to Detroit for forward Adrian Dantley and a first-round draft choice. Just four months later, the move paid off for the Pistons, as Aguirre, averaging 18.9 points, helped lead Detroit to its first-ever NBA championship, a four-game sweep over Magic Johnson and the Los Angeles Lakers, who had defeated the Pistons in the championship series the year before.

The following season, Aguirre, averaging 14.1 points per game for the Bad Boys, was instrumental in helping Detroit defend its championship with a four-games-to-one victory over the Portland Trail Blazers.

FACT FILE

Born: December 10, 1959
Height: 6' 6"
Length of NBA career:
1981–1994
Major teams:
Dallas Mavericks
Detroit Pistons
(joined 1989)
LA Clippers
(joined 1993)
Records/Awards:
Naismith Award (1980)
Member of US Olympic
Team (1980)
NBA Championships (2)

LEFT: MARK AGUIRRE'S BACK-TO-THE-BASKET MASTERY HELPED DETROIT WIN BACK-TO-BACK CHAMPIONSHIPS.

DANNY AINGE

FACT FILE

Born: March 17, 1959
Height: 6′ 4″
Length of NBA career:
  1981–95
Major teams:
  Boston Celtics
  Sacramento Kings
      (joined 1989)
  Portland Trail Blazers
      (joined 1990)
  Phoenix Suns
      (joined 1992)
Records/Awards:
  Wooden Award winner
      (1981)
  NBA Championships (2)

Tough. Smart. Talented. Those are the qualities that can best be used to describe numerous players throughout the years who have helped the Boston Celtics build their storied tradition.

Danny Ainge was one of those players. Ainge, a fiery shooting guard who came to Beantown in 1981 after averaging 20.9 points in four stellar years at Brigham Young, was a pivotal role player on the 1984 and 1986 Celtic championships squads. Though he played in the shadows of Larry Bird, Kevin McHale, Robert Parish and Dennis Johnson, Ainge won over the Celtic faithful with a penchant for making clutch three-point baskets and a gutsy in-your-face attitude that constantly got under the skin of his opponents.

Don Nelson, former head coach of the Golden State Warriors, once called Ainge "a cheap-shot artist," and during a 1983 playoff series between Boston and Atlanta, the 6-foot-4-inch Ainge got into a brawl with Atlanta's 7-foot-1-inch center, Tree Rollins, who was eventually suspended and fined for biting the scrappy Celtic. "The tree bit me," Ainge said after that game. "He almost bit my finger off, man, all the way to the tendon."

Ainge, who played in 193 post-season games with Boston, Portland and Phoenix, holds the career playoff record for most three-point field goals made (172) and most three-point field goals attempted (433). His best scoring years came in 1988–89, when he averaged 17.5 points in a split-season with Boston and Sacramento, and the following season, when he poured in 17.9 points for Sacramento. He also enjoyed a brief career as a professional baseball player, playing parts of three seasons (1979–81) as an infielder with the Toronto Blue Jays.

RIGHT: TOUGH AS NAILS, DANNY AINGE HELPED LIGHT A FIRE UNDER SOME OF THE GREAT BOSTON CELTIC TEAMS.

Kenny Anderson

A product of New York City basketball, Kenny "The Kid" Anderson dribbled his way out of the Lefrak projects in Queens, NY, and into NBA stardom. In 1989, Anderson, one of the most ballyhooed schoolboy players ever, left Archbishop Molloy High School and enrolled at Georgia Tech as the top recruit in the United States.

He posted an average of 23 points in two spectacular seasons for the Yellowjackets, made himself eligible for the 1991 draft, and was selected as the second pick overall by the New Jersey Nets.

The 6-foot-1-inch point guard, now recognized as one of the top ball-handlers in the NBA, ran the show for four and a half seasons in New Jersey before he was traded midway through the 1995–96 campaign to the Charlotte Hornets. A free agent after last season, Anderson left Charlotte and signed with the Portland Trail Blazers.

Anderson, who has racked up 3,275 assists going into 1997–98 in his career, and left New Jersey as the all-time leader in that department, finished seventh in the league in 1995–96 by averaging 8.3 assists per game.

While he prides himself as an assist-man, the flashy lefthander also provides a solid scoring punch. In the 1993–94 season—the year in which Anderson was voted as a starter in his only All-Star appearance—he finished with a career-high 18.8 scoring average.

Entering the 1997–98 season, Kenny the Kid had posted healthy averages of 15.7 points, 7.7 assists, and 3.5 rebounds per game in six NBA seasons.

FACT FILE

Born: October 9, 1970
Height: 6′ 1″
Length of NBA career:
1991–present
Major teams:
New Jersey Nets
Charlotte Hornets
(joined 1996)
Portland Trail Blazers
(joined 1996)
Records/Awards:
NBA All-Star (1)

LEFT: KENNY ANDERSON DRIBBLED HIS WAY OUT OF POVERTY AND INTO NBA STARDOM.

LONG BEFORE RUSSELL AND BIRD: THE ORIGINAL CELTICS

In 1922, a New York promoter named Jim Furey organized a band of talented and undisciplined basketball players who had been peddling their hoop skills around the city on a pay-per-game basis—and turned them into the greatest basketball team on the planet.

Furey, working on this project with his brother, Tom, signed these players to the first individual contracts in the history of the sport. Several members of this group, including Pete Barry and Johnny Witte, had previously played for a team called the New York Celtics, which was organized in 1914 and represented a settlement house on the rough streets of Manhattan's West Side. Unable to use the name New York Celtics because of legal reasons, the Fureys called their talented vagabonds the Original Celtics.

In addition to Barry and Witte, the Original Celtics added the best talent money could buy. Dutch Dehnert was a phenomenal playmaker; Nat Holman, a tremendous ballhandler with an arsenal of electrifying moves; Joe Lapchick, in a class by himself as a jumper; and Johnny Beckman, a player blessed with overall basketball smarts. Other Original Celtics included Joe Tripp, Ernie Reich, Horse Haggerty, Davie Banks, Carl Husta, and Nat Hickey.

Before long, the Celtics became the most dominant team in the New York region, making a shambles of the Metropolitan League, the Eastern League, the American Basketball League, and any other competition they met on barnstorming tours around the country.

The Celtics, who averaged more than five victories in six games for the rest of the decade, were so good that the team was eventually forced to disband.

"The Celtics were at least twenty years ahead of their time," Lapchick would say years later. "In addition to the pivot play, they also introduced the switching defense. They were magnificent ballhandlers who played completely as a unit. The individual star was unknown, in fact, not even considered."

In 1930, Lapchick reorganized the team, but the Celtics found themselves earning less money than they earned in their heyday. With the strain of traveling, injuries, and plain old age adding to the unhappy equation, the team decided it was best to finally call it quits in 1935.

The Original Celtics faded into history, but their achievements and contributions to the evolution of the sport will never be forgotten.

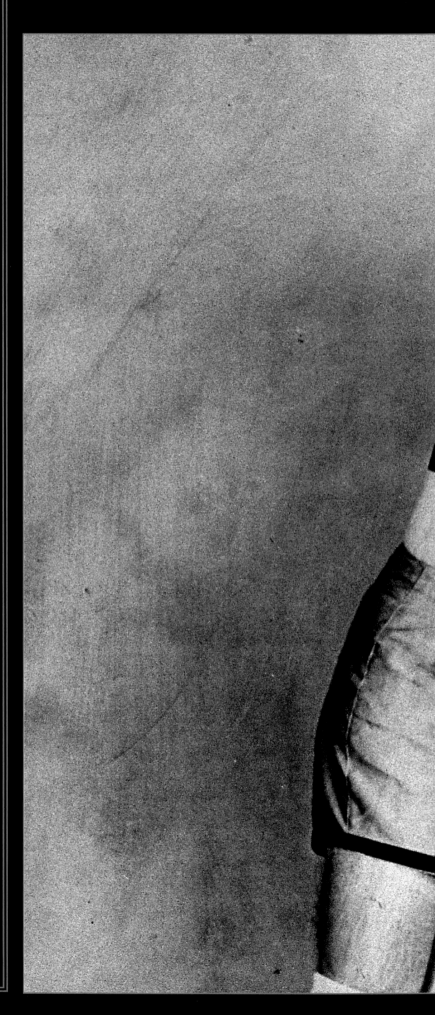

NICK ANDERSON

FACT FILE

Born: January 20, 1968
Height: 6' 6"
Length of NBA career:
   1989–present
Major team:
   Orlando Magic

Before the Orlando Magic ever played a minute of basketball, Nick Anderson was in their plans. Anderson, a 6-foot-6-inch shooting guard out of Illinois, was the first-ever college draft pick selected by the franchise in its inaugural NBA season of 1989.

Over the next seven years, Anderson became one fifth of the best starting unit in the league, teaming with Penny Hardaway, Dennis Scott, Horace Grant, and Shaquille O'Neal to form one of the most potent attacks in the game.

Anderson, an explosive leaper and long-distance threat who left Illinois after his junior season, enjoyed his best scoring seasons in 1991–92 and 1992–93, averaging 19.9 points per game in each of those campaigns.

In the 1994–95 season, Anderson averaged 16 points per game in helping the Magic to a regular-season record of 57–25, and a trip to the NBA Finals, where Orlando lost to the Houston Rockets. In that series, Anderson set a Finals single-game record for most three-point field goals attempted (12).

Four of Orlando's major team records belong to Anderson. He leads the club in points scored (9,059), most field goals made (3,479), most field goals attempted (7,582) and most steals (868).

Last season, Anderson averaged 12 points, 4.8 rebounds, and 2.9 assists per game, shooting 35 percent from three-point range, connecting on 143 of 405 long-distance attempts.

RIGHT: NICK ANDERSON, THE FIRST-EVER DRAFT PICK OF THE ORLANDO MAGIC, IS STILL AN INTEGRAL PART OF THE TEAM.

NATE "TINY" ARCHIBALD

If there was an opening, the slightest opening, on a path to the basket, Nate "Tiny" Archibald would usually find it.

Archibald, the 6-foot-1-inch lightning-quick point guard who grew up in New York City, was arguably a better penetrator to the hoop in heavy traffic than any player who ever stepped onto an NBA court.

After a one-year stint with Arizona Western and three years at Texas-El Paso, Archibald broke into the NBA in 1970 with the Cincinnati Royals. It wasn't long before he was electrifying crowds with his ball-handling ability and fearless dashes to the hoop, often colliding with much bigger defenders, often leaving them red-faced when he slithered between them for a twisting, turning layup and a trip to the free-throw line.

In 1972–73, as a member of the Sacramento Kings, Archibald became the only player in NBA history to lead the league in scoring average (34.0) and assists (11.4) in the same season.

After establishing himself as a true all-star on several poor teams, Archibald was traded in 1978 by the San Diego Clippers—a franchise which had moved from Buffalo that year—to the Boston Celtics, and his career took flight.

In 1981, Archibald teamed up with legendary Celtics Larry Bird, Robert Parish and Kevin McHale to capture the NBA championship, marked by a four-games-to-two victory over the Houston Rockets. It was Tiny who led Boston's fast-break attack and helped the fabled franchise return to glory.

A five-time NBA All-Star—he was the Most Valuable Player of the 1981 All-Star contest—Archibald finished his stellar 14-year career with a 18.8 points-per-game average, 6,476 assists, and 719 steals.

FACT FILE

Born: April 18, 1948
Height: 6' 1"
Length of NBA career:
  1970–1984
Major teams:
  Cincinnati
  Kansas City/Omaha
    (joined 1972)
  Kansas City
    (joined 1975)
  New York Nets
    (joined 1976)
  Buffalo
    (joined 1977)
  Boston
    (joined 1978)
  Milwaukee
    (joined 1983)
Records/Awards:
  NBA Championship (1)
  NBA All-Star Game (5)
  Hall of Fame (1990)

LEFT: IF THERE WAS THE TINIEST OPENING TO THE BASKET, NATE "TINY" ARCHIBALD WOULD USUALLY FIND IT.

PAUL ARIZIN

FACT FILE

Born: April 9, 1928
Height: 6′ 4″
Length of NBA career:
  1950–1962
Major team:
  Philadelphia
Records/Awards:
  NBA Championship (1)
  NBA All-Star Game (10)
  Hall of Fame (1970)

One of the great jumpshooters of the 1950s and early 1960s was Paul Arizin, a 6-foot-4-inch swingman from Villanova—he led the NCAA in scoring with 25.3 points per game in 1950 and was named College Player of the Year—who burst onto the NBA scene with the Philadelphia Warriors in 1950.

After averaging 20 points per game in three seasons at Villanova, Arizin, who was born in Philadelphia, remained home to net 17.2 points per game and lead the Warriors to a 40–26 record and the Eastern Division Crown. The following season, "Pitchin" Paul, as Arizin was called, copped the league's scoring title with a sizzling 25.4 average, wresting the scoring crown from perennial champion George Mikan, the 6-foot-10-inch center from Minneapolis.

A call from the military forced Arizin to miss the next two seasons, but he returned in the 1954–55 campaign to average 21 points per game. The next season, Arizin teamed with super-scoring teammate Neil Johnston, a 6ft 8in center, to lead Philadelphia to a four-games-to-one championship victory over the Fort Wayne Pistons.

Arizin, who was voted to the NBA's 25th Anniversary All-Time Team, played his entire 12-year NBA career with Philadelphia, averaging 22.8 points per game over that span.

From 1962–65, Arizin averaged 25 points a game playing for the Eastern Basketball League—an early-day Continental Basketball Association—and was named the EBL's Most Valuable Player in 1963.

RIGHT: A PHILLY FAVORITE, PAUL ARIZIN SPENT HIS ENTIRE CAREER IN THE CITY OF BROTHERLY LOVE.

B. J. ARMSTRONG

A baby-faced killer on the basketball court, point guard B.J. Armstrong was a key member of the Chicago Bulls teams that won three straight championships from 1991–93.

While Michael Jordan and Scottie Pippen got all the headlines during the Bulls' three peak glory years, it was Armstrong who was often asked to do the little things that didn't always show up in the boxscores. The 6-foot-2-inch playmaker was usually relied upon to bring the ball upcourt under intense pressure, shut down an opponent on defense, or hit an open shot when one of his superstar teammates was being double-teamed. More often than not, Armstrong responded to those challenges, and his clutch shooting helped keep defenses honest, and allowed Jordan and Pippen to do some serious one-on-one damage.

Armstrong, who averaged 13.1 points in four seasons at Iowa, made his only NBA All-Star appearance in 1994, when he averaged a career-high 14.8 points per game, racked up 323 assists and 80 steals.

The season before, he led the league with a .453 three-point field goal percentage, bagging 63 of 139 attempts from behind the arc.

After six solid seasons in Chicago, Armstrong was lost to the Bulls when he was selected by Toronto in the 1995 NBA Expansion Draft. He never played for Toronto, however, as he was traded before the start of the season to Golden State.

Armstrong played in all 82 games for the Warriors in 1995–96, averaging 12.3 points per contest. Last season he played in just 49 games due to injury, averaging 7.9 points per game.

FACT FILE

Born: September 9, 1967
Height: 6′ 2″
Length of NBA career:
    1989–present
Major teams:
    Chicago Bulls
    Golden State Warriors
        (joined 1995)
Records/Awards:
    NBA All-Star Game (1)
    NBA Championships (3)

LEFT: B.J. ARMSTRONG WAS A BABY-FACED KILLER ON THREE STRAIGHT CHICAGO BULLS CHAMPIONSHIP TEAMS.

CHARLES BARKLEY

FACT FILE

Born: February 20, 1963
Height: 6′ 6″
Length of NBA career:
   1984–present
Major teams:
   Philadelphia
   Phoenix (joined 1992)
   Houston (joined 1997)
Records/Awards:
   NBA All-Star Game (11)
   Most Valuable Player
      (1993)
   Olympic Gold Medal
      (1992)

BELOW: THE ROUND MOUND
OF REBOUND, CHARLES
BARKLEY, JUST 6-FEET-6-
INCHES TALL, DOMINATES
POWER FORWARDS.

A power forward trapped in a small forward's body, Charles Barkley plays a lot taller, a lot stronger and a lot tougher than most any other player in the history of the NBA. The Round Mound of Rebound, as Barkley is called, led the league in rebounds per game (14.6) as a member of the Philadelphia 76ers in the 1986–87 season, a phenomenal achievement in an era when 7-foot centers are commonplace. That same year, in a game against the Knicks on March 4, Barkley established a single-season record for most offensive rebounds in one quarter (11), and most offensive rebounds in one half (13).

A member of the 1992 United States Olympic Dream Team, which won the gold medal and is considered by many to be the greatest basketball team ever assembled, Barkley has proven himself to be much more than just a rebounder. As a rookie in 1984–85, he averaged fourteen points a game, but in each of his 11 NBA seasons that followed, Barkley averaged no less than 20 points per game, reaching a career-high 28.3 with Philadelphia in 1988.

One month before winning his gold medal in 1992, Barkley, wanting badly to play for a contender, was traded to the Phoenix Suns.

Revitalized and focused, Sir Charles led the Suns' charge toward the NBA Finals. Though Phoenix lost the championship to Chicago four games to two, Barkley, who had racked up 25.6 points a game in the regular season and brought his heart, desire and winning attitude to a club that badly needed a boost, was named the league's Most Valuable Player.

Now 35 years old, the bald-headed, 252-pound Barkley has been bothered by a bad back in recent years. However, the ex-Auburn star has showed little sign of slowing down. He led the Suns in scoring during the 1995–96 season with a 23.2 average and hauled down a team-leading 11.6 boards per game. Barkley, wanting to play for a team with a chance to win a title before he retires, was then traded to the Houston Rockets, where he averaged 19.2 points per game last season.

JIM "BAD NEWS" BARNES

His nickname was Bad News, but Jim Barnes turned out to be good news for the New York Knicks when they selected the 6-foot-8-inch forward out of Texas Western (now Texas-El Paso) in the first round of the 1964 draft (the legendary Willis Reed was chosen by the Knicks in the second round). As a rookie in New York, Barnes played in 75 games, averaging 15.5 points and nearly 10 rebounds a contest. It was the best season of his seven-year career.

On November 2, 1965, Barnes, along with Johnny Green and John Egan, was traded by the Knicks to the Baltimore Bullets for the 6-foot-11-inch center Walt Bellamy. Though he changed uniforms, Barnes' smooth game remained intact, as he averaged 12.4 points and a shade over 10 rebounds per game for Baltimore, helping the Bullets reach the Western Division semi-finals of the playoffs, where they were eliminated by the St. Louis Hawks, three games to none.

After that, Bad News traveled fast, from Baltimore to Los Angeles, Chicago, Boston and back to Baltimore, before he called it quits in 1971. Barnes finished his career with an average of 8.8 points on 43 percent shooting and 6.5 rebounds.

FACT FILE

Born: April 13, 1941
Height: 6' 8"
Length of NBA career:
    1964–1971
Major teams:
    New York Knicks
    Baltimore Bullets
        (joined 1965)
    Los Angeles Lakers
        (joined 1966)
    Chicago Bulls
        (joined 1967)
    Boston Celtics
        (joined 1968)
    Baltimore Bullets
        (joined 1970)

LEFT: BAD NEWS, AS JIM BARNES WAS CALLED, TRAVELED FAST THROUGHOUT HIS NBA CAREER, BUT CONTRIBUTED WHEREVER HE WENT.

MARVIN BARNES

FACT FILE

Born: July 27, 1952
Height: 6′ 9″
**Length of ABA and NBA
    career:** 1974–1980
Major teams:
  St. Louis, ABA
  Detroit, NBA
    (joined 1976)
  Buffalo, NBA
    (joined 1977)
  Boston, NBA
    (joined 1978)
  San Diego, NBA
    (joined 1979)
Records/Awards:
  ABA Rookie of the Year
    (1975)
  ABA All-Star Game (2)

Marvin Barnes, who had averaged 20.7 points and 18 rebounds a game at Providence College, earned his big-league reputation in the high-flying, high-scoring ABA, where he averaged 24 points and 13 rebounds for St. Louis in the 1974–75 and 1975–76 campaigns, which covered 144 regular-season contests. Barnes, who led the NCAA in rebounding in 1974, hauling down a whopping 18.7 boards per game for the Friars, made room in his trophy case a year later when he was named the ABA Rookie of the Year.

When the ABA merged with the NBA in 1976, Barnes—a player as equally known for his off-court disciplinary problems as his on-court heroics—was selected by Detroit in the first round of the ABA dispersal draft, and averaged 9.6 points and 4.7 rebounds in his first season with the Pistons. The following season, Barnes, traded in November to Buffalo, improved his scoring and rebounding averages to 11.4 and 7.3 respectively.

Barnes spent his last two seasons with Boston and San Diego, averaging 8.1 points and 4.7 rebounds for the Celtics in 1978–79, and 3.2 points and 3.9 rebounds for the Clippers in 1979–80.

Overall, Barnes finished his NBA career with a 9.2 scoring average and 5.5 rebounds in 171 games. Though he never appeared in an NBA playoff game, Barnes averaged a sensational 30.8 points and 14 rebounds in ten career ABA playoff contests. After this, he played in Italy during the 1980–81 season.

RIGHT: MARVIN BARNES WAS ONE OF THE MANY OUTSTANDING ABA STARS WHO LATER PLAYED IN THE RIVAL NBA.

DICK BARNETT

"Too late," the sleepy-eyed shooting guard would say to his opponents after sending a feathery, left-handed shot toward the net, his legs tucked under him in mid-air. "Fall back, baby," he would say to his teammates, even before the ball would drop through the cords.

Those were just a few of the confident words spoken by Dick Barnett in his heyday. A 6-foot-4-inch sharpshooter who was traded to the New York Knicks from the Los Angeles Lakers in 1965, Barnett was instrumental in helping the Knicks capture championships in 1970 and 1973.

Barnett, who started on the 1970 championship team with Willis Reed, Dave DeBusschere, Bill Bradley and Walt Frazier, and backed up Earl Monroe on the 1973 squad, played 9 of his 14 pro seasons in New York, and is best remembered for a shooting style that his coach, Red Holzman, hadn't "seen before or since."

A star at Tennessee State College, Barnett broke into the NBA with Syracuse in 1959, where he played for two seasons before he joined the Los Angeles Lakers in 1962. In his first season as a member of the Knicks, Barnett averaged a career-high 23.1 points per game, and finished his solid career with a 15.8 scoring average. Barnett's scoring touch never waned in the post-season, as he pumped in an average of 15.1 points in 102 playoff games.

Barnett's uniform No. 12, now retired by the Knicks, hangs from the Madison Square Garden rafters along with the uniform numbers of several of his teammates.

FACT FILE

Born: October 2, 1936
Height: 6′ 4″
Length of NBA career:
1959–1974
Major teams:
Syracuse
Los Angeles
(joined 1962)
New York
(joined 1965)
Records/Awards:
NBA All-Star Game (1)

LEFT: DICK BARNETT'S SHARP-SHOOTING SKILLS HELPED BRING A PAIR OF NBA CHAMPIONSHIPS TO THE BIG APPLE.

BRENT BARRY

FACT FILE

Born: December 31, 1971
Height: 6′ 6″
Length of NBA career:
 1995–present
Major team:
 Los Angeles Clippers

If Brent Barry were a thorough-bred, he'd probably be favored to win the Kentucky Derby. His rich basketball bloodline is connected to his father, Rick, a Hall of Famer, and brothers: Jon, who plays for Atlanta; Drew, who played for Georgia Tech and was drafted by Seattle in the second round of the June 1996 draft; and Scooter, who played his college ball at Kansas.

"I can only be me," said Brent. "I can't be my father. I'll just have to find my own groove and go with it."

Barry, a first-round draft pick out of Oregon State—who was acquired by the Los Angeles Clippers from the Nuggets along with Rodney Rogers in exchange for the draft rights to Antonio McDyess and Randy Woods—got into a serious groove during the 1996 All-Star festivities weekend, when he brought back fond memories of Julius Erving and Michael Jordan by leaping twice from the foul line and soaring to the rim for a gravity-defying jam that earned him the Slam Dunk crown.

Barry's amazing aerial feat was pulled off with plenty of room to spare, and he didn't even need to take off his warm-up jacket to do it.

After averaging 21 points per game in his senior season at Oregon State, Barry has become a nice fit in the Clippers' backcourt, as he averaged 10.1 points per game in 1995–96, and 7.5 points last season.

RIGHT: BRENT BARRY, WHO CAN SIMPLY FLY, IS A PRODUCT OF RICH BASKETBALL BLOODLINES.

RICK BARRY

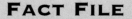

The only player in basketball history to capture NCAA, ABA and NBA scoring titles was Rick Barry, one of the greatest forwards ever to play the game.

The 6-foot-7-inch Barry, who preferred shooting his free throws underhand, was a scoring machine who averaged 29.8 points per game at the University of Miami. He led the NCAA with 37.4 points per game in 1965, and broke into pro ball spectacularly with the San Francisco Warriors of the NBA in 1966, earning the league's Rookie of the Year award on the strength of a 25.7 scoring average. The following year, Barry led the NBA in scoring with a 35.6 average, establishing a league mark that season for most field goals (1,011).

After his record-setting campaign, Barry was signed as a free agent by the Oakland Oaks of the ABA. Since he had jumped ship from one rival league to another, a court order required him to sit out his 1967–68 option season with the Warriors. Barry finally suited up for ABA action in 1968, and he proved well worth the wait for Oakland, as he led the league in scoring with a 34.0 average.

After four ABA seasons with Oakland, Washington and the New York Nets, Barry packed his duffel bags again and headed back to the NBA for the 1972–73 season, where he signed with Golden State, a franchise which had previously been known as San Francisco.

Along the path of his brilliant career, Barry helped deliver to Golden State its first-ever NBA championship in 1975, and not only established himself as a premier scorer, but a better passer than most big men who had come before him, finishing his 14-year professional stint with an average of just under 5 assists per contest.

Barry, who finished his NBA career with the Houston Rockets, left the league with a 23.2 scoring average, and posted a hefty 30.5 career scoring mark in the ABA.

FACT FILE

Born: March 28, 1944
Height: 6′ 7″
Length of NBA career:
1965-67, 1972-80
Length of ABA career:
1968–72
Major teams:
San Francisco
Oakland (joined 1968)
Washington (joined 1969)
New York (joined 1970)
Golden State
(joined 1972)
Houston (joined 1978)
Records/Awards:
NBA championship (1)
NBA All-Star Game (8)
ABA All-Star Game (4)
NBA Rookie of the Year
(1966)
Hall of Fame (1986)

LEFT: RICK BARRY, WHO STARRED IN BOTH THE ABA AND NBA, WAS ONE OF THE MOST SKILLED FORWARDS EVER TO PLAY THE GAME.

ELGIN BAYLOR

FACT FILE

Born: September 16, 1934
Height: 6′ 5″
Length of NBA career:
   1958–72
Major team:
   Minneapolis (franchise
      moved to Los Angeles)
Records/Awards:
   NBA All-Star Game (1)
   NBA Rookie of the Year
      (1959)
   Hall of Fame (1976)

Julius Erving with a jump shot, Elgin Baylor was one of the flashiest, high-flying talents of the 1950s and 1960s.

The 6-foot-5-inch forward, who poured in 31.3 points per game in two college seasons at Seattle, was the first overall pick of the Minneapolis Lakers in the 1958 draft. He justified that selection by winning the NBA Rookie of the year award in 1959, when he averaged 24.9 points and 15 rebounds per game.

Baylor, who spent his entire fourteen-year career with the Lakers (who moved from Minneapolis to Los Angeles in 1960), helped them get to NBA Finals nine times, making two of those trips with a pair of enormously talented teammates, Wilt Chamberlain and Jerry West.

In a bit of sad irony, the Lakers finally won the championship in 1972, Baylor's last season, defeating the New York Knicks four games to one. Baylor, however, was no longer on the roster. He had played just nine games that season because wear and tear to his legs had robbed him of his explosive leaping ability.

For everything he ever achieved on a basketball court, Baylor is best remembered for pumping in 61 points against arch-rival Boston in Game 5 of the 1962 NBA Finals. It was a record which still stands. In this contest, which Boston won on the way to winning the series four games to three, Baylor also set a record for the most field goals attempted in one half (25). In 1960, Baylor scored a record 71 points in one game for the Lakers. He ended his career with averages of 27.4 points and 13.5 rebounds, was selected as

RIGHT: ELGIN BAYLOR COULD DO JUST ABOUT ANYTHING ON A BASKETBALL COURT, BUT INJURIES FORCED HIM OUT OF THE GAME JUST BEFORE THE LOS ANGELES LAKERS WON A CHAMPIONSHIP.

ZELMO BEATY

A 6-foot-10-inch hulking center, Zelmo Beaty starred in an era dominated by quality pivotmen like Bill Russell, Wilt Chamberlain, Kareem Abdul-Jabbar, Wes Unseld, and Nate Thurmond. Beaty, one of many involved in the player-jumping battle between the NBA and ABA in the early 1970s, broke in with the St. Louis Hawks of the NBA in 1962 and played his last year for the franchise when it switched to Atlanta in 1968.

After averaging 17.5 points in seven seasons with the Hawks, Beaty jumped ship for the Utah Stars of the ABA in 1970, and averaged 22.9 points per game that season in helping the Stars to an ABA championship. He made 661 of 1,189 field goals that year for a league-best 55.6 field goal percentage.

Beaty, a former Prairie View star who was the number-one draft pick of St. Louis in 1962, averaged 16 points and 10.4 rebounds in eight NBA seasons, and posted 19.1 points and 11.6 boards in four ABA seasons—all spent with the Jazz. In 63 NBA playoff contests, Beaty registered 17.0 points and 11.1 rebounds per game. In 52 ABA post-season contests, Beaty averaged 19.1 points and 12.9 rebounds.

A two-time NBA All-Star and three-time ABA Star, Beaty finished his twelve-year career with the Los Angeles Lakers, averaging just 5.5 points and 4.7 rebounds as a part-time player.

FACT FILE

Born: October 25, 1939
Height: 6' 10"
Length of NBA career:
1962–69, 1974–75
Length of ABA career:
1970–74
Major teams:
St. Louis-Atlanta
Utah (joined 1970)
Los Angeles (joined 1974)
Records/Awards:
NBA All-Star Game (2)
ABA All-Star Game (3)
ABA Championship (1)

LEFT: IN AN ERA OF DOMINANT CENTERS, ZELMO BEATY WAS A STAR IN HIS OWN RIGHT.

NAT HOLMAN: THE GAME'S FIRST TRUE SUPERSTAR

Billed by the Original Celtics of the 1920s as "the world's greatest basketball player," Nat Holman was the game's first true superstar and matinee idol. His many finesse moves were often imitated, and became the foundation of the type of basketball played in New York.

A well-built, 5-foot-11-inch player with slick-backed black hair, Holman was born on the Lower East Side on October 19, 1896, in Grover Cleveland's second term as President, and about five years after the invention of basketball.

As a player, Holman described himself as "fast and a good passer and a team player, and I never gave a damn if I got my name in the paper as long as we won the game, or played well, the way the game should be played."

As a young man, he turned down a chance to sign as a pitcher with the Cincinnati Reds in order to play basketball. In his day, the game of hoops was played using chicken-wire cages, which were hoisted up around the basketball court so that rowdy fans couldn't get at the players and the referees.

"It was brutal," Holman once said of basketball in the 1920s. "The game they play today is tame compared to it. You had to be quick on your feet and fast with your fists." At the age of 21, Holman joined The Whirlwinds, a pro basketball team in Germantown, Pa. At the same time, he began his career at CCNY, as the junior varsity coach.

After a short stay with the Whirlwinds, who together with the Original Celtics were the outstanding teams of the time, Mr. Holman left at the end of the 1921 season to join the Celtics, the famous barnstorming team that helped legitimize professional basketball, playing more than 100 games a year and rarely losing. He stayed with the Celtics through 1927, two years before the team disbanded because there was no suitable opposition.

After his professional playing days were over, Holman eventually took over the reigns at CCNY, becoming one of the great college head coaches of all-time. In 1950, his CCNY teams won both the National Collegiate Athletic Association and the National Invitation Tournament championships, a feat that can no longer be duplicated because college teams in post-season play now enter one tournament or the other.

WALT BELLAMY

FACT FILE

Born: July 24, 1939
Height: 6′ 11″
Length of NBA career:
  1961–73
Major teams:
  Chicago
  Baltimore (joined 1963)
  New York Knicks
    (joined 1966)
  Detroit (joined 1968)
  Atlanta (joined 1970)
  New Orleans
    (joined 1974)
Records/Awards:
  NBA Rookie of the Year
    (1962)
  NBA All-Star Game (4)
  Olympic Gold Medal
    (1960)
  Hall of Fame (1993)

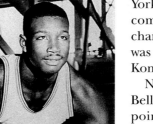

Hall of Famer Dave Bing once called Walt Bellamy "the best pick-and-roll center that ever played the game," and he certainly has an argument.

Though he was often overshadowed in his day by Wilt Chamberlain and Bill Russell, the 6-foot-11-inch Bellamy rang up some monster numbers during his career. Oddly enough, Bellamy's strongest season was his first. As a rookie in the 1961–62 season, the man his teammates called "Bells" posted averages of 31.6 points, 19 rebounds and 2.7 assists a game for the Chicago Packers, earning himself the NBA Rookie of the Year award.

Bellamy, who played 1,043 games for seven NBA teams from 1961 to 1974, including the New York Knicks, is best remembered in New York as being part of a trade that completed the 1970 Knicks' championship team puzzle, as he was sent to Detroit with Howard Komives for Dave DeBusschere.

No matter where he traveled, Bellamy played big, averaging 20.1 points and 13.7 boards in his career. A four-time All-Star, Bellamy holds the single-season record for most games played, logging in a combined 88 regular-season contests in 1968–69 for New York and Detroit.

Before he was selected by the Packers as the first pick overall in the 1961 NBA draft, Bellamy had made a name for himself at Indiana, where he averaged 20.6 points, 15.5 rebounds and earned a place on the 1960 U.S. Olympic gold-medal team.

RIGHT: HERE, WALT BELLAMY SHOWS THE EXPLOSIVE SKILLS THAT MADE HIM A FOUR-TIME ALL-STAR.

AL BIANCHI

Al Bianchi's road to professional basketball hit a nasty bump in his rookie season of 1956, when he joined the Minneapolis Lakers after a two-year stint in the Army, and was waived by the team after only a week. Bianchi survived, however, as he went on to play ten seasons as a quality reserve for the Syracuse Nationals, the predecessors of the Philadelphia 76ers.

Bianchi, a 6-foot-3-inch guard out of Bowling Green, played for Syracuse-Philadelphia his entire career, his best seasons coming in 1958–59, when he averaged 10 points and 2.2 assists per game for Syracuse, and in 1961–62, when he averaged 10.3 points and 3.5 assists per contest for the Nationals.

Over his full career, Bianchi averaged 8.1 points and 2.2 assists. He averaged 8.0 points and just under 2 assists per game in 56 post-season contests.

FACT FILE

Born: March 26, 1932
Height: 6′ 3″
Length of NBA career:
   1956–66
Major teams:
   Minneapolis Lakers
   Syracuse-Philadelphia
   (joined 1956)

LEFT: AL BIANCHI ENDURED A BUMPY RIDE TO THE PROFESSIONAL RANKS.

HENRY BIBBY

FACT FILE

Born: November 24, 1949
Height: 6′ 1″
Length of NBA career:
  1972–81
Major teams:
  New York Knicks
  New Orleans
    (joined 1975)
  Philadelphia (joined 1976)
  San Diego (joined 1980)
Records/Awards:
  NBA Championship (1)

As if being a starting guard on three NCAA championship teams (at UCLA) wasn't impressive enough on his resume, Henry Bibby also happens to be the only man ever to play for an NCAA, an NBA and a CBA championship team.

A 6-foot-1-inch sparkplug on the hardwood, Bibby broke into the big leagues with the New York Knicks in 1972–73—New York's last championship season—averaging 4.2 points per game. After two-and-a-half seasons with the Knicks, Bibby moved on to the New Orleans Jazz, the Philadelphia 76ers—whom he helped to the league's championship final in 1977 and 1980—and finally, the San Diego Clippers.

He was also a player and assistant coach for the 1982 Lancaster Lightning, which won the CBA title.

Bibby, who won three titles at UCLA from 1970–72, also holds a few other distinctions. He is one of four players in history to win an NCAA and an NBA championship in successive years. Joining Bibby in that category are Billy Thompson of Louisville and the Los Angeles Lakers, Bill Russell of San Francisco and the Boston Celtics, and Magic Johnson of Michigan State and the Los Angeles Lakers.

While Henry Bibby played professional basketball, his older brother, Jim, was a major league baseball pitcher. Henry Bibby finished his nine-year NBA career with averages of 8.6 points and 3.3 assists.

RIGHT: HENRY BIBBY IS ONE OF FOUR PLAYERS IN HISTORY TO WIN AN NCAA AND NBA CHAMPIONSHIP IN SUCCESSIVE YEARS.

DAVE BING

The first member of the Detroit Pistons to have his number retired, Dave Bing led the Motown crew in scoring five times from 1966 to 1975.

A 6-foot-3-inch shooting guard out of Syracuse, where he registered an average 24.8 points per game, Bing was the first player chosen in the 1966 draft and became the Rookie of the Year with the Pistons after averaging 20.6 points a contest.

The next season, Bing led the league in scoring with 2,142 points and a 27.1 scoring average. He played nine seasons with the Pistons, in seven of which he averaged 20 points or better . In 1975, Bing was traded from Detroit to Washington, where he scored 16.2 points and 10.6 points respectively in two seasons. Bing's final season was spent in Boston, where he averaged 13.6 points and dished out 3.8 assists per game.

For all his greatness, Bing was never blessed with many super-talented teammates, and he never did get to play in a championship series. He was, however, a seven-time All-Star selection, and earned the All-Star Game Most Valuable Player Award in 1976 on the strength of a 16-point, 4-assist performance.

Bing also did quite well in playoff competition, averaging 15.4 points and 4.3 assists in thirty-one post-season games.

FACT FILE

Born: November 24, 1943
Height: 6′ 3″
Length of NBA career:
1966–78
Major teams:
  Detroit
  Washington (joined 1975)
  Boston (joined 1977)
Records/Awards:
  NBA Rookie of the Year
    (1967)
  NBA All-Star Game (7)

LEFT: DAVE BING WAS BLESSED WITH TALENT, BUT NOT MANY TALENTED TEAMMATES.

LARRY BIRD

FACT FILE

Born: December 7, 1956
Height: 6′ 9″
Length of NBA career:
 1979–92
Major team:
 Boston Celtics
Records/Awards:
 NBA Rookie of the Year
  (1980)
 NBA Championship (3)
 NBA Most Valuable Player
  (3)
 Olympic Gold Medal
  (1992)

BELOW: THE LEGENDARY LARRY BIRD WAS ALWAYS ONE STEP AHEAD OF THE COMPETITION.

Larry Bird, one of the greatest clutch shooters in NBA history, did a lot more than just rebound, throw mind-boggling passes and lead the storied Celtics back to greatness. It was Bird, along with his college nemesis, Magic Johnson, who joined the NBA in 1979 and triggered the league's enormous rise in popularity in the 1980s.

Bird, whose undefeated Indiana State team lost to Johnson's Michigan State team in the 1979 NCAA championship game, continued his battle with Johnson in the NBA, creating one of the classic rivalries in the history of the sport: Bird's thinking-man's Celtics vs. Johnson's high-flying Los Angeles Lakers, more commonly referred to as Showtime.

He was not blessed with great leaping ability and by no means was he a speed-demon, but mentally, Bird was always one step ahead of the competition, and broke opponents' hearts with his court savvy and deadly shooting. He

was voted NBA Rookie of the Year in 1980 after leading the Celtics to a 61–21 record, a 32-game improvement over the previous season.

One of the most memorable images of Bird is from Game 5 of the 1987 Eastern Conference Finals against Detroit. Larry the Legend stole an inbounds pass from Isiah Thomas and passed to teammate Dennis Johnson for the game-winning basket with one second remaining.

Despite injuries which plagued him throughout his career—including a bad back which eventually forced him to retire in 1992 after thirteen seasons—Bird still managed to put together a phenomenal basketball resume: three NBA championships, three Most Valuable Player Awards and eleven All-Star games.

His final basketball appearance came as a member of the 1992 United States Olympic team, where Bird joined forces with Johnson, Michael Jordan, and a host of super-talented players to win the gold medal.

OTIS BIRDSONG

The soft, arching jump shot that belonged to Otis Birdsong—basketball's first $1 million guard—was on display for 12 NBA seasons. Birdsong, a 6-foot-4-inch guard with a scorer's mentality and all-around talent, was among an elite group of backcourt stars in his day that included the likes of George Gervin, David Thompson, Phil Ford, and Magic Johnson.

The son of a Southern minister, Birdsong averaged 30.3 points per game in his senior season at the University of Houston in the 1976–77 campaign. If not for an injury-riddled professional career, Birdsong might have fulfilled his Hall-of-Fame potential. Nevertheless,

he still put together a fabulous career, averaging 18.0 points per game in 12 seasons with Kansas City, the New Jersey Nets, and Boston Celtics.

Birdsong, a four-time All Star, enjoyed his best seasons in Kansas City from 1978–81, averaging 21.7, 22.7, and 24.6 points respectively. In 1981, he was traded to New Jersey, and brought to the metropolitan area the flashiness and pizzazz at the guard position that basketball fans there hadn't seen since the days of Walt "Clyde" Frazier. His best season in New Jersey was 1984–85, when he averaged 20.6 points per game. In 35 career playoff games, Birdsong tallied 15.6 points per contest.

FACT FILE

Born: December 9, 1955
Height: 6' 4"
Length of NBA career:
  1977–89
Major teams:
  Kansas City
  New Jersey (joined 1981)
  Boston (joined 1989)

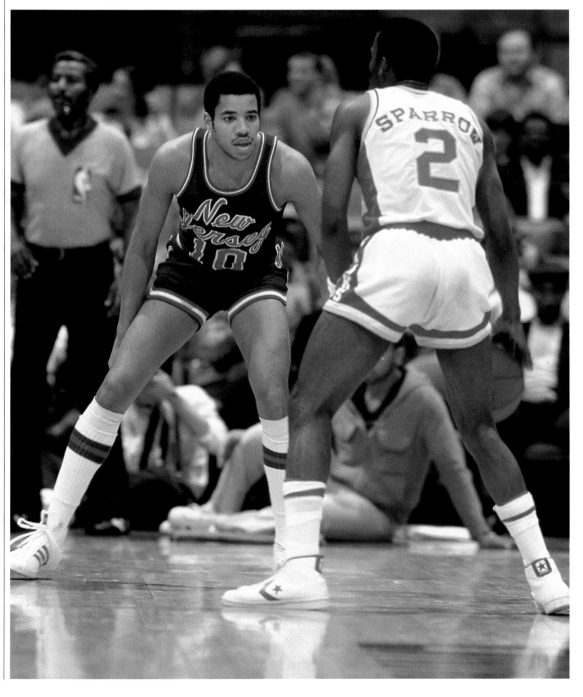

LEFT: OTIS BIRDSONG, HERE PLAYING DEFENSE, WAS BASKETBALL'S FIRST MILLION-DOLLAR GUARD.

ROLANDO BLACKMAN

FACT FILE

Born: February 26, 1959
Height: 6′ 6″
Length of NBA career:
 1981–94
Major teams:
 Dallas
 New York Knicks
  (joined 1992)
Records/Awards:
 NBA All-Star Game (4)

The young man with the big afro hairstyle gave little thought of ever making it as a pro back in the mid-1970s, back when he played his hoops at Grady High School in Brooklyn, NY. After all, there were much bigger names on the New York basketball scene at the time, names like Joe Foster, Larry Washington and Riley Clarida —none of whom ever made it to the NBA.

"This was a time when I had no goals whatsoever as far as playing basketball," Blackman once said. "I was just trying to get a scholarship and go to school. All these guys were talking about being pros."

The Panamanian-born Blackman got his scholarship, and made the best of his basketball situation at Kansas State, averaging 15.2 points per game from 1977–81.

Six-feet-six-inches tall, he established himself as one of the best big guards in the country and earned a spot on the 1980 U.S. Olympic Basketball Team, which never competed in Olympic play because the United States boycotted the Moscow Games.

The dream he never dared to dream came true for Blackman in 1981, when he was selected by the Dallas Mavericks in the first round of the NBA draft as the ninth pick overall. Blackman became a folk hero in the Dallas area through the 1980s and early 1990s, teaming with Derek Harper to form one of the most talented backcourt tandems in the history of the NBA.

Blackman, a four-time NBA All-Star, played eleven seasons in Dallas before he was traded to the New York Knicks in 1992, where he finished the final two seasons of his brilliant career on a sad, injury-plagued note. His best seasons were in Dallas, where he averaged a career-high 22.4 points in 1983–84, 21.5 points in 1985–86, and 21.0 points the following season. He finished with an 18.0 career scoring average.

RIGHT: GROWING UP, ROLANDO BLACKMAN NEVER DREAMED HE WOULD EVER PLAY IN THE NBA.

MOOKIE BLAYLOCK

Kenny Anderson was the best thing that ever happened to Mookie Blaylock. After three solid seasons as the starting point guard for the New Jersey Nets from 1989–92, Blaylock was pushed out of the job by the gifted Anderson, who the Nets were hoping would become one of the cornerstones of their franchise.

Blaylock was traded to Atlanta, and while quarterbacking the Hawks without having to look over his shoulder, has become an All-Star in his own right.

The 6-foot-1-inch playmaker out of Oklahoma has turned himself into a reliable clutch performer, not to mention one of the top defensive players in the league.

Last season, Blaylock averaged a career-high 17.4 points per game, 5.9 assists, and led the league with 2.72 steals per game. An All-Defensive First Team selection for two seasons, Blaylock has now racked up 1,460 career steals.

Grand theft was also Blaylock's speciality at the collegiate level, where he holds the NCAA Division I single-season record for most steals with 150 in 1988. He also holds the NCAA mark for most steals in a single game with 13, pulling off that feat twice, against Centenary in 1987, and then against Loyola Marymount in 1988.

In addition, Blaylock is also the only player in NCAA history to record over 200 assists and 100 steals in consecutive seasons. Blaylock's second-best scoring season came in 1994–95, when he posted 17.2 points per game.

FACT FILE

Born: March 20, 1967
Height: 6′ 1″
Length of NBA career:
  1989–present
Major teams:
  New Jersey
  Atlanta (joined 1992)
Records/Awards:
  NBA All-Defensive First
    Team (2)
  NBA All-Star Game (1)

LEFT: THE NEW JERSEY NETS DID MOOKIE BLAYLOCK A FAVOR WHEN THEY TRADED HIM TO THE ATLANTA HAWKS.

MUGGSY BOGUES

FACT FILE

Born: January 9, 1965
Height: 5′ 3″
Length of NBA career:
  1987–present
Major teams:
  Washington
  Charlotte (joined 1988)

After ten seasons in the National Basketball Association, Tyrone "Muggsy" Bogues, the shortest player in the history of the league, is still standing tall.

Bogues, a 5-foot-3-inch whirling dervish who was drafted out of Wake Forest by Washington in 1987, has been a catalyst for the Charlotte Hornets since joining the team via the 1988 NBA expansion draft.

Though he played just 65 games last season due to injury, Bogues has averaged 8.3 points and 8.4 assists per contest throughout his career. In his first seven seasons with Charlotte, Bogues joined Utah's John Stockton as the only NBA point guards to dish out over 600 assists during that span.

In 1983, Bogues was the big man—as in Most Valuable Player—on Dunbar High Schools campus in Baltimore, leading that team to an undefeated season and a national championship. That squad also featured future NBA players David Wingate, Reggie Williams, and Reggie Lewis.

Bogues, who wears number 1 because that is the only digit that will fit on his jersey, was more than up to the taller competition at Wake Forest. While there, he set career records for the Demon Deacons in assists (781) and steals (275). A two-time Most Valuable Player at Wake Forest, Bogues received First-Team All-ACC honors in 1987, when he tallied collegiate career-highs in points (14) and assists (9.5).

RIGHT: MUGGSY BOGUES, THE SMALLEST PLAYER IN NBA HISTORY, IS THE STRAW THAT STIRS THE CHARLOTTE HORNETS.

RON BOONE

A guard who played in a record 1,041 consecutive professional basketball games, Ron Boone had his illustrious streak come to a grinding halt on January 26, 1981, when he was waived by the Utah Jazz of the NBA. Boone, who was 34 years old when he was cut by Utah—a transaction that brought an end to a solid thirteen-year career—had played in all fifty-two games for the struggling Jazz that season, and was posting averages of 7.8 points per game.

"Our thinking was that we are anxious to play our younger players," General Manager Frank Layden explained at the time. "With thirteen games to go, we just had to give some time to our youngsters."

Since Boone began his career with Dallas of the ABA in 1968, the NBA refused to accept his astonishing achievement as a record. Randy Smith, a guard who played 906 consecutive games over ten NBA seasons from 1973–1983, officially holds the NBA ironman streak.

A veteran of eight ABA seasons, the 6-foot-2-inch Boone finished with a career scoring average of 18.4 points for Dallas, Utah and St. Louis from 1968–76, enjoying his best professional season in 1974–75, when he averaged 25.2 points for Utah.

He also won an ABA championship in 1970–71 with Utah, averaging 18.0 points for the Stars after they had obtained his services in a January trade with Dallas.

In 1976, Boone began his NBA career with Kansas City, averaging a career NBA-best 22.2 points that season. In five NBA seasons, Boone averaged 13.9 points per game.

FACT FILE

Born: September 6, 1946
Height: 6′ 2″
Length of ABA career:
1968–76
Length of NBA career:
1976–81
Major teams:
Dallas
Utah (joined 1971)
St. Louis (joined 1975)
Kansas City (joined 1976)
Los Angeles (joined 1978)
Utah (joined 1979)
Records/Awards:
ABA Championship (1)
ABA All-Star (3)

LEFT: RON BOONE, ONE OF PRO SPORTS' ORIGINAL IRONMEN, PLAYED IN 1,041 CONSECUTIVE GAMES.

HARRY BOYKOFF

FACT FILE

Born: July 24, 1922
Height: 6′ 9″
Length of NBA career:
  1947–51
Major teams:
  Toledo
  Waterloo (joined 1948)
  Boston (joined 1951)
  Tri-Cities (joined 1951)

New York's first basketball giant, Harry Boykoff helped St. Johns University become a national power in the 1940s, and went on to enjoy a productive four-year professional career from 1947–51.

A 6-foot-9-inch center who averaged 10.1 points per game as a pro, Boykoff enjoyed his best season as a member of the Waterloo Hawks in the 1949–50 season, averaging 12.8 points per game.

He broke into the big leagues with Toledo of the National Basketball League in 1947, posting a 9.7 scoring average as a rookie.

Boykoff, known in his day as "Big Hesh," became the first 1,000-point scorer in St. Johns' history, and the first-ever Consensus All-American choice at St. Johns in 1943, an honor which was achieved by only two other players in St. John's' history—Chris Mullin and Walter Berry.

In four seasons at St. Johns, Boykoff averaged 16.6 points per game. He averaged 16.6 points as a collegiate rookie. Then, after spending the next two years in the U.S. military, he came back to St. John's to score 16.5 points per game in 1945–46, and 16.7 points per game in 1946–47.

As a rookie at St. John's, Boykoff led the Red Storm to their first-ever NIT title and was named Most Valuable Player of the post-season tournament after scoring 56 points in three games. That same season, Boykoff also broke the Madison Square Garden record with a 45-point performance against St. Josephs.

RIGHT: HARRY BOYKOFF (SECOND FROM LEFT) WAS THE FIRST-EVER 1,000-POINT SCORER AT ST. JOHN'S UNIVERSITY.

BILL BRADLEY

A key member of the New York Knicks 1970 and 1973 championship teams, Bill Bradley, a Princeton graduate who joined the Knicks in 1967 after a two-year Rhodes Scholarship at Oxford, played all ten of his NBA seasons in New York.

A Hall-of-Fame forward who averaged 12.4 points, 3.4 assists and 3.1 rebounds in his career, Bradley—who would become a US Senator (New Jersey) long after his playing days—joined forces in his prime with Dave DeBusschere and Willis Reed to form one of the strongest frontlines in the history of the game. In the 1969–70 championship campaign—the last season the Knicks wore the NBA crown—he posted a career-high 16.1 points per contest.

One of the best fast-break passers of his era, the 6-foot-5-inch Bradley possessed great court

vision, was an excellent ballhandler and a nifty outside shooter.

At Princeton, Bradley averaged 30 points per game and was a two-time All-American. As a senior in 1965, Bradley was voted College Player of the Year, and set an NCAA Tournament one-game record with 58 points.

Bradley's number 24 has been retired by the Knicks, and currently hangs from the Madison Square Garden rafters along with the other stars from those New York championship teams.

William Warren Bradley, or "Dollar Bill" as he was sometimes known, averaged 12.9 points in 95 NBA playoff games and made one All-Star appearance in his career.

Bradley and DeBusschere, roommates in their playing days, were named to the Hall of Fame in the same year (1983).

FACT FILE

Born: July 28, 1943
Height: 6′ 5″
Length of NBA career:
 1967–1977
Major team:
 New York Knicks
Records/Awards:
 NBA Championship (2)
 NBA All-Star Game (1)
 US Olympic Gold Medal
 (1964)

LEFT: PRINCETON SCHOLAR BILL BRADLEY, MOVING IN ON A CHICAGO DEFENDER, HELPED THE KNICKS TO CHAMPIONSHIPS IN 1970 AND 1973 AND LATER WENT INTO POLITICS.

NED IRISH,
SALESMAN

Dr. James Naismith was the man who invented the game of basketball. Ned Irish was the man who sold it to the public.

Edward S. Irish, who worked as a sports reporter for the *New York World Telegram*, left that position in 1934 to take a crack at the business of promoting basketball games.

Having witnessed the success of college basketball benefit games at Madison Square Garden a few years earlier—a tripleheader on January 19, 1931, drew a capacity crowd, and a seven-game card on February 22, 1933, attracted 20,000 spectators—Irish was one of a handful of promoters who offered his ideas to General John Reed Kilpatrick, the serving president of Madison Square Garden.

Eventually, Irish's promotional vision was the one that Kilpatrick was sold on. On December 29, 1934, Irish promoted his first basketball event, a double-header in which New York University defeated Notre Dame 25–18, and Westminster edged St. John's 37–33. That double-header, which drew 16,180 fans, was a huge success, and the start of college basketball as a big-time business.

"I didn't have to put up a cent," Mr. Irish once said. "Don't forget, it was the Depression and the Garden was dark a lot of nights. The only guarantee the Garden wanted was that its percentage of the gate would average the cost of renting the building, which at the time was $4,000 a night. If I didn't meet it, my option would not be renewed."

As it turned out, Irish and the game of basketball continued to reach new levels of success. In his second season working to sell basketball at Madison Square Garden, Irish promoted eight double-headers, which included teams from all over the United States. Basketball was suddenly booming.

When General Kilpatrick went into the army in 1943, Irish was named the Garden's acting president. Under his supervision, the Garden reached an average attendance of 18,196 in 1946. That same year, he was one of the founders of the 11-team Basketball Association of America, which merged with the National Basketball League three years later to become the present NBA.

In 1969, during the feud between the NBA and ABA, Mr. Irish was one of the early leaders in the fight for a merger.

During an almost 40-year association with the Garden, Mr. Irish served as basketball director, acting president, executive vice president, president of the Knicks, and a member of the corporation's board of directors.

Irish, who died in 1982, was elected to the Basketball Hall of Fame in 1964.

FRANK BRIAN

FACT FILE

Born: May 1, 1923
Height: 6′ 1″
Length of NBA career:
   1947–1956
Major teams:
   Anderson
   Tri-Cities (joined 1950)
   Fort Wayne (joined 1951)
Records/Awards:
   NBL Championship (1)
   NBA All-Star Game (2)

"Flash" as Frank Brian was called, was one of the top performers in the old National Basketball League, which was open for business from 1937–1949 before its surviving franchises merged with the Basketball Association of America to form the National Basketball Association.

Brian, a 6-foot-1-inch guard who played just one season of college ball at Louisiana State (after spending three years in military service), helped the Anderson Packers of Indiana become the last NBL champion in 1949, averaging 9.9 points per game that season. He spent two seasons in the NBL before he and his Anderson team joined the NBA for the 1949–50 season. During that campaign, Brian averaged a career-high 17.8 points per game.

As a member of the Fort Wayne Pistons from 1951–56, Brian had his best shot at winning an NBA title in the 1954–55 season, when the Pistons were defeated by Syracuse in the NBA Finals four games to three, losing Game 4 by a single point, 92–91. That season, the playoff charge was led by Brian and a pair of talented backcourt mates, Max Zaslofsky and Andy Phillip.

A two-time All-Star, Brian retired in 1956 with a career 11.9 scoring average. In 56 professional post-season contests, Brian averaged 9.3 points per game.

RIGHT: FRANK "FLASH" BRIAN, HELPED THE ANDERSON PACKERS CAPTURE THE LAST NBL CHAMPIONSHIP.

BILL BRIDGES

Bill Bridges and the Kansas City Steers both arrived on the professional basketball scene in 1961. The Steers, and the newly formed American Basketball League in which they played, lasted just a year and a half. Bridges a 6-foot-6-inch forward out of Kansas, lasted fifteen seasons, and went on to become one of the NBA's all-time greats.

After averaging 23.6 points in his brief ABL tenure – he holds the league mark for most points in a single game with 55 – Bridges hooked up with the St. Louis Hawks of the NBA, and got stronger in each of his first five seasons in St. Louis. He averaged 6.1 points in 1962-63, 8.5 in 1963-64, 11.5 in 1964-65, 13.0 in 1965-66, and a career-high 17.4 in 1966-67.

One of the top defenders in the league during his era, Bridges remained with the Hawks for three and a half more seasons after the franchise moved to Atlanta in 1968. After brief stints with Philadelphia and Los Angeles at the tail-end of his carrer, Bridges was signed as a free agent by the championship-bound Golden State Warriors in 1975, and waved goodbye to professional basketball that season wearing a championship ring.

A three-time NBA All-Star, Bridges averaged 11.9 points and 11.9 rebounds throughout his career, and posted 10.5 points per game in 113 post-season contests.

FACT FILE

Born: April 4, 1939
Height: 6′ 6″
Length of NBA career:
1961–1975
Major teams:
 Kansas City
 St. Louis (joined 1962)
 Philadelphia (joined 1971)
 Los Angeles (joined 1972)
 Golden State
  (joined 1975)
Records/Awards:
 NBA Championship (1)
 NBA All-Star Game (3)
 US Olympic Gold Medal
  (1964)
 NBL All-Star Game (1)

LEFT: WITH EACH PASSING SEASON IN ST. LOUIS, BILL BRIDGES SEEMED TO GET BETTER.

FRED BROWN

FACT FILE

Born: July 7, 1948
Height: 6′ 3″
Length of NBA career:
  1971–1984
Major team:
  Seattle SuperSonics
Records/Awards:
  NBA Championship (1)
  NBA All-Star Game (1)

They called him "Downtown" Fred Brown because his sweet outside shot was measured in yards instead of feet. "Downtown's the best shooter in the NBA," longtime coach Dick Motta said in 1978. "His misses are closer than some guy's makes."

Brown, who averaged 14.6 points per game in his career, helped lead the 1978–79 Seattle SuperSonics—the only team he played for in 13 NBA seasons—to their only world championship.

A 6-foot-3-inch marksman out of Iowa, Brown enjoyed his best scoring seasons in 1974–75, when he averaged 21.0 points per game, and 1975–76, when he posted a career-high 23.1. In 1980, he led the NBA in three-point field goal percentage, connecting on 39 of 88 long-distance tries for 44 percent. He spent long hours sharing the secrets of his soft, outside shooting touch with Vinnie Johnson, a teammate who also played the shooting guard position. Johnson went on to become an NBA star.

A 22.7 points-per-game scorer at Iowa from 1967–69, Brown was selected by Seattle as the sixth overall pick in the first round of the 1971 draft. After achieving his career-best scoring average in 1976, Downtown made his first—and only—All-Star appearance. In 83 NBA playoff games, he averaged 14.4 points.

RIGHT: "DOWNTOWN" FRED BROWN, LOOKING FOR AN OPEN TEAMMATE HERE, COULD BURY BASKETS FROM LONG RANGE.

KOBE BRYANT

One of the most electrifying young talents in the NBA, Kobe Bryant, at age 17, made a giant leap from Lower Merion High School in Pennsylvania to the Los Angeles Lakers, and he has already shown enough promise on the basketball court to suggest that he might be the heir-apparent to Michael Jordan's throne.

Bryant, who concluded his high school career as the all-time leading scorer in Southeastern Pennsylvania history (2,883 points), breaking the previous record held by Wilt Chamberlain (2,359) and Carlin Warley (2,441), turned heads all over the world in his professional rookie campaign.

Originally selected by Charlotte in the 1996 NBA Draft, Bryant's Draft rights were traded by the Hornets to the Lakers for center Vlade Divac. It was not long before Charlotte management started thinking twice about having traded Bryant, who won over the hearts of many skeptics with an explosive performance in the NBA's Slam Dunk contest, becoming the first player in Los Angeles Laker history to win the celebrated event.

During the season, Bryant's open-court brilliance jelled nicely with young teammates like Shaquille O'Neal, Nick Van Exel, and Eddie Jones. After averaging 7.6 points per game, Bryant was named to the NBA's All-Rookie Second Team, becoming just the second player in the history of the NBA—along with Kevin Garnett of Minnesota in 1995–96—to earn All-Rookie team honors after entering the league directly out of high school.

Bryant, the son of Jelly Bean Bryant, who played eight seasons in the NBA with Philadelphia, San Diego and Houston before retiring in 1983, is the second-youngest player to appear in an NBA game. Kobe was just 18 years, two months and 11 days old when he stepped onto the floor against Minnesota on November 3, 1996. Jermaine O'Neal of Portland, who also skipped college for the NBA, was 18 years, one month and 22 days old when he made his big-league debut last season.

FACT FILE

Born: August 23, 1978
Height: 6′ 6″
Length of NBA career:
    1996–present
Major teams:
    Los Angeles Lakers

LEFT: KOBE BRYANT'S VAST TALENTS SUGGEST THAT HE MIGHT ONE DAY FILL MICHAEL JORDAN'S TALENTED SHOES.

MARCUS CAMBY

FACT FILE

Born: March 22, 1974
Height: 6' 11"
Length of NBA career:
    1996–present
Major team:
    Toronto

The 1996 College Player of the Year, Marcus Camby has already brought a winning attitude to the young Toronto Raptors, who are playing in just their third NBA season.

Camby, a 6-foot-11-inch fluid scorer and shot-blocking wizard who was selected as the second pick overall by the Raptors in the 1996 NBA Draft, played three super seasons for the University of Massachusetts, leading the Minutemen to a 35–2 record, and their first-ever berth in the Final Four.

In his initial NBA season, Camby earned all-rookie first team honors by averaging 14.8 points, 6.3 rebounds and tallying 130 blocks.

At the college level, Camby proved he could roam the court with a quickness and slickness rarely seen in a big man. He averaged 20.5 points, 8.2 rebounds and 3.9 blocks last season in leading Massachusetts to the semifinals of the NCAA Tournament, where the Minutemen lost to the eventual-champion Kentucky Wildcats, 81–74, wasting a 25-point, 8-rebound, 6-block performance by Camby. Along the way, Camby was named Most Valuable Player of the NCAA East Regionals.

During his remarkable senior campaign, Camby became the first Massachusetts player to surpass 300 career blocks, posting 336 rejections in 92 career games.

He was equally dominant on the defensive end in the NCAAs, setting a tournament career-record with 43 blocks in 11 games.

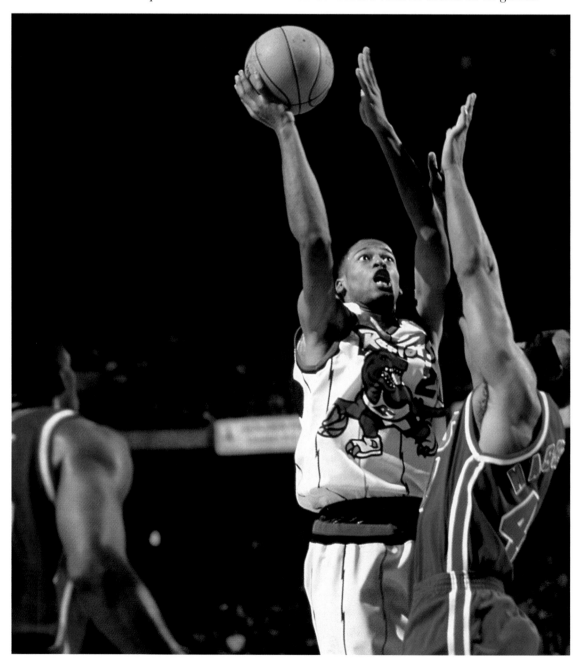

RIGHT: THE MULTI-DIMENSIONAL MARCUS CAMBY HAS A BRIGHT FUTURE WITH THE TORONTO RAPTORS.

ANTOINE CARR

Before there ever was a Glenn Robinson, Antoine Carr was the NBA's "Big Dog." Carr, a 6-foot-9-inch, 255-pound freight train in tank top and shorts, has rediscovered his scoring touch in the twilight of his 13-year NBA career.

For the past three seasons, the reserve power forward has helped the Utah Jazz into the playoffs, posting 9.6 points and 3.4 rebounds per game in 1994–95, 7.3 points and 2.5 boards per contest in 1995–96, and 7.4 points and 2.4 rebounds last season.

A standout at Wichita State from 1979–83, Carr was drafted by the Detroit Pistons as the eighth pick overall in the 1983 NBA draft. But rather than sign a four-year deal with the Pistons worth $250,000 per season, Carr chose

to play his first season of professional basketball in Italy, signing a one-year deal with Milano estimated at $350,000.

After averaging a professional career-best 21.1 points per game with Milano, Carr returned to the NBA and played six and a half seasons with the Atlanta Hawks before he was traded in 1990 to the Sacramento Kings.

The following season, the only full-season Carr would spend in Sacramento, he posted an NBA career-high 20.0 points average per contest. Carr spent the next four seasons in a reserve role with the San Antonio Spurs before signing with Utah in 1994, and proving to the world that the Big Dog still has some bite left in his game.

FACT FILE

Born: July 23, 1961
Height: 6′ 9″
Length of NBA career:
  1984–present
Major teams:
  Atlanta
  Sacramento (joined 1990)
  San Antonio (joined 1991)
  Utah (joined 1994)

LEFT: WILL THE REAL BIG DOG PLEASE STAND UP? BEFORE GLENN ROBINSON, ANTOINE CARR WAS THE TOP DOG IN THE NBA.

AUSTIN CARR

FACT FILE

Born: March 10, 1948
Height: 6′ 4″
Length of NBA career:
 1971–81
Major teams:
 Cleveland
 Dallas (joined 1980)
 Washington (joined 1980)
Records/Awards:
 NBA All-Star (1)

One of the most explosive scorers in the history of college basketball, Austin Carr kept his keen shooting-touch in high-gear for the better part of ten NBA seasons.

Carr, a 6-foot-4-inch guard from Notre Dame, is the greatest scorer in NCAA Tournament history, having averaged 41.3 points in seven career NCAA games.

Selected as the National Player of the Year in 1971, Carr finished his college career with a blistering 34.6 scoring average, placing second all-time in that category behind the legendary Pistol Pete Maravich (44.2).

The Cleveland Cavaliers selected Carr as the first pick overall in the 1971 NBA draft, and the scoring machine responded by torching opponents for 21.2 points per game that season and consequently earning a place for himself on the NBA's All-Rookie Team.

The following season, Carr posted 20.5 points per game for the Cavs, and in 1973–74, earned his one and only NBA All-Star selection by averaging a career-high 21.9 points.

Carr, who played nine seasons in Cleveland and split his last year with Dallas and Washington, finished with a 15.4 career scoring average. He averaged 11.8 points in 18 career playoff contests.

RIGHT: AUSTIN CARR IS THE GREATEST SCORER IN NCAA TOURNAMENT HISTORY.

BILL CARTWRIGHT

The Chicago Bulls of Michael Jordan and Scottie Pippen reeled off three straight championships from 1991–93, and in the middle of all the hoopla and history-making stood the 7-foot-1-inch veteran center, Bill Cartwright.

Traded from the arch-enemy New York Knicks to Chicago in 1988, Cartwright was already 34 years old when he helped the Bulls to their first-ever world championship.

For Cartwright, three championship rings hardly seemed possible when he was mired in mediocrity as a member of the Knicks from the time New York drafted him out of San Francisco in 1979. An NBA All-Rookie with the Knicks, Cartwright teamed with fellow-center Patrick Ewing in his prime to form a Twin-Towers attack that gave opposing front lines major problems, but was never quite powerful enough to spearhead a championship charge.

In Chicago, Cartwright was surrounded by much more talent, and his reliable, short-range shot, which he often released from way atop his head, helped soften defenses around Jordan and Pippen, giving both more room on the court to work their magic.

A 16-year NBA veteran, Cartwright averaged 13.2 points and 6.3 rebounds in his career, and in 124 career playoff games, tallied 8.9 points and 5.4 rebounds per game.

FACT FILE

Born: July 30, 1957
Height: 7′ 1″
Length of NBA career:
  1979–95
Major teams:
  New York
  Chicago (joined 1988)
  Seattle (joined 1994)
Records/Awards:
  NBA Championship (3)
  NBA All-Star Game (1)

LEFT: IN THE MIDDLE OF CHICAGO'S THREE STRAIGHT CHAMPIONSHIPS FROM 1991–93 STOOD THE 7-1 CENTER, BILL CARTWRIGHT.

SAM CASSELL

FACT FILE

Born: November 18, 1969
Height: 6′ 3″
Length of NBA career:
  1993–present
Major teams:
  Houston
  Phoenix (joined 1996)
  Dallas (joined 1996)
  New Jersey (joined 1997)
Records/Awards:
  NBA Championship (2)

Sam Cassell went two-for-two in his first two NBA seasons, helping the Houston Rockets win back-to-back championships in 1994 and 1995.

A fiery point guard with bold moves to the basket, the 6-foot-3-inch Cassell shared Houston's quarterbacking duties with veteran Kenny Smith, but was called upon more often during crucial stages down the stretch of both championship seasons.

A product of powerful Dunbar High School in Baltimore, Md, Cassell made a name for himself as a scorer at San Jacinto Junior College, where he averaged 22.3 points in two seasons. He spent the next two years at Florida State, posting 18.3 points per game and leading the ACC in steals in his senior campaign. One of Cassell's greatest NBA games took place in Game 2 of the 1995 NBA Finals against Orlando. In that contest, Cassell rolled up 31 points on 8 of 12 shooting from the field, including 4 of 6 buckets from three-point range.

Last season, Cassell played for Pheonix, Dallas and finally, New Jersey, averaging 15.9 points and 5.0 assists per game.

RIGHT: SAM CASSELL, TRYING TO WORK HIS WAY AROUND MICHAEL JORDAN, BAGGED 31 POINTS IN GAME 2 OF THE 1995 NBA FINALS.

AL CERVI

One of the greatest back-court stars of his generation, and one of the few early pros who didn't go to college, Al Cervi dominated the game from the mid-1940s through the early 1950s.

A superb 5-foot-11-inch guard who broke into professional hoops with Buffalo of the National Basketball League in 1937—he played just nine games with Buffalo that season—Cervi gained valuable playing experience with independent teams from 1935–1937, and 1938–1945 while serving in the U.S. Army.

Upon his return to the NBL in the 1945–46 season, Cervi helped the Rochester Royals win the championship by contributing 10.7 points per game and his own brand of tenacious defense. The following season, the man known as "Digger" led the NBL in scoring with a career-high 14.4 average and was named the league's Most Valuable Player.

After three seasons in Rochester, Cervi became a player-coach for the Syracuse Nationals in 1948—Syracuse joined the NBA in 1949—and retired as a player in 1953 with a 10.1 career scoring average. In 57 post-season NBL and NBA playoff games, Cervi averaged 9.3 points per game. Also regarded as one of the game's leading coaches in his time, Cervi piloted the Nationals until early in the 1956-57 season.

BELOW: AL CERVI, WHEELING AROUND THE NEW YORK KNICKS' DEFENSE, LED ROCHESTER TO A NBL CHAMPIONSHIP.

FACT FILE

Born: February 12, 1917
Height: 5′ 11″
Length of NBL career:
 1937–37, 1945–49
Length of NBA career:
 1949–53
Major teams:
 Buffalo
 Rochester (joined 1945)
 Syracuse (joined 1948)
Records/Awards:
 NBL All-Star (3)
 NBL Championship (1)
 Hall of Fame (1984)

WILT CHAMBERLAIN

FACT FILE

Born: August 21, 1936
Height: 7′ 1″
Length of NBA career:
1959–73
Major teams:
Philadelphia-San
Francisco Warriors
Philadelphia '76ers
(joined 1965)
Los Angeles (joined 1968)
Records/Awards:
NBA Championship (2)
NBA Rookie of the Year
(1960)
NBA All-Star (13)
NBA Most Valuable Player
(4)
Hall of Fame (1978)
All-Defensive First Team
(2)

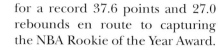

The unstoppable scoring machine, Wilt "The Stilt" Chamberlain was, in his heyday, the greatest offensive force the game of basketball had ever seen. Twenty-four years after he played his last NBA game, the 7-foot-1-inch, 275-pound Chamberlain still holds scores of records, many of which are near-impossible to break.

For all of his amazing feats, like most career games with 50 or more points (118) or most seasons leading the league in field goal percentage (9), perhaps the most unapproachable record in Chamberlain's fourteen-year NBA career is his 50.4 per-game scoring average with the Philadelphia Warriors in the 1961–62 season.

Chamberlain, who used a smooth finger-roll over smaller defenders to score many of his points, is the only center in NBA history ever to lead the league in scoring (7 times), rebounding (11 times) and assists (702 assists in 1967–68). He played his college ball at Kansas for three seasons, and before embarking on a legendary NBA journey, signed with the Harlem Globetrotters for the 1958–59 season. He broke in with Philadelphia in a huge way in 1959, tearing up the league for a record 37.6 points and 27.0 rebounds en route to capturing the NBA Rookie of the Year Award.

After spending his first five-and-a-half seasons with the Philadelphia Warriors—two-and-a-half after the franchise moved to San Francisco in 1962—the great Chamberlain was traded to the Philadelphia 76ers in 1965, and two seasons later, won his first NBA Championship. "The Big Dipper," as Chamberlain was also called, was traded to the Los Angeles Lakers in 1968. He finished his career in Los Angeles, but not before helping the 1971–72 Lakers to an NBA title.

Throughout the years, Chamberlain detractors have criticized the big man for racking up points against much-smaller competition in his era—Boston's 6-foot-11-inch Bill Russell was his arch-rival—but Chamberlain's whopping scoring totals had as much to do with his fine outside shooting, agility, and overall knowledge of the game as it did with his height advantage.

A four-time Most Valuable Player and 13-time All-Star, Chamberlain finished his career with averages of 30.1 points and 22.9 rebounds. He was named to the NBA's 35th Anniversary All-Time Team in 1980.

RIGHT: WILT CHAMBERLAIN, IN HIS PHILADELPHIA UNIFORM, WAS AN OFFENSIVE TERROR THE LIKES OF WHICH PROFESSIONAL BASKETBALL HAD NEVER SEEN BEFORE.

TOM CHAMBERS

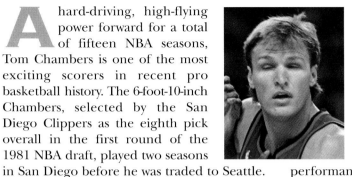

A hard-driving, high-flying power forward for a total of fifteen NBA seasons, Tom Chambers is one of the most exciting scorers in recent pro basketball history. The 6-foot-10-inch Chambers, selected by the San Diego Clippers as the eighth pick overall in the first round of the 1981 NBA draft, played two seasons in San Diego before he was traded to Seattle.

Although he never won a scoring title, Chambers was often among the top-ten scorers in the league in his prime, chasing that crown with the likes of Michael Jordan, Karl Malone, Larry Bird, and Chris Mullin. He could drain the outside shot, and if a defender overplayed him, Chambers had the quickness to blow by his man, and the explosiveness to soar toward the rim for a thunderous dunk.

Chambers, a four-time All-Star, enjoyed his best scoring seasons with Seattle and Phoenix from 1986–1990, when he posted 23.3, 20.4, 25.7 and 27.2 points, respectively. His 34-point performance in the 1987 All-Star Game earned him the Most Valuable Player Award.

After posting NBA career averages of 18.3 points and 6.1 rebounds, through 1995, Chambers signed to play basketball in Israel in 1996 with Maccabi Tel Aviv, but returned to play 12 games with Charlotte last season.

FACT FILE

Born: June 21, 1959
Height: 6′ 10″
Length of NBA career:
  1981–95
  1996–present
Major teams:
  San Diego
  Seattle (joined 1983)
  Phoenix (joined 1988)
  Utah (joined 1993)
  Charlotte (joined 1996)
Records/Awards:
  NBA All-Star Game (4)

LEFT: HE NEVER WON A SCORING TITLE, BUT HIGH-FLYING TOM CHAMBERS WAS ALWAYS IN THE HUNT.

NEW YORK-TORONTO: THE FIRST GAME

The NBA, celebrating its 50th anniversary, kicked off the 1996–97 season with a meeting between New York and Toronto, the same two cities that met in the first game of the league's inaugural season in 1946.

The New York Knicks and Toronto Huskies, both members of the 11-team Basketball Association of America formed in 1946—the NBA's predecessor—squared off on November 1 of that year at Maple Leaf Gardens, where Toronto of the National Hockey League would win three consecutive Stanley Cups between 1947–49.

The story of the Knicks' train ride up to Toronto for that historic game showed how little interest Canadians had for the game of basketball, one of the major reasons why the Huskies folded after just one season of play.

As the story goes, a Canadian customs inspector walked over to a group of Knicks on the train on the evening of October 31, and asked "What are you?"

"We're the New York Knicks," Coach Neil Cohalan answered.

"We're familiar with the New York Rangers," said the inspector. "Are you anything like them?"

"They play hockey," said an irritated Cohalan, "we play basketball."

The next night, the two teams met before an estimated crowd of 8,000. With the exception of Toronto's Canadian-born Hank Biasetti, all 22 players from both squads were American.

The Knicks, led by Leo Gottlieb and Ozzie Schechtman, who scored the first basket of the game, raced out to a 6–0 lead in the first two minutes, and held a 16–12 lead at the 12-minute mark.

Toronto, led by the 6-foot-8-inch George Nostrand and Ed Sadowski, who combined for 35 points, stormed back to take a 29–27 lead. The Knicks, however, reeled off ten straight points to close out the first half with a 37–29 lead.

In a rugged, seesaw second half, the Knicks hung on for a 68–66 victory.

By season's end, the Huskies' franchise, a failure at the ticket window, went out of business, proving that the customs inspector was correct. Toronto was indeed a hockey town, at least for the next 50 years, anyway.

DON CHANEY

FACT FILE

Born: March 22, 1946
Height: 6′ 5″
Length of NBA career:
 1968–75, 1976–80
Length of ABA career:
 1976–77
Major teams:
 Boston
 St. Louis (joined 1975)
 Los Angeles (joined 1976)
 Boston (joined 1978)
Records/Awards:
 NBA Championship (2)

Don Chaney lives in Boston Celtic lore as the only man to play alongside two great Celtics from two different eras: Bill Russell and Larry Bird.

A 6-foot-5-inch guard out of the University of Houston, the man his teammates called "Duck" won two world championships with the Celtics, the first in 1969, when Boston defeated the Los Angeles Lakers, four games to three, and the second in 1974, when the Celtics took four out of seven from Milwaukee.

A five-time NBA All-Defensive Second-Team selection, Chaney averaged 8.4 points and 2.1 assists in a 12-year career which started in 1968 with Boston, and ended there in 1980 after a second tour of duty in Beantown.

In between, Chaney played for the ABA's Spirits of St. Louis and the NBA's Los Angeles Lakers. His career scoring year was 1972–73, when he averaged 13.1 points for the Celtics. In 70 career NBA playoff games, Chaney averaged 8.1 points per game.

At the University of Houston, Chaney averaged 12.6 points in four years, helping the Cougars to an 81–12 record during that span and two trips to the NCAA Final Four. On January 20, 1968, Houston pulled a memorable, 71–69 upset over top-ranked UCLA. In that game, Chaney played the entire 40 minutes.

He finished with 11 points, 6 rebounds and 3 key steals down the stretch.

RIGHT: DON CHANEY WAS A TEAMMATE OF CELTIC GREATS BILL RUSSELL AND LARRY BIRD.

MAURICE CHEEKS

The legendary Julius Erving once said this about his teammate, Maurice Cheeks: "Mo is a very creative passer. Anyone can get you the ball, but the trick is to get it to you when you're in the maximum scoring position. If his man lays off him, he can hit the jumper. If his man crowds him, he just blows right by him and penetrates all the way."

One of the quickest guards in NBA history, "Mo" Cheeks teamed with Dr. J to help the Philadelphia 76ers win the 1983 NBA Championship. He wasn't a prolific scorer, but Cheeks was a true floor general who possessed excellent court vision and the ability to run a fast-break offense. For most of his 15 NBA seasons—the first 11 of which were spent in Philadelphia—Cheeks was the standard by which point guards were measured.

A four-time All-Star and four-time All Defensive First Team selection, Cheeks averaged 11.1 points and 6.7 assists in his career. He retired at the end of the 1992–93 season after playing just 35 games with the New Jersey Nets, and Cheeks still holds the NBA record for most career steals with 2,130.

Cheeks, who was drafted out of West Texas State by Philadelphia as the 36th pick overall in the second round of the 1978 NBA draft, averaged 14.4 points and 6.9 rebounds in 133 career playoff games.

FACT FILE

Born: September 8, 1956
Height: 6′ 1″
Length of NBA career:
1978–93
Major teams:
Philadelphia
San Antonio (joined 1989)
New York (joined 1990)
Atlanta (joined 1991)
New Jersey (joined 1993)
Records/Awards:
NBA Championship (1)
NBA All-Star (4)
NBA All-Defensive First
Team (4)

LEFT: MAURICE CHEEKS, A TRUE FLOOR LEADER, TEAMED WITH JULIUS ERVING TO HELP PHILADELPHIA WIN THE 1983 NBA CHAMPIONSHIP.

ARCHIE CLARK

FACT FILE

Born: July 15, 1941
Height: 6' 2"
Length of NBA career:
  1966–76
Major teams:
  Los Angeles
  Philadelphia (joined 1968)
  Baltimore (joined 1972)
  Capital (joined 1973)
  Seattle (joined 1974)
  Detroit (joined 1975)
Records/Awards:
  NBA All-Star (2)

Despite a career filled with injuries and contract disputes, despite playing in the shadows of two future Hall-of-Famers, Archie Clark proved himself to be one of the top backcourt men of his era.

Clark, a 6-foot-2-inch guard out of Minnesota, began his pro career in the 1966–67 season with the Los Angeles Lakers. Overshadowed in the Lakers backcourt by the great Jerry West, Clark nonetheless averaged 10.5 points and 19.9 points in his first two seasons with the Lakers. He was traded to the Philadelphia 76ers in 1968 as part of the deal that brought Wilt Chamberlain to the Lakers.

In Philadelphia, Clark was overshadowed by yet another high-profiled teammate, Hal Greer, but still managed to produce. He raised his scoring average in each of his three-and-a-half seasons with the 76ers, posting 13.5 points in 1968–69, 19.7 in 1969–70, 21.3 in 1970–71, and a career high 25.2 points in the 1971–72 season, which he split between Philadelphia and Baltimore.

In 1972–73, Clark found himself in a contract dispute at Baltimore, sat out 43 games, but came back to average 18.3 points per game. The following season, Clark missed 26 games for that franchise, which became the Capital Bullets, while recuperating from a broken collarbone.

A two-time All-Star, Clark averaged 16.3 points per game during his 10-year NBA career.

RIGHT: ARCHIE CLARK MAY HAVE BEEN OVERSHADOWED THROUGHOUT HIS CAREER BY BETTER-KNOWN PLAYERS, BUT HIS TALENTS AND CONTRIBUTIONS TO THE GAME CAN NEVER BE OVERLOOKED.

NAT "SWEETWATER" CLIFTON

One of the first black players in the National Basketball Association, Nathaniel "Sweetwater" Clifton was a talented and popular star with the New York Knick teams of the 1950s.

Clifton, who played his college basketball at Xavier University in New Orleans, came to the Knicks after playing for the New York Rens, the Dayton Metropolitans and the world-famous Harlem Globetrotters. A 6-foot–7-inch forward and center who had the flashy moves of a point guard, Clifton played seven seasons in New York, helping the Knicks reach the NBA Finals three times during his career.

In eight NBA seasons, his last spent with Detroit, Clifton averaged 10 points and 8.2 rebounds per game. His best season in New York was 1954–55, when he averaged 13.1 points on a team that included star players like Carl Braun, Harry Gallatin, Ray Felix and Dick McGuire. In the 1956–57 season, "Sweetwater," who got his nickname because he loved drinking soda pop as a kid, was named to the NBA All-Star team, averaging 10.7 points. He scored 8 points and grabbed 11 rebounds in that year's All-Star game.

FACT FILE

Born: October 13, 1922
Height: 6′ 7″
Length of NBA career:
 1950–58
Major teams:
 New York
 Detroit (joined 1957)
Records/Awards:
 NBA All-Star (1)

LEFT: NAT "SWEETWATER" CLIFTON WAS THE FIRST BLACK PLAYER TO SUIT UP WITH THE NEW YORK KNICKS.

DERRICK COLEMAN

FACT FILE

Born: June 21, 1967
Height: 6' 10"
Length of NBA career:
   1990–present
Major teams:
   New Jersey
   Philadelphia (joined 1995)
Records/Awards:
   NBA Rookie of the Year
      (1991)
   NBA All-Star (1)

One of the most gifted power forwards in the NBA today, Derrick Coleman is one of those rare players who have the ability to singlehandedly take control of a game. Though he is often criticized for being undisciplined and out of playing shape, Coleman is a terrific scorer and rock-solid rebounder who frustrates opponents with an arsenal of smooth moves around the basket.

After breaking in with the New Jersey Nets as the first overall pick in the 1990 NBA draft, the 6-foot-10-inch Coleman averaged roughly 20 points and 10 rebounds per game in five and a half seasons with the Nets before he was traded to the Philadelphia 76ers.

In his first season with the Nets, Coleman was named NBA Rookie of the Year after he led all first-year players in scoring (18.4) and rebounding (10.3). He averaged a career-high 20.7 points for the Nets in 1992–93, and the following season was named to his first All-Star team en route to a 20.2 scoring season.

On an international level, Coleman won a gold medal in the 1994 World Championships as a member of Dream Team II, dominating the opening minutes of the gold medal game against Russia. A legendary performer at Syracuse University, Coleman is the first player in NCAA history to notch at least 2,000 points, 1,500 rebounds and 300 blocks in his career.

RIGHT: WHILE DERRICK COLEMAN'S ATTITUDE IS OUT OF LINE, HIS GAME IS OUT OF SIGHT.

DOUG COLLINS

If not for numerous injuries that slowed his career, Doug Collins could have been one of the NBA's all-time greats. Nevertheless, Collins enjoyed a productive eight-year career in Philadelphia, helping the 76ers reach the NBA Finals twice during his tenure with the team.

A 6-foot-6-inch shooting guard from Illinois State, Collins averaged 18.3 points per game in 1976–77, teaming with first-year NBA superstar Julius Erving to steer the 76ers to the Finals, where Philadelphia was defeated by Portland, four games to two.

Foot and knee injuries limited Collins to just 36 games in 1979–80, when Philadelphia lost the NBA Championship to the Los Angeles Lakers, four games to two.

A three-time All-Star who averaged 17.9 points as a pro, Collins enjoyed his best season in 1975–76, when he registered a career-high 20.8 points per contest. In 32 playoff games, he averaged 21.5 points. The first pick overall in the 1973 NBA draft, Collins averaged 29.1 points per game in four seasons at Illinois State.

He was a member of the 1972 U.S. Olympic Basketball Team which lost the gold medal to the Soviet Union at Munich in controversial fashion, losing the contest on a court-length pass, catch and layup at the buzzer.

It was the first time the United States had failed to win a gold medal since basketball was introduced to the Olympics in 1936.

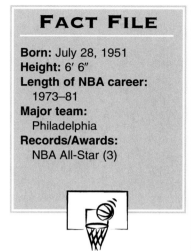

FACT FILE

Born: July 28, 1951
Height: 6′ 6″
Length of NBA career:
  1973–81
Major team:
  Philadelphia
Records/Awards:
  NBA All-Star (3)

LEFT: DOUG COLLINS WAS A MEMBER OF THE 1972 US OLYMPIC BASKETBALL TEAM WHICH LOST TO THE SOVIET UNION IN CONTROVERSIAL FASHION.

CHARLES COOPER

FACT FILE

Born: August 30, 1907
Height: 6′ 4″
Length of Pro career:
  1925–45
Major teams:
  Philadelphia Panther Pros
  Philadelphia Giants
  New York Renaissance
  Washington Bears
Records/Awards:
  Championships (2)
  Hall of Fame (1976)

Joe Lapchick, a Hall-of-Fame coach and a member of the Original Celtics, often said that Charles "Tarzan" Cooper was the best center he ever saw.

Cooper, a 6-foot-4-inch pivotman, was a member of the all-black New York Renaissance Five of the 1930s, a traveling team which became the arch-rival of the Original Celtics.

A twenty-year pro, Cooper played eleven seasons with the "Rens," and spent the rest of his career playing for the Philadelphia Panther Pros, the Philadelphia Giants and the Washington Bears.

During Cooper's tenure with the Rens, the team won 1,303 games and lost just 203. In the 1932–33 season, Cooper led the Rens to 88 straight victories before that string was snapped by the Celtics. (The Rens defeated the Celtics in seven other contests that season, including the first basketball game between blacks and whites in the South.)

When the Rens won the World Pro Championship Tournament in 1939, Cooper was their Most Valuable Player.

Four years later, Cooper would help the Washington Bears win the World Pro Title.

RIGHT: CHARLES COOPER WAS A DOMINANT CENTER WITH THE LEGENDARY HARLEM RENS.

MICHAEL COOPER

One of the greatest "sixth" men in NBA history, Michael Cooper came off the bench to spark the Los Angeles Lakers to five championships during their dynasty in the 1980s.

Kareem Abdul-Jabbar, Magic Johnson and James Worthy got most of the publicity during the Laker's glory years, but it was Cooper, running the floor like a cheetah and leaping as if he had mighty springs built into his muscular legs, who added top-flight defense and a decent scoring punch to L.A.'s fast-break, Showtime attack, which racked up NBA titles in 1980, 1982, 1985, 1987, and 1988.

The 6-foot-7-inch Cooper, a third-round draft pick out of New Mexico in 1978, played all 11 of his NBA seasons in a Laker uniform. He never made an All-Star team, but Cooper was a five-time All-Defensive First Team selection, and in 1987, was the NBA's Defensive Player of the Year.

During his career, Cooper averaged 8.9 points per game for the Lakers, and tallied 9.4 points per contest in 168 playoff games. His best scoring season came in 1981–82, when he averaged 11.9 points.

Growing up in California, Cooper admired John Havlicek, the great sixth man on the Boston Celtics of the 1960s and 1970s.

"As a kid, I'd sit and watch the Celtics, and I just admired that guy so much," said Cooper. "I wanted to be just like him. When I was playing in high school and college, I even told my coaches that I'd rather come off the bench than start because that's what Havlicek did."

FACT FILE

Born: April 15, 1956
Height: 6' 7"
Length of NBA career:
 1978–90
Major team:
 Los Angeles Lakers
Records/Awards:
 NBA All-Defensive First
  Team (5)
 NBA Defensive Player of
  the Year (1987)
 Championships (5)

LEFT: A BRILLIANT "SIXTH MAN," MICHAEL COOPER HELPED THE LOS ANGELES LAKERS RACK UP FIVE CHAMPIONSHIPS IN THE 1980S.

BOB COUSY

FACT FILE

Born: August 9, 1928
Height: 6′ 1″
Length of NBA career:
  1950–70
Major teams:
  Boston
  Cincinnati (joined 1969)
Records/Awards:
  NBA Most Valuable Player
    (1957)
  NBA Championship (6)
  All-Star (13)
  Hall of Fame (1970)

Known in his day as "Houdini of the Hardwood," Bob Cousy's slick ball-handling, blind, behind-the-back and lookaway passes brought entertainment and excitement to the NBA—and six championships to the Boston Celtics.

Cousy, a 6-foot-1-inch guard out of Holy Cross who broke into pro ball with the Celtics in 1950, played 13 of his 14 NBA seasons with Boston, and his backcourt wizardry wowed not only spectators, but teammates and opponents alike. He led the NBA in assists for eight consecutive years from 1952–60, and proved himself an accomplished shooter as well, posting season scoring averages of 20 or more points four times in his career, and hanging up his sneakers with a career 18.4 average.

A thirteen-time NBA All-Star, Cousy helped the Celtics to a championship in 1957—the same year he was named the league's Most Valuable Player—and five straight crowns from 1959–63. He shares the NBA Finals single-game record for most assists in one quarter, racking up 8 dishes against St. Louis on April 9, 1957. Cousy also holds the NBA single-game playoff record for most free-throws made, 30, and most free-throws attempted, 32, setting those marks on March 21, 1953 against Syracuse.

For years after he retired in the 1969–70 season (after playing just 7 games with Cincinnati), Cousy was the standard by which all backcourt players were measured. He was selected to the NBA's 25th Anniversary All-Time Team in 1970, and made the cut again in 1980 as a member of the league's 35th Anniversary All-Time Team.

RIGHT: BOB COUSY WORKED MAGIC WITH A BASKETBALL IN HIS HANDS.

DAVE COWENS

lthough only 6-foot-8-inches tall, Dave Cowens became one of the NBA's premier centers, using speed and aggressiveness to neutralize an opponent's height advantage.

For 11 seasons—10 of which he spent in Boston—the red-headed Cowens played the game with reckless abandon. He began his pro career as the Celtics 1970 top draft choice out of Florida State and made an immediate impact, averaging 17 points and 15 rebounds per game en route to earning a co-Rookie of the Year Award, which he shared with Portland's Geoff Petrie.

A seven-time All-Star—he was the MVP of the 1973 All-Star Game—Cowens enjoyed his best season as a Celtic in 1972–1973, when he averaged career-highs in points (20.5) and rebounds (16.2), and was named the NBA's Most Valuable Player.

Cowens, a tough defensive player who averaged 17.6 points and 13.6 rebounds in his career, and added 18.9 points and 14.4 boards in 89 playoff games, helped the Celtics to NBA titles in 1974 and 1976 before retiring in 1980. Two years later, Cowens was coaxed out of retirement—and traded to the Milwaukee Bucks for Quinn Buckner. He played in Milwaukee for one final season, averaging 8.1 points and 6.9 rebounds in 40 games.

Despite his height disadvantage, Cowens shares the single-game playoff record for most defensive rebounds, 20, pulling off that remarkable feat twice in his career, once on April 22, 1975, against Houston, and again on May 1, 1977, against Philadelphia.

FACT FILE

Born: October 25, 1948
Height: 6′ 8″
Length of NBA career:
 1970–80, 1982–83
Major teams:
 Boston
 Milwaukee (joined 1982)
Records/Awards:
 NBA Most Valuable Player
  (1973)
 NBA All-Defensive First
  Team (1)
 NBA Rookie of the Year
  (1971)
 NBA Championship (2)
 NBA All-Star (7)
 Hall of Fame (1990)

LEFT: DAVE COWENS WAS A HARD-NOSED PERFORMER WHO EXCELLED AS A LEADER OF THE BOSTON CELTICS FOR AN ENTIRE DECADE.

TERRY CUMMINGS

FACT FILE

Born: March 15, 1961
Height: 6′ 9″
Length of NBA career:
1982–present
Major teams:
San Diego
Milwaukee (joined 1984)
San Antonio (joined 1989)
Milwaukee (joined 1995)
Seattle (joined 1996)
Records/Awards:
NBA Rookie of the Year
(1983)
NBA All-Star (2)

Grace and power. Those two words best describe what Terry Cummings has been bringing to the game of professional basketball for the past fifteen seasons.

Cummings, a 6-foot-9-inch power forward out of DePaul, has established a reputation over the years as one of the NBA's most consistent and most dangerous scorers.

Selected by San Diego as the second pick overall in the 1982 NBA draft, Cummings sizzled in his rookie season with the Clippers, averaging a career-high 23.7 points per game en route to winning the league's Rookie of the Year award.

On December 15 of his rookie season, Cummings, after complaining of dizziness, and shortness of breath, collapsed in the middle of the court at the Salt Palace in Salt Lake City during a game against the Utah Jazz. A series of tests showed that Cummings had suffered from arrhythmia—an irregular rhythm in the heartbeat. The problem was controlled by medication, and Cummings has been able to continue a career that has featured seven seasons of scoring 20 or more points per game.

After two seasons in San Diego, Cummings was traded to Milwaukee, where he played five more years before he was dealt to San Antonio in 1989.

He played six seasons for the Spurs before he resurfaced with Milwaukee for the 1995–96 season. After one season with the Bucks, Cummings signed as a free agent with Seattle.

RIGHT: AFTER ALL THESE YEARS, TERRY CUMMINGS IS STILL ONE OF THE NBA'S MOST DANGEROUS SCORERS.

BILLY CUNNINGHAM

H e could jump clear out of a gymnasium, and that is why Billy Cunningham was nicknamed the "Kangaroo Kid." Cunningham, a flashy 6-foot-7-inch forward drafted out of North Carolina in 1965, teamed with Wilt "The Stilt" Chamberlain to lead the Philadelphia 76ers to the 1967 NBA Championship, a four-games-to-two victory over San Francisco.

The smooth-shooting, high-flying Cunningham played his first seven seasons with the 76ers before jumping to the Carolina Cougars of the ABA in 1972. His best NBA season was 1969–70, when he averaged a career-high 26.1 points, 13.6 rebounds, and 4.3 assists.

A four-time NBA All-Star by the time he reached the ABA, Cunningham's mere presence boosted the image of the rival league. He played two seasons for Carolina, and after averaging 24.1 points, 12 rebounds, 6.3 assists and a league-leading 216 steals in his first season with the Cougars, earned the ABA's Most Valuable Player award.

After his brief ABA stint, Cunningham re-signed with Philadelphia of the NBA, playing two more seasons before a knee injury forced him to retire. In eleven professional seasons, Cunningham finished with averages of 21.2 points, 10.4 rebounds, and 4.3 assists.

FACT FILE

Born: June 3, 1943
Height: 6′ 7″
Length of NBA career:
  1965–72, 1974–76
Length of ABA career:
  1972–74
Major teams:
  Philadelphia
  Carolina (joined 1972)
  Philadelphia (joined 1974)
Records/Awards:
  NBA All-Star (4)
  ABA All-Star (1)
  ABA Most Valuable Player
    (1973)
  NBA Championship (1)
  Hall of Fame (1985)

LEFT: BILLY CUNNINGHAM, WHO COULD PRACTICALLY LEAP OUT OF THE GYM, WAS NICKNAMED THE "KANGAROO KID."

DELL CURRY

FACT FILE

Born: June 25, 1964
Height: 6′ 5″
Length of NBA career:
  1986–present
Major teams:
  Utah
  Cleveland (joined 1987)
  Charlotte (joined 1988)
Records/Awards:
  NBA Sixth Man Award
    (1994)

There are only a handful of players in the NBA who possess the shooting range of Dell Curry, a 6-foot-5-inch swingman with the Charlotte Hornets. Curry, who has averaged 13.2 points in eleven NBA seasons, is the Hornet's all-time scoring leader with 10,461 points through last season.

With the ability to hit a jumper from the parking lot, the slick-shooting Curry, who bagged 14.8 points per game last season, has been one of the most effective sixth-men in the league in recent years.

At the conclusion of the 1996–97 season, Curry and Muggsy Bogues were the only two players left from Charlotte's expansion season of 1988–89. He had spent his first two seasons as a limited role player with Utah and Cleveland. In the 1993–94 campaign, Curry averaged a career-high 16.3 points per game—placing him first among all NBA bench scorers—and won the NBA's Sixth Man Award.

A standout athlete at Virginia Tech from 1982–86, Curry averaged 19.0 points during his college career. He was also a pitcher on the baseball team at Virginia Tech and was selected by the Baltimore Orioles in the 14th round of the 1985 free-agent draft.

RIGHT: THE PARKING LOT IS NOT OUT OF DELL CURRY'S SHOOTING RANGE.

HOWARD DALLMAR

Howard Dallmar, a 6-foot-5-inch forward with a solid all-around game, teamed in his rookie season with shooting-sensation Joe Fulks to lead the 1946–47 Philadelphia Warriors to the Basketball Association of America championship. The Warriors won that championship by defeating Chicago, four games to one.

Dallmar, who starred at Stanford, contributed 8.8 points per game in his rookie season, complementing the talents of Fulks—the league's scoring champion that season with 23.2 points per game—and other talented teammates like guards Angelo Musi, Jerry Fleishman, and George Senesky.

The following season, Dallmar racked up a career-high average of 12.2 points per contest and led the BAA in assists with 120 in forty-eight games.

His efforts helped Philadelphia to get back to the championship round, but the Warriors were defeated by Baltimore, four games to two.

In three BAA seasons, Dallmar averaged 9.6 points and racked up 340 assists. In twenty-five career playoff games, he averaged 8.0 points.

BELOW: THE ALL-AROUND TALENTS OF HOWIE DALLMAR (THIRD FROM LEFT) HELPED THE PHILADELPHIA WARRIORS CAPTURE THE 1946–47 BAA CHAMPIONSHIP.

FACT FILE

Born: May 24, 1922
Height: 6′ 5″
Length of BAA career:
  1946–49
Major team:
  Philadelphia
Records/Awards:
  BAA Championship (1)

Tick, Tick, Tick . . . The Longest Game ever Played

There were two five-overtime games in league history. The first took place on November 24, 1949, when Syracuse squeaked past Anderson, 125–123. The second five-overtime marathon took place on November 9, 1989, at the Bradley Center in Milwaukee, where the Bucks, despite a 53 point performance by Xavier McDaniel, slipped past the Seattle SuperSonics, 155–154.

One game in history lasted longer—the six-overtime affair staged between the Indianapolis Olympians and the Rochester Royals on January 6, 1951.

With the 24-second clock still three years away, the going was a lot slower, but no less dramatic, on that historic evening.

Playing before a sparse crowd of 3,300 spectators at the Edgerton Park Arena in Rochester, the Royals' 6-foot-9-inch center, Arnie Risen had delighted the home crowd with a game-high 26 points, but the contest was tied, 65–65, at the end of regulation time.

In the first five-minute overtime session, each team scored just one basket, sending the game into a second overtime, which went scoreless.

In the third extra session, each team again scored one basket apiece, and the score was knotted at 69–69 after 63 minutes of play. The fourth quarter came and went with nary a point scored between the two clubs.

In the fifth overtime session, as players from both sides began to tire, the scoring opened up a bit, as each team registered four points to send the game into a sixth overtime deadlocked at 73–73.

Once again, the scoreboard was silent, and a seventh overtime seemed likely until a high-arcing, last-second shot by Indianapolis' Ralph Beard nestled through the cords to give the Olympians a long-awaited, and much-deserved, 75–73 victory.

Rochester, however, would get the last laugh. The Royals got their second wind and went sailing into the championship round, where they defeated the New York Knicks in seven games to win the title.

75

Below: Xavier McDaniel's 53 points were not enough to help Seattle in its five-overtime loss to Milwaukee in 1989.

LOUIE DAMPIER

FACT FILE

Born: November 20, 1944
Height: 6' 0"
Length of ABA career:
 1967–76
Length of NBA career:
 1976–79
Major teams:
 Kentucky
 San Antonio (joined 1976)
Records/Awards:
 ABA Championship (1)
 ABA All-Star (7)

Louie Dampier was the last original ABA player to suit up for an NBA team. The 6ft Dampier, a jump-shooting guard out of Kentucky who broke in with the ABA's Kentucky Colonels in the league's inaugural 1967–68 campaign, played 12 professional seasons, spending his last three years with the NBA's San Antonio Spurs.

Dampier, who averaged 18.9 points in his ABA career and 16.9 in 94 playoff games—he spent all nine of his ABA seasons with Kentucky—is the league's career leader in games played (728), minutes played (27,770) and points scored (13,726). He once scored 55 points in a game against Dallas. Overall, he made seven ABA All-Star appearances.

"I don't exactly walk down Park Avenue and say 'Here I am.' But I'm proud of those records," Dampier said during the 1976–77 season in San Antonio, his first year in the NBA. "They'll always be there, and they're something I can show my grandkids."

Often asked to take the crucial shot with the game on the line, Dampier, who teamed with better-known stars like Artis Gilmore and Dan Issel, helped Kentucky win the 1974–75 ABA Championship, averaging 16.8 points that season.

In his three NBA seasons with San Antonio, Dampier averaged 6.7 points per game, and 4.5 points in 15 career playoff contests.

At the University of Kentucky, Dampier was a member of the team that was drubbed by predominantly black Texas Western in the national championship game that paved the way for future black players.

BELOW: THOUGH HE WAS OFTEN UNDERRATED, LOUIE DAMPIER, HERE SLIPPING PAST THE GREAT JULIUS ERVING, WAS OFTEN CALLED UPON TO TAKE THE CRUCIAL SHOT.

BOB DANDRIDGE

One week before the Washington Bullets opened their training camp in the 1977–78 season, head coach Dick Motta was drooling over the arrival of Bob Dandridge.

"It's up to Dandridge," said Motta. "We could be among the elite teams in the NBA by the end of the season, but so much depends on what Dandridge does. If he comes and plays and does what we think he can do, we will be one of the premier teams."

Indeed, Dandridge came to play. Teaming with Elvin Hayes and Wes Unseld to form one of the most powerful front lines in the league, Dandridge averaged 19.3 points that season—and helped Washington win the NBA Championship by defeating Seattle, four games to three.

For Dandridge, a 6-foot-6-inch small forward with great scoring instincts and a tough defensive game, the championship ring he helped Washington win was the second of his career.

A college star at Norfolk State, Dandridge broke into the big leagues with the Milwaukee Bucks in 1969.

Two years later, he and the legendary Kareem Abdul-Jabbar teamed to help the Bucks cash in on an NBA title, sweeping Baltimore that season, four games to none.

In thirteen NBA seasons, the last three plagued by injuries, Dandridge averaged 18.5 points per game. A four-time All-Star, he averaged 20.1 points in 98 playoff games.

FACT FILE

Born: November 15, 1947
Height: 6′ 6″
Length of NBA career:
  1969–82
Major teams:
  Milwaukee
  Washington (joined 1977)
Records/Awards:
  NBA Championship (2)
  NBA All-Star (4)
  NBA All-Defensive First
    Team (1)

LEFT: BOB DANDRIDGE TEAMED WITH GREATS ELVIN HAYES AND WES UNSELD TO GIVE WASHINGTON ONE OF THE PREMIER FRONT-LINE ATTACKS IN ALL OF BASKETBALL.

MEL DANIELS

FACT FILE

Born: July 20, 1944
Height: 6' 9"
Length of ABA career:
  1967–75
Length of NBA career:
  1976–77
Major teams:
  Minnesota
  Indiana (joined 1968)
  Memphis (joined 1974)
  New York Nets
    (joined 1976)
Records/Awards:
  ABA Championship (3)
  ABA Most Valuable Player
    (2)
  ABA All-Star (7)

The first ABA player in history to reach the 10,000-point plateau was Mel Daniels, a 6-foot-9-inch center who shot fall-away jumpers with incredible accuracy, rebounded with a ferocious tenacity, and also wrote poetry in his spare time.

Daniels, who played his college ball at New Mexico, started his ABA career with Minnesota in 1967, and when he was dealt to Indiana the following season, he turned the Pacers into an immediate contender. With Daniels in the fold, Indiana won three ABA Championships, the first in 1969–70, and back-to-back championships from 1971–73.

A two-time ABA Most Valuable Player and seven-time All-Star, Daniels averaged 18.7 points and an astounding 15.1 rebounds in eight ABA seasons. He finished his ABA career with 11,739 regular-season points, and he also averaged 17.4 points in 109 ABA playoff contests.

Daniels, who found it difficult to sleep after games and stayed up writing poems instead—he wrote hundreds of them during his brilliant career—played his last season with the New York Nets of the NBA, appearing in just 11 games and posting a 3.5 scoring average.

RIGHT: MEL DANIELS WAS, LITERALLY, POETRY IN MOTION ON THE BASKETBALL COURT.

ADRIAN DANTLEY

One of the most exciting and prolific scorers in NBA history, Adrian Dantley won two scoring crowns during his 15-year career.

Dantley, a heavily muscled, 6-foot-5-inch small-forward and sometimes big guard, was a shooting star at Notre Dame, where he averaged 25.8 points from 1973–76. He helped the U.S. Basketball Team win a gold medal at the 1976 Olympics with a 30-point effort against Yugoslavia. During his long NBA tenure, Dantley was asked by seven different teams to fill the role of instant point-producer that he had played so brilliantly as an amateur—and he rarely disappointed.

After averaging 20.3 points in his first season with Buffalo, Dantley, whose strong moves to the basket often resulted in easy points from the free-throw line, captured the NBA's Rookie of the Year award.

He bounced around the next two seasons, spending half of a year with Indiana, and a season and a half with Los Angeles. In 1979, he was traded from Los Angeles to Utah, where he became a scoring fixture and bonafide star.

In six seasons with the Jazz, Dantley averaged no less than 26.6 points per season and was voted to the All-Star squad six straight times. His best seasons with the Jazz were 1980–81, when he rang up 30.7 points per game and won his first scoring title, and in 1983–84, when he fired away for 30.6 points per contest en route to winning his second scoring title.

Dantley was traded by Utah to Detroit in 1986 and enjoyed two-and-a-half seasons with the Pistons before his job was taken over by a young leaper and tenacious rebounder named Dennis Rodman. For his career, Dantley averaged 24.3 points per game.

FACT FILE

Born: February 26, 1956
Height: 6′ 5″
Length of NBA career:
   1976–91
Major teams:
   Buffalo
   Indiana (joined 1977)
   Los Angeles (joined 1978)
   Utah (joined 1979)
   Detroit (joined 1986)
   Dallas (joined 1989)
   Milwaukee (joined 1991)
Records/Awards:
   NBA Rookie of the Year
      (1977)
   Olympic Gold Medal
      (1976)
   NBA All-Star (6)

LEFT: THE PROLIFIC SCORING OF ADRIAN DANTLEY NETTED HIM A PAIR OF SCORING CROWNS.

BOB DAVIES

FACT FILE

Born: January 15, 1920
Height: 6′ 1″
Length of ABL career:
  1943–45
Length of NBL career:
  1945–48
Length of BAA career:
  1948–49
Length of NBA career:
  1949–55
Major teams:
  Brooklyn
  New York (joined 1944)
  Rochester (joined 1945)
Records/Awards:
  NBL Championship (2)
  NBA Championship (1)
  NBL All-Star (1)
  NBL Most Valuable Player
    (1947)
  NBA All-Star (4)

Considered one of the first true superstars of modern pro basketball, Bob Davies, who electrified crowds with his behind-the-back dribbling, enjoyed a magnificent 12-year professional career, winning three championships during that span. A 6-foot-1-inch guard who was named All-American twice at Seton Hall, Davies broke into the big leagues with the Brooklyn Indians of the ABL in 1943 and played briefly for the New York Gothams the following season.

In the 1945–46 campaign, Davies was signed as a free agent by the Rochester Royals of the NBL and averaged 9.0 points in helping the Royals to a championship.

Davies, who played the last ten seasons of his career with Rochester (which transferred to the BAA for the 1948–49 season), averaged 13.7 career points per game with the Royals, and led the league in assists for six straight years.

A five-time All-Star and the game's second-biggest attraction in his day behind George Mikan, Davies earned the NBL's Most Valuable Player award in 1947, averaging 14.4 points and leading the Royals to a second straight championship. He also helped Rochester to an NBA championship in 1950–51—the BAA was transformed into the NBA in 1949—by scoring 15.2 points per game. The following season, he averaged a career-high 16.2 points per contest with the Royals. The Harrisburg Houdini, as Davies, who grew up in Harrisburg, PA, was called, posted a 13.5 scoring average in 67 career playoff games.

RIGHT: IN HIS HEYDAY, BOB DAVIES WAS JUST AS BIG A SUPERSTAR AS THE GIANT GEORGE MIKAN.

BRAD DAVIS

Brad Davis is one of many players who took the NBA's underground railroad to stardom.

A 6-foot-3-inch guard out of Maryland, Davis bounced around the NBA for three seasons with Los Angeles, Indiana and Utah before making a name for himself in the minor-league CBA, where he led Anchorage to a CBA championship in the 1979–80 season. (The season before, Davis had paved his road to eventual NBA success by keeping his skills sharp as a member of the Montana Sky in the Western Basketball Association.)

After honing his skills in the CBA—where he was also named Newcomer of the Year and Second-Team All-Star—Davis was signed as a free agent by the Dallas Mavericks in 1980, and spent his last twelve seasons in Dallas. In fifteen NBA seasons, he averaged 8.2 points and 4.9 assists. In 1983, Davis set a then-record for highest field goal percentage by a guard, bagging 359 of 628 field goal attempts for a .572 percentage.

Davis, who averaged 12.2 points in three seasons at Maryland, had his best NBA scoring season in 1981–82, posting an average of 12.1 points per game. He averaged 7.6 points and 3.7 rebounds in 45 career playoff games.

FACT FILE

Born: December 17, 1955
Height: 6′ 3″
Length of NBA career:
  1977–92
Major teams:
  Los Angeles
  Indiana (joined 1979)
  Utah (joined 1980)
  Dallas (joined 1980)
Records/Awards:
  CBA Championship (1)

LEFT: BRAD DAVIS TOOK THE UNDERGROUND RAILROAD, OTHERWISE KNOWN AS THE CBA, TO NBA STARDOM.

JOHNNY DAVIS

FACT FILE

Born: October 21, 1955
Height: 6′ 2″
Length of NBA career:
　1976–86
Major teams:
　Portland
　Indiana (joined 1978)
　Atlanta (joined 1982
　Cleveland (joined 1984)
　Atlanta (joined 1986)
Records/Awards:
　NBA Championship (1)

Quickness was one of Johnny Davis's main assets, and that quickness paid handsome dividends in his rookie season of 1976–77, when he was one of Bill Walton's fast-break partners on a Portland Trail Blazers team that won the NBA championship.

Davis, a 6-foot-2-inch speedster out of Dayton, averaged 8 points per game in his rookie season with the Trail Blazers. He played two seasons in Portland before he was dealt to Indiana in 1978. In his first season with the Pacers, Davis produced a career-high 18.3 points per game. He was never an All-Star, but Davis's surehanded skills in the backcourt plus his ability to score

points kept opponents honest, and a number of general managers around the NBA interested in his services throughout his ten-year career. Davis's all-round basketball smarts helped him become head coach of the Philadelphia 76ers in the 1996–97 season.

On a basketball journey that took him from Portland to Indiana, to Atlanta and Cleveland, and then back to Atlanta, Davis averaged 12.9 points per game. He posted a 10.3 scoring average in 43 playoff games.

At Dayton, Davis averaged 19.3 points in three seasons, including a 22.3 scoring campaign in 1974–75.

RIGHT: JOHNNY DAVIS' COURT SMARTS HELPED HIM BECOME A NBA HEAD COACH WHEN HIS PLAYING DAYS WERE OVER.

WALTER DAVIS

Instant offense. For 13 seasons, that's what Walter Davis brought with him onto NBA courts.

Davis, a 6-foot-6-inch shooting guard out of North Carolina, rode his picture-perfect jump shot to an Olympic gold medal in 1976, the NBA Rookie of the Year award in 1978 and six All-Star appearances. He played 11 seasons in Phoenix before joining the Denver Nuggets for the last two years of his career.

In his rookie campaign, Davis averaged a career-high 24.2 points per game, and when he was selected to the star-studded game that season, he became just the 26th rookie named to play in an All-Star game since its inception in 1951, joining such exclusive company as Jerry West, Wilt Chamberlain, Oscar Robertson and Elgin Baylor.

Throughout his glittering career, which was tarnished slightly by substance abuse problems, Davis never averaged below 15 points in a season. An uncle of Toronto's Hubert Davis, a sharpshooter himself who also played at North Carolina, Walter Davis was a collegiate All-American who averaged 15.7 points in four seasons with the Tar Heels.

During his NBA career, Davis averaged 19.8 points per game, and 21.6 points in 65 career playoff games.

FACT FILE

Born: September 9, 1954
Height: 6′ 6″
Length of NBA career:
 1977–90
Major teams:
 Portland
 Denver (joined 1988)
Records/Awards:
 NBA Rookie of the Year
  (1978)
 Olympic Gold Medal
  (1976)
 NBA All-Star (6)

LEFT: AS A ROOKIE, SLICK-SHOOTING WALTER DAVIS FOUND HIMSELF IN THE ALL-STAR GAME.

DARRYL DAWKINS

FACT FILE

Born: January 11, 1957
Height: 6′ 11″
Length of NBA career:
  1975–89
Major teams:
  Philadelphia
  New Jersey (joined 1982)
  Utah (joined 1987)
  Detroit (joined 1987)

Chocolate Thunder. Double D. Dr. Dunk. Sir Slam. Dr. D. Master of Disaster.

Those are just some of the nicknames which belonged to Darryl Dawkins during a 14-year career in which he established himself as one of the most powerful and intimidating centers in the history of the league.

Dawkins, a 6-foot-11-inch center who did not play college ball but was still talented enough to be drafted by the Philadelphia 76ers in 1975, played his first seven seasons in the City of Brotherly Love.

He quickly gained a reputation as a ferocious dunker—shattering several backboards during the course of his career—and as an extremely physical defender—setting an NBA record in 1984 for most personal fouls in a season (386).

After his stint in Philadelphia, Dawkins went on to terrorize backboards for five more seasons with the New Jersey Nets, and split the last two seasons of his career between Utah and Detroit. He enjoyed nicknaming some of his favorite dunks, like In Your Face Disgrace, Spine-Chiller Supreme, Flop A Dop, Sexophonic, Earthquake Breaker and Backboard Swaying.

The best season of Dawkins's colorful career came with New Jersey in the 1983–84 season, when he averaged 16.8 points and 6.7 rebounds per game. He averaged 12.6 points and 6.1 rebounds in 109 playoff games.

RIGHT: DARRYL DAWKINS' CAREER WAS FILLED WITH THUNDEROUS DUNKS AND COLORFUL NICKNAMES.

JOHNNY DAWKINS

Best known in Philadelphia for being half of the Hawk-and-Dawk show with Hersey Hawkins for four seasons, John Dawkins enjoyed a productive nine-year career in the NBA.

A 6-foot-2-inch penetrating point guard out of Duke, Dawkins teamed with Hawkins from 1989–92, thrilling home-and-away crowds with their slick passing, clutch shooting and open-court brilliance.

Dawkins, who played his first three seasons in San Antonio, enjoyed his best scoring season with Philadelphia in 1989–90, averaging 14.3 points per game. After five seasons with the 76ers—he only played four games in 1990–91 because of reconstructive knee surgery—Dawkins played his last NBA season with the Detroit Pistons in 1994–95.

After a brilliant career at Duke, where he posted a 19.2 scoring average in four seasons and led the Blue Devils to the 1986 NCAA championship game (won by Lousville), Dawkins's vast talents were sometimes wasted on very poor teams. For his career, Dawkins averaged 11.1 points and 5.5 assists. In his nine seasons, he only appeared in 13 playoff games, averaging 12.1 points and 7.5 rebounds in those games.

FACT FILE

Born: September 28, 1963
Height: 6′ 2″
Length of NBA career:
  1986–95
Major teams:
  San Antonio
  Philadelphia (joined 1989)
  Detroit (joined 1994)

LEFT: ALONG WITH HIS TEAMMATE HERSEY HAWKINS, JOHNNY DAWKINS WAS ONE-HALF OF THE HAWK AND DAWK SHOW.

DAVE DEBUSSCHERE

Born: October 16, 1940
Height: 6′ 6″
Length of NBA career:
  1962–74
Major teams:
  New York (joined 1968)
  Detroit
Records/Awards:
  NBA Championship (2)
  NBA All-Star (7)
  NBA All Defensive First
    Team (6)
  Hall of Fame (1982)

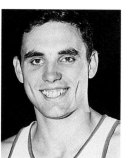

One of the greatest defensive forwards in NBA history, Dave DeBusschere proved to be the last piece of the New York Knicks 1970 Championship puzzle when he was traded by Detroit in 1968 for center Walt Bellamy and guard Howard Komives. Upon his arrival in New York, DeBusschere averaged 16.3 points and a career-high 11.7 rebounds. He teamed with Willis Reed, Walt Frazier, Dick Barnett and Bill Bradley to take the Knicks past the first round of the playoffs for the first time in sixteen years.

The following season, DeBusschere and the Knicks won 23 of their first 24 games and never looked back, knocking off the Los Angeles Lakers in a tough series, four games to three. Three seasons later, DeBusschere and company, this time joined by the great Earl Monroe, topped Los Angeles four games to one for another NBA crown.

An outstanding all-round player, the 6-foot-6-inch DeBusschere averaged 16.1 points and 11 rebounds in a 12-year career split between Detroit and New York. A six-time All Defensive First Team selection and seven-time All Star, DeBusschere posted averages of 16 points and 12 boards in 96 career playoff games.

A three-time All-American at the University of Detroit, where he averaged 24.8 points in four seasons, DeBusschere, at the age of 24, became the youngest player-coach in NBA history when he took over the Pistons early in the 1964–65 season.

A baseball player as well, he also pitched for parts of two seasons with the Chicago White Sox in 1962 and 1963.

RIGHT: WHEN THE NEW YORK KNICKS DEALT FOR DAVE DEBUSSCHERE, THE FINAL PIECE OF THEIR CHAMPIONSHIP PUZZLE WAS IN PLACE.

VLADE DIVAC

Vlade Divac had one of the toughest acts to follow in NBA history, filling in at center for the Los Angeles Lakers the season after the legendary Kareem Abdul-Jabbar retired.

The 7-foot-1-inch Divac, who played professionally for five years in his native Yugoslavia before he was drafted by Los Angeles in 1989, filled in admirably for Abdul-Jabbar for seven years before he was traded to the Charlotte Hornets after the 1996 season.

During his stay in Los Angeles, Divac averaged 12.5 points and 8.7 rebounds. Early in his career with the Lakers, Divac was surrounded by most of the same all-stars who surrounded Kareem: Magic Johnson, James Worthy, Sam Perkins, Byron Scott. In just his second NBA season, Divac was good enough in the pivot to help Los Angeles to the 1991 Finals, where they were defeated by the Chicago Bulls, four games to one.

Divac, who won a silver medal with the Yugoslavian Olympic team in 1988, was an NBA All Rookie in 1990, averaging 8.5 points and 6.2 rebounds. From there, his scoring average went up every year for six straight seasons, topping off at a career-high 16 points per game in 1994–95.

That same season, Divac joined Hakeem Olajuwon, David Robinson and Shawn Kemp as the only NBA players to qualify for the exclusive "100 Club," registering at least 100 points, 100 rebounds, 100 steals, 100 assists and 100 blocked shots.

FACT FILE

Born: February 3, 1968
Height: 7′ 1″
Length of NBA career:
  1989–present
Major teams:
  Los Angeles
  Charlotte (joined 1996)

LEFT: VLADE DIVAC DID A SUPER JOB FILLING THE HUGE SHOES OF KAREEM ABDUL-JABBAR.

FATHER TIME: HOW DANNY BIASONE SAVED THE NBA

On November 22, 1950, the Fort Wayne Pistons defeated the Minneapolis Lakers, 19–18, in the lowest scoring game in NBA history. That contest epitomized the slow-down game that was commonplace in the early 1950s, when teams relied on their slick, ball-handling guards to dribble away the game-clock, while fans yawned in their seats or turned their attention to stories in their game programs.

The game became slower, duller, riddled with fouls, and ever lower scoring. With attendance suffering, the game of basketball seemed destined to self-destruct.

That's when Danny Biasone stepped in, and saved the NBA.

Biasone, then the owner of the Syracuse Nationals, invented the 24-second shot clock, forcing a team in possession of the basketball to attempt a field goal within 24 seconds.

"Basketball needed a time," Biasone would say years later. "In baseball you get three outs and in football you have to gain ten yards in four plays or give up the ball. But in basketball, if you had the lead and a good ball-handler, you could play around all night. It was dull."

Biasone's 24-second shot clock changed all of that. The clock was used initially on a trial basis during the 1954 exhibition games, but the device became extremely popular with fans, who were thrilled to see more scoring and less dribbling and foul shooting. Late-game stall tactics all but disappeared.

By the time the Rochester Royals played the Boston Celtics to open the regular season on October 30, 1954, the 24-second clock was an official NBA rule.

"The adoption of the clock was the most important event in the NBA," Maurice Podoloff, then-league president, once said, "and Danny Biasone is the most important man in the NBA."

JOHN DREW

FACT FILE

Born: September 30, 1954
Height: 6′ 6″
Length of NBA career:
  1974–85
Major teams:
  Atlanta
  Utah (joined 1982)

Before John Drew burst onto the NBA scene with the Atlanta Hawks in 1978, not many college or pro basketball fans had ever heard of Gardner Webb College in Boiling Springs, North Carolina.

A big fish from a small pond, Drew put the tiny school on the basketball map forever after a solid eleven-year NBA career in which he averaged 20.7 points per game.

A 6-foot-6-inch sweet-shooting forward, Drew earned a place on the NBA's All-Rookie team in 1975 after posting averages of 18.5 points and 10.7 rebounds.

He would average 20 points or more in his next four seasons in Atlanta, including a career-high 24.2 points in 1976–77.

Unfortunately for Drew, problems with drugs plagued him during his stellar career, but he still managed to put up healthy scoring averages during eight seasons with the Hawks, and two and a half more with the Utah Jazz.

A two-time NBA All-Star, Drew gained national attention at little-known Gardner Webb by producing whopping scoring and rebounding totals in back-to-back seasons there.

In the 1972–73 campaign, he lit up scoreboards for 24.4 points and 8.5 rebounds per game. As a senior the following season, he increased those numbers, averaging 25.9 points and 13 rebounds per game. In 29 career playoff contests, Drew averaged 14 points and 4.8 boards.

RIGHT: JOHN DREW, FROM LITTLE-KNOWN GARDNER WEBB COLLEGE, BECAME AN NBA ALL-STAR.

LARRY DREW

arry Drew, who stood 6-feet-1½-inches, was one of those players trapped between two positions, more commonly referred to in NBA parlance as a "tweener." He had the skills to be a shooting guard, but a lack of height often kept him at point guard.

Nevertheless, Drew, a backcourtsman, who loved to penetrate to the hoop, played nine productive seasons in the NBA, and while he never won a championship on American soil, he did win one during a season he spent in Italy.

A product of the University of Missouri, Drew broke into the NBA quietly with the Detroit Pistons in 1980–81, averaging 6.6 points and 3.2 assists as a part-time player in the motor city.

The following season, Drew was traded to the Kansas City Kings and spent four of the best seasons of his career there.

In 1982–83, Drew's second season with the Kings, he averaged career highs with 8.1 rebounds and 20.1 points per game.

After a one-year stint with Sacramento and two more with the Los Angeles Clippers, Drew packed his bags and headed to Italy for the 1988–89 season, helping Pesaro Scavollini to an Italian League Championship on the strength of a professional career-high 23 points per game.

The next season, Drew went back to the NBA, signing with the Lakers for a last hurrah in which he averaged 5.2 points and 2.7 assists per game.

FACT FILE

Born: April 2, 1958
Height: 6′ 1¹⁄₂″
Length of NBA career:
1980–90
Major teams:
  Detroit
  Kansas City (joined 1981)
  Sacramento (joined 1985)
  L.A. Clippers (joined 1986)
  L.A.Lakers (joined 1990)

LEFT: TRAPPED BETWEEN TWO POSITIONS, LARRY DREW STILL EXCELLED AT THE NBA LEVEL.

CLYDE DREXLER

FACT FILE

Born: June 22, 1962
Height: 6' 7"
Length of NBA career:
  1983–present
Major teams:
  Portland
  Houston (joined 1995)
Records/Awards:
  NBA Championship (1)
  NBA All-Star (10)
  Olympic Gold Medal
    (1992)

A member of the University of Houston's Phi Slamma Jamma fraternity of the early 1980s, Clyde "The Glide" Drexler graduated to the NBA, where, in his prime, he was the slammingest, high-flyingest shooting guard in the league.

Drexler, who completed his fourteenth NBA campaign as a member of the Houston Rockets in the 1996–97 season, flew onto the big-league scene with the Portland Trail Blazers in 1983.

He spent eleven and a half seasons in Portland carving an image for himself as one of the great superstars and marquee attractions in league history.

At 6-feet-7-inches, Drexler can jump over the moon, let alone smaller shooting guards who have trouble defending him. During his long stint in Portland, Drexler twice led the Trail Blazers to the NBA Finals. In the 1989–90 season, Portland lost the NBA Championship to Detroit, four games to one. In 1991–92, the Trail Blazers were defeated in the championship series by the Chicago Bulls, four games to two.

During the 1994–95 season, Drexler finally got his championship ring. He was traded to Houston, and teamed with Hakeem Olajuwon to give the Rockets a much-needed boost toward capturing their second straight title.

A member of Dream Team I in 1992, Drexler teamed with the likes of Michael Jordan, Larry Bird and Magic Johnson to help the United States capture an Olympic gold medal.

A ten-time All-Star, averaging 20.6 points throughout his career, Drexler is a guaranteed future member of the Hall of Fame.

RIGHT: CLYDE "THE GLIDE" DREXLER SPENT HIS ENTIRE CAREER SOARING OVER DEFENDERS AND DUNKING BASKETBALLS.

JOE DUMARS

The last remaining member of the Detroit Piston Bad-Boy teams that won back-to-back NBA championships in 1989 and 1990, Joe Dumars, entering his thirteenth season in the league, remains Detroit's unflappable and consistent leader, both offensively and defensively.

Dumars, a 6-foot-3-inch shooting guard out of McNeese State, wasn't the baddest of the Bad Boys, but he was their most reliable player, and in big moments, he was always asked to guard the opposing team's best backcourt player. When the Pistons swept the Los Angeles Lakers to win the 1989 NBA championship, it was Dumars—who averaged 27.3 points per game in the series and kept the great Magic Johnson in check—who was voted Most Valuable Player.

The following season, Dumars, with help from his super-talented backcourt mates, Isiah Thomas and Vinnie Johnson, smothered Portland's All-Star guard Clyde Drexler and the rest of the Portland backcourt, and easily won that championship series, four games to one.

A six-time All Star and four-time First Team Defensive Player, Dumars averaged 14.7 points last season, and has averaged 16.6 points throughout his illustrious career. His best scoring season was 1992–93, when he averaged 23.5 points per game. He shares the single-game record for most three-point field goals made, knocking down ten treys on November 8, 1994 against Minnesota, and most three-point field goals made in one half, bagging seven on April 5, 1995, against Orlando.

FACT FILE

Born: May 24, 1963
Height: 6′ 3″
Length of NBA career:
   1985–present
Major team:
   Detroit
Records/Awards:
   NBA Championship (2)
   NBA All-Star (6)
   NBA All-Defensive First
      Team (4)

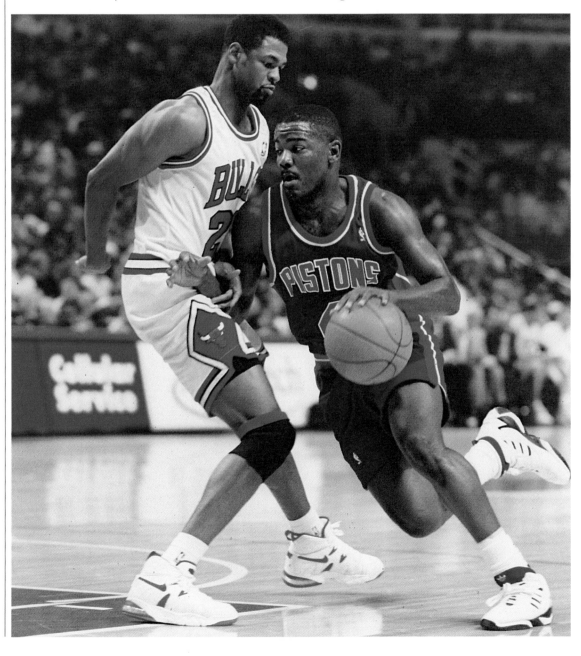

LEFT: STEADY-AS-HE-GOES JOE DUMARS HELPED LEAD THE DETROIT PISTONS TO BACK-TO-BACK CHAMPIONSHIPS.

MARIO ELIE

FACT FILE

Born: November 26, 1963
Height: 6′ 5″
Length of NBA career:
1990–present
Major teams:
Philadelphia
Golden State (joined 1991)
Portland (joined 1992)
Houston (joined 1993)
Records/Awards:
NBA Championship (2)

Mario Elie, a dependable 6-foot-5-inch swingman who overcame long odds to get to the NBA, was instrumental in helping the Houston Rockets win unlikely back-to-back world championships in 1994 and 1995.

Elie, a seventh-round draft choice of the Milwaukee Bucks back in 1985, played his college ball at little-known American International (Massachusetts), and after he was waived by the Bucks, took his blue-collar game to Portugal, Argentina, Ireland, the World Basketball League and the CBA.

Finally, in 1990, Elie got his first taste of NBA life by signing a ten-day contract with the Philadelphia 76ers. Later that season, he signed a ten-day contract with Golden State, eventually re-signing with the Warriors for the remainder of the season. He played his first full NBA campaign with Golden State in 1991–92, averaging 7.8 points per game.

After spending the 1992–93 season with the Portland Trail Blazers, Elie was traded to the Rockets, and his hard-nosed play and clutch-shooting proved to be missing ingredients in their championship recipe. He averaged 9.1 points and 3.1 assists in 1993–94, the year Houston defeated the New York Knicks for the NBA title, four games to three. The following season, Elie averaged 8.8 points per contest en route to Houston's championship sweep of the Orlando Magic.

RIGHT: MARIO ELIE STRUGGLED TO GET TO THE NBA, THEN EXPLODED WITH THE ROCKETS.

SEAN ELLIOTT

One of the top shooting-forwards in the NBA, Sean Elliott's scoring average has grown as fast as his reputation in recent years.

Elliott, a 6-foot-8-inch long-distance marksman drafted out of Arizona in 1989, averaged a career-high 20 points per game for the San Antonio Spurs in 1995–96. In each of his first four seasons with the Spurs, Elliott's average climbed considerably: 10 points, 15.9, 16.3 and 17.2.

He was traded to the Detroit Pistons for the outlandish Dennis Rodman in 1993. When Rodman began to fall out of favor with San Antonio management, the Spurs, who had deeply missed Elliott's athleticism and open-floor scoring prowess, brought him back in a trade the following season.

After a sparkling four-year career at Arizona in which he averaged 19.2 points per game and won the 1989 Wooden Award as the nation's top Division I player, Elliott earned a spot on the NBA's All-Rookie second team in 1990, averaging 10 points, 3.7 rebounds and 1.9 assists coming off the bench. He made his two All-Star appearances in 1993 and 1996.

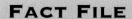

FACT FILE

Born: February 2, 1968
Height: 6′ 8″
Length of NBA career:
 1989–present
Major teams:
 San Antonio
 Detroit (joined 1993)
 San Antonio (joined 1994)
Records/Awards:
 NBA All-Star (2)

LEFT: SEAN ELLIOTT IS ONE OF THE BETTER LONG-DISTANCE SHOOTERS IN THE NBA TODAY.

DALE ELLIS

FACT FILE

Born: August 6, 1960
Height: 6′ 7″
Length of NBA career:
  1983–present
Major teams:
  Dallas
  Seattle (joined 1986)
  Milwaukee (joined 1991)
  San Antonio (joined 1992)
  Denver (joined 1994)
Records/Awards:
  NBA All-Star (1)

One of the most dangerous long-distance shooters in the history of the NBA, Dale Ellis leads the league in career three-point field goals made with 1,461, and career three-pointers attempted with 3,675.

Ellis, a 6-foot-7-inch forward out of Tennessee, averaged 16.6 points last season—his fourteenth NBA campaign—as a member of the Denver Nuggets. He was up to his old three-point tricks again, canning 192 of 528 shots from beyond the arc. After averaging 17.5 points in four seasons at Tennessee, Ellis broke into the NBA with the Dallas Mavericks in 1983. He played three quiet seasons in Dallas, averaging 8.2, 9.3 and 7.1 points, respectively, before he was traded to the Seattle SuperSonics, where he became a household name.

In his first season with Seattle, Ellis exploded for 24.9 points per game and was named the NBA's Most Improved Player. It marked the first of four seasons in which he would post an average of no less than 23.5 points. He was named to his only All-Star team during the 1988–89 season, when he averaged a career-high 27.5 points per game.

Now with his fifth NBA club, Ellis has racked up an average of 16.7 points during his career so far. He was the winner of the NBA's Long Distance Shootout during All-Star festivities weekend in 1988.

RIGHT: NEED A THREE-POINTER? DIAL LONG-DISTANCE FOR DALE ELLIS.

WAYNE EMBRY

Wayne Embry, a 6-foot-8-inch, 255-pound center, muscled his way to the basket for three teams in an 11-year NBA career, starting with the Cincinnati Royals in 1958 and ending with the Milwaukee Bucks in 1969.

In between, it was with the Boston Celtics that Embry earned his only championship ring. He did it by spelling Bill Russell, the Celtics player-coach, at center in the 1967–68 season, averaging 14 minutes, 6.3 points and 4 rebounds a game for a team that went 54–28 in the regular season and beat the Los Angeles Lakers, four games to two, in the championship round of the playoffs.

Over his career, the first eight years of which were spent in Cincinnati, Embry averaged 12.5 points, with a career-high of 19.8 in 1961–62. He also averaged 9 rebounds, and set countless picks and screens for shooters like Jack Twyman and Oscar Robertson. The "Goose," as Embry was called in his playing days, played two seasons in Boston, and closed out his career in Milwaukee, averaging 13.1 points in his final campaign. Embry, who played college ball at Miami of Ohio, was a four-time All-Star during his career. He averaged 10.1 points in 56 career playoff games.

FACT FILE

Born: March 26, 1937
Height: 6′ 8″
Length of NBA career:
   1958–69
Major teams:
   Cincinnati
   Boston (joined 1966)
   Milwaukee (joined 1968)
Records/Awards:
   NBA Championship (1)
   NBA All-Star (4)

LEFT: WAYNE EMBRY'S MUSCULAR PRESENCE HELPED BILL RUSSELL AND THE BOSTON CELTICS CAPTURE THE 1967–68 CHAMPIONSHIP.

ALEX ENGLISH

FACT FILE

Born: January 5, 1954
Height: 6′ 7″
Length of NBA career:
  1976–91
Major teams:
  Milwaukee
  Indiana (joined 1978)
  Denver (joined 1980)
  Dallas (joined 1990)
Records/Awards:
  NBA All-Star (8)

One of the most explosive scorers in NBA history, Alex English played 15 seasons in the league, and currently ranks seventh on the all-time scoring list with 25,613 points.

English, a 6-foot-7-inch small forward out of South Carolina, played the first two years of his career with the Milwaukee Bucks, having been selected by the Bucks in the second round of the 1976 NBA draft. He went one and a half seasons with Indiana before his career took flight in Denver, where he was traded in 1980.

In his first full season with the Nuggets, English averaged 23.8 points per game. The following season, he averaged 25.4 points, and began a streak of eight consecutive seasons with 2,000 or more points. In the 1982–83 season, English led the league in scoring with 28.5 points per contest.

Amazingly enough, English's best scoring seasons were yet to come. He posted a career-high 29.8 points per game in 1985–86, and in 1986–87, put up a 28.6 scoring average.

An eight-time All Star, English averaged 21.5 points per game in his career. After his last NBA campaign with Dallas in 1991, he played one season with Depi Napoli in the Italian League, averaging 13.9 points per game.

In 68 career playoff games, English averaged 24.4 points.

RIGHT: ALEX ENGLISH, WHO PILED UP MORE THAN 25,000 CAREER POINTS, WAS ONE OF THE MOST DYNAMIC SCORERS IN NBA HISTORY.

JULIUS ERVING

Julius Winfield Erving, II, the incomparable Dr. J, was one of the most electrifying performers in the history of professional basketball. Erving, an acrobatic scorer with a tall afro hairstyle and long, graceful strides, was the Michael Jordan of the bell-bottom generation. From 1971–87, Erving wowed capacity crowds with gravity-defying dunks and an arsenal of innovative moves to the hoop which helped his reputation and the image of the sport soar to immeasurable artistic heights. Erving, who left the University of Massachusetts as a sophomore in 1971, bolted to the Virginia Squires of the American Basketball Association—a league which rivaled the National Basketball Association—and played two seasons with the Squires before coming home to sign with the New York Nets of the ABA.

Erving, who averaged a career record 28.7 points per game in the ABA, led the Nets to championships in 1974 and 1976, winning the ABA's Most Valuable Player Award in both of those seasons. The popularity and legitimacy

Erving brought to the ABA helped some of its teams gain a merger with the NBA in 1976. That same year, Erving, locked in a contract dispute with the Nets, joined the Philadelphia 76ers of the NBA, and for 11 more seasons, proved that he could be a shining star in any league.

Erving averaged 22 points per game during his career with Philadelphia, which was highlighted by a championship in 1983, and he was an All-Star selection in each of his NBA seasons. One of the most thrilling moments in sports occurred during the 1976 ABA All-Star festivities, when Erving won the Slam Dunk contest—and raised eyebrows around the globe—by leaping from the foul line for an improbable jam that spawned an entire generation of dunkers.

Erving was the NBA's Most Valuable Player in 1981, averaging 24.6 points per game that year, and was named MVP of the league's All-Star squad in 1977 and 1983. Dr. J was voted onto the NBA's 35th Anniversary All-Time Team in 1980.

FACT FILE

Born: February 22, 1950
Height: 6′ 7″
Length of ABA career:
1971–76
Length of NBA career:
1976–87
Major teams:
Virginia Squires
New York Nets (joined 1973)
Philadelphia 76ers (joined 1976)
Records/Awards:
ABA All-Star squad (5)
ABA Championships (2)
ABA Most Valuable Player (2)
ABA All-Defensive team (1)
ABA Slam Dunk Competition (1)
NBA Championship (1)
NBA Most Valuable Player (1)
NBA All-Star squad (11)
Hall of Fame (1993)

LEFT: JULIUS ERVING, A.K.A. DOCTOR J, WAS THE MICHAEL JORDAN OF THE BELL-BOTTOM GENERATION.

PATRICK EWING

FACT FILE

Born: August 5, 1962
Height: 7′ 0″
Length of NBA career:
   1985–present
Major team:
   New York Knicks
Records/Awards:
   NBA Rookie of the Year,
      1986
   NBA All-Star (11)
   Olympic Gold Medal
      (1984, 1992)

The cornerstone of the New York Knicks franchise since he was selected out of Georgetown as the first pick overall in the 1985 NBA draft, Patrick Ewing, still searching for his first NBA championship, has proven himself to be one of the elite centers of his era.

Ewing, a 7-footer who led Georgetown to the NCAA championship in 1985, led New York to the NBA Finals in 1994, where the Knicks lost to the Houston Rockets, four games to three.

In that series, Ewing established a Finals record for most blocked shots with 30, and tied a Finals record for most blocked shots in a single game with eight. In each of his NBA seasons, Ewing, an eleven-time All-Star, has never failed to average below 20 points. He averaged 20 points per contest in his first season with the Knicks en route to winning the Rookie of the Year award. He also established a career-high 28.6 points per game in 1989–90, and a career-high 12.1 rebounds per game in 1992–93.

In his trophy case, Ewing displays two Olympic gold medals. He won the first as a collegian in 1984, and the second as a member of Dream Team I in 1992.

With 12 NBA seasons under his elastic drawstrings, Ewing has shown little signs of slowing down. Last season, he averaged a team-leading 22.4 points and 10.7 rebounds per game.

RIGHT: THOUGH HE STILL HASN'T WON A CHAMPIONSHIP, PATRICK EWING'S MANY TALENTS HAVE MADE THE NEW YORK KNICKS PERENNIAL CONTENDERS.

When the Phoenix Suns selected Wisconsin's Michael Finley in the first round of the 1995 NBA draft (21st pick overall), it raised the eyebrows of many average basketball fans. Who was this guy? One season later, Finley showed the basketball world why Phoenix was so interested in his services.

Finley, a 6-foot-7-inch, 215-pound swingman who averaged 18.7 points in four seasons at Wisconsin, quickly worked his way into the Suns' starting lineup, and into the hearts of Phoenix fans everywhere with his smooth shooting touch, explosive leaping ability, and a talent for slashing to the tin and making things happen.

"To be starting for this team feels real good for me," said Finley, whose 15 points per game in 1995–96 placed him third on the squad in scoring behind the veterans Charles Barkley (23.2) and Kevin Johnson (18.7). "It's my first time for everything, but if you go in the game thinking that you're a rookie, you're going to play like a rookie."

Indeed, Finley played the game as if he were a veteran instead of a rookie, powering his way to the basket on numerous occasions, and never shying away from a tough shot in critical stages of games.

Finley, traded to Dallas last season, matched his scoring average from his rookie campaign, tallying 15 points per game.

FACT FILE

Born: March 6, 1973
Height: 6' 7"
Length of NBA career:
 1995–present
Major team:
 Phoenix
 Dallas (joined 1996)

LEFT: IN PHOENIX, MICHAEL FINLEY BECAME A HOUSEHOLD NAME IN A HURRY.

Clash of the Titans: The First Chamberlain-Russell Meeting

BILL RUSSELL AND WILT CHAMBERLAIN STAGED SOME OF THE MOST CLASSIC ONE-ON-ONE BATTLES IN NBA HISTORY. BELOW: RUSSELL JAMS FOR TWO POINTS OVER CHAMBERLAIN.

Instant offense vs. stop-right-there defense. The first-ever meeting between Philadelphia's Wilt Chamberlain and Boston's Bill Russell was one of the most anticipated events in the history of sport.

It finally happened on November 7, 1959, when the 7-foot-2-inch Chamberlain, a 21-year-old rookie center who crushed smaller defenses, went head-to-head with the shot-blocking, defensive-minded Russell at the Boston Garden. The game, talked about and debated for weeks, was sold out. A few remaining tickets were scalped for a whopping $15 each.

"They billed that first meeting between me and Bill Russell," Chamberlain once said, "as the unstoppable offensive force versus the immovable defensive object."

When the clash of the titans finally began, a confident Chamberlain immediately went to his patented, one-handed jump shot, but had it blocked by the 6-foot-10-inch Russell for the first time in his career.

As the game wore on, Russell, a three-year veteran, had broken Chamberlain's confidence, forcing him to misfire on numerous occasions, and leaving Wilt the Stilt no choice but to fall back on his less-reliable hook shot.

With Chamberlain in shackles, Boston stormed out to a 76–61 halftime lead, and eventually won the contest, 115–106.

In the end, Chamberlain had outscored Russell, 30–22, but took twice as many shots from the field, 39–18.

When it was announced that the smaller Russell had out-rebounded Chamberlain, 35–28, Celtic fans cheered wildly.

At least for a day, the immovable defensive object had stopped the unstoppable offensive force.

VERN FLEMING

FACT FILE

Born: February 4, 1962
Height: 6′ 5″
Length of NBA career:
  1984–present
Major teams:
  Indiana
  New Jersey (joined 1995)
Records/Awards:
  Olympic Gold Medal
  (1984)

There are a number of quality guards from New York City currently performing in the NBA: Mark Jackson, Rod Strickland, Kenny Anderson, Stephon Marbury, Mario Elie.

Vern Fleming made it to the big show before all of them.

Fleming, a 6-foot-5-inch guard who played college ball at Georgia, has been one of the steadiest backcourt performers in the league since he was selected by the Indiana Pacers in the first round of the 1984 NBA draft. He spent his first eleven seasons in Indiana before he joined the New Jersey Nets in the 1995 season. As a member of the Pacers, Fleming averaged no less than 12 points per game in his first seven seasons. His career-high scoring average of 14.3 points was achieved in the 1988–89 season and duplicated in the 1989–90 campaign.

A level-headed floor leader who is smart enough to know his limitations on the court, Fleming chipped in 7.7 points per game with the Nets in 1995. He has averaged 11.3 points per game throughout his career, and 7.7 points in thirty-seven playoff games.

Fleming, who averaged 14.2 points per game in four seasons at Georgia, was a member of the 1984 Olympic gold-medal winning team.

RIGHT: VERN FLEMING PAVED THE WAY FOR THE CURRENT GROUP OF NEW YORK CITY POINT GUARDS IN THE NBA.

ERIC "SLEEPY" FLOYD

Eric "Sleepy" Floyd was one of the most prolific scoring point guards in NBA history.

A 6-foot-3-inch playmaker who helped turn Georgetown into a collegiate power, Floyd played thirteen seasons in the NBA. He was originally selected by the Nets in the first round of the 1982 NBA draft, but was traded in mid-season to the Golden State Warriors.

Floyd would play four and one half seasons in Golden State, making a name for himself as a guard who could sink big shots in an up-tempo, transition offense. In 1983–84, his first full season with the Warriors, Floyd netted 16.8 points per game. The following season, he bagged a career-high 19.5 points per contest.

Sleepy's perkiest season came in 1986–87, when he posted 18.8 points per game and a career-high 10.3 assists per contest. He was named to his only All-Star team that season, and in the playoffs, set four records in a single game against the Lakers: most points in one half (39), most points in one quarter (29), most field goals in one quarter (12), most field goals made in one half (15).

Midway through the 1987–88 season, Floyd was traded to Houston, where later he fueled the Rockets' backcourt through the 1992–93 season. He spent the next season in San Antonio, and his final year right back where he started his pro career—with the New Jersey Nets.

Floyd finished his NBA career with averages of 12.8 points and 5.4 assists. At Georgetown, he finished as the Hoyas' top career scorer with 2,304 points.

FACT FILE

Born: March 6, 1960
Height: 6′ 3″
Length of NBA career:
 1982–95
Major teams:
 New Jersey
 Golden State (joined
  1983)
 Houston (joined 1987)
 San Antonio (joined 1993)
 New Jersey (joined 1994)
Records/Awards:
 NBA All-Star (1)

LEFT: ERIC "SLEEPY" FLOYD, SEEN HERE WITH THE NEW JERSEY NETS, WAS WIDE-EYED AND DANGEROUS ON THE BASKETBALL COURT.

CHRIS FORD

FACT FILE

Born: January 11, 1949
Height: 6′ 5″
Length of NBA career:
1972–82
Major teams:
Detroit
Boston (joined 1978)
Records/Awards:
NBA Championship (1)

What Chris Ford lacked in physical talent during his ten-year NBA career, he made up for with a fierce competitiveness and dive-on-the-floor mentality.

Ford, a 6-foot-5-inch guard who starred at Villanova, played six and one half seasons with the Detroit Pistons before he was traded to the Boston Celtics in 1978.

Three years after joining the Celtics, Ford, along with Tiny Archibald and Gerald Henderson, fed the basketball to the Hall-of-Fame trio Robert Parish, Kevin McHale and Larry Bird. Those Celtics went on to capture a world championship, knocking off the Houston Rockets, four games to two.

After averaging 15.7 points in four seasons at Villanova, Ford, an emotional player whose towel and arm-waving was often interpreted by fans as hotdogging, was drafted by Detroit in the second round of the 1972 NBA draft.

With an uncanny ability to knock down the open shot, Ford racked up 12.3 points per game for the Pistons in 1976–77, 10.5 points in 1977–78 and a career-high 15.4 points per game in the 1978–79 season, which he split between Detroit and Boston. In 1979, when the NBA implemented the 3-point shot, it was Ford who became the first player in the league to connect from that range.

For his career, Ford averaged 9.2 points and 3.4 assists. In 58 career playoff games, he averaged 7.5 points and 2.6 assists.

RIGHT: CHRIS FORD DIDN'T PUT UP BIG NUMBERS, BUT HIS COURT SAVVY HELPED LARRY BIRD AND THE BOSTON CELTICS CAPTURE A CHAMPIONSHIP.

LARRY FOUST

Larry Foust was one of the quality big men of the 1950s and early 1960s, finishing his 12-year NBA career with averages of 13.7 points and 9.8 rebounds.

The 6-foot-9-inch Foust, who played his college ball at LaSalle, spent his first seven NBA seasons with the Fort Wayne Pistons, and two and one half seasons each with Minneapolis and St. Louis.

A seven-time All-Star, Foust enjoyed his best seasons with Fort Wayne. As a rookie in 1950–51, he netted 13.5 points per game, and, in just his second campaign with the Pistons, averaged 15.9 points and tied Milwaukee's Mel Hutchins for the league-lead in rebounding, hauling down 880 boards for a 13.3 average.

In the 1954–55 campaign, Foust averaged a career-high 17 points per game for Fort Wayne, and led the league in field goal percentage, bagging 298 of 818 field goal attempts for 48 percent.

Foust joined Minneapolis in the 1957–58 season and was named team captain. That season, he led by example on the court, posting 16.8 points per game for the Lakers, which placed him second on the squad in scoring behind Vern Mikkelsen (17.3).

In 73 career playoff games, Foust finished with a career-high 12.4 points and 9.6 rebounds.

FACT FILE

Born: June 24, 1928
Height: 6′ 9″
Length of NBA career:
1950–62
Major teams:
Fort Wayne
Minneapolis (joined 1957)
St. Louis (joined 1959)
Records/Awards:
NBA All-Star (7)

LEFT: WHEN LARRY FOUST JOINED MINNEAPOLIS FOR THE 1957-58 SEASON, HE BECAME THE LAKERS' CAPTAIN.

WALT FRAZIER

FACT FILE

Born: March 29, 1945
Height: 6′ 4″
Length of NBA career:
 1967–80
Major teams:
 New York
 Cleveland (joined 1977)
Records/Awards:
 NBA Championship (2)
 NBA All-Star (7)
 Hall of Fame (1986)

Off the court, Walt "Clyde" Frazier wore wide-brimmed hats, expensive fur coats and sports clothes of the latest fashion.

On the court, he was even flashier. Frazier, a 6-foot-4-inch guard who electrified fans, and opponents, with slick shake-and-bake moves and a deft shooting touch, helped the New York Knicks win NBA championships in 1970 and 1973.

A first-round draft pick of the Knicks in 1967 after an outstanding career at Southern Illinois University that included selection that year as the most valuable player in the National Invitation Tournament, Frazier earned a place on the NBA's All-Rookie Team with averages of 9 points, 4.1 assists and 4.2 rebounds.

Two seasons later, Frazier and his talented teammates, Willis Reed, Bill Bradley, Dave DeBusschere and Dick Barnett, found themselves in a championship series battle with the Los Angeles Lakers. In the seventh and deciding game of that series, Frazier scored 36 points and was credited with 19 assists as the Knicks won their first title.

A seven-time All-Star and seven-time NBA All-Defensive First Team selection, Frazier averaged 18.9 points and 6.1 assists in a 13-year pro career. He spent ten of those years with the Knicks—he set a club record in New York with 4,791 assists—and the last three with the Cleveland Cavaliers.

Frazier's career-high scoring season came with the Knicks in 1971–72, when he averaged 23.2 points per game. In 93 playoff games, the flashy backcourtsman averaged 20.7 points, 6.4 assists and 7.2 rebounds.

BELOW: ON AND OFF THE COURT, FEW PLAYERS WERE AS STYLISH AS WALT "CLYDE" FRAZIER.

WORLD B. FREE

The flamboyant and outspoken World B. Free backed up his loud act with a stellar 13-year career in which he proved himself to be one of the most prolific scorers the NBA had ever seen.

Free, a 6-foot-3-inch guard named Lloyd, out of little-known Guilford College, played the game above the rim. He thought so highly of his game—"I'm moving up in the world, so I thought I better do something to commemorate it," he said in 1981—that he legally changed his first name to World B. And what did the "B" stand for? "B," he answered.

World B Free, a super leaper who broke into the NBA with the Philadelphia 76ers in 1975, averaged 20 or more points in eight different seasons. He never turned the 20-plus point trick in Philadelphia, but reached that plateau twice in San Diego, twice in Golden State, once in a split season between Golden State and Cleveland, and three times in Cleveland.

In the 1978–79 season, Free had a banner year for San Diego. He averaged 28.8 points and led the league in free throws made (654) and free throws attempted (865).

The following season, he averaged a career-high 30.2 points per game for San Diego, one of the few times in league history that a player who reached an average of 30 points or better did not lead the league in scoring—George Gervin won the scoring crown in 1979–80 with a 33.1 average. Free also led the league that season in free throws made (572), and earned his first and only trip to the All-Star game.

Over the course of his long and colorful career, Free averaged 20.3 points and 3.7 assists per game. He averaged 14 points and 3 assists in 34 career playoff games.

FACT FILE

Born: December 9, 1953
Height: 6′ 3″
Length of NBA career:
1975–88
Major teams:
Philadelphia (joined 1975)
San Diego (joined 1978)
Golden State (joined 1980)
Cleveland (joined 1982)
Philadelphia (joined 1986)
Houston (joined 1987)
Records/Awards:
NBA All-Star (1)

LEFT: LLOYD FREE THOUGHT SO MUCH OF HIS GAME THAT HE DECIDED TO CHANGE HIS NAME.

JOE FULKS

FACT FILE

Born: October 26, 1921
Height: 6′ 5″
Length of BAA career:
  1946–49
Length of NBA career:
  1949–54
Major teams:
  Philadelphia
Records/Awards:
  BAA All-Star (1)
  BAA Championship (1)
  NBA All-Star (2)
  Hall of Fame (1977)

One of the first great jump shooters, "Jumpin' Joe" Fulks of the Philadelphia Warriors, a 6-foot-5-inch forward/center, led the BAA in scoring in each of his first two seasons.

After starring at Murray State, Fulks spent three seasons in the military before averaging a league-leading 23.2 points per game in his rookie campaign of 1946–47, helping Philadelphia to the BAA Championship.

Fulks, who averaged a league-best 22.1 points the following season, and a career-high 26.0 points per game in 1948–49, including a whopping 1,560 points, played his entire eight-year career with Philadelphia.

One of Fulks's greatest feats was his 63-point effort against the Indianapolis Jets in 1949, a record that stood for ten years. He also reeled off 49 consecutive free throws twice in his career. One of the first BAA and NBA stars, Fulks scored 30 or more points 12 times in his career and 41 once.

A one-time BAA All-Star and two-time NBA All-Star, Fulks averaged 16.4 points in his career. Voted onto the NBA's 25th Anniversary All-Time Team in 1970, he averaged 19 points in 31 career playoff games.

At Murray State, Fulks averaged 13.2 points per game in two seasons.

RIGHT: JOE FULKS, A GREAT JUMP SHOOTER, NETTED 63 POINTS AGAINST THE INDIANAPOLIS JETS IN 1949.

HARRY GALLATIN

ne of the NBA's original ironmen, Harry "The Horse" Gallatin once held the league record for most consecutive games played with 746, which included 64 post-season contests.

Gallatin, a 6-foot-6-inch forward/center who played his college ball at Northeast Missouri State, was the epitome of durability during his playing days, never missing a game in ten seasons—nine of which he spent with the New York Knicks, the last with the Detroit Pistons.

A seven-time All-Star, Gallatin averaged 13.0 points in his career, and 12.0 points in post-season play. His best scoring season came in his last year with the Knicks, when he averaged 15.0 points per game. In the 1953–54 season,

Gallatin led the league in rebounding with 1,098 for a 15.3 average.

Traded to Detroit in the 1957–58 season, Gallatin's 10.4 rebounds per game was a considerable help to his super-shooting teammate George Yardley, who led the league that season with 2,001 points and a 27.8 scoring average.

At Northeast Missouri State, Gallatin averaged 13.2 points in two seasons, before Ned Irish, the founder and former president of the New York Knicks and one of basketballs most famous promoters, signed him to a professional contract.

BELOW: HARRY "THE HORSE" GALLATIN (FAR LEFT) WAS ONE OF THE NBA'S ORIGINAL IRONMEN.

FACT FILE

Born: April 26, 1927
Height: 6′ 6″
Length of BAA career:
 1948–49
Length of NBA career:
 1949–58
Major teams:
 New York
 Detroit (joined 1957)
Records/Awards:
 NBA All-Star (7)
 Hall of Fame (1990)

KEVIN GARNETT

FACT FILE

Born: May 19, 1976
Height: 6' 11"
Length of NBA career:
 1995–present
Major team:
 Minnesota
 NBA All-Star (1)

Kevin Garnett's senior prom pictures still weren't developed when he signed an NBA contract with the Minnesota Timberwolves in 1995.

Selected by Minnesota as the fifth pick overall in the 1995 draft, Garnett, the big man on the Farragut High School campus in Chicago, became just the fourth player to leap from high school to the NBA. In that special department, he joined Moses Malone, Bill Willoughby and Darryl Dawkins.

Garnett's decision to turn pro very early in his life may have spawned a new generation of high school hot-shots skipping college for the fortune and fame of the NBA. In 1996, Kobe Bryant of the Los Angeles Lakers became the fifth player in history to go directly from high school to the pros.

The 6-foot-11-inch, 220-pound Garnett, who possesses a short-range shooting touch, and the ability to handle the ball and steam to the hoop, proved in the 1995 season that he could indeed compete with the big boys.

In 80 games, Garnett scored 835 points for a 10.4 scoring average. He shot splendidly from the field, bagging 361 of 735 field goal attempts for 49 percent, and hauled down 6.3 rebounds per contest.

Last season, Garnett increased his overall productivity, averaging 17 points, 8 rebounds and 3.1 assists per game while racking up 163 blocks.

RIGHT: KEVIN GARNETT WAS ONE BABE WHO WAS THROWN TO THE WOLVES—AND BECAME AN NBA STAR.

GEORGE GERVIN

George "Iceman" Gervin, who earned his nickname by shooting cool under pressure, was one of the most lethal scorers in NBA history.

A 6-foot-7-inch shooting guard out of Eastern Michigan who could also play small forward, Gervin led the NBA four times in scoring, winning his first scoring crown in amazingly dramatic fashion.

On the last day of the 1977–78 campaign, Denver's David Thompson, who had been battling Gervin for the scoring lead all season, scored 73 points to finish with a 27.1 average. With the Iceman needing to tally a near-impossible 63 points to regain the title, it seemed as if Thompson couldn't lose. But later that night, Gervin, whose wicked fingerroll was one of his deadliest offensive weapons, lit up the scoreboard for 63 points, and won the scoring war with a 27.2 average.

Gervin, who began his professional career with the Virginia Squires of the ABA in 1972, played one and a half seasons with Virginia before joining San Antonio in 1974. By the time the Spurs had joined the NBA in 1976, Gervin was already a proven commodity, having averaged 21.9 points in four ABA seasons.

After winning his first NBA scoring title, Gervin won two more scoring crowns in a row. He posted 29.6 points per game in 1978–79 and a career-high 33.1 points in 1979–80, becoming the first guard in league history to win three straight scoring titles. He won his fourth and last scoring title in 1981–82, ringing up 32.3 points per contest.

In a 14-year career that included ten seasons in San Antonio, Gervin averaged 26.2 points per game. A 12-time All-Star, he averaged 27.0 points in 59 career playoff games. He still holds the single-game record for most points in one quarter, piling up 33 points in a single stanza on April 9, 1978, against New Orleans.

After his brilliant career, Gervin played for one season in Italy, averaging 26.1 points for Banco Roma in 1986–87. He made a brief comeback for Quad City of the CBA in 1989–90, posting 20.3 points per game.

FACT FILE

Born: April 27, 1952
Height: 6' 7"
Length of ABA career:
 1972–76
Length of NBA career:
 1976–86
Major teams:
 Virginia
 San Antonio (joined 1974)
 Chicago (joined 1985)
Records/Awards:
 ABA All-Star (3)
 NBA All-Star (9)

LEFT: GEORGE "THE ICEMAN" GERVIN, WHO WON FOUR SCORING TITLES, EARNED HIS NICKNAME BY SHOOTING COOL UNDER PRESSURE.

ARTIS GILMORE

FACT FILE

Born: September 21, 1949
Height: 7' 2"
Length of ABA career:
   1971–76
Length of NBA career:
   1976–88
Major teams:
   Kentucky
   Chicago (joined 1976)
   San Antonio (joined 1982)
   Chicago (joined 1987)
   Boston (joined 1988)
Records/Awards:
   ABA Championship (1)
   ABA Most Valuable Player
      (1972)
   ABA Rookie of the Year
      (1972)
   ABA All-Defensive Team
      (4)
   ABA All-Star (5)
   NBA All-Star (6)

One of the most underrated centers of his time, Artis Gilmore had a rock-steady seventeen-year professional career.

A 7-foot-2-inch rebounding machine out of Jacksonville College—he holds the NCAA career record for average rebounds per game with 22.7—Gilmore began his career in spectacular fashion with the Kentucky Colonels of the ABA in 1971–72. He was both the Rookie of the Year and Most Valuable Player that season, leading the league in field goal percentage (.598) and rebounds per game (17.8), and finishing the season with a 23.8 scoring average.

Gilmore, a First-Team All-League center in each of his five ABA seasons, helped the Colonels capture the ABA title in 1975 with 23.6 points and 16.2 rebounds per game. The following season—the league's last—Gilmore won the rebounding title for the fourth time in five seasons and finished fourth in scoring with a career-high 24.6 points per game.

When the ABA went out of business, Gilmore hooked up with the Chicago Bulls. Despite the fact that he kept his rebounding and scoring numbers healthy for six seasons in Chicago, the spotlight dimmed on Gilmore for two primary reasons. One, he was playing on mediocre teams. Also, by the time he reached the NBA, he had to settle in the shadows of established and better-known centers like Kareem Abdul-Jabbar, Bob Lanier and Robert Parish.

Gilmore, a five-time ABA All-Star and four-time All-Defensive Team selection, holds the ABA single-game record for most rebounds, hauling down 40 boards against the New York Nets on Feb. 3, 1974, and also holds the ABA's single-season mark for most blocked shots with 422 in 1972.

After 12 NBA seasons—he was with San Antonio from 1982–88 and split the 1987–88 campaign between Chicago and Boston—Gilmore finished with averages of 17.1 points, 10.1 rebounds, and a career record .599 field goal percentage. A six-time NBA All-Star, Gilmore spent his last professional season in Italy, averaging 12.3 points and 11 rebounds per game for Bologna Arimo of the Italian League.

RIGHT: ARTIS GILMORE WAS AN ABA STAR WHO LATER SETTLED IN THE SHADOWS OF SOME OF THE BETTER-KNOWN NBA CENTERS LIKE KAREEM ABDUL-JABBAR AND BOB LANIER.

Gail Goodrich

A quick, left-handed shooting guard, Gail Goodrich teamed with Jerry West on the Los Angeles Lakers to form one of the most explosive backcourts in NBA history. The slick-shooting tandem helped the 1972 Lakers win the world championship.

A 6-foot-1-inch dynamo out of UCLA, where he averaged 19.0 points and helped the Bruins win back-to-back championships in 1964 and 1965, Goodrich was selected by the Los Angeles Lakers in the 1965 NBA draft. He played 14 seasons in the NBA, averaging 18.6 points and 4.7 assists over that time.

Goodrich played three quiet seasons in Los Angeles before he was picked up by the Phoenix Suns in the 1968 Expansion Draft. As a member of the Suns, he became a shooting star, averaging 23.8 points in 1968–69 and 20.0 points in 1969–70.

The following season, Los Angeles brought Goodrich back in a trade, and he soon became one-fifth of a starting lineup that would win the title, joining forces with West in the backcourt, Wilt Chamberlain at center, and Happy Hairston and Jim McMillan at forwards. In that championship season, Goodrich averaged a career-high 25.9 points, while West was ringing up 25.8 points per contest.

A five-time All-Star, Goodrich posted scoring averages of 20 or more points six times in his career. He averaged 18.1 points in 80 career playoff games.

Fact File

Born: April 23, 1943
Height: 6' 1"
Length of NBA career:
   1965–79
Major teams:
   Los Angeles
   Phoenix (joined 1968)
   Los Angeles (joined 1970)
   New Orleans (joined
   1976)
Records/Awards:
   NBA Championship (1)
   NBA All-Star (5)

LEFT: GAIL GOODRICH, DRIVING TO THE BASKET HERE FOR LOS ANGELES, TEAMED WITH JERRY WEST TO GIVE THE LAKERS ONE OF THE MOST EXPLOSIVE BACKCOURTS IN NBA HISTORY.

HORACE GRANT

FACT FILE

Born: July 4, 1965
Height: 6′ 10″
Length of NBA career:
 1987–present
Major teams:
 Chicago
 Orlando (joined 1994)
Records/Awards:
 NBA Championship (3)
 NBA All-Star (1)

He's strong. He's aggressive. He can score when he needs to and play good defense when he has to. Horace Grant is everything an NBA power-forward is supposed to be.

Grant, a 6-foot-10-inch workhorse out of Clemson, was the muscle behind the Chicago Bulls' three straight NBA titles from 1991–93. During those three glory seasons in the Windy City, Michael Jordan and Scottie Pippen enjoyed most of the spotlight, but Grant contributed with 8.4 rebounds and 12.8 points per game in 1990–91, a career-high 10.0 rebounds and 14.2 points in 1991–92 and 9.5 boards and 13.2 points in 1992–93.

An unsung hero with big biceps and thick goggles who played for seven seasons in Chicago from 1987–94, Grant was signed as a free agent by the Orlando Magic in 1994. In just his first season with the Magic, Grant helped Shaquille O'Neal and Penny Hardaway reach the NBA Finals, but Orlando was defeated in four straight games by the Houston Rockets.

After averaging 12.6 points and 9.0 rebounds for Orlando last season, Grant's career scoring average is at 12.7 points per game. Horace and his twin brother Harvey, who also plays in the NBA, were born on the Fourth of July.

RIGHT: BEFORE HE BOLTED TO THE ORLANDO MAGIC, HORACE GRANT PROVIDED THE MUSCLE THAT HELPED MICHAEL JORDAN AND THE CHICAGO BULLS WIN THREE CHAMPIONSHIPS.

A. C. GREEN

O ne of the most durable players in NBA history, A. C. Green ranks first among active players with a streak of 896 consecutive regular-season games played through the 1996–97 season. He is second all-time in that category, trailing only Randy Smith (906).

A 6-foot-9-inch power forward who helped the Los Angeles Lakers win back-to-back titles in 1987 and 1988, Green, now in his 12th NBA campaign and a member of the Phoenix Suns, cracked the 10,000-point and 7,000-rebound barriers in 1995–96.

During the Lakers Showtime Era, it was Green, a tremendous leaper who excels in a quick transition game, who was often ahead of the field for breakaway slams. Teaming with the likes of Kareem Abdul-Jabbar, Magic Johnson and James Worthy, Green appeared in four championship series with Los Angeles during his career.

After putting up 7.2 points and 7.9 rebounds per game last season, Green has now averaged 10.9 points and 7.9 rebounds during the course of his career. His best scoring seasons came with the Lakers in 1991–92, when he averaged 13.6 points per game, and with Phoenix in 1993–94, when he posted a career-high 14.7 points per contest.

A product of Oregon State, where he averaged 14.7 points in four seasons, Green was an NBA All-Defensive Second Team selection in 1989, and the following season, was named to his only All-Star squad. In 127 career playoff games, Green averaged 9.6 points and 7.7 rebounds. He is now with Dallas.

FACT FILE

Born: October 4, 1963
Height: 6′ 9″
Length of NBA career:
1985–present
Major teams:
Los Angeles
Phoenix (joined 1993)
Dallas (joined 1996)
Records/Awards:
NBA Championship (2)
NBA All-Star (1)

LEFT: A. C. GREEN, BEING WATCHED HERE BY DENNIS RODMAN, WAS USUALLY AHEAD OF THE FIELD FOR AN EASY BASKET DURING THE LAKERS' SHOWTIME DAYS.

WILT CHAMBERLAIN'S 100-POINT GAME

Most records are made to be broken, but the one Wilt Chamberlain set on March 2, 1962, in Hershey, PA, remains untouchable, and is widely considered the most remarkable achievement in the history of professional sports.

On that cold, slushy Friday night, Chamberlain, the 7-foot-2-inch goateed Goliath of the Philadelphia Warriors, scored one hundred points against the visiting New York Knicks. With the exception of Chamberlain himself, no other player in basketball history has come remotely close to matching it.

The 4,124 spectators who attended that historic Knicks-Warriors game had no idea they would be witness to the greatest one-man offensive show in the history of the league.

Chamberlain, just twenty-five years old at the time, squared off for the opening tip against New York's 6-foot-10-inch pivotman, Darrell Imhoff. The big fella had been out late the night before and had had no sleep entering the game, which made the next forty-eight minutes of play even more improbable, even more phenomenal.

After winning the tip, Chamberlain followed a missed shot by teammate Paul Arizin and jammed the ball through the rim for his first 2 points.

From there, Wilt the Stilt began lighting it up. He bagged his next five shots to give the Warriors a 19–3 lead, and by the end of the first quarter, had racked up 23 points. A poor free-throw shooter in his day, Chamberlain was even clicking from the foul line, as he hit nine straight free throws in the opening quarter.

Continuing his scoring spree on an assortment of jump shots, fingerrolls, dunks, and free throws, Chamberlain had boosted his halftime total to 41 points, connecting on 13 of 14 free-throw attempts.

When Chamberlain reached the 50-point plateau early in the third quarter, the tiny crowd went wild. With Imhoff in foul trouble and his 6-foot-7-inch replacement, Cleveland Buckner, helpless on defense against the rampaging giant,

ABOVE: WILT CHAMBERLAIN, DOING BATTLE AT LEFT WITH HIS NUMBER ONE NEMESIS, BILL RUSSELL OF THE BOSTON CELTICS, DROPS IN TWO POINTS

Chamberlain ran off 28 points in the quarter, bringing his total to 69 points with twelve minutes left to play in the contest.

Entering the fourth quarter, the Warriors led, 125–106, but with the crowd sensing history and chanting "Give it to Wilt. Give it to Wilt . . ." the final score was becoming a mere footnote on what was shaping up to be an historic evening.

With 7:51 left in the game, Chamberlain hit a one-handed shot from the foul line for his 78th and 79th points. His teammates, also sensing history, began feeding Chamberlain the ball on every offensive possession, which infuriated the Knicks.

With 2:45 left to play, Chamberlain had tallied 94 points, and moments later added two more on a jumper. With time running out, points number 97 and 98 came on an easy layup off a feed from York Larese.

With under a minute to play, the Knicks brought the ball down court and missed a shot. The Warriors quickly set up on offense, and Joe Ruklick tossed the ball to Chamberlain in the pivot.

Chamberlain launched a shot and missed, got his own rebound, put up another shot, and missed again. Philadelphia, however, fought for the offensive rebound.

With forty-six seconds left on the clock, Ruklick spotted Chamberlain under the basket and flipped a high lob-pass over the rim. Chamberlain leaped high, and in one swift motion, grabbed the ball with two hands and stuffed it through the cords for his 100th point.

Chamberlain's historic basket sent the sparse crowd into the outer limits of hysteria. Paper cups and newspapers were thrown onto the floor, and some 200 people rushed onto the court to congratulate him.

"When I made my first nine free throws, I thought I'd be heading for some kind of foul-shooting record," Chamberlain remembered. "But never in my fondest dreams did I ever expect I would score a hundred points going into that game."

HAL GREER

FACT FILE

Born: June 26, 1936
Height: 6′ 2″
Length of NBA career:
   1958–1973
Major teams:
   Syracuse–Philadelphia
Records/Award:
   NBA Championship (1)
   NBA All-Star (10)
   Hall of Fame (1981)

The 1966–67 Philadelphia 76ers are widely considered one of the NBA's greatest teams, and Hal Greer was one of their best players.

Greer, a 6-foot-2-inch quick guard with a sensational jump shot, teamed with Wilt Chamberlain, Chet Walker and Billy Cunningham to lead Philadelphia to a four-games-to-two championship victory over the San Francisco Warriors. While Chamberlain led the 76ers that season with 24.1 points per contest, Greer was a close second, contributing 22.1 points per game.

The first black scholarship athlete at Marshall University, Greer was selected by the Syracuse Nationals in the second round of the 1958 NBA draft. He played his entire 15-year career with the Nationals' franchise, moving with it from Syracuse to Philadelphia in 1963 (the team was also renamed 76ers that season).

A ten-time All-Star and seven-time All-NBA Second Team selection, Greer averaged 19.2 points, 5.0 rebounds and 4.0 assists during his career, and 20.4 points, 5.5 rebounds and 4.3 assists in 92 career playoff games. He was voted the NBA All-Star Game Most Valuable Player in 1968, setting a record in that contest for most points in one quarter with 19. That same season, he averaged a career-high 24.1 points per game.

At Marshall, Greer averaged 19.4 points in four seasons, and 23.6 as a senior in 1958, earning All-American honors.

BELOW: HAL GREER WAS A STAR ON THE 1966–67 PHILADELPHIA 76ERS, WIDELY CONSIDERED ONE OF THE NBA'S GREATEST TEAMS.

DARRELL GRIFFITH

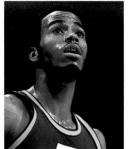

Throughout the 1980s, Darrell Griffith of the Utah Jazz was one of the most exciting guards in the NBA. His forte was outside shooting, and he wasted little time showing off that talent, gunning his way to the NBA Rookie of the Year award in 1981 with a 20.6 scoring average.

Selected by Utah as the second pick overall in the 1980 NBA draft, Griffith had an outstanding college career at Louisville. He averaged 18.5 points in four seasons with the Cardinals, leading them in his senior season to the NCAA Championship.

Griffith, a 6-foot-4-inch shooting guard, kept his long-distance skills intact at the pro level. He followed up his stellar rookie season with 19.8 points per game in 1981–82. He then scored 20 or more points in each of his next three seasons with the Jazz, including a career-high 22.6 points per game in 1984–85.

He also led the NBA, in three-point field goal percentage twice, knocking down 91 of 252 trifectas for a .361 percentage in 1983–84, and 92 of 257 treys for a .358 shooting clip in 1984–85.

Despite missing the entire 1985–86 season because of a broken bone in his foot, Griffith returned to the Jazz for five more productive seasons from 1986–91. He averaged 16.2 points in his career, tallying an average of 15.1 points in 37 career playoff games.

FACT FILE

Born: June 16, 1958
Height: 6′ 4″
Length of NBA career:
  1980–1991
Major team:
  Utah
Records/Awards:
  NBA Rookie of the Year
  (1981)

LEFT: DARRELL GRIFFITH GUNNED HIS WAY TO THE 1981 ROOKIE OF THE YEAR AWARD.

ERNIE GRUNFELD

FACT FILE

Born: April 24, 1955
Height: 6′ 6″
Length of NBA career:
1977–1986
Major teams:
Milwaukee
Kansas City (joined 1979)
New York (joined 1982)

At Tennessee in the early 1970s, Ernie Grunfeld, who averaged 22.3 points in four seasons there, was co-host of the "Bernie and Ernie Show." He teamed with Bernard King to form one of the most explosive offensive tandems in the college game.

Grunfeld, a gifted outside shooter who played a thinking-man's brand of basketball, was selected by the Milwaukee Bucks in the first round of the 1977 NBA draft. He played two seasons in Milwaukee, averaging 6.9 points and 10.3 points, respectively.

For the next three seasons, Grunfeld found himself in Kansas City, and after scoring 5.9 points in 1979–80 and 7.5 points in 1980–81,

he bounced back to average a career-high 12.7 points per game with the Kings the following season. His next (and last) NBA stop was with the New York Knicks, where he played from 1982–86 and was reunited with his old college teammate, King. Grunfeld later returned to the New York Knicks franchise as the team's General Manager.

Over the course of his nine-year NBA career, Grunfeld averaged 7.4 points per contest, and posted 8.9 points in 42 career playoff games.

Grunfeld and King, who combined for 50.6 points per game in 1975–76 at Tennessee, were inducted together into the New York City Basketball Hall of Fame in 1994.

RIGHT: ERNIE GRUNFELD, NOW THE GENERAL MANAGER OF THE NEW YORK KNICKS, PLAYED A THINKING-MAN'S BRAND OF BASKETBALL.

RICHIE GUERIN

From the late 1950s into the 1960s, the New York Knicks made the playoffs just once during a ten-year span. At the time, there was nothing much for New York fans to cheer about, unless of course, Richie Guerin was having another of his terrific shooting nights.

Guerin, a 6-foot-4-inch native New Yorker who played his college ball at Iona, spent the first seven and a half seasons of his NBA career in New York, three and a half seasons with St. Louis, and parts of two other campaigns with the Hawks franchise, which had moved to Atlanta.

It was with New York, however, that the fiery Guerin enjoyed his best seasons. He averaged four seasons of 20 or more points with the Knicks, including a career-high 29.5 scoring average in 1961–62. He finished sixth among NBA scorers that season.

A scrappy player who fought for every loose ball, Guerin lit up the scoreboard on numerous occasions. He was the first Knick to score 50 points, firing in 57 points on February 11, 1959, against Syracuse. That feat was just one of 11 40-plus point-performances in Guerin's career.

A six-time All-Star and three-time All-NBA Second Team selection, Guerin was traded by the Knicks to St. Louis in 1963, and averaged roughly 14.5 points during his tenure with the Hawks. He retired during the 1967–68 season, but came out of retirement in 1968 to play with the Atlanta Hawks.

Over his 13-year playing career, Guerin averaged 17.3 points per game, and racked up 15.6 points in 42 career playoff contests.

FACT FILE

Born: May 29, 1932
Height: 6′ 4″
Length of NBA career:
 1956–1967, 1968–70
Major teams:
 New York
 St. Louis–Atlanta (joined
 1963)
Records/Awards:
 NBA All-Star (6)

LEFT: AT A TIME WHEN THE NEW YORK KNICKS WERE PLAYING POOR BASKETBALL, RICHIE GUERIN WAS ONE OF THE ONLY TALENTS WORTH WATCHING ON BROADWAY.

CLIFF HAGAN

FACT FILE

Born: December 9, 1931
Height: 6′ 4″
Length of NBA career:
 1956–66
Length of ABA career:
 1967–70
Major teams:
 St. Louis
 Dallas (joined 1967)
Records/Awards:
 NBA Championship (1)
 NBA All-Star (5)
 ABA All-Star (1)
 Hall of Fame (1977)

Long before Kareem Abdul-Jabbar was shooting the sky hook, Cliff Hagan was using it as one of the weapons in his offensive arsenal.

Hagan, a 6-foot-4-inch forward out of Kentucky, broke into the NBA with the St. Louis Hawks in 1956. He spent ten of his 13 professional seasons with the Hawks, averaging 18 points per game over that span while helping St. Louis win six Western Division titles and the 1958 NBA Championship. In 90 career NBA playoff games, he averaged 20.4 points, 8.3 rebounds and 3.4 assists per game.

"Li'l Abner," as Hagan was called in his playing days, had one of his best NBA seasons in 1959–60, averaging 24.8 points, 10.7 rebounds and 4.0 assists. He averaged 20 or more points per game in four straight seasons from 1958–62. After his stint in St. Louis, Hagan went on to be a player-coach for the ABA's Dallas Chaparrals from 1967–70.

A six-time All-Star—he was the Most Valuable Player of the 1958 All-Star game—and two-time All-NBA Second Team selection, Hagan averaged 15.1 points, 4.7 rebounds and 4.3 assists in his three seasons with Dallas.

A Kentucky All-American in 1952 and 1954, Hagan helped the 1951 Wildcats win the NCAA Championship, and the 1954 team was undefeated in 25 games. He averaged 19.2 points in four seasons at Kentucky, and, in 1952, set an NCAA single-season record for rebounds with 528.

RIGHT: CLIFF HAGAN, FINISHING OFF A LAYUP HERE, HELPED THE ST LOUIS HAWKS WIN THE 1958 NBA CHAMPIONSHIP.

ANFERNEE "PENNY" HARDAWAY

One of the most explosive and talented players ever to have arrived on the NBA scene, Anfernee "Penny" Hardaway of the Orlando Magic has established himself as one of the premier attractions in the game. With smooth all-round skills, he is capable of playing every position on the floor except center.

A 6-foot-7-inch swingman with incredible leaping ability and an electric dribble, Hardaway's scoring average improved in each of his first three NBA seasons. He posted 16 points per game as a rookie, 20.9 points in his second season, and a career-high 21.7 points per game in 1995–96.

"Penny," who was given his nickname by his grandmother, Louise—"When I was a kid, she used to say I was pretty as a penny," he says—helped Shaquille O'Neal and the rest of his Orlando Magic teammates reach the NBA Finals in 1994–95, where Houston took the title in four straight games.

"In this league, you just have to keep getting better and better, and not pay attention to what people are saying about you," said Hardaway, an NBA All-Rookie First Team selection who has already been voted onto three All-Star squads. "That's my goal, to just keep getting better and better."

A standout at Memphis, where he averaged 20 points per game in two seasons and was twice named Great Midwest Conference Player of the Year, Hardaway was selected by the Golden State Warriors in the first round of the 1993 NBA draft. In one of the blockbuster deals of the 1990s, his draft rights were traded by the Warriors to the Orlando Magic for the draft rights to power forward Chris Webber.

Hardaway, who averaged 20.5 points per game last season, survived a major scare several years ago in his hometown of Memphis, TN, where a robber threatened to shoot him, is savoring every moment of his stellar NBA career.

"I'm just thankful that I'm still around to enjoy all of this," he said.

FACT FILE

Born: July 18, 1972
Height: 6′ 7″
Length of NBA career:
   1993–present
Major team:
   Orlando
Records/Awards:
   NBA All-Star (3)
   Olympic Gold Medal
   (1996)

LEFT: ANFERNEE "PENNY" HARDAWAY'S EXPLOSIVE TALENTS MAKE HIM ONE OF THE NBA'S GREATEST ATTRACTIONS.

TIM HARDAWAY

FACT FILE

Born: September 1, 1966
Height: 6′ 0″
Length of NBA career:
1989–present
Major teams:
Golden State
Miami (joined 1996)
Records/Awards:
NBA All-Star (4)

The crossover dribble. No one in the NBA does it better or uses it more effectively than Tim Hardaway of the Miami Heat.

Hardaway, a 6-foot point guard with an amazing ability to penetrate to the hoop, has been crossing up opponents since he was drafted by the Golden State Warriors out of Texas-El Paso in 1989.

In five seasons with Golden State—he missed the 1993–94 campaign due to a knee injury—Hardaway, with help from teammate Chris Mullin, ran the show. During that span, he averaged 20.5 points, 9.6 assists, and 3.1 rebounds per game.

Midway through the 1995–96 season, Hardaway was traded by Golden State to the Miami Heat, and helped the Heat earn a play-off berth by averaging 15.2 points per game, which placed him second on the team in scoring behind Alonzo Mourning (23.2).

An All-Rookie selection in 1990—he averaged 14.7 points and 8.7 assists as a rookie—and three-time NBA All-Star, Hardaway enjoyed his best season with Golden State in 1991–92, averaging a career-high 23.4 points and 10.0 assists per contest.

During the course of his NBA career, Hardaway has averaged 19.7 points and 9.2 assists per game. He shares the single-game playoff record for most steals with 8, pulling off that feat on May 8, 1991, against Los Angeles, and again on April 30, 1992, against Seattle. Hardaway is also the holder of one of the league's bizarre records. On December 27, 1991, he attempted 17 field goals, and did not make any of them.

Last season, Hardaway averaged 20.5 points per game.

RIGHT: TIM HARDAWAY, MOVING IN HERE ON A DEFENDER, IS THE MASTER OF THE CROSSOVER DRIBBLE.

DEREK HARPER

After starring on Broadway for two and a half seasons, Derek Harper is back in Dallas, where his long and productive career started.

A 6-foot-4-inch point guard with overall court savvy, great defensive skills and a penchant for hitting the clutch outside shot, Harper was drafted by the Dallas Mavericks out of Illinois in the first round of the 1983 NBA draft. Harper, who averaged 10.9 points and 4.7 assists in three seasons at Illinois, played his first ten and a half seasons in Dallas before he was traded to New York in 1994.

That same season, he helped lead the Knicks to their first world championship appearance in twenty-one years. In that title clash, which was won by the Houston Rockets in seven thrilling games, Harper shared an NBA Finals single-series record for most three-point field goals made with 17. His best scoring campaign in a Knicks uniform was 1995–96, when he posted 14.0 points per game.

For nine years in Dallas, Harper teamed in the backcourt with Rolando Blackman to form one of the flashiest offensive attacks in the league. Harper's best season with the Mavericks came in 1990–91, when he averaged 19.7 points and 7.1 assists per game.

A two-time NBA All-Defensive Second Team selection, Harper has averaged 13.9 points and 5.7 assists throughout his career.

He was brought back by Dallas in 1996 in hopes that his vast experience will help steer the young and talented Mavericks in a winning direction.

FACT FILE

Born: October 13, 1961
Height: 6′ 4″
Length of NBA career:
 1983–present
Major teams:
 Dallas
 New York (joined 1994)
 Dallas (joined 1996)

LEFT: DEREK HARPER'S SOLID BACKCOURT PLAY HELPED THE NEW YORK KNICKS REACH THE NBA FINALS.

RON HARPER

FACT FILE

Born: January 20, 1964
Height: 6′ 6″
Length of NBA career:
1986–present
Major teams:
Cleveland
Los Angeles (joined 1989)
Chicago (joined 1994)
Records/Awards:
NBA Championship (2)

When the Chicago Bulls returned to championship glory in 1995–96, Ron Harper was a significant contributor.

Harper, a 6-foot-6-inch shooting guard whose spectacular leaping ability has been slowed by injuries in recent years, helped Michael Jordan quarterback the Bulls to a record 72 wins in 1995–96 en route to sweeping the Orlando Magic in the NBA Finals for Chicago's fourth championship in six years.

Last season, Harper and the Bulls were back in championship business, defeating Utah in six games to win another title.

An open-court demon in his early NBA days with the Cleveland Cavaliers, Harper was mired in mediocrity for eight seasons with Cleveland and the Los Angeles Clippers before joining the Bulls in 1994. With Cleveland and Los Angeles, he had never advanced beyond the first round of the playoffs.

After averaging 19.8 points in four seasons at Miami of Ohio, Harper was selected by Cleveland in the first round of the 1986 NBA draft. In his first season with the Cavs, he averaged a career-high 22.9 points per game and was named to the league's All-Rookie team. He averaged 22.8 points in a split season with Cleveland and Los Angeles in 1989–90, and enjoyed his last 20-point scoring season with the Clippers in 1993–94.

RIGHT: RON HARPER, WHOSE GREAT SKILLS WERE WATERED DOWN BY INJURIES, REGAINED HIS HEALTH JUST IN TIME TO HELP THE 1995–96 CHICAGO BULLS CAPTURE A CHAMPIONSHIP.

CLEM HASKINS

C lem "The Gem" Haskins, one of the first black scholarship players at Western Kentucky, played nine solid seasons in the NBA.

A quick guard with the ability to penetrate to the hoop through traffic, the 6-foot-3-inch Haskins broke into the NBA with the Chicago Bulls in the 1967–68 season, averaging 8.9 points and 2.1 assists per game in his rookie season.

He played three seasons in Chicago, averaging 17.2 points and 3.8 assists per game in his second campaign with the Bulls, and a career-high 20.3 points and 2.9 assists in 1969–70.

The following season, Haskins brought his cut-and-slash driving style of play to Phoenix, posting 17.8 points and 4.6 assists per contest in his first season with the Suns.

After averaging 15.7, 10.5 and 11.1 points in his next three seasons in Phoenix, Haskins was off to Washington, where he played the last two seasons of his NBA career. He averaged 4.0 points and 6.4 points as a part-time player in those seasons.

For his career, Haskins averaged 12.8 points and 3.5 assists per contest. In 28 playoff games, he posted 5.9 points and 1.4 assists per contest.

FACT FILE

Born: August 11, 1944
Height: 6' 3"
Length of NBA career:
1967–76
Major teams:
Chicago
Phoenix (joined 1970)
Washington (joined 1974)

LEFT: CLEM "THE GEM" HASKINS, A QUICK GUARD WITH THE ABILITY TO PENETRATE TO THE HOOP, KEEPS HIS EYES FIXED ON THE BASKET.

JOHN HAVLICEK

FACT FILE

Born: April 8, 1940
Height: 6′ 5″
Length of NBA career:
  1962–78
Major team:
  Boston
Records/Awards:
  NBA Championship (8)
  NBA All-Star (13)
  NBA All-Defensive First
  Team (5)
  Hall of Fame (1983)

BELOW: IN HIS PRIME, JOHN HAVLICEK WAS THE HEART AND SOUL OF THE BOSTON CELTICS.

For sixteen seasons in Beantown, the man they called "Hondo" was the heart and soul of the Boston Celtics.

John Havlicek, a 6-foot-5-inch defensive-minded swingman who was a picture of perpetual motion on the hardwood, helped Boston capture eight championships throughout the course of his legendary career.

During his first four seasons with the Celtics from 1962–66, Havlicek made a name for himself as the NBA's preeminent Sixth Man, coming off the bench to help fabled teammates like Bob Cousy, Bill Russell and Sam Jones keep Boston's championship tradition intact. In those four seasons, the Celtics won four straight titles.

Havlicek, a star at Ohio State who helped the Buckeyes win the 1960 NCAA title and compile a 78–6 record in three seasons, was a starter on the Celtics 1968 and 1969 championship teams. After years of hard work and hustle, he was team captain by the time Boston had returned to championship glory in 1974 and 1976.

A thirteen-time All-Star and five-time NBA All-Defensive First Team selection, Havlicek averaged 20.8 points, 6.3 rebounds and 4.8 assists in a career spent entirely in Boston. Considered a defensive specialist in his early NBA years, Havlicek proved himself a big-league scorer as well, scoring 20 or more points in eight straight seasons from 1966–74.

In 172 career playoff games, Havlicek averaged 22.0 points, 6.9 rebounds and 4.8 assists. He was the NBA Finals Most Valuable Player in 1974, and shares the NBA Finals single-game record for most points in an overtime period, scoring 9 points on May 10, 1974, against the Milwaukee Bucks. He also shares the single-game playoff record for most field goals made, bagging 24 shots from the field on April 1, 1973, against Atlanta.

In addition to his NBA career, Havlicek also played football and was selected as a wide-receiver by the Cleveland Browns in the 1962 NFL draft. He was voted onto the NBA's 35th Anniversary All-Time team in 1980.

CONNIE HAWKINS

A New York City playground legend, Connie Hawkins overcame adversity to become one of professional basketball's all-time greats.

Hawkins, a 6-foot-8-inch forward/center who grew up in Brooklyn and played just one season of college ball at Iowa, had been banned from the NBA for his alleged involvement in the college betting scandals of 1961. Despite his NBA banishment, Hawkins found a number of stages to showcase his tremendous talent.

After his brief college tenure, "The Hawk," as the high-flying Hawkins was known in his playing days, signed a contract to play for the Pittsburgh Rens of the ABL. He led the league in scoring as a rookie with 27.5 points per game, and racked up 27.9 points per contest in his second and last season with the Rens.

From 1963–67, Hawkins suited up with the Harlem Globetrotters, and in 1967, he inked a contract with the Pittsburgh Pipers of the upstart ABA. In his rookie season in the new league, Hawkins led the league with a 26.8 scoring average —and led the Pipers to the 1967–68 ABA Championship, a four-games-to-three victory over New Orleans.

After averaging a career-high 30.2 points per game for the Pipers —who had relocated to Minnesota—the following season, Hawkins had sued the NBA to gain reinstatement in the league, and won his case.

From 1969 through the middle of the 1973–74 season, Hawkins played with the Phoenix Suns of the NBA, and later played for the Los Angeles Lakers and the Atlanta Hawks.

A four-time NBA All-Star, Hawkins averaged 16.5 points and 8.0 rebounds in seven seasons in the league. He finished his career with combined ABA and NBA averages of 18.7 points, 8.8 rebounds and 4.1 assists.

FACT FILE

Born: July 17, 1942
Height: 6′ 8″
Length of ABL career:
1961–63
Length of ABA career:
1967–69
Length of NBA career:
1969–76
Major teams:
Pittsburgh (ABL)
Pittsburgh–Minnesota
(joined 1967)
Phoenix (joined 1969)
Los Angeles (joined 1973)
Atlanta (joined 1975)
Records/Awards:
ABA Championship (1)
ABA All-Star (2)
ABA Most Valuable Player
(1)
NBA All-Star (4)

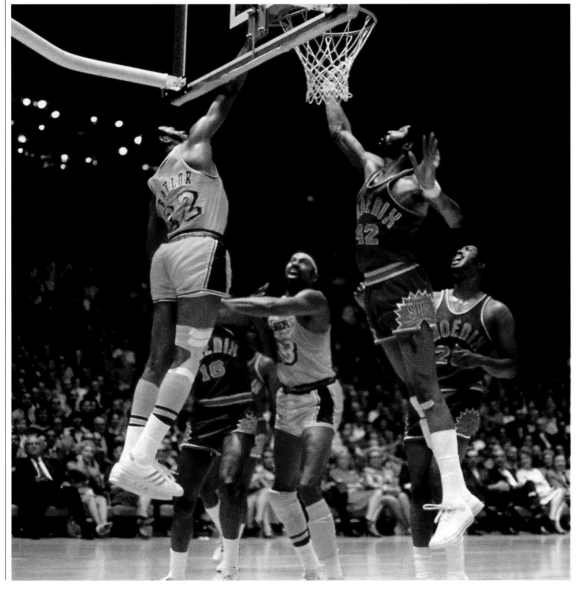

LEFT: PERSONAL PROBLEMS FORCED CONNIE HAWKINS TO BLOOM LATE, BUT HE IS STILL CONSIDERED ONE OF PRO BASKETBALL'S ALL-TIME GREATS.

BEFORE JORDAN, BAYLOR WAS THE STAR OF POST-SEASON THEATER

Only one player in NBA history has scored more points in a single playoff game than Elgin Baylor. That player is Michael Jordan of the Chicago Bulls, who poured in 63 points against the Boston Celtics in two overtimes on April 20, 1986.

Twenty-four years before Jordan's eruption—he connected on 22 field goals and added 19 free throws—it was Baylor stunning a capacity crowd at the Boston Garden. On April 14, 1962, with the Celtics-Lakers championship series tied at two games apiece, Baylor launched shots from everywhere, torching the Celtics' defense and the man who was guarding him, Tom "Satch" Sanders. "Elgin was just a machine in that game," Sanders said later.

When it was over, Baylor had scored 61 points and added 22 rebounds, in regulation, to give the Lakers a 126–121 victory and a three-games-to-two lead in the Finals. Boston would come back to win the series, but Baylor's performance—he bagged 22 field goals and added 17 free throws for his 61 points—earned him an everlasting place in the NBA's folklore.

"You wouldn't believe it," said the Boston playmaker Bob Cousy after Baylor's magnificent performance, "but Satch played great defense against Elgin. I recall telling him after the game that he did a heck of a job. He made Baylor work for every shot and take shots he didn't want to take."

Jerry West, who teamed with Baylor on the Lakers, remembered the historic evening.

"It was one of those nights where Baylor's every effort seemed to guide him to just the right spot on the floor," said West. "He was without a doubt truly one of the great people to play the game."

ELVIN HAYES

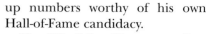

FACT FILE

Born: November 17, 1945
Height: 6′ 9″
Length of NBA career:
1968–84
Major teams:
San Diego–Houston
Baltimore–Capital–
Washington (joined
1972)
Houston (joined 1981)
Records/Awards:
NBA Championship (1)
NBA All-Star (12)
Hall of Fame (1989)

One of the greatest outside shooting centers in the history of the NBA, Elvin Hayes led the 1977–78 Washington Bullets to an NBA Championship.

Hayes, a 6-foot-9-inch center who also played forward during his stellar sixteen-year career, teamed with Wes Unseld and Bob Dandridge to help Washington knock off Seattle four games to three for the 1978 NBA crown.

A sizzling collegiate star at the University of Houston—where he averaged 36.8 points in his senior season and was named the 1968 College Player of the Year—Hayes was selected by the San Diego Rockets as the first overall pick in the 1968 NBA draft. He tore up the NBA in his All-Rookie campaign of 1968–69, ringing up a league-high 28.4 points per game, burying many of his league-leading 2,327 points from deep in the corners of the court. Often overshadowed in his day by the phenomenal Kareem Abdul-Jabbar, Hayes put up numbers worthy of his own Hall-of-Fame candidacy.

The "Big E," as Hayes was often called, averaged 20 or more points ten times in his career. In his second season in San Diego, he averaged 27.5 points and a league-leading 16.9 rebounds per game. He played four seasons with the Rockets—who moved to Houston in 1971—before he was traded in 1972 to the Baltimore Bullets—who eventually moved to Washington—and in his second season with the franchise, again led the league in rebounding with a career-high 18.1 boards per game.

A 12-time All-Star, Hayes averaged 21.0 points and 12.5 rebounds in his career, racking up 22.9 points and 13 rebounds in 96 career playoff games. He holds the single-season record for most minutes played by a rookie, logging in 3,695 minutes in 1968–69. He also holds the NBA Finals single-game record for most offensive rebounds, hauling down 11 boards on May 27, 1979, against Seattle.

RIGHT: THE "BIG E", AS ELVIN HAYES WAS KNOWN, AVERAGED 20 OR MORE POINTS 10 TIMES IN HIS CAREER.

SPENCER HAYWOOD

efore embarking on a sensational 12-year NBA career, Spencer Haywood played one season in the ABA, putting together one of the most remarkable campaigns in the history of professional basketball.

A product of Detroit University, where he averaged 32.1 points and led the NCAA with 22.1 rebounds per game in 1969, Haywood signed with the Denver Rockets of the ABA. In one season with the Rockets, the 6-foot-9-inch center/forward, who had a load of quickness and a feathery touch for a big man, led the league in scoring (30.0), rebounding (19.5), points scored (2,519) and minutes played (3,808). He averaged 36.7 points in 12 playoff games en route to winning both the Rookie of the Year and Most Valuable Player awards.

The following season, Haywood hooked up with the Seattle SuperSonics, averaging 20.6 points and 12.0 rebounds in his initial NBA season. He played five seasons in Seattle, averaging more than 20 points in each of them.

After spending three and a half seasons with the New York Knicks and a half season with the New Orleans Jazz, Haywood was traded to the Los Angeles Lakers for the 1979–80 season. He teamed with a veteran named Kareem Abdul-Jabbar and a rookie named Magic Johnson to help Los Angeles defeat the Philadelphia 76ers in six games for the NBA title.

The following season, Haywood took his act to Italy, averaging 23.5 points for Venezia of the Italian League. He returned to the NBA with Washington in 1981, and spent his last two seasons with the Bullets.

A five-time All-Star, Haywood averaged 20.3 points and 10.3 rebounds in his combined ABA and NBA careers.

FACT FILE

Born: April 22, 1949
Height: 6′ 9″
Length of ABA career:
 1969–70
Length of NBA career:
 1970–83
Major teams:
 Denver
 Seattle (joined 1970)
 New York (joined 1975)
 New Orleans (joined 1979)
 Los Angeles (joined 1979)
 Washington (Joined 1981)
Records/Awards:
 ABA Most Valuable Player (1)
 ABA Rookie of the Year (1970)
 ABA All-Star (1)
 NBA Championship (1)
 NBA All-Star (4)
 Olympic Gold Medal (1968)

LEFT: SPENCER HAYWOOD'S ONE SEASON IN THE ABA PROVED TO BE A REMARKABLE CAMPAIGN.

AL HEERDT

FACT FILE

Al Heerdt's Fact File is incomplete as very little information concerning professional basketball was documented around the turn of the century.

In the early days of basketball, Al Heerdt was the captain of the Buffalo Germans, a team which played from the years 1895–1929 and compiled an incredible 792–86 record during that time.

According to the *NBA Encyclopedia*, Heerdt, along with his teammate Eddie Miller, led the Germans, who were organized in a Buffalo YMCA and started playing an amateur schedule when most of them were just fourteen years old.

The Germans dominated amateur tournaments, including the 1901 Pan American Exposition where the basketball competition was staged on a grass court. Heerdt and his Buffalo team also fared well against professional competition. As a touring team, the Germans reeled off 111 consecutive victories before a 26–21 loss to a team from Herkimer, NY. One of their many opponents was the Carlisle Indians, featuring the legendary Jim Thorpe, an Olympic athlete and football star.

The long-sleeved uniforms worn by the Buffalo Germans and many other basketball teams from their era bear a close resemblance

BELOW: AL HEERDT, CENTER OF MIDDLE ROW, WAS THE CAPTAIN OF THE BUFFALO GERMANS, ONE OF THE EARLIEST, AND BEST, PROFESSIONAL TEAMS.

TOM HEINSOHN

Tom Heinsohn, a rugged 6-foot-7-inch forward and accomplished artist, painted a picturesque career with the Boston Celtics, winning a remarkable eight championships in nine seasons.

After averaging 22.1 points in four seasons at Holy Cross, Heinsohn won Rookie of the Year honors in 1956–57, averaging 16.2 points and 9.8 rebounds as he and Celtic teammates Bill Russell, Bill Sharman and Bob Cousy defeated St. Louis in seven games to win the NBA title.

The following season, Heinsohn raised his scoring (17.8) and rebounding (10.2) averages to help Boston get back to the championship series. However, that year St. Louis, led by the All-Star forward Bob Pettit, stormed back to win the title in six games.

From there, Heinsohn and the Celtics won seven straight titles. His most productive seasons were 1959–62. In those three campaigns, Heinsohn averaged 21.7 points and 10 rebounds per game.

A ten-time All-Star and four-time All-NBA Second Team selection, Heinsohn posted 18.6 points and 8.8 rebounds in his career with the Celtics, adding 19.8 points and 9.2 rebounds in 104 career playoff games.

Off the court, Heinsohn is an artist who has had many gallery exhibitions.

TOM HEINSOHN

TOM HEINSOHN

TOM HEINSOHN

TOM HEINSOHN

TOM HEINSOHN

TOM HEINSOHN

Tom Heinsohn, a rugged 6-foot-7-inch forward and accomplished artist, painted a picturesque career with the Boston Celtics, winning a remarkable eight championships in nine seasons.

After averaging 22.1 points in four seasons at Holy Cross, Heinsohn won Rookie of the Year honors in 1956–57, averaging 16.2 points and 9.8 rebounds as he and Celtic teammates Bill Russell, Bill Sharman and Bob Cousy defeated St. Louis in seven games to win the NBA title.

The following season, Heinsohn raised his scoring (17.8) and rebounding (10.2) averages to help Boston get back to the championship series. However, that year St. Louis, led by the All-Star forward Bob Pettit, stormed back to win the title in six games.

From there, Heinsohn and the Celtics won seven straight titles. His most productive seasons were 1959–62. In those three campaigns, Heinsohn averaged 21.7 points and 10 rebounds per game.

A ten-time All-Star and four-time All-NBA Second Team selection, Heinsohn posted 18.6 points and 8.8 rebounds in his career with the Celtics, adding 19.8 points and 9.2 rebounds in 104 career playoff games.

Off the court, Heinsohn is an artist who has had many gallery exhibitions.

FACT FILE

Born: August 26, 1934
Height: 6' 7"
Length of NBA career:
1956–65
Major team:
Boston
Records/Awards:
NBA Rookie of the Year
(1957)
NBA All-Star (6)
NBA Championship (8)
Hall of Fame (1985)

LEFT: TOM HEINSOHN, WHO WON EIGHT CHAMPIONSHIPS WITH THE BOSTON CELTICS, WHOOPING IT UP IN HIS DAYS AT HOLY CROSS.

GERALD HENDERSON

FACT FILE

Born: January 16, 1956
Height: 6′ 2″
Length of NBA career:
  1979–92
Major teams:
  Boston
  Seattle (joined 1984)
  New York (joined 1986)
  Philadelphia (joined 1987)
  Milwaukee (joined 1989)
  Detroit (joined 1989)
  Houston (joined 1991)
  Detroit (joined 1992)
Records/Awards:
  NBA Championship (3)

Every championship team has its pivotal role players, and Gerald Henderson filled that description on three different teams during his thirteen-year career with the NBA.

Henderson, a 6-foot-2-inch point guard out of Virginia Commonwealth, contributed to two championships as a member of the Boston Celtics in 1981 and 1984, and a third crown with the Detroit Pistons in 1990.

After being drafted by the San Antonio Spurs in the third round of the 1978 NBA draft, Henderson was eventually cut by the Spurs. He played one season with the Tucson Gunners of the Western Basketball Association before he signed as a free agent with Boston in 1979.

As a backup to Boston's backcourt wizard, Nate "Tiny" Archibald, Henderson, a reliable ball-handler who could penetrate to the hoop, came off the bench to help the Celtics defeat the Houston Rockets, four games to two, and capture the 1981 championship.

By 1984, Dennis Johnson was running the show in Boston, but Henderson shared the spotlight, averaging 11.6 points and 3.8 assists in helping the Celtics to a four-games-to-three championship over the rival Los Angeles Lakers.

After stops in Seattle, New York, Philadelphia and Milwaukee, Henderson's vast experience and leadership qualities were called upon by the Detroit Pistons, who signed him as a free agent in December 1989. As a backup to Isiah Thomas and Joe Dumars, Henderson helped the Pistons win their second straight championship, a four-games-to-one thumping of the Portland Trail Blazers.

For his career, Henderson averaged 8.9 points and 3.6 rebounds per contest. He posted 7.2 points and 2.6 assists in 88 career playoff contests.

RIGHT: EPITOME OF A ROLE PLAYER—GERALD HENDERSON.

GRANT HILL

When Julius Erving retired as one of the NBA's most exciting, most gravity-defying players ever, Michael Jordan came soaring along to fill his winged shoes. As Jordan enters the twilight of his career, Grant Hill of the Detroit Pistons is a major candidate to be his Air-apparent.

Hill, a 6-foot-8-inch skywalker out of Duke University, plays an above-the-rim game much the way Erving and Jordan did in their primes. He inherited much of his athleticism from his father, Calvin, a former NFL running back.

After helping Duke win back-to-back NCAA championships in 1991 and 1992, Grant was selected by Detroit as the third pick in the first round of the 1994 NBA draft. A gifted shooter, passer and ball-handler who averaged 14.9 points, 6.0 rebounds and 3.6 assists in four seasons at Duke, Hill took his act to another level as a pro, averaging 19.9 points, 6.4 rebounds and 5.0 assists per game in his initial season in the Motor City.

Those numbers earned Hill Co-Rookie of the Year honors, which he shared with Jason Kidd of the Dallas Mavericks.

Last season, Hill led the Pistons in scoring with 21.4 points per game, and also added 9.0 rebounds and 7.3 assists. Grant was also voted onto the All-Star squad in each of his first three NBA seasons.

FACT FILE

Born: October 5, 1972
Height: 6′ 8″
Length of NBA career:
 1994–present
Major team:
 Detroit
Records/Awards:
 NBA Co-Rookie of the
  Year (1995)
 NBA All-Star (3)
 Olympic Gold Medal
  (1996)

LEFT: GRANT HILL, WHO CAN SOAR LIKE AN EAGLE, APPEARS TO BE THE AIR-APPARENT TO MICHAEL JORDAN.

CRAIG HODGES

FACT FILE

Born: June 27, 1960
Height: 6′ 2″
Length of NBA career:
  1982–92
Major teams:
  San Diego
  Milwaukee (joined 1984)
  Phoenix (joined 1988)
  Chicago (joined 1988)
Records/Awards:
  NBA Championship (2)

One of the most prolific three-point shooters in NBA history, Craig Hodges helped Michael Jordan and the Chicago Bulls win a pair of championships in 1991 and 1992.

Hodges, a 6-foot-2-inch guard from Long Beach State who was selected by the San Diego Clippers in the third round of the 1982 NBA draft, led the league in trifecta perfection twice. As a member of the Milwaukee Bucks in 1986, he bagged 73 of 162 three-point tries for 45 percent, and, in a split 1987–88 season with Milwaukee and Phoenix, Hodges nailed 86 of 175 shots from behind the three-point stripe for 49 percent.

The following season, "Hodge," as he was called in his playing days, brought his long-distance magic to Chicago, and proved himself to be a solid backup behind Jordan, John Paxson and B. J. Armstrong in the Bulls' backcourt. In the 1990–91 championship season, he chipped in with 5.0 points, hitting 44 of 115 shots for 38 percent, and in 1991–92, scored 4.3 points per contest, making 9 of 20 three-pointers for 45 percent.

A winner of three straight three-point shooting contests—which are staged each season as part of All-Star weekend festivities—Hodges finished his ten-year NBA career with an 8.5 scoring average, adding 7.2 points per game in 101 career playoff contests. He shares the single-game playoff record for most steals in one game, tallying eight steals against Philadelphia on May 9, 1986.

RIGHT: THREE-POINT SPECIALIST CRAIG HODGES, LOOKING TO PASS THE BALL IN THIS SITUATION, CAPTURED A PAIR OF NBA CHAMPIONSHIPS AND THREE STRAIGHT THREE-POINT SHOOTING CONTESTS.

RED HOLZMAN

One of the top guards of the 1940s, and one of the first great backcourt players to come out of New York City, William "Red" Holzman helped the Rochester Royals win two world championships.

A 5-foot-10-inch playmaker with slick ball-handling skills, Holzman helped Rochester win the 1946 NBL championship in just his first season with the team, averaging 10.7 points in 34 games. He also helped the Royals to an NBA Championship in the 1950–51 season, posting 7.3 points per game.

Holzman, who played two seasons at then-powerful City College in New York from 1940–42, had plenty of basketball experience before he joined Rochester. After averaging 11.6 points in two college seasons, he joined the military from 1942–45, and played basket-ball at the Naval Training Station in Norfolk, VA. Holzman's last stop before joining Rochester was a non-military four-game stint with New York of the ABL, where he averaged 12 points per game.

After spending eight straight seasons with Rochester—his best season coming in 1946–47, when he averaged a career-high 12.0 points per game—Holzman joined the Milwaukee Hawks for the 1953–54 season, his last, averaging 3.8 points per contest.

A two-time All-Star, Holzman averaged 7.4 points in a combined NBL and NBA nine-year career. He posted 7.3 points in a total of fifty-six career playoff games.

He went on to become a successful coach, piloting the New York Knicks to NBA titles in 1970 and 1973.

FACT FILE

Born: August 10, 1920
Height: 5′ 10″
Length of ABL career:
  1945–46
Length of NBL career:
  1945–48
Length of BAA career:
  1948–49
Length of NBA career:
  1949–54
Major teams:
  New York
  Rochester (joined 1945)
  Milwaukee (joined 1953)
Records/Awards:
  NBL Championship (1)
  NBL All-Star (2)
  NBA Championship (1)
  Hall of Fame (1985)

LEFT: RED HOLZMAN WAS THE ARCHITECT OF THE GREAT NEW YORK KNICKS TEAMS OF THE EARLY 1970S.

JEFF HORNACEK

FACT FILE

Born: May 3, 1963
Height: 6′ 4″
Length of NBA career:
 1986–present
Major teams:
 Phoenix
 Philadelphia (joined 1992)
 Utah (joined 1994)
Records/Awards:
 NBA All-Star (1)

One of the most dangerous shooters in the NBA today, Jeff Hornacek helped the Utah Jazz reach the NBA finals last season, where the Jazz lost to the Chicago Bulls in six games.

Hornacek, a 6-foot-4-inch shooting guard from Iowa State, averaged 14.5 points last season for the Jazz.

A veteran of eleven NBA seasons, Hornacek was selected by the Phoenix Suns in the second round of the 1986 NBA draft. He played six seasons in Phoenix, scoring a career-high 20.1 points in 1991–92, his last season with the Suns. The following season, Hornacek was traded to the Philadelphia 76ers, and shot his way to a 19.1 scoring average, finishing second in that department behind Hersey Hawkins's 20.3 points.

Midway through the 1993–94 season, Hornacek was traded to Utah, and kept his keen shooting eye intact, ringing up 15.9 points per game.

In his first full season with the Jazz, Hornacek tied a single-season record for most consecutive three-point field goals without a miss, sinking 11 straight treys from December 30, 1994, through January 11, 1995. He also set the single-game record for most three-point field goals without a miss, bagging eight straight three-pointers on November 23, 1994, against Seattle. At Iowa State, Hornacek averaged 10.7 points, 5.4 assists, and 3.3 rebounds in four seasons.

RIGHT: FOR MORE THAN A DECADE, JEFF HORNACEK HAS BEEN BURNING UP THE CORDS ON NBA FLOORS.

ROBERT HORRY

On February 4, 1994, the Houston Rockets made a deal with Detroit that involved trading Robert Horry to the Pistons for Sean Elliott. The deal was voided, however, when Elliott failed his physical examination.

Horry's return to Houston was a blessing for the Rockets, as the 6-foot-10-inch power forward became an integral part of back-to-back world championship teams.

Four months after the trade that never happened, Horry helped Hakeem Olajuwon and company knock off the New York Knicks in seven games to win the title. In a low-scoring, defense-oriented series, Horry averaged 10.3 points and 6.1 rebounds per game, second in that category behind Olajuwon (9.1).

The following season, it was Horry who provided both key baskets and a suffocating brand of defense to help the Rockets sweep the Orlando Magic to capture their second straight NBA crown. In Game 1 of the series, Horry blocked a last-second shot by Orlando's Dennis Scott to send the game into overtime. In Game 2, Horry finished with 11 points, 10 rebounds and a Finals-record 7 steals. In Game 3, with Houston up by a single point in the closing seconds, Horry buried a clutch three-pointer to put the game—and the series—out of reach. In Game 4, he finished with 21 points and 13 rebounds. At the conclusion of the series, coaches from both Orlando and Houston agreed that Horry had been the difference.

Last season, Horry, an Alabama product drafted by Houston in 1992, was traded by the Rockets to the Phoenix Suns, and shortly after was dealt to Los Angeles.

Horry's trade to Phoenix brought Charles Barkley to Houston.

FACT FILE

Born: August 25, 1970
Height: 6′ 10″
Length of NBA career:
1992–present
Major teams:
Houston
Phoenix (joined 1996)
Los Angeles Lakers
(joined 1997)
Records/Awards:
NBA Championship (2)

LEFT: IT WAS A BLESSING IN DISGUISE FOR HOUSTON WHEN ITS 1994 TRADE OF ROBERT HORRY TO DETROIT WAS VOIDED.

ALLAN HOUSTON

FACT FILE

Born: April 4, 1971
Height: 6' 6"
Length of NBA career:
1993–present
Major teams:
Detroit
New York (joined 1996)

BELOW: WITH EACH PASSING SEASON, ALLAN HOUSTON GETS A LITTLE CLOSER TO JOINING THE RANKS OF THE NBA'S ELITE SHOOTING GUARDS.

Watch out, Michael Jordan and Reggie Miller—Allan Houston of the New York Knicks is slowly becoming one of the top shooting guards in the NBA.

Houston, a 6-foot-6-inch smooth-as-silk performer out of Tennessee, played his first three professional campaigns with the Detroit Pistons before he signed with the Knicks in 1996.

In the Motor City, Houston's scoring average climbed every season. Selected in the first round of the 1993 draft, he posted 8.5 points per contest as a rookie. The following season, he improved to 14.5 points per game, tying a single-game record that season for most three-point field goals made in one half—connecting for seven three-pointers in 24 minutes against Chicago on February 17, 1995.

In the 1995 season, Houston reached a career-high 19.7 points per game, and also established career-highs in assists (3.0) and rebounds (3.7). Besides his scoring, Houston's height also helps the Knicks defend big guards, something they had trouble doing in previous seasons.

The Knicks, who waved goodbye to veteran backcourt players Derek Harper and Hubert Davis after the 1995–96 season, were helped considerably by Houston's 14.8 points per game last season.

At Tennessee, Houston showed his explosive scoring ability, averaging 21.9 points in four seasons from 1989–93.

His best season with Tennessee came as a sophomore in 1990–91, when he tallied 23.7 points per game.

PHIL HUBBARD

A lanky 6-foot-8-inch forward, Phil Hubbard enjoyed a successful ten-year career in the NBA.

Hubbard, a Michigan star and a member of the 1976 U.S. Olympic Basketball Team that won a gold medal in Montreal, was selected by the Detroit Pistons in the first round of the 1979 NBA draft. He spent his first two and a half seasons on poor Piston teams and the rest of his career on Cleveland Cavalier squads that weren't much better.

With a body better suited for playing a finesse game than a physical one, Hubbard averaged 10.9 points and 5.3 rebounds in his NBA career. His best scoring season was with Cleveland in 1984–85, when he totaled 15.8 points per contest. His best scoring campaign in a Piston uniform came in 1980–81, his second season in the Motor City, when he posted 14.5 points per contest. Overall, Hubbard averaged double-digit scoring totals in six of his ten pro seasons. Despite playing in the league for an entire decade, Hubbard participated in just eight career playoff games —all with Cleveland—through which he averaged 8.0 points per game.

At Michigan, Hubbard averaged 16.5 points per game over three seasons. He missed the 1977–78 college basketball season because of a knee injury. After his freshman year at Michigan, he hooked up with the U.S. Olympic Basketball Team. In the gold-medal game against Yugoslavia, he scored ten second-half points to help the U.S. to a 95–74 victory.

FACT FILE

Born: December 13, 1956
Height: 6' 8"
Length of NBA career:
1979–89
Major teams:
Detroit
Cleveland (joined 1982)
Records/Awards:
Olympic Gold Medal (1976)

LEFT: PHIL HUBBARD WAS ONE OF MANY TALENTED PLAYERS WHO HAD THE MISFORTUNE OF PLAYING ON POOR TEAMS.

JOHN ISAACS

FACT FILE

Born: September 30, 1915
Height: 6′ 3″
**Length of professional
  career:** 1936–51
Major teams:
  Harlem Renaissance
    (1936–43)
  Washington Bears
    (1941–46)
  Philadelphia Bears
    (1943–46)
  Utica Pics (1943–46)
Records/Awards:
  BAA Championship (1)

In 1923, when John Isaacs was just seven years old, a black businessman named Bob Douglas organized an all-black barnstorming team, originally calling it the "Harlem Renaissance Big Five."

At the time, Douglas's team used the Renaissance Casino ballroom in Harlem as its home court, sharing the floor with the big bands of Count Basie and Jimmy Lunsford. Traveling was tough on the Rens, as they often had to eat on their own bus because white-owned establishments would not serve them.

Before Isaacs arrived on the scene, the Rens had won eighty-eight consecutive games, many of these victories ending in fist fights with opposing white players and fans, who could not accept being defeated by black players.

Isaacs, who was Panamanian-born and learned his game on the playgrounds of Harlem, NY, was offered a contract by Douglas straight out of Manhattan-based Textile High School to help carry on the Rens' winning tradition—and Isaacs, a 6-foot-3-inch guard, did not fail him.

Douglas, who paid Isaacs $150 per month with an additional $3 per day for meal money, once said that Isaacs had "the most natural ability of any man ever to play for me." "Wonder Boy," as Isaacs was called during his playing days, became a key member of the 1939–40 Renaissance squad which captured the first World Professional Championship in a Chicago tournament made up of the country's top professional teams. In the final, the Rens defeated the Oshkosh All-Stars of the fledgling National Basketball League. John Wooden, the legendary UCLA basketball coach, later described the 1939–40 Harlem Rens team as "the greatest team I ever saw."

By 1943, the great Renaissance teams had started to fade into history, and Isaacs had joined the Washington Bears. An all-black team, the Bears carried five former Rens, including the hall-of-famer, "Pop" Gates, one of the few Rens still living today.

That same year, Isaacs led the Bears to the World Professional Championship, scoring a game-high 11 points in the final to help his new team defeat Oshkosh, 43–31.

Following his playing career, Isaacs was inducted into the New York City Hall of Fame.

"Maybe one day, history will forget us altogether," said Isaacs. "But as long as I'm walking this earth, I will always speak proudly of the Harlem Rens.

"Dead or alive," John Isaacs said, "we will always be a family."

RIGHT: "WONDER BOY," AS JOHN ISAACS WAS KNOWN, WAS A KEY MEMBER OF THE 1939–40 HARLEM RENS, WHO WON THE FIRST WORLD PROFESSIONAL CHAMPIONSHIP IN CHICAGO.

DAN ISSEL

He was several inches shorter than most centers, not noted for his jumping, shot-blocking or intimidation. Despite those shortcomings, Dan Issel went on to be one of the NBA's all-time greats. He currently ranks fifth on the combined ABA – NBA scoring list with a total of 27,482 points, trailing only Kareem Abdul-Jabbar, Wilt Chamberlain, Julius Erving and Moses Malone.

Issel, a 6-foot-9-inch center/forward who established 23 records at the University of Kentucky, was the first pick of the Kentucky Colonels in the 1970 ABA draft. He was Rookie of the Year that season, leading the league with 29.9 points per game. In his first four NBA seasons, Issel averaged 28 points a game. In his fifth year, coach Hubie Brown switched him to power forward to play alongside the 7-foot-2-inch center, Artis Gilmore, and that combination led Kentucky to an ABA Championship.

The following season, Issel was traded to Denver, and averaged 20.5 points per game. Denver joined the NBA in 1976, and playing in a new league did not affect Issel's scoring ability.

Making up in effort and intelligence what he lacked in physical attributes, Issel rang up 20 points or better in five of the next seven seasons.

"Dan was the perfect pro player," Brown once said. "He's an outstanding perimeter and free-throw shooter. A very intelligent player. The scouts have been wrong before, and Dan has proven that."

A six-time All-Star, Issel holds the ABA's single-season record for most points, racking up 2,538 in 1972.

FACT FILE

Born: October 25, 1948
Height: 6′ 9″
Length of ABA career:
1970–76
Length of NBA career:
1976–85
Major teams:
Kentucky
Denver (joined 1975)
Records/Awards:
ABA Rookie of the Year
(1971)
ABA Championship (1)
ABA All-Star (6)
NBA All-Star (1)

LEFT: DAN ISSEL, HERE PLAYING WITH THE DENVER NUGGETS, OVERCAME A LACK OF HEIGHT, AND OTHER SHORTCOMINGS, TO BECOME ONE OF THE ALL-TIME GREATS.

CAZZIE MEETS BILL

One of the most talked about games in college basketball history is "The night Cazzie met Bill." It happened on December 30, 1964, when the two best college players on the planet, Bill Bradley of Princeton, and Cazzie Russell of mighty Michigan, met at the old Madison Square Garden in the semifinal round of the Holiday Festival.

With a capacity crowd of 18,499 cheering wildly from the outset, Bradley staged a one-man show for the first 35 minutes and 23 seconds of the contest. The 6-foot-5-inch senior, scoring from all angles, rebounding and running the floor like a man possessed, brought the screaming spectators to their feet, chanting, "Go, Tiger go!"

Bradley finished with 23 points by halftime, and Princeton, a 12-point underdog, had a 39–37 lead at the intermission.

As the second half started, most everyone at the game felt Michigan would come out and deliver the knockout blow. But Bradley kept scoring, the Wolverines couldn't get their offense on track, and one of the greatest upsets in the history of the sport seemed in the making.

As the game wore on, however, Bradley began to tire. In the later stages, he missed a pair of free throws, was called for traveling, and was absolutely exhausted by the time he fouled out with 4:37 left to play in the contest.

As he walked wearily back to the Princeton bench, trying to catch his breath after registering 41 points, nine rebounds, and four assists, staking his team to a 75–63 lead, the crowd stood and cheered for a full two minutes.

Now it was Cazzie's turn.

Russell, known throughout his college career for late, game-saving heroics, lived up to his reputation.

After Michigan had fallen behind by 14 points, 77–63, Russell went to work. He scored one basket, stole the ball, and scored another. Princeton tried to go into a stall, but Russell stole the ball again and dished it off to John Thompson for another Michigan basket.

Quick buckets by Russell and Thompson gave the Wolverines five baskets in a 66-second span, and, with Bradley watching helplessly from the bench, closed Princeton's lead to just four points.

With the Tigers clinging to a three-point lead, 78–75, Russell drove for a layup, was fouled, and hit the free throw to tie the score at 78 apiece with 51 seconds left to play.

After a Princeton miss, the last shot of the game belonged to Russell, and he promptly buried it to give Michigan an 80–78 victory.

When the final buzzer sounded, players from both teams congratulated Russell and consoled Bradley.

"I didn't think that any one fellow on any club could dominate a game against another team," Dave Strack, the Wolverine coach, said of Bradley's performance after that memorable game. "I knew he was great, but I just never thought that one man could control a game like that."

ALLEN IVERSON

FACT FILE

Born: June 7, 1975
Height: 6′ 0″
Length of NBA career:
1996–present
Major team:
Philadelphia
Awards:
NBA Rookie of the Year
(1996–97)

The lightning-quick Allen Iverson was selected as the first overall pick in the 1996 NBA draft by the Philadelphia 76ers, and Iverson did not disappoint, capturing the Rookie of the Year award last season.

Iverson, a phenomenal athlete who electrified crowds with his great moves, average 23.5 points, 7.5 assists, and 4.1 rebounds per game in his first tour of NBA duty.

A speed-demon with a scorer's mentality, one of Iverson's biggest challenges was adjusting to the role of ball-distributor and he responded brilliantly.

"All my life I've been put in tough situations, and this is just another one of them," said Iverson before his rookie season.

Iverson came to the NBA with glittering college credentials. In each of his two seasons at Georgetown, he was selected as the Big East Defensive Player of the Year. During the summer of 1995, he helped the United States win a gold medal at the World University Games in Japan, leading the team in scoring, assists and steals in seven straight victories.

As a freshman with the Hoyas, Iverson was named the Big East Rookie of the Year after leading the team with averages of 20.4 points and 4.5 assists.

"I know my attitude, this organization, my coach's attitude," he said. "My teammates have a great attitude. These guys want to win . . . and I want to contribute to that."

RIGHT: THE SPECTACULAR ALLEN IVERSON CAME TO THE NBA WITH GLITTERING CREDENTIALS.

JIM JACKSON

Jim Jackson is healthy again, and that's unhealthy news for opponents of the Dallas Mavericks. After missing thirty-one games with an ankle sprain in 1994–95, Jackson, a 6-foot-6-inch shooting guard out of Ohio State, was the only Maverick to play in 82 games, in 1995–96, leading the team in scoring with 19.6 points per contest.

Selected by Dallas in the first round of the 1992 NBA draft, Jackson raised his scoring average in each of his first three seasons in the professional league.

As a rookie, he posted 16.3 points in just twenty-eight games. The following season, his scoring improved to 19.2 points per game, and in 1994–95, he reached a career-high 25.7 scoring mark.

At Ohio State, Jackson averaged 19.2 points in three seasons, declaring himself eligible for the NBA draft after his junior year. His best scoring season as a Buckeye was 1991–92, when he tallied 22.4 points per game.

In five NBA seasons, Jackson has averaged 19.3 points, 5.0 rebounds, and 3.9 assists.

Jackson, who has great shooting range and the ability to beat his man off the dribble, was traded from Dallas to New Jersey, but he kept up his stellar shooting, averaging 15.9 points per game last season.

FACT FILE

Born: October 14, 1970
Height: 6′ 6″
Length of NBA career:
1992–present
Major teams:
Dallas
New Jersey (joined 1997)

LEFT: JIM JACKSON DRIVING HARD AROUND REGGIE MILLER OF THE INDIANA PACERS.

LUKE JACKSON

FACT FILE

Born: October 31, 1941
Height: 6′ 9″
Length of NBA career:
 1964–72
Major team:
 Philadelphia
Records/Awards:
 NBA Championship (1)
 NBA All-Star (1)

During the late 1960s, when the raiding of players by the ABA and NBA was intense, Luke Jackson jumped from the Philadelphia 76ers to the Carolina Cougars and back to Philadelphia, all within a span of 48 hours.

As it turned out, Jackson, a 6-foot-9-inch forward out of Pan American, played his entire eight-year NBA career with Philadelphia. He teamed with Wilt Chamberlain, Billy Cunningham and Hal Greer to help the 1966–67 76er team capture the NBA crown in six games over the San Francisco Warriors.

Jackson averaged 9.9 points and 8.3 rebounds in his career. As a rookie in the 1964–65 season, Jackson posted career-high averages with 14.8 points and 12.9 rebounds. Those numbers earned him the only All-Star selection of his career.

On four occasions in his career, Jackson—who worked the corners of the court along with teammate Chet Walker, opening up the middle for Chamberlain to dominate—finished in double-digit scoring. He averaged better than ten points per game in three straight seasons from 1966–69, posting 12 points per game during Philadelphia's championship season, 11.8 in 1967–68, and 14.4 in 1968–69.

In 56 career playoff games, Jackson averaged 9.7 points and 9.1 rebounds per contest.

RIGHT: LUKE JACKSON'S STELLAR CORNER-WORK OPENED UP THE MIDDLE FOR TEAMMATE WILT CHAMBERLAIN TO DOMINATE.

MARK JACKSON

A pure point guard with a pass-first-shoot-later mentality, Mark Johnson is an underrated star in the NBA. Jackson, a 6-foot-3-inch sparkplug out of St. Johns University who led the NCAA Division I with 9.1 assists per game in 1986, has racked up at least 600 assists and 100-plus steals in all but two of his ten NBA seasons. His characteristic unselfishness on the court has usually resulted in more publicity for higher-scoring teammates than for himself.

Two years after helping St. Johns reach the Final Four of the 1985 NCAA Tournament, Jackson, a native of Queens, New York City, was drafted by his hometown New York Knicks. He turned in a phenomenal first-year performance with the Knicks, averaging 13.6 points and 10.6 assists per game en route to winning the Rookie of the Year Award. That same year, he set the single-season record for most assists by a rookie with 868.

The following season, Jackson posted a career-high 16.9 points per game and was voted onto the All-Star squad. But after five seasons in New York in which he and the Knicks failed to win a championship, Jackson was traded to the Los Angeles Clippers, where he helped lead the downtrodden franchise to a playoff appearance in 1993.

After two seasons in Los Angeles, Jackson was traded by the Clippers to Indiana. Jackson spent two seasons with Indiana before he was dealt to the Denver Nuggets, who traded him back to Indiana midway through last season.

Jackson's return to Indiana was a success, as he led the NBA with 935 assists.

FACT FILE

Born: April 1, 1965
Height: 6' 3"
Length of NBA career:
    1987–present
Major teams:
    New York
    Los Angeles Clippers
        (joined 1992)
    Indiana (joined 1994)
    Denver (joined 1996)
    Indiana (joined 1997)
Records/Awards:
    NBA Rookie of the Year
        (1988)
    NBA All-Star (1)

LEFT: NEED AN ASSIST? JUST DIAL MARK JACKSON'S NUMBER.

PHIL JACKSON

FACT FILE

Born: September 17, 1945
Height: 6′ 8″
Length of NBA career:
   1967–80
Major teams:
   New York
   New Jersey (joined 1978)
Records/Awards:
   NBA Championship (2)

A defensive specialist on the great New York Knicks teams of the late 1960s and early 1970s, Phil Jackson helped the Knicks win championships in 1970 and 1973.

An All-American center at the University of North Dakota, where he averaged 27 points a game, Jackson was selected by the Knicks in the second round of the 1967 NBA draft.

A bearded, long-haired, 6-foot-8-inch power forward with 42-inch arms and extremely wide shoulders—his teammate, Earl Monroe, once called him a flower child—Jackson appeared awkward on the court. However, despite this clumsy appearance, whether he was taking a hook shot or trying to prevent an inbounds pass, he filled his limited role to perfection. "He was a very, very intelligent player," said former Knicks coach Red Holzman in his autobiography, *Red on Red.*

In twelve NBA seasons, the first ten of which were spent in New York, Jackson averaged 6.7 points and 4.2 rebounds per game. His best scoring seasons in a Knicks uniform came in 1973–74, when he averaged a career-high 11.1 points per game, and in 1974–75, when he posted 10.8 points per contest.

Jackson, who spent his last two seasons with the New Jersey Nets, averaged 7.7 points in 67 career playoff games.

"Phil always had an impact on the game," said Willis Reed, who teamed with Jackson on both Knicks championship squads. "He was an excellent defensive player. He really knew how to defend."

RIGHT: DEFENSIVE SPECIALIST PHIL JACKSON GIVES OFFENSE A TRY HERE, STEAMING TO THE BASKET AS WILT CHAMBERLAIN (FAR LEFT) LOOKS ON.

DENNIS JOHNSON

One of the greatest defensive guards of all time, Dennis Johnson, or just "DJ" to his teammates, was the sturdy quarterback on three NBA championship teams. Johnson, a 6-foot-4-inch point guard out of Pepperdine, had few weaknesses in his game. He could handle the ball, penetrate to the basket, find the open man, or shoot the outside jumper.

Selected by Seattle in the second round of the 1976 NBA draft, Johnson was the Most Valuable Player for the SuperSonics in the 1978–79 Finals, which resulted in a four-games-to-one victory over the Washington Bullets.

He spent his first four seasons playing with the Sonics—establishing a career-high total of 19.0 points per game there in the 1979–80 campaign—and three more seasons in Phoenix before he was traded to the Boston Celtics in 1983.

In his first season with the Celtics, Johnson orchestrated an offensive unit that included team members Larry Bird, Kevin McHale and Robert Parish.

That nucleus won a championship, and remained intact to win another NBA title in 1986.

A five-time All-Star and six-time All Defensive First Team selection, Johnson averaged 14.1 points, 5.0 assists and 3.9 rebounds per game in fourteen NBA seasons, adding averages of 17.3 points, 5.6 assists and 4.3 rebounds in 180 career playoff games.

He also shares the NBA Finals single-game record for most free throws made in one half, making 12 shots from the charity stripe on June 12, 1984, against the Los Angeles Lakers.

FACT FILE

Born: September 18, 1954
Height: 6′ 4″
Length of NBA career:
1976–90
Major teams:
Seattle
Phoenix (joined 1980)
Boston (joined 1983)
Records/Awards:
NBA Championships (3)
NBA All-Star (5)
NBA All-Defensive First
Team (6)

LEFT: DENNIS JOHNSON RAN THE SHOW FOR SEATTLE AND BOSTON, BRINGING CHAMPIONSHIPS TO EACH CITY.

EARVIN "MAGIC" JOHNSON

FACT FILE

Born: August 14, 1959
Height: 6' 9"
Length of NBA career:
  1979–91,1995–96
Major team:
  Los Angeles
Records/Awards:
  NBA Championship (5)
  NBA All-Star (12)
  NBA Most Valuable
    Player (3)
  Olympic Gold Medal
    (1992)

Earvin "Magic" Johnson, one of the most celebrated athletes of the twentieth century, revolutionized the game of basketball, winning at every level of the sport and lifting it to global popularity with a wide smile and an even-wider range of talent and raw athletic ability.

A flashy 6-foot-9-inch point guard out of Michigan State, Johnson put the Show in the Lakers Showtime attack, helping Los Angeles reach the NBA Finals nine times, and win five championships, during a twelve-year period from 1979–91.

Just before the start of the 1991–92 season, Johnson sent shockwaves around the world when he announced he was retiring because he was infected with the AIDS virus. He did make a brief comeback last season, averaging 14.2 points in thirty-two games, but decided to re-retire after realizing he no longer fit into the Lakers' plans.

A three-time Most Valuable Player and twelve-time All-Star, Johnson was the master of the no-look pass, and his coast-to-coast trips on the basketball court brought fans of all ages—and all cultures—to their feet in jubilant celebration at the sight of him playing.

Despite missing the entire 1991–92 NBA season, Johnson starred with Larry Bird and Michael Jordan on the 1992 U.S. Olympic Basketball team which won a gold medal for the U.S. in Barcelona, Spain.

Selected by the Lakers in the first round of the 1979 NBA draft, Johnson's arrival into the league had been highly trumpeted, as he had previously defeated Bird's Indiana State squad to win the NCAA championship.

In 1980, Johnson became the first rookie in league history to be named Most Valuable Player in the playoffs. He earned that award on the strength of a legendary performance in Game 6 of the championship series against the Philadelphia 76ers. With teammate Kareem Abdul-Jabbar unable to play center in the sixth game because of injury, Johnson played all five positions and finished with 42 points, 15 rebounds and 7 assists to clinch the title. It was the beginning of a run that made the Lakers the team of the 1980s.

When he retired, Johnson was the NBA's all-time leader in assists with a total of 9,921, a record which would eventually be broken by Utah's John Stockton. A three-time NBA Finals Most Valuable Player, Johnson still holds numerous regular-season and post-season records. He led the league with an average of 3.43 steals per game in 1981, and again in 1982, when he finished with 2.67 swipes per game. In post-season play, Johnson still holds the mark for most assists (2,320) and most steals (358). He finished his remarkable NBA career with averages of 19.5 points, 11.1 assists and 7.2 rebounds.

RIGHT: THROUGHOUT MOST OF HIS CAREER, JOHNSON (NO. 32) WAS MORE MAGIC THAN EARVIN.

EDDIE JOHNSON

It's hard for any team to find a big man with outside range, but the teams that Eddie Johnson has played for throughout the years didn't have to look very far.

Johnson, a 6-foot-9-inch forward out of Illinois, has been a rare commodity since entering the NBA with the Kansas City Kings in 1981. He averaged 9.3 points per game in his rookie season, and in each of the next 12 seasons, averaged double digits in scoring.

After spending his fifteenth professional season with the Indiana Pacers in the 1995 season, Johnson's NBA resume now includes six seasons with the Kings—who moved from Kansas City to Sacramento for the 1985–86 campaign—three and a half seasons with the Phoenix Suns, two and a half seasons with the Seattle SuperSonics, and one season with the

Charlotte Hornets. He spent the 1994–95 campaign playing professionally in Greece.

Johnson, who is not afraid to take the three-point shot, had banner years with the Kings in 1983–84, when he averaged 21.9 points, 5.5 rebounds and 3.6 assists, and the following season, when he posted a career-high 22.9 points, 5.0 rebounds and 3.3 assists per contest. As a member of the Phoenix Suns in 1988–89, he received the NBA's Sixth Man Award, coming off the bench to score 21.5 points per game. He has led his team in scoring three times in his career.

Last season, Johnson averaged 7.7 points, 2.5 rebounds and 1.1 assists in 62 games. Through fourteen NBA seasons, he has now tallied 18,133 points, and his averages stand at 16.9 points per game, 4.2 rebounds and 2.2 assists.

FACT FILE

Born: May 1, 1959
Height: 6′ 9″
Length of NBA career:
1981–present
Major teams:
Kansas City–Sacramento
Phoenix (joined 1987)
Seattle (joined 1990)
Charlotte (joined 1993)
Indiana (Joined 1995)
Records/Awards:
NBA Sixth Man Award
(1989)

LEFT: EDDIE JOHNSON IS A RARE TALENT IN THAT HE IS A BIG MAN WHO CAN SHOOT THE BALL FROM LONG DISTANCE.

EDDIE JOHNSON, JR.

FACT FILE

Born: February 24, 1955
Height: 6′ 2″
Length of NBA career:
 1977–87
Major teams:
 Atlanta
 Cleveland (joined 1986)
 Seattle (joined 1986)
Records/Awards:
 NBA All-Star (2)

For eight and a half seasons in Atlanta, Eddie Johnson, Jr., ran the Hawks fast-break. A super-quick point guard who kept defenders off balance with a variety of hesitation moves, Johnson averaged double digits in scoring in nine of his NBA seasons.

Legal and substance abuse problems plagued him during and after his career, but he still managed to put together an extraordinary decade of basketball.

A third-round draft pick of the Hawks out of Auburn in 1977, "Fast Eddie," as Johnson was called, averaged 10.5 points per game in his rookie season. His scoring average climbed steadily the next three seasons, as he posted 16.0 points in 1978–79, 18.5 points in 1979–80, and a career-high 19.1 points per game in 1980–81. He was named to the NBA All-Star squad after the 1980 and 1981 campaigns. In the 1984–85 season, Johnson set an Atlanta Hawk record for most assists in a single season with 566, breaking Walt Hazzard's mark of 561.

For six years in Atlanta, Johnson teamed with the high-scoring forward Dan Roundfield, but he was always center-stage with the Hawks. He split the 1985–86 season between Atlanta and Cleveland, and the 1986–87 campaign, his last, with the Seattle SuperSonics.

The brother of former NBA guard Frank Johnson, Eddie Johnson was a two-time NBA All-Defensive Second Team selection. He averaged 15.1 points over the course of his career and 11.9 points in 37 career playoff games.

At Auburn, Johnson averaged 19.5 points in four years. His best season with the Tigers came as a freshman in 1973–74 when he scored 21.8 points per game, leading the nation's freshman players in scoring.

RIGHT: EDDIE JOHNSON JR. FINISHING OFF A FAST BREAK HERE FOR THE ATLANTA HAWKS.

GUS JOHNSON

One of the great all-round forwards in the history of pro basketball, Gus Johnson of the Baltimore Bullets teamed with stars like Earl Monroe, Kevin Loughery, Jack Marin and Wes Unseld in the 1960s to form one of the greatest teams never to win a world championship.

Johnson, a 6-foot-6-inch super leaper out of Idaho, was selected by the Bullets in the second round of the 1963 NBA draft. In his first season with Baltimore, Johnson earned a place on the All-Rookie team by averaging 17.3 points and 13.6 rebounds per game.

A five-time NBA All-Star and two-time All Defensive First Team selection who did battle with the likes of Elgin Baylor and Dave DeBusschere in his prime, "Honeycomb," as Johnson was called in his playing days, averaged no less than 16.5 points per game in his first eight seasons with Baltimore. He averaged a career-high 20.7 points per game in the 1966–67 season, and turned in a blockbuster 1970–71 campaign, dominating the competition with 18.2 points and a career-high average of 17.1 rebounds per game.

Trapped in the same conference with the great New York Knicks teams of that era, Johnson and the Bullets were never able to get themselves into a championship series.

In 1972–73, his last professional season, Johnson played in just twenty-four games for the Phoenix Suns before signing as a free agent with the ABA's Indiana Pacers. Johnson won his only championship that season, helping the Pacers with 6.0 points and 4.9 rebounds per game. In nine and a half NBA seasons, Johnson averaged 17.1 points and 12.7 rebounds per game. He also racked up averages of 13.3 points and 9.7 rebounds in thirty-four career NBA playoff games.

FACT FILE

Born: December 13, 1938
Height: 6′ 6″
Length of NBA career:
1963–73
Length of ABA career:
1972–73
Major teams:
Baltimore
Phoenix (joined (1972)
Indiana (joined 1972)
Records/Awards:
NBA All-Star (5)
NBA All-Defensive First
Team (2)
ABA Championship (1)

LEFT: SUPER-LEAPER GUS JOHNSON, WHO WON HIS ONLY CHAMPIONSHIP WITH THE ABA'S INDIANA PACERS, FADING AWAY FOR A JUMPER.

JOHN JOHNSON

FACT FILE

Born: October 18, 1947
Height: 6′ 7″
Length of NBA career:
 1970–81
Major teams:
 Cleveland
 Portland (joined 1973)
 Houston (joined 1975)
 Seattle (joined 1977)
Records/Awards:
 NBA Championship (1)
 NBA All-Star (2)

With John Johnson and Lonnie Shelton flanking Jack Sikma on the Seattle front line in the 1978–79 season, the SuperSonics went on to defeat Wes Unseld and the Washington Bullets in five games to capture the NBA title.

Johnson, a 6-foot-7-inch forward out of Iowa, played 12 seasons in the NBA with four different teams. He began his career with the Cleveland Cavaliers in 1970, averaging 16.6 points in his rookie year and a career-high 17.0 points the following season.

After three seasons in Cleveland, Johnson was traded to Portland, where he averaged 16.4 points and 16.1 points per game in his first two seasons with the Trail Blazers. Midway through the 1975–76 season, Portland dealt Johnson to Houston, and in back-to-back seasons with the Rockets, his average dipped below ten points per game for the first time in his NBA career.

Midway through the 1977–78 season, Houston gave up on Johnson. So did the Boston Celtics. Seattle, however, had a hunch that Johnson would be a nice fit in their championship plans, and his acquisition helped bring the city its only championship in any major sport.

A two-time NBA All-Star, Johnson averaged 12.9 points and 5.4 rebounds in his career. He posted averages of 9.7 points and 4.9 rebounds in 73 career playoff games.

When Johnson's career was over at Seattle, the Sonics waived him at the age of 34, prompting Johnson to quip: "I'm looking forward to a future in the business world now that I have to get off fantasy island." At Iowa, Johnson averaged 23.9 points and 10.3 boards in two seasons.

Before that, Johnson attended North West Community College, Powell, Wyoming.

RIGHT: THE SEATTLE SUPERSONICS HAD A HUNCH THAT JOHN JOHNSON WOULD FIT IN NICELY WITH THEIR CHAMPIONSHIP PLANS IN 1978-79.

KEVIN JOHNSON

njuries are the only thing that stand between Kevin Johnson and NBA super-stardom.

Johnson, a 6-foot-1-inch point guard out of California, has been running the show for the Phoenix Suns since joining the club midway through the 1987–88 season. After averaging 9.2 points per game in that split rookie season, the little man with the quick first step, wicked cross-over dribble and tremendous leaping ability, burst into the national spotlight the following season. He averaged 20.4 points, 12.2 assists, and 4.2 rebounds per game en route to winning the NBA's Most Improved Player Award.

In each of the next three seasons, Johnson continued to roll up double-digit scoring and assist averages. In the 1989–90 season, he averaged a career-high 22.5 points and a career-high 11.4 assists per game. In 1990–91, he posted 22.2 points and 10.1 assists per contest, and in 1991–92, he put up 19.7 points and dished out 10.7 assists per game.

Injuries began taking their toll on Johnson in the 1992–93 season. He missed thirty-three games that season, but made it back in time to help steer the Suns into the NBA Finals, where they were defeated by the Chicago Bulls, four games to two. In that series, he set the NBA Finals single-game record for most minutes played, logging in 62 minutes in a three-overtime contest on June 13, 1993.

Johnson, who averaged 20.1 points and 9.3 assists in 70 games last season, has missed 121 games the past five years due to various injuries. A three-time All-Star and four-time All-NBA Second Team selection, Johnson still remains one of the top point guards in the game, and certainly one of its most dangerous one-on-one performers.

FACT FILE

Born: March 4, 1966
Height: 6′ 1″
Length of NBA career:
  1987–present
Major teams:
  Cleveland
  Phoenix (joined 1988)
Records/Awards:
  NBA All-Star (3)

LEFT: IF NOT FOR INJURIES, KEVIN JOHNSON WOULD EASILY GO DOWN AS ONE OF THE GREATEST POINT GUARDS IN NBA HISTORY.

WILLIS REED: LIMPING INTO HISTORY

The morning after the Los Angeles Lakers crushed the New York Knicks 135–113 in Game 6 of the 1970 NBA Finals, a blaring headline in the *New York Post* read: "There's a 7th Game—is there a Reed?"

No one really knew the answer to that question until the evening of May 8, 1970, the night Willis Reed became a legend. Reed, a 6-foot-9-inch center and the heart and soul of the Knicks' team, had injured himself after tripping over Wilt Chamberlain in Game 5 of the championship series, his right hip taking the weight of his 255 pounds.

Without Reed in the lineup for Game 6, Chamberlain dominated his replacement, Nate Bowman, in the pivot, connecting on 20 of 27 shots from the field and hauling down 27 rebounds.

With Reed limping on the sidelines and the Knicks limping into a seventh and deciding game, the basketball world, uncertain if Reed could make it back in time, held its collective breath.

When the Knicks trotted out onto the floor at Madison Square Garden just minutes before the opening tip of the biggest game in franchise history, Reed was nowhere to be found. Back in the Knicks' training room, the injured center was receiving a last-second injection of pain-killing drugs in his right hip.

A few seconds later, Reed was ready to go. The sight of him limping out of the runway sent the capacity crowd at Madison Square Garden into a frenzy, rocking the World's Most Famous Arena.

"As I came out of the runway from the dressing room, I remember the crowd standing, cheering, and going crazy," said Reed. "I guess they felt the Captain was here and everything was going to be all right."

His teammates felt the same way. Inspired by Reed's heroics,—the one-legged captain scored the first two baskets for New York and played outstanding defense against Chamberlain—the rest of the Knicks turned up their intensity.

By the time Reed left the game with 3:05 remaining in the first half, the Knicks had surged to a 61–37 lead. When the emotional night was over, the Knicks, who got 36 points from Walt Frazier, had captured their first-ever championship by a score of 113–99.

"It wasn't only Willis Reed who wanted this championship," Reed would say years later. "It was Bill Bradley, Dave DeBusschere, Clyde Frazier, everybody on the team. Most of all the fans. They had waited a very long time for our first championship."

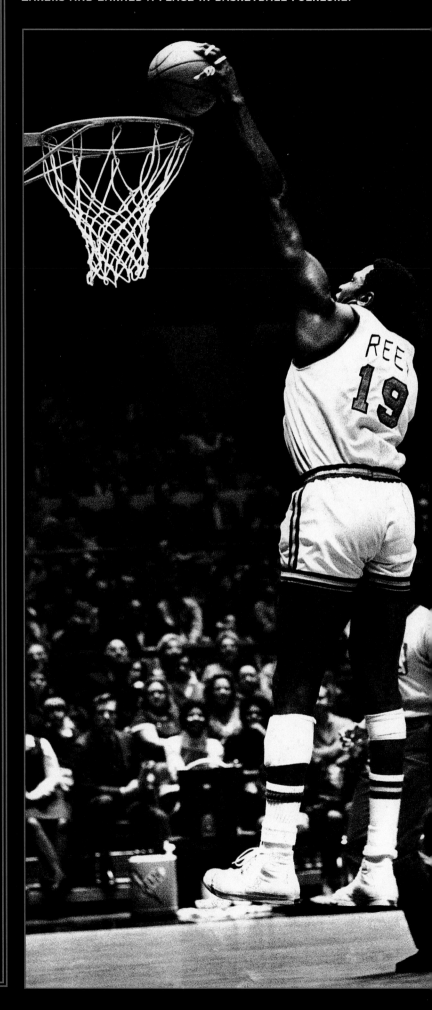

LARRY JOHNSON

FACT FILE

Born: March 14, 1969
Height: 6′ 7″
Length of NBA career:
  1991–present
Major teams:
  Charlotte
  New York (joined 1996)
Records/Awards:
  NBA Rookie of the Year
  (1992)
  NBA All-Star (2)

When Larry Johnson's back is not bothering him, he is one of the most dominant power-forwards in the game. The 6-foot-7-inch, 263-pound Johnson has a sweet-shooting touch for a big man, and, if need be, can bruise an opponent on his way to scoring a basket.

After spending his first five NBA seasons with the Charlotte Hornets, Johnson was traded to New York in the 1996 season, and the Knicks were hoping that his intimidating presence on their front line, alongside Patrick Ewing and Charles Oakley, would be enough to help them dethrone the defending NBA champion Chicago Bulls, but it has not worked out that way yet for the New Yorkers.

"Larry is just an awesome player," said Scott Burrell, a former teammate of Johnson on the Hornets. "There aren't too many players in the league that possess his all-round talents."

The NBA's Rookie of the Year in 1991–92, Johnson averaged 19.2 points, 11.0 rebounds, and 3.6 assists per game that year. The following season, Johnson averaged a career-high 22.1 points per game and 10.5 rebounds, and was on his way to the first of two All-Star games.

After the 1992–93 season, Johnson was awarded a twelve-year $84 million contract by the Hornets. At the time, Johnson's deal was the richest in basketball history.

In 1993–94, back pains kept Johnson out of 31 games, but despite the pain, he still averaged 16.4 points and 8.8 boards.

Although Charlotte was leery about his health, he played 81 games in each of the next two seasons, and finished the 1995 season with averages of 20.5 points and 8.4 rebounds. A former star at UNLV, Johnson, selected by Charlotte as the first overall pick in the 1991 NBA draft, helped the Runnin' Rebels to the 1990 NCAA championship.

RIGHT: AFTER BUZZING AROUND WITH THE CHARLOTTE HORNETS FOR FIVE SEASONS, LARRY JOHNSON AND HIS ACHING BACK WAS TRADED TO THE NEW YORK KNICKS.

MARQUES JOHNSON

I n his prime, Marques Johnson was considered one of the NBA's three most gifted forwards along with Julius Erving and Larry Bird.

Johnson, a 6-foot-7-inch small forward with the ability to score from the outside or slip past defenders off the dribble, was selected by the Milwaukee Bucks in the first round of the 1977 NBA draft.

An All-American at UCLA who helped the powerful Bruins capture the 1975 NCAA championship, Johnson was an instant star in the NBA. He earned a place on the league's All-Rookie team by averaging 19.5 points, 10.5 rebounds and 2.3 assists per game in the 1977–78 season. He would play his first seven years in Milwaukee, averaging better than 20 points per game in five of those seasons. His career-scoring year came in his second season with the Bucks, That year he lit up scoreboards around the country for 25.6 points per game.

A five-time All-Star, Johnson was traded to the Los Angeles Clippers in 1984, and in his second season with the team, averaged 20.3 points per game and was named the 1986 NBA Comeback Player of the Year.

In ten NBA seasons, Johnson averaged 20.3 points and 7.0 rebounds per game. He closed the curtain on a decade of fantastic basketball with averages of 21.5 points and 7.9 boards in fifty-four career playoff games.

At UCLA, Johnson produced an average of 14.4 points in four seasons.

FACT FILE

Born: February 8, 1956
Height: 6′ 7″
Length of NBA career:
  1977–87
Major teams:
  Milwaukee
  Los Angeles Clippers
  (joined 1984)
Records/Awards:
  NBA Comeback Player of
  the Year (1986)
  NBA All-Star (5)

LEFT: THREE'S COMPANY:
MARQUES JOHNSON, PASSING
THE BALL HERE IN MID-AIR,
WAS OFTEN MENTIONED IN THE
SAME BREATH AS JULIUS
ERVING AND LARRY BIRD.

VINNIE JOHNSON

FACT FILE

Born: September 1, 1956
Height: 6′ 2″
Length of NBA career:
 1979–92
Major teams:
 Seattle
 Detroit (joined 1981)
 San Antonio (joined 1991)
Records/Awards:
 NBA Championship (2)

They called him "Microwave," because when Vinnie Johnson heated up on the basketball court, he was unstoppable. Johnson, a 6-foot-2-inch, stocky guard from Brooklyn, NY, was a key contributor to the Bad-Boy Detroit Pistons' back-to-back championships in both 1989 and 1990. A streaky shooter out of Baylor who possessed tremendous shooting range, Johnson came off the bench for much of his nine and a half years in Detroit to add firepower to the Pistons' attack.

His mission was two-fold: add instant scoring punch to the defensive-minded, physically intimidating Bad Boys, and also, allow star teammates like Isiah Thomas and Joe Dumars some time to breathe during games.

After playing his last two college seasons at Baylor, Johnson was selected by Seattle in the first round of the 1979 NBA draft, and played two and a half quiet seasons with the SuperSonics before joining the Pistons via a trade and becoming a shooting star in Motown.

In 1982–83, his first full season in Detroit, Johnson averaged a career-high 15.8 points per contest, beginning a string of seven consecutive seasons of double-digit scoring.

After spending his last season in San Antonio, Johnson finished his career with averages of 12.0 points and 3.2 assists per game. He posted 12.0 points and 2.6 assists per game in 116 career playoff games.

RIGHT: VINNIE JOHNSON, KNOWN AROUND THE BASKETBALL WORLD AS "MICROWAVE," OFTEN HELPED DETROIT HEAT UP ITS OFFENSE.

NEIL JOHNSTON

A lantern-jawed center for the Philadelphia Warriors who was a three-time NBA scoring leader in the league's early years, Neil Johnston was voted into the Hall of Fame by the veterans committee in 1990.

Johnston, a 6-foot-8-inch center who starred for Philadelphia from 1951 to 1959, led the Warriors to the 1956 NBA championship, teaming with stars like Paul Arizin and Joe Graboski to defeat the Fort Wayne Pistons, four games to one.

After playing two seasons at Ohio State, Johnston signed a pro baseball contract in 1948 and became ineligible for his last two college seasons. He eventually chose basketball as a profession, and after joining the Warriors, averaged 6.0 points in his rookie campaign.

From there, Johnston's hoop career took flight. He captured three straight scoring crowns with averages of 22.3 points in 1952–53, a career-high 24.4 points in 1953–54, and 22.7 points in 1954–55—a season in which he also led the league in rebounding with 15.1 boards per game.

A five-time NBA All-Star, Johnston scored 20 or more points in five of his seven seasons with Philadelphia. Two years after he played his last game with the Warriors, Johnston was signed as a player-coach by the Pittsburgh Rens of the ABA. He played in just five games for the Rens in the 1961–62 season, posting an average of 9.8 points per contest.

Overall, Johnston averaged 19.4 points and 11.3 rebounds in eight seasons with Philadelphia. He posted averages of 15.0 points and 11.1 rebounds in twenty-three career playoff contests as a member of the Warriors.

FACT FILE

Born: February 4, 1929
Height: 6′ 8″
Length of NBA career:
  1951–59
Length of ABA career:
  1961–62
Major teams:
  Philadelphia
  Pittsburgh (joined 1961)
Records/Awards:
  NBA Championship (1)
  NBA All-Star (5)
  Hall of Fame (1990)

LEFT: PHILADELPHIA'S NEIL JOHNSTON, LAUNCHING A HOOK SHOT HERE, WON THREE STRAIGHT SCORING TITLES IN THE 1950S.

BOBBY JONES

FACT FILE

Born: December 18, 1951
Height: 6′ 9″
Length of ABA career:
  1974–76
Length of NBA career:
  1976–86
Major teams:
  Denver
  Philadelphia (joined 1978)
Records/Awards:
  ABA All-Star (1)
  NBA Championship (1)
  NBA All-Star (4)
  NBA Sixth Man Award
    (1983)
  NBA All-Defensive First
    Team (8)

Opponents of his rarely found Bobby Jones with the basketball. The 6-foot-9-inch forward spent his entire twelve-year professional career for both ABA and NBA leagues in fast and constant motion on the court, setting screens for talented teammates like Julius Erving, or using his long arms and quick hands to steal an important rebound.

"Bobby can complement anybody's game," Erving once said. "I'm learning from him. So many of the things he does are difficult for the fans to understand or appreciate. His contributions can't always be measured by what shows up in the stats."

Jones, who starred at North Carolina from 1970–74 and was a member of the 1972 U.S. Olympic Basketball team that lost the gold-medal game to Russia in controversial fashion, broke into professional basketball with the Denver Nuggets of the ABA.

He earned a place on the All-Rookie team in the 1974–75 season by averaging 14.8 points and 8.2 rebounds per game. He played four seasons in Denver—which joined the NBA in 1976—and posted a career-high 15.1 points per game in the 1976–77 season. After his stay in Denver, the slender Jones was traded to Philadelphia in 1978. He was a starter in his first season with the 76ers, but after the team had been eliminated by the San Antonio Spurs in the 1979 Eastern Conference playoffs, coach Billy Cunningham decided to move Jones to the bench and use him primarily as a sixth man.

The strategy paid off, as Philadelphia won the 1983 NBA championship, sweeping the Los Angeles Lakers in four games. Not coincidentally, Jones, who averaged 9.0 points and 4.6 rebounds per game that season, received the NBA's Sixth Man Award.

A five-time All-Star, Jones averaged 11.5 points and 5.5 rebounds in twelve professional seasons, and 11.6 points and 4.9 rebounds in 125 career playoff games. He holds the ABA single-season record for highest field-goal percentage, shooting .605 from the field in 1975.

An eight-time All Defensive First Team selection, Jones was always one of the leading vote-getters on the all-defensive team, selected by the coaches. His role as the sixth man did not change the coaches' thinking.

RIGHT: WHEN PHILADELPHIA COACH BILLY CUNNINGHAM MADE BOBBY JONES HIS SIXTH MAN, HE CAME OFF THE BENCH TO SPARK THE 76ERS TO A CHAMPIONSHIP.

CALDWELL JONES

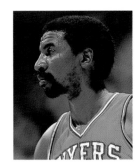

A shot-blocking and rebounding demon, Caldwell Jones played sixteen seasons of professional basketball, earning a reputation in his heyday as one of the professional game's top defensive players.

Jones, a 6-foot-11-inch center out of Albany State College, GA, began his career with San Diego of the ABL in 1973. A third-round draft choice, he didn't take long to prove that he belonged at the pro level, averaging 15.0 points and 13.8 rebounds per game in his rookie year. The following season, Jones averaged a career-high 19.5 points per contest, and tied the ABA record for most blocked shots in one game, racking up 12 rejections against Carolina on January 6, 1974.

After three years in the ABA, Jones jumped to Philadelphia of the NBA, and for the next six seasons, became an invaluable defensive weapon for the 76ers, as he helped the Philadelphia team reach the NBA Finals three times during that span.

In his first season with the 76ers, Jones averaged just 6.0 points per game, but at the other end of the floor, posted 8.2 rebounds per contest and a career-high 200 blocks. Those numbers helped Philadelphia get to the NBA championship series, which was won by Portland in six games.

Three seasons later, Jones, still filling his role to perfection on a team that included stars like Julius Erving, Darryl Dawkins and Bobby Jones, helped Philadelphia return to the NBA Finals. This time around, it was the Los Angeles Lakers who spoiled the 76ers' fun, capturing the title in six games.

In 1981–82, his last season with Philadelphia, Jones again came close to puffing on a championship cigar. But once again, Los Angeles took the crown in six games.

Jones, who spent the last eight years of his career with Houston, Chicago, Portland and San Antonio, finished his fourteen-year NBA stint with averages of 6.4 points, 7.4 rebounds and 1,490 blocks.

BELOW: CALDWELL JONES' BRILLIANT CAREER, SPENT IN BOTH THE ABA AND NBA, SPANNED SIXTEEN SEASONS.

FACT FILE

Born: August 4, 1950
Height: 6' 11"
Length of ABA career:
 1973–76
Length of NBA career:
 1976–90
Major teams:
 San Diego
 Kentucky (joined 1975)
 St. Louis (joined 1975)
 Philadelphia (joined 1976)
 Houston (joined 1982)
 Chicago (joined 1984)
 Portland (joined 1985)
 San Antonio (joined 1989)
Records/Awards:
 ABA All-Star (1)
 NBA All-Defensive First
  Team (2)

DONTAE JONES

FACT FILE

Born: June 2, 1975
Height: 6′ 7″
Length of NBA career:
1996–present
Major team:
New York

A Bulldog in tank top and shorts, Dontae Jones was one of three forwards selected by the championship-starved New York Knicks in the 1996 NBA draft. Unfortunately for Jones, injuries sidelined him for the entire 1996–97 season.

A 6-foot-7-inch banger out of Mississippi State who made himself eligible for the draft after his junior year, Jones, along with teammate Erick Dampier, led the Bulldogs' in 1995–96 to their first-ever trip to the NCAA Final Four, NCAA Regional Championship, SEC Tournament title and SEC Western Division title. He was named Most Outstanding Player of the SEC Tournament after posting averages of 21.3 points, 6.7 rebounds, and 2.7 blocks per game.

Jones, who averaged 14.7 points and 6.8 rebounds in thirty-three games with the Bulldogs, has impressed the Knicks with his aggressive style of play and ability to score from all areas of the floor. The only question mark remains his health, as he is trying to recover fully from a broken foot.

Having played just one season of major college basketball before being drafted by the Knicks, Jones honed his skills on the junior-college circuit. He played two seasons at Northeast Mississippi Community College, finishing as the school's all-time leading scorer (1,648 points) and rebounder (751). As a freshman at Northeast Mississippi, Jones finished as the nation's fifth-leading scorer, pouring in 25.2 points per game.

RIGHT: THE NEW YORK KNICKS ARE HOPING THAT DONTAE JONES RECOVERS FROM INJURY AND FULFILLS HIS GREAT POTENTIAL.

JIMMY JONES

A do-it-all-guard with a sweet-scoring touch, Jimmy Jones was one of the ABA's marquee attractions from the late 1960s through the early 1970s.

Selected by New Orleans of the ABA out of Grambling in 1967, Jones was one of many lesser-known college players who never would have had a chance to showcase their talents in the more-established NBA.

When given his chance, Jones strutted his stuff in New Orleans, averaging 18.8 points per game in his rookie season with the Buccaneers. The next season, he exploded for a career-high 26.6 points per contest, and posted 20.7 points per game for New Orleans in 1969–70.

The following season, Jones and the rest of the New Orleans franchise was moved to Memphis and renamed the Sounds, but the change of scenery didn't affect Jones's loud shooting tune, as he registered 19.6 points per contest. From 1971–74, Jones played three seasons for the Utah Stars and continued his scoring onslaught, averaging 15.5, 16.7 and 16.8 points per game, respectively, in each of those campaigns.

After his stint with the Stars, Jones jumped to the NBA, where he played two seasons for the Washington Bullets from 1974–76, and the last three games of his career with the team in the 1976–77 campaign.

A six-time ABA All-Star, Jones averaged 19.2 points per game in seven ABA seasons, adding an average 21.7 points per contest in seventy-one career ABA playoff games.

FACT FILE

Born: January 1, 1945
Height: 6' 4"
Length of ABA career:
1967–74
Length of NBA career:
1974–77
Major teams:
New Orleans–Memphis
Utah (joined 1971)
Washington (joined 1974)
Records/Awards:
ABA All-Star (6)

LEFT: JIMMY JONES, HERE SEEN ATTEMPTING A STEAL, WAS A MULTI-TALENTED GUARD AND ONE OF THE ABA'S MARQUEE ATTRACTIONS.

K. C. JONES

FACT FILE

Born: May 25, 1932
Height: 6' 1"
Length of NBA career:
  1958–67
Major team:
  Boston
Records/Awards:
  Olympic Gold Medal
    (1956)
  NBA Championship (8)
  Hall of Fame (1988)

One of the best defensive guards in the history of the NBA, K. C. Jones of the Boston Celtics played on eight championship teams during his nine-year professional career.

Jones, a 6-foot-1-inch guard who combined with Bill Russell to lead the University of San Francisco to two national championships, teamed again with Russell on the great Celtic teams of the late 1950s and 1960s.

A member of the gold-medal winning 1956 U.S. Olympic Basketball team, Jones's collegiate success carried over to pro basketball with the NBA. He won eight straight championships with the Celtics. His best offensive season came midway through that phenomenal stretch, as he averaged a career-high 9.2 points per game in the 1961–62 season, adding 4.3 assists and 3.7 rebounds per contest.

For his career, Jones averaged 7.4 points, 4.3 assists and 3.5 rebounds per contest. In 105 career playoff games, he averaged 6.4 points, 3.8 assists and 3.0 rebounds. When his NBA playing days were over, Jones hooked up with the Hartford Capitols of the Eastern Basketball League, posting 6.5 points and 6.8 assists in just six games with the team.

At the University of San Francisco, Jones tallied an average 8.8 points as a basketball player, and also starred on the college's football team. He was also selected by the Los Angeles Rams in the 30th round of the 1955 National Football League draft.

RIGHT: A TWO-TIME NCAA CHAMPION AT THE UNIVERSITY OF SAN FRANCISCO, K.C. JONES HAD JUST ENOUGH FINGERS LEFT FOR EIGHT MORE RINGS HE WOULD WIN WITH THE BOSTON CELTICS.

LARRY JONES

hen the ABA's first national television audience tuned into the league's 1970 All-Star game at Indianapolis, Larry Jones gave them a show.

Jones, a 6-foot-3-inch guard out of Toledo, set an All-Star game record that day by scoring 30 points, dishing out 5 assists and hauling down 6 rebounds to help the West stars crush their East counterparts, 128–98.

A four-time ABA All-Star, Jones actually began his career with Philadelphia of the NBA in the 1964–65 season. He averaged just 5.7 points in twenty-three games that year, but joined the ABA's Denver Rockets the next season and became a shooting star, averaging 22.9 points per game.

Jones played three seasons in Denver—averaging a career-high 28.4 points per contest in 1968–69—before joining the Floridians for two seasons between 1970–72. He split his last ABA season with Utah and Dallas, and in the 1973–74 campaign went back to where he launched his first professional shot, re-joining the Philadelphia 76ers.

The following season, Jones took his shooting act to Europe, joining Germany of the European Pro Basketball League. There, he played alongside and against a number of former ABA and NBA players now playing basketball in the European League.

In his seven ABA seasons, Jones averaged 21.2 points per game, adding 21.5 points per contest in thirty career playoff games. In his two NBA seasons, Jones posted an average of 9.0 points per game.

Jones, an all Mac performer in 1961 and 1962, became the first ABA player to score 5000 points. He later moved on to coaching with Detroit in the NBA and in a European League in Munich, Germany.

BELOW: LARRY JONES, SEEN HERE IN HIS COLLEGE DAYS AT TOLEDO, WAS A FOUR-TIME ABA ALL-STAR.

FACT FILE

Born: September 22, 1941
Height: 6' 3"
Length of ABA career:
1967–73
Length of NBA career:
1964–65, 1973–74
Major teams:
Philadelphia
Denver (joined 1967)
Floridians (joined 1970)
Utah (joined 1972)
Dallas (joined 1972)
Philadelphia (joined 1973)
Records/Awards:
ABA All-Star (4)

SAM JONES

FACT FILE

Born: June 24, 1933
Height: 6' 4"
Length of NBA career:
  1957–69
Major team:
  Boston
Records/Awards:
  NBA Championship (10)
  NBA All-Star (5)
  Hall of Fame (1983)

BELOW: MASTER OF THE BANK
SHOT, LITTLE-KNOWN SAM
JONES BECAME A DRIVING
FORCE BEHIND TEN BOSTON
CELTIC CHAMPIONSHIPS.

Hardly anyone had ever heard of Sam Jones when he joined the Boston Celtics in 1957 out of little-known North Carolina Central College. Twelve years, 15,380 points and ten championships later, Jones was being hailed as one of the greatest Celtics in the history of the storied franchise.

A 6-foot-4-inch guard who loved to use the bank shot, Jones was one of the greatest shooters of his era. In all but one of his dazzling dozen years with Boston, Jones averaged double digits in scoring. His greatest season was 1964–65, when he burned up the cords for 25.9 points per game, adding 2.8 assists and 5.1 rebounds per contest.

It was Jones who hit one of the biggest shots of the 1968–69 post-season, connecting on an off-balance flip at the buzzer to give the Celtics an 89–88 victory over the Los Angeles Lakers in Game 4 of the NBA Finals. That shot tied the series at two games apiece, and gave the underdog Celtics the confidence and momentum they needed to upset the mighty Lakers in Game 7. That championship flag would be the last one waved by the great Boston teams in the 1960s. It was also the end of another era, as the 36-year-old Jones retired shortly thereafter.

A five-time All-Star and three-time All-NBA Second Team selection, Jones averaged 17.7 points, 2.5 assists and 4.9 rebounds throughout his glorious stint in Beantown. He added 18.9 points, 2.3 assists and 4.7 rebounds in 154 career playoff games.

Although he teamed with superstars like Bob Cousy, Bill Russell and John Havlicek in his career, Jones retired as the Celtics all-time leading scorer. The man Bostonians had never heard of was voted onto the NBA's 25th Anniversary All-Time team in 1970, and elected to the Hall of Fame thirteen years later.

STEVE JONES

Steve Jones is a 6-foot-5-inch swingman who made his professional debut in the ABA in the 1967–68 season, the same year that the league rolled out the red-white-and-blue balls and opened for business.

Jones, who played his college basketball at Oregon, electrified crowds for eight years in the ABA, amassing more than 10,000 points with six different teams before finishing his career in the rival NBA.

A three-time ABA All-Star, Jones broke into the ABA with the Oakland Oaks in 1967, posting averages of 10.1 points, 4.5 rebounds and 1.4 assists per game.

The following year, Jones hooked up with New Orleans, and was one of the franchise's marquee attractions for three seasons, including the 1970–71 campaign when the franchise moved to Memphis. In those three seasons, Jones's scoring numbers continued to grow. He tallied up 19.9 points in 1968–69, 21.5 in 1969–70 and a career-high 22.1 points in the 1970–71 seasons.

Over the next four years, Jones took his act to Dallas, Carolina, Denver and St. Louis. Wherever Jones went, Jones scored. In each of his eight ABA seasons, he averaged double digits in scoring.

The last professional season of Jones's career was spent in Portland, where he scored 6.5 points per game for the Trail Blazers. He averaged 16.0 points per game during his ABA career, adding 15.3 points per game in thirty–seven post-season contests.

At Oregon, Jones finished with a three-year scoring average of 12.1, leading the team in his senior season with a 16.1 scoring average.

BELOW: WHEREVER HE DRIBBLED A BASKETBALL, STEVE JONES ATTRACTED HUGE CROWDS.

FACT FILE

Born: October 17, 1942
Height: 6' 5"
Length of ABA career:
1967–76
Major teams:
  Oakland
  New Orleans–Memphis
    (joined 1968)
  Dallas (joined 1971)
  Carolina (joined 1972)
  Denver (joined 1973)
  St. Louis (joined 1974)
  Portland (joined 1975)
Records/Awards:
  ABA All-Star (3)

MICHAEL JORDAN

FACT FILE

Born: February 17, 1963
Height: 6' 6"
Length of NBA career:
  1984–93, 1994–present
Major team:
  Chicago Bulls (joined
  1984)
Records/Awards:
  NBA Rookie of the Year
  1985
  NBA Championships (5)
  NBA Most Valuable Player
  (3)
  NBA Slam-Dunk
  Competition (2)
  Olympic Gold Medal
  (1984, 1992)

BELOW: SIMPLY PUT, MICHAEL JEFFREY JORDAN IS THE MOST CELEBRATED PLAYER IN THE HISTORY OF PROFESSIONAL BASKETBALL.

The most celebrated player in the history of the NBA, Michael Jeffrey Jordan, known around the globe as "Air Jordan," is a performer without equal. Jordan, who helped North Carolina win an NCAA championship in 1982, has established himself as a larger-than-life, living legend since joining the Chicago Bulls in 1984 and leading the team to three straight world championships from 1991–93, and two more the past two seasons. A Picasso in tank top and shorts, Jordan holds the career record for highest points-per-game average (31.7), and holds the career record for most seasons leading the league in scoring (9).

Jordan, the NBA Rookie of the Year in 1985, a three-time Most Valuable Player and two-time winner of the NBA's Slam-Dunk Competition, is with little argument the most dominant and dangerous one-on-one player in the history of the league. In his prime, Jordan, his long tongue slithering out of his mouth like a deadly snake, played the game above the rim like no other player before him. While he has lost an inch or two on his vertical leap during the last few years, he can still single-handedly control the outcome of games with an assortment of other weapons. Defensively, Jordan is also one of the league's best; he was voted eight times to the NBA's All-Defensive First Team.

A teammate of Larry Bird and Magic Johnson on the 1992 US gold-medal Olympic team, Jordan has, in a manner of speaking, carried the torch for the NBA since Bird retired in 1992, and Johnson entered the twilight of his career. NBA basketball, which he, Bird and Johnson helped popularize in the 1980s, has experienced an unprecedented global boom in total viewing figures and advertising dollars during Jordan's colorful, high-flying tenure.

The NBA is a league filled with some of the most acrobatic and talented athletes in the world, but when Jordan retired from basketball in 1993 to give professional baseball a whirl, the game of roundball wasn't as enjoyable without him.

Near the end of the 1994–95 season, Jordan returned to basketball, and again established himself as the league's marquee attraction, creating a second dynasty in Chicago.

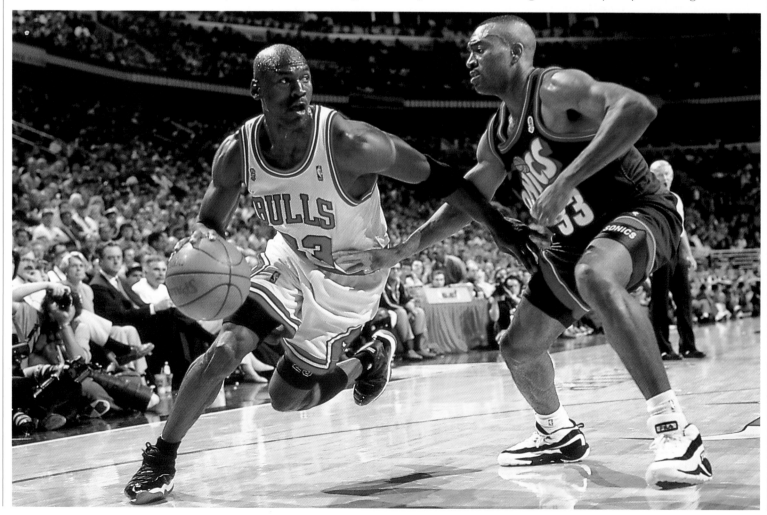

SHAWN KEMP

One of the most explosive power forwards ever to play the game, Shawn Kemp has gotten better in each of his first eight NBA seasons.

The 6-foot-10-inch "Rain Main," as Kemp is called, earned his nickname over the years by slamming down thunderous dunks from way above the rim. He averaged a career-high 19.6 points and 11.4 rebounds per game in the 1995–96 season in helping the Seattle SuperSonics reach the NBA Finals, where they were defeated by the Chicago Bulls.

Kemp, who made it into the NBA without having played major college basketball, played one season at Trinity Valley Community College before he was selected by Seattle in the first round of the 1989 NBA Draft.

In his first season with the SuperSonics, Kemp started slowly, averaging just 6.5 points and 4.3 rebounds per contest. With one year of experience under his belt, the Man-Child, as Kemp is also called, began blossoming into an NBA star. He averaged 15.0 points and 8.4 rebounds in 1990–91, and his scoring and rebounding totals have steadily risen since: 15.5 points and 10.4 boards per game in 1991–92, 17.8 and 10.7 in 1992–93, 18.1 and 10.8 in 1993–94, and 18.7 and 10.9 in 1994–95.

An all-Star in each of the past five seasons and a three-time All-NBA Second Team selection, Kemp was just 27 years old when he began his eighth year with the SuperSonics last season. He has now averaged 16.2 points, 9.6 rebounds, and 1.8 assists per game throughout his career.

FACT FILE

Born: November 26, 1969
Height: 6′ 10″
Length of NBA career:
  1989–present
Major teams:
  Seattle
  Cleveland (joined 1997)
Records/Awards:
  NBA All-Star (5)

LEFT: THE EXPLOSIVE SHAWN KEMP COMES RAINING DOWN HERE ON SCOTTIE PIPPEN AND THE CHICAGO BULLS.

JUST WIN, BABY: THE LOS ANGELES LAKERS' 33-GAME WINNING STREAK

BELOW: JERRY WEST, PULLING UP FOR A JUMPER, WAS AN INTEGRAL MEMBER OF THE LOS ANGELES LAKER TEAM THAT REELED OFF THIRTY-THREE CONSECUTIVE VICTORIES.

Kareem Abdul-Jabbar was waiting in Milwaukee. John Havlicek was waiting in Boston. Walt Frazier was waiting in New York.

Those are just some of the opponents that the Los Angeles Lakers visited, and conquered, en route to putting together their 33-game winning streak in the 1971–72 season—the longest winning streak in NBA history—which ultimately led to the franchise's first championship since it had moved from Minneapolis to Los Angeles for the 1960–61 season.

The streak started on November 5th—the day after Elgin Baylor retired—when the Lakers got past the Baltimore Bullets, 110–106.

From there, the Lakers, led by Wilt Chamberlain and Jerry West, ran off a string of lopsided victories, but hit a speed-bump in Game 20 on December 10, when they were taken into overtime by the Phoenix Suns. On the strength of Gail Goodrich's 32 points, seven of which came in the extra session, the Lakers kept the streak alive with a 126–117 victory.

Two nights later, the Lakers beat the Atlanta Hawks 104–95 for a record-breaking 21st victory. When Los Angeles stretched its streak to 33 games on January 8 with a 134–98 trashing of the Hawks, it seemed as if the winning would never end.

But the very next night, the Milwaukee Bucks ended the party with a 120–104 thumping of the Lakers. Abdul-Jabbar, who would later star for Los Angeles, scored 39 points in that contest, and the Bucks reeled off an 18–2 spurt in the fourth quarter that put the contest out of reach and gave new meaning to the phrase "the Buck stops here."

STEVE KERR

FACT FILE

Born: September 27, 1965
Height: 6′ 3″
Length of NBA career:
  1988–present
Major teams:
  Phoenix
  Cleveland (joined 1989)
  Orlando (joined 1992)
  Chicago (joined 1993)
Records/Awards:
  NBA Championship (2)

When the baby-faced, blond-haired Steve Kerr is in action for the Chicago Bulls, you could get the impression that you're watching a high school basketball game.

Kerr, however, has grown into a bona fide pro in Chicago's backcourt. His clutch outside shooting is one of the keys to the Bulls' enormously successful triangle offense, and it was one of the main reasons why Michael Jordan and company won the NBA championship the past two seasons.

A nine-year pro out of Arizona, the 6-foot-3-inch Kerr broke into the big leagues with the Phoenix Suns in 1989. He played just 26 games for the Suns before he was traded to Cleveland the following year. In his first season with the Cavaliers, Kerr averaged 6.7 points per game but proved his worth behind the three-point stripe, leading the NBA with a .507 shooting percentage.

After three and a half seasons with Cleveland and one half-season with Orlando, Kerr settled in Chicago, where he has become a fan-favorite. He averaged a career-high 8.6 points for the Bulls in 1993–94, and the following year set the single season record for highest field goal percentage, knocking down 89 of 170 trifectas for a .524 percentage. He entered the 1997–98 season with the career record for highest three-point field goal percentage—based on a minimum of 250 made—connecting on his treys at a .477 clip. Last season, Kerr averaged 8.1 points per game.

BELOW: HE MAY LOOK LIKE YOUR AVERAGE SCHOOLBOY HOOPSTER, BUT STEVE KERR IS A BONA FIDE PRO.

JEROME KERSEY

A valuable member of the Portland Trail Blazer teams that made appearances in the 1990 and 1992 NBA Finals, Jerome Kersey will be entering his fourteenth professional season as a member of the Los Angeles Lakers. High-flying Kersey, a 6-foot-7-inch forward out of Division II's Longwood College in Virginia, spent his first eleven NBA seasons with Portland, averaging 12.1 points, 6.1 rebounds, and 2.1 assists during that span.

Kersey's best season in a Trail Blazer uniform was 1987–88, when he averaged 19.2 points, 8.3 rebounds, and 3.1 assists per game. He posted 17.5 points per game the following season, and in 1989–90, came up big in the post-season during Portland's championship run, averaging 17.9 points and 6.9 rebounds in 16 playoff games. However, Portland lost the title to Detroit in five games.

For seven straight years in Portland, Kersey averaged double digits in scoring. He posted 12.6 points per game in the 1991–92 campaign, helping the Trail Blazers back to the Finals, where they were defeated by the Chicago Bulls in six games.

Selected by the Toronto Raptors in the 1995 NBA Expansion draft, Kersey signed instead as a free agent with the Golden State Warriors in 1995–96, averaging 6.7 points per contest. He was traded to the Lakers last season, averaging 11.3 points per game.

At Longwood, Kersey averaged 17.0 points in four seasons. He led all NCAA Division II players in rebounding his senior year, averaging 14.7 boards per game.

FACT FILE

Born: June 26, 1962
Height: 6' 7"
Length of NBA career:
  1984–present
Major teams:
  Portland
  Golden State (joined 1995)
  Los Angeles (joined 1996)

LEFT: HIGH-FLYING JEROME KERSEY TEAMED WITH CLYDE DREXLER IN TWICE LEADING PORTLAND TO THE NBA FINALS.

JASON KIDD

FACT FILE

Born: March 23, 1973
Height: 6′ 4″
Length of NBA career:
  1994–present
Major teams:
  Dallas
  Phoenix (joined 1996)
Records/Awards:
  NBA Co-Rookie of the
    Year (1995)
  NBA All-Star (1)

Jason Kidd has been one of the most exciting players in the NBA since joining the Dallas Mavericks in 1994.

One of the great ball-handlers in the game today, the 6-foot-4-inch playmaker out of California is one of only six players in NBA history to rack up 700 assists and 500 rebounds in one season.

He turned both of those tricks in the 1995–96 season, finishing with averages of 16.6 points, 9.7 assists, and 6.8 rebounds per game. He also led all guards in rebounds in 1995–96 season with 553, and set a Maverick's team record with 9 triple-doubles.

After two seasons at California, where he averaged 14.9 points, 8.4 assists, and 5.9 rebounds per contest, Kidd was selected after his sophomore campaign by Dallas as the second pick overall in the 1994 NBA draft.

He had a smashing rookie season with the Mavericks, averaging 11.7 points, 7.7 assists, and 5.4 rebounds per game en route to being named co-Rookie of the year, an honor he shared with Grant Hill of the Detroit Pistons.

In two full seasons running the show for the young and talented Mavericks before he was traded to Phoenix, Kidd posted averages of 14.2 points, 8.7 assists, and 6.1 rebounds per game. An all-around player with raw athletic ability, Kidd has also blocked 70 shots and made 450 steals in his young career.

At California, Kidd led the NCAA Division I with 3.8 steals per game in 1993, and in 1994, led Division I with 9.1 assists per game. He is now with Phoenix.

RIGHT: A MODERN-DAY BOB COUSY? JASON KIDD IS ONE OF THE MOST PHENOMENAL BALL-HANDLERS IN THE NBA TODAY.

ALBERT KING

Injury was the only opponent that ever stopped Albert King. A 6-foot-6-inch shooting guard who grew up on basketball courts in Brooklyn, NY, King went on to a brilliant four-year career at Maryland before he was selected by the New Jersey Nets in the first round of the 1981 NBA draft.

In his rookie season with the Nets, King, who had missed all of training camp with an injured right knee, came back to average 12.1 points per game, haul down 312 rebounds, and dish out 142 assists.

The following season, King, who loved to catch the basketball, wheel around, and shoot in one fluid motion, averaged a career-high 17.0 points per game. In his first five seasons playing in New Jersey, King's shooting and play-making ability helped the downtrodden Nets reach the playoffs five straight times. In the 1986–87 season, however, his sixth with the Nets, injuries began to affect King's game and sent his career into a tailspin.

He missed a total of twenty games that season with ankle and knee injuries, and, after posting averages of 13.6 points in six seasons with New Jersey, he signed his name to a free-agent deal with Philadelphia.

King played one season in Philadelphia, averaging 7.2 points per game, and closed out his career with the San Antonio Spurs in 1988–89, posting a career-low 7.1 points in just forty-six contests.

The younger brother of Bernard King, Albert King averaged 12.2 points per game in eight NBA seasons, adding an average 15.6 points per contest in twenty-one career playoff games.

During his four-year career at Maryland, King averaged 17.4 points in four seasons and retired as the school's all-time leading scorer with a total of 2,058 career points.

FACT FILE

Born: December 17, 1959
Height: 6′ 6″
Length of NBA career:
1981–89
Major teams:
New Jersey
Philadelphia (joined 1987)
San Antonio (joined 1988)

LEFT: ALBERT KING'S SUPER SKILLS HELPED THE DOWNTRODDEN NEW JERSEY NETS REACH THE PLAYOFFS IN EACH OF HIS FIRST FIVE SEASONS WITH THE TEAM.

BERNARD KING

FACT FILE

Born: December 4, 1956
Height: 6′ 7″
Length of NBA career:
1977–93
Major teams:
New Jersey
Utah (joined 1979)
Golden State (joined 1980)
New York (joined 1982)
Washington (joined 1987)
New Jersey (joined 1993)
Records/Awards:
NBA All-Star (4)
NBA Comeback Player of the Year (1981)

One of the most prolific scorers in NBA history, Bernard King lit up scoreboards in every arena he played during a professional career that spanned sixteen seasons.

A 6-foot-7-inch forward who grew up in New York and starred in the "Bernie and Ernie" show at Tennessee with Ernie Grunfeld, King was selected by the New Jersey Nets in the first round of the 1977 NBA draft.

In his first season with the Nets, King, who exploded in the open court, proved himself a legitimate scorer. He averaged 24.2 points per game, earning a place for himself on the league's All-Rookie squad.

After scoring 21.6 points in his second season with the Nets, King was traded to Utah, where he played nineteen games in an injury-plagued season. He was then shipped by the Jazz to the Golden State Warriors, where he regained his health and recaptured his scoring stroke. He averaged 21.9 points per game and was named the NBA Comeback Player of the Year.

King's comeback campaign started a string of six straight seasons in which he would average 20 or more points per game. That scoring string went through New York, where King returned as a free agent in 1982 and enjoyed some of the greatest moments in his career.

As a Knick, King averaged a career-high 32.9 points per game in 1984–85, capturing the league's scoring crown. He missed the entire 1986–87 season due to a serious knee injury, but came back the following season, his last in New York, to make a scoring average of 22.7 points per game.

From 1987–91, King enjoyed four more solid seasons with the Washington Bullets before injuries sidelined him continuously for the entire 1991–92 campaign.

A four-time NBA All-Star and two-time All-NBA First Team Selection, King finished his NBA career where it had started. He averaged 7 points in just thirty-two games for the New Jersey Nets in 1992–93.

Through his career, King averaged 22.5 points, 5.8 rebounds, and 3.3 assists per game, posting 24.5 points per contest in twenty-eight career playoff games.

RIGHT: A SHOOTING SENSATION, BERNARD KING, DRIVING HARD TO THE BASKET HERE, LIT UP SCOREBOARDS IN EVERY ARENA HE PLAYED IN.

KERRY KITTLES

After a dismal 1995–96 campaign, the New Jersey Nets realized they desperately needed a money shooter—and hoped to cash in on Kerry Kittles of Villanova, whom they selected in the first round of the 1996 NBA draft.

Kittles, a 6-foot-5-inch shooting guard who possesses great shooting range and tremendous leaping ability, paid handsome dividends for the Nets by turning in a spectacular rookie performance, averaging 16.4 points, 3.9 rebounds, and 3.0 assists per game.

Kittles, who set the single season record with most three-point field goals made by a rookie (158), also finished with 157 steals, and was selected to the NBA's all-rookie second team.

"Kerry the Cat," as Kittles is sometimes called, left Villanova as the school's all-time leader in points scored with 2,243 and also finished as its career-steals leader with 277. He is the only player in Villanova history to ring up 2,000 points, 700 rebounds, 400 assists, and 200 steals. In addition, Kittles was named to the Big East Conference First Team for three straight seasons from his sophomore year through his senior season.

As a junior at Villanova, Kittles averaged a collegiate, career-high 21.4 points per game, and was named Big East Player of the Year after helping the Wildcats capture the Big East Tournament title. As a sophomore, Kittles led Villanova in scoring with a 19.7 point average en route to leading the Wildcats to the NIT Championship.

FACT FILE

Born: June 12, 1974
Height: 6' 5"
Length of NBA career:
  1996–present
Major team:
  New Jersey Nets

BELOW: KERRY KITTLES, VILLANOVA'S ALL-TIME LEADER IN POINTS SCORED, WILL LIKELY BECOME A CORNERSTONE OF THE NEW JERSEY NETS' FRANCHISE.

MITCH KUPCHAK

FACT FILE

Born: May 24, 1954
Height: 6′ 9″
Length of NBA career:
  1976–86
Major teams:
  Washington
  Los Angeles Lakers
  (joined 1981)
Records/Awards:
  NBA Championship (2)
  Olympic Gold Medal
  (1976)

One of the great inspiration stories in league history, Mitch Kupchak made it back from a severe knee injury to help the Los Angeles Lakers defeat the Boston Celtics in six games to win the 1985 NBA championship.

Kupchak, a bruising 6-foot-9-inch backup center and power forward who had helped the Washington Bullets win the 1978 NBA title, blew his knee apart early in the 1981–82 season. He missed the entire 1982–83 campaign, and, on his slow journey back to good health, played only 324 minutes in 1983–84.

The following season, Kupchak returned to the Laker lineup. As the muscleman who complemented the finesse game of Kareem Abdul-Jabbar, Kupchak averaged 5.3 points and 3.1 rebounds per game during the regular season. In the championship series, Laker coach Pat Riley used Kupchak more than he ever had,

asking him to lean on and agitate Boston's Kevin McHale and Robert Parish, and Kupchak had filled his role to perfection. In the final game of the series, Kupchak played 20 minutes, hauled down 5 rebounds, had 2 assists, and made 4 of 6 free throws for 6 points.

A star formerly at North Carolina who was selected by Washington in the first round of the 1976 NBA draft—the same year that he helped the US Olympic Basketball Team win a gold medal—Kupchak averaged 10.4 points per game in his first season with the Bullets, earning a spot on the All-Rookie team. The following season, he averaged a career-high 15.9 points per game.

In a ten-year NBA career split between Washington and Los Angeles, Kupchak averaged 10.2 points and 5.3 rebounds per game. He posted 7.7 points and 4.7 boards in sixty-eight career playoff games.

RIGHT: MITCH KUPCHAK, LEFT, WAS ONE OF THE GREAT INSPIRATION STORIES IN LEAGUE HISTORY.

BILL LAIMBEER

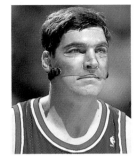

During his fourteen-year NBA career, opponents of Bill Laimbeer have called him a cheater, a cheap-shot artist, and an instigator.

Most of them, however, would all agree that the 6-foot-11-inch center, who won a pair of championships with Detroit, was one of the most mobile and talented big men ever to play the game.

After three quiet seasons at Notre Dame, Laimbeer was a third-round selection of the Cleveland Cavaliers in the 1979 NBA draft. He played his first year of professional basketball in Italy, averaging 21.1 points per game for Brescia of the Italian League.

The following season, Laimbeer broke into the NBA with Cleveland, averaging 9.8 points and 8.6 rebounds as a rookie. Midway through the 1981–82 season, Laimbeer was traded by Cleveland to Detroit, and he became a fixture, if not a hero, in the Motor City.

A 260-pound banger who loved to run the floor and break opponents' hearts with a feathery but oh-so-deadly jumper from the top of the key, Laimbeer played twelve and a half seasons in Detroit. There, he teamed with stars like Isiah Thomas, Dennis Rodman, and Joe Dumars to help Detroit's Bad-Boy Piston teams capture back-to-back world championships in the years 1989 and 1990.

Laimbeer, whose retirement just eleven games into the 1993–94 season shocked the basketball world, averaged 12.9 points and 8.6 rebounds in his career.

A four-time NBA All-Star, Laimbeer added 12.0 points and 9.7 rebounds in 113 career playoff games.

FACT FILE

Born: May 19, 1957
Height: 6′ 11″
Length of NBA career: 1980–94
Major teams:
 Cleveland
 Detroit (joined 1982)
Records/Awards:
 NBA Championship (2)
 NBA All-Star (4)

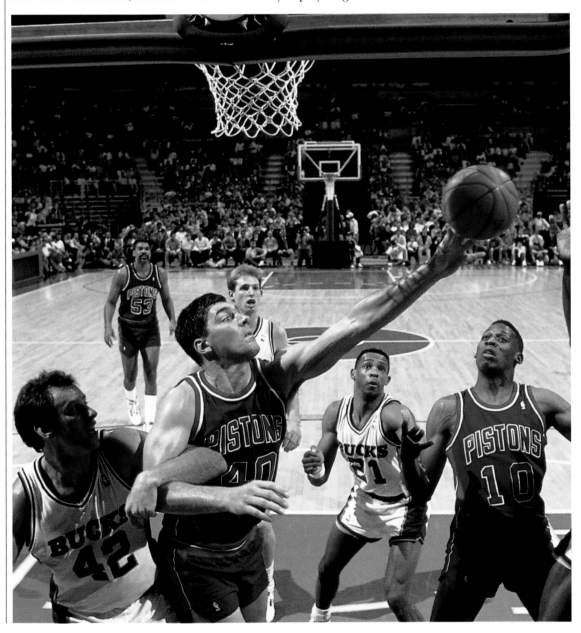

LEFT: PERHAPS THE BADDEST OF THE BAD BOYS, BILL LAIMBEER HAD AN AWFUL LOT OF TALENT TO GO ALONG WITH HIS ROUGH-AND-TUMBLE ATTITUDE.

BOB LANIER

FACT FILE

Born: September 10, 1948
Height: 6′ 11″
Length of NBA career:
 1970–84
Major teams:
 Detroit
 Milwaukee (joined 1980)
Records/Awards:
 NBA All-Star (8)
 Hall of Fame (1991)

Shaquille O'Neal with a jump shot, Bob Lanier was one of the most talented centers in NBA history never to win an NBA Championship.

After averaging 27.6 points per game in four seasons at St. Bona-venture, he was selected by the Detroit Pistons in the first round of the 1970 NBA draft. For fourteen seasons, the 6-foot-11-inch, 265-pounder, who teamed with stars like Dave Bing and Jimmy Walker in his day, dominated the competition.

In his first year with the Pistons, Lanier averaged 15.6 points and 8.1 rebounds en route to securing a place for himself on the All-Rookie team of that year.

The following season, Lanier posted a career-high 25.7 points per game, the first of eight straight seasons in which the left-handed shooting pivotman would average 20 or more points per contest.

His best all-around season was 1972–73, when he averaged 23.8 points, a career-high 14.9 rebounds, and 3.2 assists.

Midway through the 1979–80 season, Lanier, starting to slow down because of bad knees, was traded by Detroit to Milwaukee, and played out his career with the Bucks through the 1983–84 campaign.

An eight-time All-Star—he was the MVP of the 1974 All-Star game after scoring 24 points—Lanier averaged 20.1 points and 10.1 rebounds throughout his career. He averaged 18.6 points and 9.6 boards in 67 career playoff games. In each of his fourteen seasons with Detroit and Milwaukee, Lanier finished with double-digit scoring averages.

RIGHT: BOB LANIER, WHO WAS SHAQUILLE O'NEAL WITH A JUMP SHOT, WAS ONE OF THE MOST TALENTED CENTERS IN HISTORY NEVER TO WIN A CHAMPIONSHIP.

JOE LAPCHICK

In an era of few six-footers among basketball players, Joe Lapchick, a 6-foot-6-inch center, was considered a giant.

Lapchick, whose professional playing career spanned fourteen years from 1920–34, was a member of the Original Celtics, a New York team that dominated the game of basketball so thoroughly in the 1920s that no effective league could be formed around it.

Although he never played high school or college basketball, Lapchick learned his craft by playing for local club teams shortly after graduating from grammar school. He negotiated fees of up to $75 for a single game, a huge payday in that era.

Lapchick's big break came in the early 1920s, when he got to play against the Celtics and their experienced center, Horse Haggarty.

When Haggarty retired, the skinny, but extremely tough Lapchick became his replacement. "The Big Indian," as Lapchick was affectionately called, had a career in basketball that virtually spanned the game from its beginnings to its full growth.

After his playing days, he became a hugely successful college and pro head coach with the St. John's Redmen (which explains his nickname) and the New York Knicks in the 1940s and 1950s, watching players get bigger, stronger, and faster with each passing year. He retired from coaching in 1965.

"Consider the shooting," Lapchick once said, comparing modern styles of play with the moves of the past. "Years ago, we had two basic shooting plays, the set shot, from the chest, and the lay-up. Today, the set shot is passe. The one-handed shot and the jump shot are all the rage and have revolutionized the game. Nobody, in our day, could duplicate what these kids do with one hand today. If you tried that stuff when we were playing, you'd be accused of throwing the ball away."

FACT FILE

Born: April 12, 1900
Height: 6' 6"
Length of Pro career:
1920–34
Major teams:
  Original Celtics
  Holyoke (joined 1920)
  Schenectady (joined 1921)
  Troy (joined 1922)
  Brooklyn (joined 1922)
  Holyoke (joined 1922)
  Brooklyn (joined 1923)
  Troy (joined 1923)
  Holyoke (joined 1923)
  Original Celtics (1924–26)
  Brooklyn (joined 1926)
  New York (joined 1927)
  Cleveland (joined 1928)
  Toledo (joined 1931)
  Yonkers (joined 1932)
  Plymouth (joined 1933)
Records/Awards:
  Hall of Fame (1966)

LEFT: JOE LAPCHICK HAD A CAREER IN BASKETBALL THAT VIRTUALLY SPANNED THE GAME FROM ITS BEGINNINGS TO ITS FULL GROWTH.

LAFAYETTE "FAT" LEVER

FACT FILE

Born: August 18, 1960
Height: 6′ 3″
Length of NBA career:
1982–94
Major teams:
Portland
Denver (joined 1984)
Dallas (joined 1990)
Records/Awards:
NBA All-Star (2)

One of the best rebounding guards ever, Lafayette "Fat" Lever played eleven seasons in the National Basketball Association before knee injuries forced him out of the game.

Lever, a 6-foot-3-inch standout at Arizona State, was selected by Portland in the first round of the 1982 NBA draft. He played his first two seasons with the Trail Blazers, establishing a reputation as an all-around player who could rebound, shoot, pass, and cause extreme damage in the open floor.

Traded from Portland to Denver in 1984, Lever led all guards in rebounding as a member of the Nuggets from 1986–90. His career-high rebounding total was 734 in the 1989–90 season, his last with the Nuggets. Only Oscar Robertson, Tom Gola, and Magic Johnson have ever hauled down more rebounds as a guard in a single season. In addition, Lever ranked among the league's top-ten in assists from the 1986–87 through the 1988–89 campaign, averaging 7.8 assists per game during that span. He also was among the league's steals leaders in seven of his eleven seasons in the NBA.

A two-time All-Star and a member of the NBA's All-Defensive Team in 1988, Lever, who finished his career with the Dallas Mavericks from 1990–94, averaged 13.9 points, 6.2 assists, and 6.0 rebounds by the time he called it quits. He added averages of 12.4 points, 6.2 assists, and 5.8 rebounds per game in forty-eight career playoff contests.

RIGHT: FOR A GUARD, LAFAYETTE "FAT" LEVER WAS A TREMENDOUS REBOUNDER.

FREDDIE LEWIS

Often under-appreciated by the hometown fans and underestimated by the opposition, Freddie Lewis had enough talent and floor leadership to lead the Indiana Pacers of the ABA to three championships in the early 1970s.

Lewis, a 6-foot guard out of Arizona State, broke into professional basketball with Cincinnati of the NBA in the 1966–67 season. He received little playing time behind the great Oscar Robertson, but learned valuable lessons watching the future Hall-of-Famer perform.

The following season, Lewis was running the show in Indiana, and he responded by averaging 20.6 points per game.

In the 1968–69 campaign, Lewis tallied up avergaes of 20.3 points per game en route to leading the Pacers to their first of three ABA titles.

Often resembling a waterbug when he scurried around the hardwood dribbling a basketball, Lewis helped Indiana capture back-to-back championships in the 1971–72 and 1972–73 seasons.

Despite all the winning, Lewis was often booed by the Indiana fans, who would have rather been witness to the sight of home-grown products Billy Keller and Rick Mount running the club.

After seven seasons in Indiana, Lewis was traded to the Memphis Sounds. Ironically, he would finish his career with Indiana in the 1976–77 season. By then, the Pacers had joined the NBA.

A four-time All-Star, Lewis averaged 17.0 points in nine ABA seasons.

FACT FILE

Born: January 7, 1943
Height: 6' 0"
Length of ABA career:
   1967–76
Length of NBA career:
   1966–67, 1976–77
Major teams:
   Cincinnati
   Indiana (joined 1967)
   Memphis (joined 1974)
   St. Louis (joined 1975)
   Indiana (joined 1976)
Records/Awards:
   ABA Championship (3)
   ABA All-Star (4)

LEFT: OFTEN UNDER APPRECIATED BY HOMETOWN FANS, FREDDIE LEWIS LEAD THE PACERS TO THREE ABA TITLES IN THE EARLY 1970S.

OLYMPIC SHOCK

Three of the most bizarre seconds in the history of sport cost the 1972 United States Olympic basketball team a gold it thought it had won—twice.

The incident occurred in the Olympic Final between the U.S. and the Soviet Union. The American team, a heavy favorite, had entered the contest without a basketball loss in thirty-six years of Olympic competition.

With three seconds left in the contest, the American squad, which had trailed throughout the contest, took its first lead of the evening, 50–49, on a pair of free throws by Doug Collins.

From there, things got downright weird, if not suspicious. In the final three seconds, the Soviets would get three opportunities to win the contest. The first play, an inbounds pass, was deflected at mid-court. Thinking the Americans had won the gold medal by a single point, a crowd rushed onto the court in celebration. Officials working the game, however, ruled that one second was still left on the game clock, and ordered the court cleared and play resumed.

Once again, the Soviet squad attempted to put the ball in play. With the 6-foot-11-inch American Tom McMillan waving his arms to protect against an inbounds pass, a Soviet player tossed in a pass that fell short of a receiver. The final horn sounded, and once again, players and fans joined at midcourt, hugging and celebrating their apparent come-from-behind victory.

This time, officials working the game ruled that the game clock had not been reset. To add insult to injury, play was not only ordered to resume, but three seconds, not one, were put back onto the game clock, setting the stage for the darkest moment in U.S. Olympic history.

McMillan, whose sole task it was to interrupt the inbounds pass, was told to back off of his pressure-position by a referee. When he stepped back, a Soviet player wound up and threw a baseball pass the length of the court to a streaking Aleksander Belov, a muscular, 6-foot-8-inch player.

As Belov ran under the ball, he was met by the American players Kevin Joyce, 6 feet 3 inches in height, and Robert Forbes, a sinewy 6-foot-7-inch player.

As all three players went up for the ball, the two Americans were knocked off balance by Belov, who caught the pass and found himself wide open for an easy layup that gave the Soviet squad a 51–50 victory. Replays of the game-winning play showed the Soviets were guilty of two violations. First, the passer had stepped on the baseline while making his pass, which should have negated the play. Second, Belov had stationed himself in the lane much longer than the three-second lane violation rule permits.

The Americans immediately protested the game, and some players lingered at courtside some four hours after the game, awaiting some word of their protest.

When the International Amateur Basketball Federation upheld the Soviet victory, the American players refused to accept the silver medal.

ALTON LISTER

FACT FILE

Born: October 1, 1958
Height: 7′ 0″
Length of NBA career:
   1981–93, 1994–present
Major teams:
   Milwaukee
   Seattle (joined 1986)
   Golden State (joined
    1989)
   Milwaukee (joined 1994)
   Boston (joined 1995)
Records/Awards:
   US Olympic Team (1980)

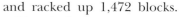

A 7-foot defensive specialist out of Arizona State, Alton Lister has played fifteen seasons in the NBA.

Selected by Milwaukee in the first round of the 1981 NBA Draft, Lister played his first five seasons with the Bucks before he was traded to Seattle in 1986 for Jack Sikma. He spent his last four NBA seasons with the Golden State, Milwaukee and Boston.

A center who also performed well at the power forward position, Lister adds a spark off the bench on both ends of the court. He has averaged 6.7 points in his career and racked up 1,472 blocks.

Lister's best season was with Seattle in 1986–87, when he averaged a career-high 11.6 points and 9.4 rebounds per game, and established a career-high 180 blocks. In eighty-five career playoff games, he averaged 7.2 points per contest.

At Arizona State, Lister's fine play helped earn him a spot on the 1980 US Olympic Basketball Team, but that was the year the US boycotted the Moscow Olympics. In his senior season at Arizona State, Lister posted 15.4 points per contest.

RIGHT: SEVEN-FOOT ALTON LISTER, LEFT, PLAYING HIS SPECIAL BRAND OF TOUGH DEFENSE.

A pure-shooter who spent eight fine seasons with poor Detroit teams from 1978–86, John Long was brought back by the Pistons in 1989 to help them capture a world championship.

A 6-foot-5-inch shooting guard out of the University of Detroit, Long was selected by the Motor City's Pistons in the second round of the 1978 NBA draft.

As a rookie at Detroit, Long averaged 16.1 points per game, starting a streak of ten straight seasons in which he would average double digits in scoring. He teamed in the Piston backcourt with Isiah Thomas and Terry Tyler to form an explosive scoring combination.

John Long, whose professional career overlapped with the career of his nephew, Grant Long, enjoyed his best season with the Pistons in 1981–82, when he posted a career-high 21.9 points per game.

After spending two and a half seasons with the Indiana Pacers, Long was reunited with Thomas and the Pistons in 1989. He averaged 5.5 points that season, ending his string of double-digit scoring seasons, but helping his old mates win the first of two straight championships. Long moved on to Atlanta for one season before coming back for a third tour of duty with Detroit in 1991. After a five year absence from the NBA, Long returned to the league as a member of the Toronto Raptors, averaging 4.0 points and 1.3 rebounds per game.

In his career, Long has averaged 13.6 points and 2.8 rebounds per game.

FACT FILE

Born: August 28, 1956
Height: 6' 5"
Length of NBA career:
  1978–91
  1996–present
Major teams:
  Detroit
  Indiana (joined 1986)
  Detroit (joined 1989)
  Atlanta (joined 1990)
  Detroit (joined 1991)
  Toronto (joined 1996)
Records/Awards:
  NBA Championship (1)

LEFT: JOHN LONG, AN AWESOME SHOOTER WHO PLAYED ON A NUMBER OF POOR TEAMS, WAS STILL IN THE NBA WHEN HIS NEPHEW, GRANT LONG, JOINED THE LEAGUE.

LUC LONGLEY

FACT FILE

Born: January 19, 1969
Height: 7′ 2″
Length of NBA career:
   1991–present
Major teams:
   Minnesota
   Chicago (1994-present)
Records/Awards:
   NBA Championship (1)

The first Australian ever to play in the NBA, Luc Longley was a key member of the 1995-96 Chicago Bulls' team that set the league mark for best-ever regular-season record (72-10), helping Michael Jordan and company at the Bulls sail on to championship glory.

Longley, at 7-feet-2-inches in height, was the focal point of Chicago's three-center alignment the entire season, finishing with averages of 9.1 points, 5.1 rebounds and 84 blocked shots.

The red-headed "Wonder from Down Under", as Longley is sometimes called, started in all eighteen playoff games for the Bulls, averaging 8.3 points and 4.6 rebounds.

With an honorable mention All-America following his junior season at University of New Mexico, Longley was drafted by the Minnesota Timberwolves in the first round (seventh overall) of the 1991 NBA draft.

Midway through the 1993-94 season, Longley was traded by Minnesota to Chicago for Stacey King. At the Bulls Longley has been a mainstay, and a Chicago fan-favorite, ever since.

A member of Australia's 1988 and 1992 Olympic Basketball team, Longley says that if not for professional basketball, he would have become a marine biologist.

Through his first five professional seasons, Longley averaged 6.5 points and 4.8 rebounds per game, adding averages of 7.1 points and 4.2 boards in 38 career playoff contests. Longley's contributions to the Bulls is helping to open the door for other basketball players from Australia wanting to be noticed by colleges and professional teams in the United States.

RIGHT: LUC LONGLEY, THE WONDER FROM DOWN UNDER, IS THE FIRST AUSTRALIAN TO PLAY IN THE NBA.

JIM LOSCUTOFF

One of the most underrated Boston Celtics in the history of the fabled franchise, Jim Loscutoff helped the green machine win seven championships during his career.

Loscutoff, a muscular 6-foot-5-inch, 230-pound forward, added strength, hustle, and overall chemistry to a Boston lineup that featured better-known stars like Bill Russell, Tom Heinsohn, Bob Cousy, and Bill Sharman.

"Jungle Jim," as the feisty Loscutoff was known to his teammates, starred at Oregon before breaking into the NBA with the Celtics in the 1955–56 season.

After averaging 8.3 points per game in his rookie season, Loscutoff posted a career high 10.6 points per contest the following year, help-ing his more-publicized teammates win the title.

Loscutoff, who played his entire nine-year career in a Celtic uniform, would win six straight championships with Boston from 1958 until he retired in 1964, making room on the roster for up-and-coming stars like John Havlicek.

For his career, Loscutoff averaged 6.2 points and 5.4 rebounds. He added 5.5 points and 5.1 rebounds in 58 career playoff contests.

Every successful team in the history of the NBA, or any other sport, had a role player who took with him onto the court many of the important intangibles that often did not surface in the box scores, but made the difference in the overall balance of their teams' attack. Jim Loscutoff, never an All-Star, was one of those players.

FACT FILE

Born: February 4, 1930
Height: 6' 5"
Length of NBA career:
  1955–64
Major team:
  Boston
Records/Awards:
  NBA Championship (7)

LEFT: DURING BOSTON'S GLORY YEARS, "JUNGLE" JIM LOSCUTOFF WAS THE BRAWN BEHIND THE CELTICS' BRAINS.

KEVIN LOUGHERY

FACT FILE

Born: March 28, 1940
Height: 6′ 3″
Length of NBA career:
1962–72
Major teams:
Detroit
Baltimore (joined 1964)

One of many outstanding guards who went from the playgrounds of New York City to the pro ranks, Kevin Loughery enjoyed an outstanding ten-year career in the NBA before moving on to a twenty-three year career as a coach.

Loughery, a 6-foot-3-inch sharpshooter who played his schoolboy hoops in the Bronx, NY, split his college playing days between St. John's University and Boston College.

A hard-working, aggressive performer, Loughery was selected by the Detroit Pistons in the second round of the 1962 NBA draft. He averaged 6.4 points per game for the Pistons as a rookie before being traded to the Baltimore Bullets midway through his second season.

In 1964–65, his first full season in Baltimore, Loughery posted 12.8 points per game, starting a streak of eight straight seasons in which he would average double digits in scoring. His best season for the Bullets came in 1968–69, when he finished with a career-high 22.6 points per contest.

The season before, Earl Monroe, a flashy guard out of Winston-Salem State, had joined Loughery in Baltimore's backcourt. Together, Loughery and Monroe formed a dynamic duo. They combined for 48.4 points per game in 1968–69, 45.4 points in 1969–70, and 36.5 points in 1970–71.

For his career, Loughery averaged 15.4 points per game, adding 12.4 points in 43 career playoff contests.

RIGHT: KEVIN LOUGHERY WAS AN OUTSTANDING PLAYER BEFORE HE PICKED UP A CLIPBOARD AND BECAME AN OUTSTANDING COACH.

BOB LOVE

A slender forward who led the Chicago Bulls in scoring seven straight seasons beginning in 1969–70, Bob Love retired as the number two scorer in club history with 12,623 points, second in that department to none other than Michael Jordan.

Love, who played his college ball at Southern University, averaged 21.9 points per game in nine seasons with the Bulls. He began his NBA career with Cincinnati, averaging 6.7 points per game as a rookie with the Royals. After two seasons in Cincinnati, Love split the 1968–69 campaign with Milwaukee and Chicago, completing his first three seasons with a scoring average of fewer than 7 points.

In his first full season with the Bulls, however, Love's talents were discovered by coach Dick Motta and he soon blossomed into a star.

"Butterbean," as Love was called in his playing days, averaged 21.0 points per game in 1969–70, the first of six straight seasons in which he would average 20 points or better. His best season came in 1971–72, when he posted a career-high 25.8 points and ripped down 6.5 boards per contest.

"I'm striving for recognition," Love said earlier in his career. "On the basketball floor, I don't intend to have anyone show me up."

A three-time All-Star, Love averaged 17.6 points and 5.8 rebounds in 11 NBA seasons, the last of which was spent with Chicago, the New York Nets, and the Seattle SuperSonics. In forty-seven career playoff games, Love averaged 22.9 points per contest.

FACT FILE

Born: December 8, 1942
Height: 6′ 8″
Length of NBA career:
1966–77
Major teams:
Cincinnati
Chicago (joined 1969)
New York Nets (joined 1976
Seattle (joined 1977)
Records/wards:
NBA All-Star (3)

LEFT: BOB LOVE IS THE GREATEST SCORER IN CHICAGO BULLS' HISTORY NOT NAMED MICHAEL JORDAN.

CLYDE LOVELLETTE

FACT FILE

Born: September 7, 1929
Height: 6′ 9″
Length of NBA career:
    1953–64
Major teams:
    Minneapolis
    Cincinnati (joined 1957)
    St. Louis (joined 1958)
    Boston (joined 1962)
Records/Awards:
    Olympic Gold Medal
        (1952)
    NBA Championship (3)
    NBA All-Star (3)

Clyde Lovellette was an All-American center at Kansas, a member of the 1952 United States Olympic basketball team, which won the gold medal, and a member of the 1954 Minneapolis Lakers and the 1963 and 1964 Boston Celtics, who won NBA Championships.

Lovellette, a 6-foot-9-inch center with a feathery shot who broke into the NBA with Minneapolis in 1953, was an understudy to George Mikan for two seasons before taking over for the legendary pivotman.

Lovellette spent four outstanding seasons in Minneapolis, teaming with Mikan in his rookie campaign to help the Lakers defeat Syracuse in seven games for the championship. After one season in Cincinnati—he averaged a career-high 23.4 points per game for the Royals in 1958–59—and four more in St. Louis, Lovellette hooked up with the Celtics during the Bill Russell dynasty years. At Boston, he averaged 6.5 points and 6.7 points in his two seasons with the team, picking up a pair of championship rings.

A three-time All-Star, Lovellette averaged 17.0 points per game in eleven NBA seasons, adding 14.0 points per contest in sixty-nine career playoff games. At Kansas, Lovellette had a record-breaking career. He led the Jayhawks to the 1952 NCAA title, scoring a game-high 33 points in a 80–63 victory over St. John's in the championship game.

RIGHT: CLYDE LOVELLETTE, GOING STRONG TO THE GLASS HERE, WAS A UNDERSTUDY TO GEORGE MIKAN BEFORE TAKING OVER FOR THE LEGENDARY PIVOT MAN.

Jerry Ray Lucas

If ever an NBA player deserved to wear a championship ring, it was Jerry "Ray" Lucas, who had to wait ten long years before winning a title with the New York Knicks in 1972–73, his last season in the league.

The 6-foot-8-inch Lucas, a forward who sometimes played center, was one of the better scorers and rebounders in the history of the game. Lucas had a brilliant career at Ohio State before he was selected by the Cincinnati Royals as a territorial pick in the 1962 NBA draft. He won the Rookie of the Year Award with the Royals in 1963–64 on the strength of 17.7 points and a whopping 17.4 rebounds per game.

Incredibly, Lucas's scoring and rebounding numbers grew the next two seasons. He averaged 21.4 points and 20 rebounds in 1964–65, and a career-high 21.5 points and 21.1 boards in 1965–66. A seven-time All-Star, Lucas was dealt to San Francisco midway through the 1969–70 season, and in 1971, the Warriors traded him to the Knicks for forward Cazzie Russell.

In his two seasons in New York, Lucas played extremely well. He racked up averages of 16.7 points and 13.1 rebounds per game in 1971–72, and 9.9 points and 7.2 rebounds per contest during the Knicks' championship campaign. These were also the final two seasons of his NBA career.

At Ohio State, Lucas averaged 24.3 points and 17.2 rebounds in three seasons. As a sophomore in 1960, he scored 26.3 points per game in leading the Buckeyes to an NCAA championship. That same season, Lucas was also a member of the gold-medal winning US Olympic basketball team.

BELOW: JERRY LUCAS WAITED A DECADE BEFORE FINALLY WINNING A TITLE WITH THE NEW YORK KNICKS IN 1972–73.

FACT FILE

Born: March 30, 1940
Height: 6' 8"
Length of NBA career:
  1963–73
Major teams:
  Cincinnati
  San Francisco (joined 1969)
  New York Knicks (joined 1971)
Records/Awards:
  NBA Championship (1)
  NBA All-Star (7)
  NBA Rookie of the Year (1964)
  Olympic Gold (1960)
  Hall of Fame (1979)

JOHN LUCAS

FACT FILE

Born: October 31, 1953
Height: 6′ 3″
Length of NBA career:
  1976–90
Major teams:
  Houston
  Golden State (joined
  1978)
  Washington (joined 1981)
  San Antonio (joined 1983)
  Houston (joined 1984)
  Milwaukee (joined 1987)
  Seattle (joined 1988)
  Houston (joined 1989)

One of the smartest point guards ever to step onto a basketball court, John Lucas, not nearly the six-feet-three-inches he's listed at, stood tall for fourteen NBA seasons.

Despite battling drug problems throughout most of his career, Lucas, blessed with tremendous athleticism, always managed to keep his act together on the hardwood. A standout at the University of Maryland, he was selected by the Houston Rockets, as the first overall pick in the 1976 NBA draft.

It didn't take long for Lucas to assert himself at the pro level. He earned a spot on the All-Rookie Team by averaging 11.1 points and 5.6 assists per game in his first season with the Rockets. After two years in Houston, Lucas was traded to Golden State, and his first season with the Warriors was one of his best, as he averaged 16.1 points and 9.2 assists per game.

Lucas's NBA journey would take him through Washington, San Antonio, back to Houston, Milwaukee, Seattle, and back to Houston for a third stint to complete his final season in 1989–90. His best year was 1986–87, when he averaged a career-high 17.5 points and 6.7 assists per game for Milwaukee.

For his career, Lucas averaged 10.7 points and 6.9 assists, adding 11.2 points in forty-five playoff games.

Lucas once compared the game of basketball to the game of life: "Basketball is a game of ego," he said. "You have to go out on the court thinking that you're going to destroy that person who's guarding you. And the way a guy plays is usually the way he lives. If he runs up and down the floor making blind passes, he's probably a happy-go-lucky type, always taking chances and defying you to say he's wrong.

"But if he's fundamentally sound, working to run the game the way it is supposed to be, then he won't take any risks. Not on the court and not in his life."

RIGHT: JOHN LUCAS, LOOKING FOR AN OPEN TEAMMATE HERE, WAS AN EXTREMELY SMART AND TALENTED POINT GUARD WHO HAD A HISTORY OF DRUG TROUBLES.

MAURICE LUCAS

The term "power forward" emerged to describe the style of strong, physical, and powerful frontcourt players such as Maurice Lucas, who convinced observers of the game that basketball was still very much a contact sport.

A self-described "aggressive, physical" player, the 6-foot-9-inch Lucas played with a fierceness and intensity rarely found on basketball courts. After starring at Marquette, Lucas broke into the professional ranks with St. Louis of the ABA, averaging 13.2 points and 10.1 rebounds per game.

The following season, Lucas improved significantly, finishing second in the ABA in rebounding with an 11.3 average, and was chosen by Portland in the dispersal draft when the league was absorbed by the NBA in 1976.

In his first season with Portland, Lucas averaged 20.2 points and 11.3 rebounds, teaming with star center Bill Walton to form a rock-solid, super-talented, one-two punch that led the Trail Blazers to the world championship.

A five-time All-Star, Lucas played 12 professional seasons, the last ten of which he spent in the NBA glaring at opposing players or protecting his domain with a shove. He averaged 16.4 points and 10.7 boards in the ABA, adding 16.4 points in 20 playoff games. In addition, Lucas posted 15.8 points and 9.5 rebounds during his NBA tenure, posting 16.4 points in sixty-four career playoff games.

At Marquette, Lucas averaged 15.7 points in three seasons.

FACT FILE

Born: February 18, 1952
Height: 6' 9"
Length of ABA career:
  1974–76
Length of NBA career:
  1978–87
Major teams:
  St. Louis
  Kentucky (joined 1975)
  Portland (joined 1976)
  New Jersey (joined 1980)
  Phoenix (joined 1982)
  L.A. Lakers (joined 1985)
  Seattle (joined 1986)
Records/Awards:
  ABA All-Star (1)
  NBA Championship (1)
  NBA All-Star (4)
  NBA All-Defensive First
    Team (1)

LEFT: MAURICE LUCAS, A PHYSICAL PRESENCE ON THE BASKETBALL COURT, DEFENDING HERE AGAINST HAKEEM OLAJUWON.

ED MACAULEY

FACT FILE

Born: March 22, 1928
Height: 6′ 8″
Length of BAA career:
  1949–50
Length of NBA career:
  1950–59
Major teams:
  St. Louis
  Boston (joined 1950)
  St. Louis (joined 1956)
Records/Awards:
  NBA Championship (1)
  NBA All-Star (7)
  Hall of Fame (1960)

One of the great big men of the 1950s, Ed Macauley, a hero in his hometown of St. Louis, helped the Hawks win the 1958 NBA Championship.

"Easy Ed," as the 6-foot-8-inch Macauley was called in his playing days, was an All-American at the University of St. Louis before he was selected by the St. Louis Bombers in the 1949 Basketball Association of America draft.

Macauley, who played both center and forward, averaged 16.1 points in his rookie season with the Bombers before he was selected by the Boston Celtics in the NBA Dispersal draft of 1950. He enjoyed a full six tremendous scoring and rebounding seasons with the Celtics, and was named to the All-Star squad in each of those years.

A three-time All-NBA First-Team Selection, Macauley topped the 20-point barrier twice with the Celtics, a major accomplishment in that era considering that the 24-second shot clock had not yet been invented. He averaged 20.4 points per game for Boston in the 1950–51 season, and 20.3 points in 1952–53. Also that same season, Macauley scored a career-high 46 points in one contest against the Minneapolis Lakers' legendary center, George Mikan.

In the 1956–57 campaign, Macauley was traded back home to the St. Louis Hawks. In his second season with the Hawks, which turned out to be his last year in the NBA Macauley teamed with St. Louis greats Bob Pettit and Cliff Hagan to defeat Boston in six games for the championship.

For his career, Macauley averaged 17.5 points per game, adding 13.8 points in forty-seven career playoff games.

RIGHT: ED MACAULEY WAS ONE OF THE GREAT BIG MEN OF THE 1950s, JUST ASK GEORGE MIKAN.

RICK MAHORN

The key to Rick Mahorn's success the past sixteen seasons has been his willingness to play the role of enforcer on the basketball court, and not be afraid to take his lumps in return.

Mahorn, a 6-foot-10-inch forward out of Division II's Hampton Institute, was selected by the Washington Bullets in the second round of the 1980 NBA draft.

In 1981–82, his second year with the Bullets, Mahorn averaged a career-high 12.2 points per game and hauled down 8.8 rebounds per contest. The following season, Mahorn posted 11.0 points per game and ripped down a career-best 9.5 rebounds per contest.

After five seasons in Washington, Mahorn was traded to Detroit, and his physical style of play fitted perfectly into the Pistons' Bad-Boy brand of basketball, which roughed up and intimidated opponents on the defensive end of the court. Mahorn's best season in Detroit was 1987–88, when he finished with averages of 10.7 points and 8.4 rebounds. The following season, Mahorn's last in Detroit, he teamed with other talented bullies like Dennis Rodman, Bill Laimbeer, and Isiah Thomas to help the Pistons capture the first of back-to-back championships.

After playing two seasons in Philadelphia, Mahorn played for Il Messaggero Roma and Virtus Roma of the Italian league before coming back to the NBA with the New Jersey Nets, where he played for four years before re-signing with Detroit in 1996.

Through sixteen NBA seasons, Mahorn has averaged 7.3 points and 6.5 rebounds per game, adding 6.0 points and 5.7 boards in 101 career playoff games.

At Hampton, Mahorn led all Division II players with 15.8 rebounds per game in 1980.

FACT FILE

Born: September 21, 1958
Height: 6′ 10″
Length of NBA career:
   1980–91, 1992–present
Major teams:
   Washington
   Detroit (joined 1985)
   Philadelphia (joined 1989)
   New Jersey (joined 1992)
   Detroit (joined 1996)
Records/Awards:
   NBA Championship (1)

LEFT: RICK MAHORN, WHO PLAYED DIVISION II COLLEGE BASKETBALL, BECAME A ROCK-SOLID PRO.

DAN MAJERLE

FACT FILE

Born: September 9, 1965
Height: 6′ 6″
Length of NBA career:
  1988–present
Major teams:
  Phoenix
  Cleveland (joined 1995)
  Miami (joined 1996)
Records/Awards:
  NBA All-Star (3)

One of the NBA's deadliest three-point threats, Dan Majerle has averaged double digits in scoring for eight straight seasons.

Majerle, a 6-foot-6-inch super leaper who explodes in the open court, was selected by the Phoenix Suns out of Central Michigan in the first round of the 1988 NBA draft.

"Thunder Dan," as the super-leaping, long-bombing Majerle is known around the league, had his best years in Phoenix. He averaged 14.3 points and 4.8 rebounds as a rookie, and in 1991–92, enjoyed career-highs in scoring, 17.3 points per game, and rebounding, 5.9 per game.

The following season, Majerle, teaming with Kevin Johnson and newcomer Charles Barkley, helped lead the Suns to the NBA Finals, which was won by Michael Jordan and the Chicago Bulls. In that series, Majerle tied a record for most three-point field goals made with 17.

After seven seasons in Phoenix, Majerle was traded to Cleveland. He posted averages of 10.6 points and 3.7 rebounds for the Cavaliers in 1995–96, helping the club reach the first round of the playoffs.

A three-time All-Star and two-time All-Defensive Second Team selection, Majerle was signed as a free agent by Miami Heat in 1996.

Through nine NBA seasons, Majerle has averaged 13.9 points, 4.8 rebounds, and 3.2 assists. In 103 career playoff games, he has registered averages of 12.7 points, 4.8 rebounds, and 2.5 assists. He once held the single-game playoff record for most three-point field goals made, connecting on 8 trifectas against Seattle on June 1, 1993.

Majerle, who averaged 21.8 points in four seasons at Central Michigan, was a member of the 1988 bronze-medal winning US Olympic Basketball Team.

RIGHT: DAN MAJERLE IS BOTTLED UP AT THE MOMENT, BUT IT WON'T BE LONG BEFORE HE IS EXPLODING IN THE OPEN COURT.

JEFF MALONE

For the past thirteen seasons, Jeff Malone has been one of the most underrated shooting guards in the NBA. While shooting guards like Reggie Miller and Michael Jordan have received most of the publicity in recent years, Malone has been quite an effective shooter playing in their shadows.

A standout at Mississippi State, Malone was selected by the Washington Bullets in the first round of the 1983 NBA draft. He earned a place on the All-Rookie team by averaging 12.1 points per game in 1983–84, starting a streak of twelve straight seasons in which he would average double figures in scoring.

Twice during his seven-year stint in Washington, Malone, who loves to shoot off of screens, was voted onto the All-Star team. His best seasons in a Bullets' uniform were 1985–86, when he averaged 22.4 points per game, and 1989–90, when he posted a career-high 24.3 points per contest.

The following season, Malone was traded by Washington to the Utah Jazz. The benefactor of Karl Malone screens and pinpoint passes from John Stockton, Malone averaged 18.6, 20.2, and 18.1 points in three straight seasons for the Jazz before he was traded to Philadelphia midway through the 1993–94 season.

He played with the 76ers until joining the Miami Heat late last season.

For his career, Malone has averaged 19.0 points, 2.6 rebounds, and 2.4 assists, adding 18.7 points, 2.8 boards, and 2.2 assists in 51 career playoff games.

FACT FILE

Born: June 28, 1961
Height: 6′ 4″
Length of NBA career:
1983–present
Major teams:
  Washington
  Utah (joined 1990)
  Philadelphia (joined 1994)
  Miami (joined 1996)
Records/Awards:
  NBA All-Star (2)

LEFT: WHILE OTHER SHOOTING GUARDS GET MORE INK, JEFF MALONE JUST KEEPS MAKING BASKETS.

REMEMBERING THE ABA

A red, white, and blue basketball. A three-point shot. A no-foul out rule. Those were just some of the gimmicks that helped keep the American Basketball Association in business from 1967 until 1976, when the league folded, and four of its teams—Indiana, Denver, New York, and San Antonio—merged with the National Basketball Association.

ABA alumni made a tremendous impact in the NBA. In the first seven seasons following the merger, former ABA star Moses Malone won three NBA Most Valuable Player awards, and Julius Erving, the ABA's version of Michael Jordan, won yet another.

George "Iceman" Gervin, a scoring machine in the ABA, lit up NBA scoreboards to win four scoring titles in five seasons. Gervin, David Thompson, and Erving (twice), each were named All-Star game MVPs.

In six of those first seven seasons since the merger, at least two former ABA players each year were named to the All-NBA First Team, and forty-eight percent of the players who were selected to the All-Defensive First Team were ABA graduates.

Some of the shiniest ABA stars to sparkle in the NBA galaxy were players like George McGinnis, Mel Daniels, Roger Brown, Rick Barry, Artis Gilmore, Bobby Jones, Dan Issel, Connie Hawkins, Charlie Scott, and Maurice Lucas.

Before the merger, both leagues competed for the services of many players, and the competition got so ugly at times that it needed to be settled in another court—the court of law.

Nevertheless, the ABA rolled on for nine seasons. During that time, the Indiana Pacers were the class of the league, making five appearances in the Finals. The Pacers won titles in 1970, 1972, and 1973, and lost in the 1969 and 1975 championship series.

The New York Nets, led by Erving, defeated David Thompson's Denver Nuggets in six games to capture the ninth and final ABA championship.

"Some of the greatest players in the history of professional basketball played in the ABA," said Moses Malone, who played with Utah and St. Louis in the ABA, and was the league's last surviving member before retiring after the 1994–95 season.

"That league was filled with so many great memories," Malone added. "It's a shame it had to come to an end."

KARL MALONE

FACT FILE

Born: July 24, 1963
Height: 6′ 9″
Length of NBA career:
  1985–present
Major team:
  Utah
Records/Awards:
  NBA All-Star (10)
  Olympic Gold Medal (2)
    (1992, 1996)

They call him the "Mailman" simply because Karl Malone delivers. Malone, a 6-foot-9-inch power forward, is one of the best ever to come along at his position, bringing speed, strength, and a nice outside shooting touch onto the floor.

He has teamed with John Stockton for each of his twelve seasons in the league to form one of the most potent one-two punches in the history of the game.

A gold-medal winner on both the 1992 and 1996 US Olympic basketball teams, Malone has put together Hall-of-Fame numbers since joining the Jazz as a first round draft pick out of Louisiana Tech in the 1985 NBA draft.

In twelve seasons, Malone has averaged 26.1 points, 10.8 rebounds, and 3.2 assists per game, adding 27.1 points, 11.4 boards, and 2.8 assists in 117 career playoff games. He holds the career record for most consecutive seasons with 2,000 or more points, pulling off that feat ten straight times between the 1987–88 and 1996–97 seasons. He also shares the career record for most seasons with 2,000 or more points.

A ten-time All-Star and nine-time All-NBA First Team Selection, Malone, who helped Utah get to the Finals last season, enjoyed his best year in 1989–90, when he averaged a career-high 31.0 points, adding 11.1 rebounds and 2.8 assists.

The MVP of the 1989 All-Star game and co-MVP of the 1993 All-Star contest, Malone also shares the single-game playoff record for most free-throws made in one half, connecting on 19 attempts from the charity stripe on May 9, 1991, against Portland.

RIGHT: KARL "MAILMAN" MALONE ABOUT TO DELIVER AT THE EXPENSE OF FRANK BRICKOWSKI.

MOSES MALONE

A dinosaur in tank top and shorts, Moses Malone was the last player of the old ABA to play in the NBA. He played professionally for twenty-one seasons before injuries and Father Time forced him out of the game.

Malone, an offensive rebounding machine and extremely tough inside player, teamed in his prime with stars like Julius Erving and Bobby Jones on the Philadelphia 76ers, and it was Moses who led that group of stellar players to a world championship in 1983.

One of only five players in NBA history to leap from high school to the professional ranks, Malone holds scores of combined ABA and NBA records. He holds the career record for most consecutive games without a disqualification (1,212), most free throws made (8,531), and most offensive rebounds (6,731). He also holds the single-season record for most offensive rebounds (587 in 1979), and the single-game record for most offensive rebounds (21 on February 11, 1982, against Seattle).

A three-time NBA Most Valuable Player and twelve-time All-Star, Malone broke into professional basketball with the Utah Stars of the ABA, averaging an eye-opening 18.8 points and 14.6 rebounds per contest and earning a spot in the league's All-Star game. The following season, his last in the ABA, Malone was sold to the Spirits of St. Louis, and finished the year with averages of 14.3 points and 9.6 rebounds.

After the ABA closed shop in 1976, Malone jumped to the NBA, splitting his rookie year between Buffalo and Houston. He hauled down 437 offensive boards that season, beginning a streak of seven straight seasons in which he would lead the league in that department.

A future Hall-of-Famer without question, Malone averaged 20.6 points, 12.2 rebounds, 1.4 assists, and racked up 1,733 blocks in his legendary NBA career, adding 22.1 points and 13.8 rebounds in 94 career playoff games. He was voted MVP of the 1983 Finals, in which Philadelphia swept Los Angeles in four straight games, outscoring Kareem Abdul-Jabbar of the Lakers, 103–94, and overwhelming Jabbar on the boards, 72–30.

FACT FILE

Born: March 23, 1955
Height: 6′ 10″
Length of ABA career: 1974–76
Length of NBA career: 1976–95
Major teams:
 Utah
 St. Louis (joined 1975)
 Buffalo (joined 1976)
 Houston (joined 1976)
 Philadelphia (joined 1982)
 Washington (joined 1986)
 Atlanta (joined 1988)
 Milwaukee (joined 1991)
 Philadelphia (joined 1993)
 San Antonio (joined 1994)
Records/Awards:
 ABA All-Star (1)
 NBA All-Star (1)
 NBA All-Star (12)
 NBA Most Valuable Player (3)
 NBA Championship (1)
 NBA All-Defensive First Team (1)

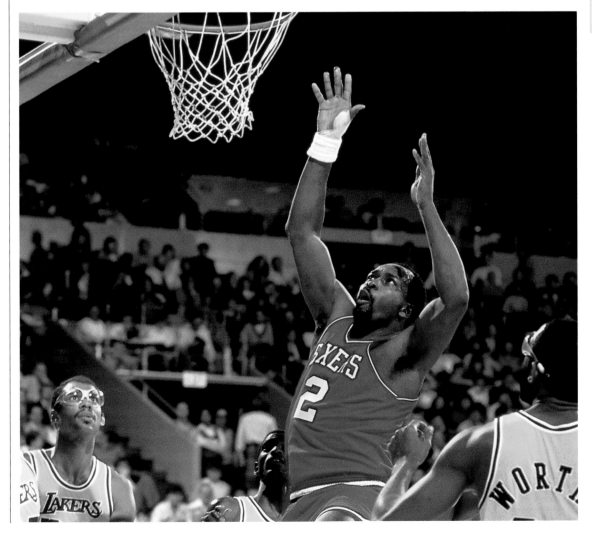

LEFT: FOR THE BETTER PART OF TWENTY-ONE SEASONS, MOSES MALONE WAS A DOMINANT FIXTURE IN PROFESSIONAL BASKETBALL.

DANNY MANNING

FACT FILE

Born: May 17,1966
Height: 6′ 10″
Length of NBA career:
  1988–present
Major teams:
  Los Angeles Clippers
  Atlanta (joined 1994)
  Phoenix (joined 1994)
Records/Awards:
  NBA All-Star (2)

Injuries have cut short three of Danny Manning's eight NBA seasons, but the 6-foot-10-inch forward/center has still had enough time on the hardwood to prove that he is one of the most gifted all-around performers in the league today.

Manning, who led Kansas to an NCAA Championship in 1988, was selected by the Los Angeles Clippers as the first overall pick in the 1988 NBA draft. A knee injury limited Manning to just 26 games in his rookie campaign, but he bounced back strong in his second season, averaging 16.3 points,5.9 rebounds, and 2.6 assists per game.

A two-time All-Star, Manning, who can shoot, pass, and handle the basketball extremely well for a big man, played his first five and a half seasons with Los Angeles. He earned his first All-Star appearance in 1992–93, the year he averaged a career-high 22.8 points per contest, and added 6.6 rebounds and 2.6 assists per game as a member of the Clippers.

Midway through the 1993–94 season, Manning was traded to the Atlanta Hawks, and the following season, signed a free agent contract with the Phoenix Suns.

Unfortunately for Manning, a nagging knee injury and an assortment of other injuries forced him to miss parts of the 1994–95 and 1995–96 seasons.

Through his first eight NBA seasons, Manning averaged 18.4 points, 6.2 rebounds, and 3.0 assists per game. He has added 18.9 points, 6.1 rebounds, and 2.6 assists in twenty-five career playoff games.

RIGHT: DESPITE PLAYING IN CONSTANT PAIN, DANNY MANNING HAS PROVEN HIMSELF TO BE ONE OF THE GAME'S GREAT ALL-AROUND PLAYERS.

PETE MARAVICH

The greatest scorer in the history of college basketball, "Pistol Pete" Maravich gunned down NBA opponents for ten seasons, a decade of rapid-fire shooting highlighted by the scoring crown he won with the New Orleans Jazz in the 1976–77 season.

Maravich, a 6-foot-5-inch shooting guard with unlimited range and wizard-like ball-handling skills, was chosen out of Louisiana State by the Atlanta Hawks in the first round of the 1970 NBA draft.

At LSU, Maravich—who played under his father, Press Maravich—set scores of records, none more impressive than the career mark for most points scored, 3,667, and highest points-per-game average, a sizzling 44.2.

A five-time All-Star who liked to wear floppy socks on the basketball court, Maravich played four seasons with the Hawks before he was traded to New Orleans. He earned a place on the All-Rookie Team in 1970–71 after averaging 23.2 points per game, and went on to score 20 or more points in seven of his last nine seasons. In the 1976–77 campaign, Maravich won the NBA's scoring crown with an amazing average of 31.1 points per game, easily outdistancing Billy Knight of Indiana, who averaged 26.6 points per game that season.

For his career, which ended with a short stint on the Boston Celtics in 1980, Maravich averaged 24.2 points, 5.4 assists, and 4.2 rebounds. He added 18.7 points, 3.8 assists, and 3.7 rebounds in 26 career playoff games.

FACT FILE

Born: June 22, 1947
Height: 6′ 5″
Length of NBA career:
1970–80
Major teams:
  Atlanta
  New Orleans (joined 1974)
  Boston (joined 1980)
Records/Awards:
  NBA All-Star (5)
  Hall of Fame (1986)

LEFT: THE GREATEST SCORER IN THE HISTORY OF COLLEGE BASKETBALL, "PISTOL" PETE MARAVICH CONTINUED TO ROLL UP BIG NUMBERS ON THE PRO LEVEL.

STEPHON MARBURY

FACT FILE

Born: February 20, 1977
Height: 6′ 2″
Length of NBA career:
1996–present
Major team:
Minnesota

The latest in a long line of New York City point guards who made it to the NBA, Stephon Marbury played just one season of college basketball at Georgia Tech before making his leap to the big show.

Marbury, a 6-foot-2-inch play-maker with super leaping ability and dizzying ball-handling skills, was selected by the Milwaukee Bucks in the first round of the 1996 NBA draft. He wore a Bucks cap for about thirty minutes on draft night before he learned he had been traded to the Minnesota Timberwolves for the draft rights to the Connecticut guard Ray Allen.

The trade was fine with Marbury, who went off to play with close friend Kevin Garnett, one of only five players in NBA history never to have played college basketball. In his first NBA season, Marbury made the NBA's all-rookie first team, averaging 15.8 points, 7.8 assists, and 2.7 rebounds per game. Many basketball experts felt Marbury should have won the Rookie of the Year Award instead of Philadelphia's Allen Iverson.

At Georgia Tech, Marbury led the Yellow Jackets with 18.9 points per game, ranking him third overall in the ACC in scoring. He became the first freshman to lead Georgia Tech in scoring since Mark Price, scoring 20 or more points fifteen times in the 1995–96 season.

Marbury, who became a basketball prodigy at Brooklyn's Lincoln High School, was named to the ACC First Team as a freshman, becoming only the fifth freshman in ACC history to do so. The others were Antawn Jamison, Kenny Anderson, Joe Smith, and Skip Wise. At Lincoln, Marbury led his team to a 24–3 record, a Public School Athletic League Championship, and a New York State Federation "A" Division Championship, scoring 28 points in the championship contest.

RIGHT: THE MILWAUKEE BUCKS WILL PROBABLY REGRET TRADING STEPHON MARBURY'S DRAFT RIGHTS TO THE MINNESOTA TIMBERWOLVES.

SLATER MARTIN

One of the greatest small men ever to play the game, Slater Martin was a part of five championship teams in his eleven NBA seasons.

Martin, an All-American at the University of Texas in 1949, joined George Mikan and the Minneapolis Lakers that same season, forming the nucleus of a basketball dynasty.

As a rookie, the 5-foot-10-inch Martin shut down opposing guards with a suffocating brand of defense. On the offensive end, he averaged 4.0 points and 2.2 assists in helping Mikan and company defeat Syracuse for the NBA Championship.

"Dugie," as Martin was called in his playing days, increased his scoring average in each of the next three seasons, averaging 8.5 points per game in 1950–51, and 9.3 points per contest in 1951–52 en route to winning his second championship with the Lakers. For Martin and the Lakers, two more championships would follow in the next two seasons. He would spend seven seasons in Minneapolis—he averaged a career-high 13.6 points per game with the Lakers in the 1954–55 season—before joining St. Louis and helping that franchise to a world championship in 1958.

The 1958 championship season was Martin's best in a St. Louis uniform, as he averaged 12 points per game. A seven-time All-Star, Martin posted averages of 9.8 points and 4.2 assists throughout his Hall-of-Fame career. He added averages of 10.0 points and 3.8 assists in ninety-two career playoff games.

FACT FILE

Born: October 22, 1925
Height: 5′ 10″
Length of NBA career:
1949–60
Major teams:
Minneapolis
New York (joined 1956)
St. Louis (joined 1957)
Records/Awards:
NBA Championship (5)
NBA All-Star (7)
Hall of Fame (1981)

LEFT: THE DIMINUTIVE SLATER MARTIN, SEEN HERE IN HIS ST. LOUIS HAWKS UNIFORM, TEAMED WITH THE GIANT GEORGE MIKAN TO FORM A DYNASTY IN MINNEAPOLIS.

CEDRIC MAXWELL

FACT FILE

Born: November 21, 1955
Height: 6′ 8″
Length of NBA career:
1977–88
Major teams:
Boston
L.A. Clippers (joined 1985)
Houston (joined 1987)
Records/Awards:
NBA Championship (2)

Red Auerbach, president and general manager of the Boston Celtics, remembered the first time he saw Cedric Maxwell play.

"It was during the NIT at Madison Square Garden," said Auerbach. "His talent for dribbling caught my eye, behind his back and between his legs, an extraordinary feat for someone 6–8. He had great body control, quickness, and very fluid moves."

Maxwell, eventually selected by Auerbach out of North Carolina-Charlotte in the first round of the 1977 NBA draft, was instrumental in helping the Celtics win championships in 1981 and 1984.

A strong inside player with the ability to finish shots from all angles of the basketball court, Maxwell led the league in field-goal percentage in 1979 and 1980.

"Cornbread," as Maxwell was known to his teammates, averaged a career- high 19.0 points per game in 1978–79, connecting on 472 of 808 field goal attempts for 58 percent. The following season, Maxwell improved his field goal percentage to 60 percent, bagging 457 of 750 shots from the field while posting an average of 16.9 points per game.

In the 1981 championship series between Boston and Houston, the Rockets geared their defense to stop Larry Bird, Robert Parish, and Tiny Archibald, and that's when Maxwell took over offensively and on the boards at each end of the floor. He was named MVP of the playoffs.

Maxwell, who spent his first eight seasons with Boston and his last three years with the L.A. Clippers and Houston, averaged 12.5 points and 6.3 rebounds per game in his career, adding averages of 10.9 points and 5.2 rebounds in 102 career playoff games.

RIGHT: AS HE HAD DONE HIS WHOLE CAREER, CEDRIC MAXWELL GOES HARD TO THE TIN.

VERNON MAXWELL

A hot-tempered, high-scoring guard, Vernon Maxwell helped Hakeem Olajuwon and the Houston Rockets win back-to-back NBA Championships in 1994 and 1995.

"Mad Max," as the 6-foot-4-inch Maxwell is sometimes called, broke into the NBA with the San Antonio Spurs in 1988, averaging 11.7 points, 3.8 assists, and 2.6 rebounds per game. He split his second season between San Antonio and Houston, averaging a career-low 9.0 points per game.

In his first full season with the Rockets, however, Maxwell bounced back in a big way, averaging 17.0 points per game, which started a streak of seven straight seasons in which he would average double digits in scoring.

Maxwell, who averaged a career-high 17.2 points per game for the Rockets in 1991–92, was a major reason why Houston stormed through the 1994 NBA Playoffs, eventually defeating the New York Knicks in seven games to capture the championship. In 23 post-season games, Maxwell averaged 13.8 points, 4.2 assists, and 3.5 rebounds.

After five and a half seasons in Houston, Maxwell was signed by the Philadelphia 76ers as a free agent and enjoyed one of his best seasons in the league, averaging 16.2 points, 4.4 assists, and 3.1 rebounds per game. After that season, he signed as a free agent with the San Antonio Spurs in 1996.

Through his first nine NBA seasons, Maxwell averaged 13.9 points per game, adding 14.6 points in 40 career playoff contests.

At The University of Florida, Maxwell averaged 18.8 points, 3.0 assists, and 3.7 rebounds in four seasons.

FACT FILE

Born: September 12, 1965
Height: 6' 4"
Length of NBA career:
  1988–present
Major teams:
  San Antonio
  Houston (joined 1990)
  Philadelphia (joined 1995)
  San Antonio (joined 1996)
Records/Awards:
  NBA Championship (2)

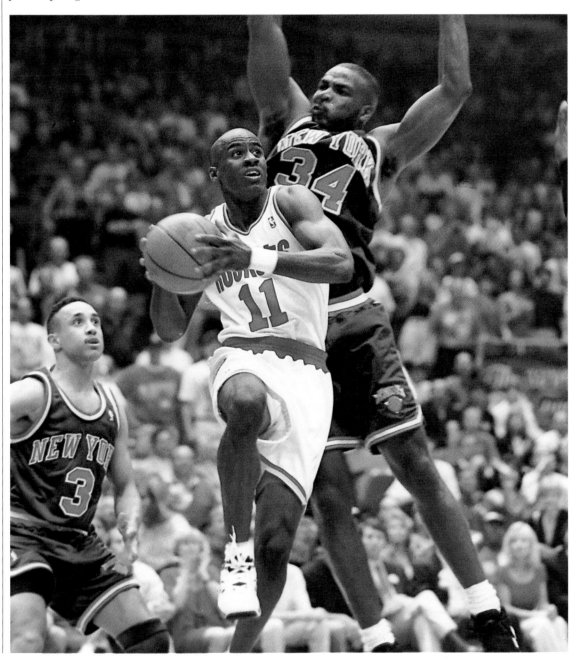

LEFT: VERNON MAXWELL'S ONLY PROBLEM MAY BE THAT HIS BLOOD PRESSURE IS HIGHER THAN HIS SCORING AVERAGE.

BOB MCADOO

FACT FILE

Born: September 25, 1951
Height: 6′ 9″
Length of NBA career:
 1972–86
Major teams:
 Buffalo
 New York Knicks (joined
  1976)
 Boston (joined 1979)
 Detroit (joined 1979)
 New Jersey (joined 1981)
 Los Angeles (joined 1981)
 Philadelphia (joined 1986)
Records/Awards:
 NBA Rookie of the Year
  (1973)
 NBA All-Star (5)
 NBA Most Valuable Player
  (1)
 NBA Championship (2)

After the Los Angeles Lakers defeated the Philadelphia 76ers to win the 1982 NBA Championship, Bob McAdoo proclaimed, "Now I've done it all."

McAdoo, a 6-foot 9-inch center/forward who wasn't so much a shooter as he was a scorer, was the NBA Rookie of the Year in 1973, the league's Most Valuable Player in 1975, and won a pair of championships with the Lakers, his second in 1985.

After he was selected out of North Carolina by the Buffalo Braves in the 1972 NBA draft, McAdoo made a big splash in his rookie season, averaging 18.0 points and 9.1 rebounds per game. The following season, McAdoo won the first of three straight scoring crowns, averaging 30.6 points and a career-high 15.1 rebounds per game. He exploded for a career-high 34.5 points per game in 1974–75 en route to winning the league's MVP Award, and in 1975–76, he won his third straight scoring crown on the strength of 31.1 points per game.

After four and a half seasons in Buffalo, McAdoo was traded to the New York Knicks. He also made stops in Boston, Detroit, and New Jersey before landing in Los Angeles.

Late in his career, McAdoo was often injured, but he became a valuable reserve for the Lakers in both championship seasons. After four seasons in Los Angeles, McAdoo finished his NBA career with the Philadelphia 76ers in 1985–86, and then moved on to Italy, where he played from 1986 through 1993.

In fourteen NBA seasons, McAdoo averaged 22.1 points and 9.4 rebounds per contest, adding 18.3 points and 7.6 rebounds in 94 career playoff games.

RIGHT: WINNER OF THREE SCORING CROWNS, BOB MCADOO (NO. 11) ACHIEVED ALL OF HIS OTHER MAJOR GOALS IN THE NBA.

RODNEY McCRAY

A versatile, unselfish player, Rodney McCray enjoyed ten successful seasons in the NBA, averaging double digits in scoring in each of his first eight seasons in the league, and ending his career as a member of the 1993 world champion Chicago Bulls.

McCray, a 6-foot-8-inch forward who helped Louisville win an NCAA Championship in 1980, was selected by the Houston Rockets in the first round of the 1983 NBA draft. As a rookie, he averaged 10.8 points and 5.6 rebounds per game. He played five solid seasons for the Rockets—he was an All-Defensive Second Team Selection in 1987 and an All-Defensive First Team Selection in 1988—before he was traded to the Sacramento Kings in 1988.

McCray enjoyed his best season as a member of the Kings in 1988–89, logging in a league-high 3,238 minutes played, and averaging a career-high 16.6 points per game. He was traded to Dallas in 1991 and played with the Mavericks for two seasons before teaming up with Michael Jordan and the Bulls to defeat Phoenix in the Finals, four games to two.

For his career, McCray averaged 11.7 points and 6.6 rebounds, adding 10.9 points and 5.8 boards in 46 career playoff contests.

A member of the 1980 Olympic Basketball Team, McCray averaged 9.2 points per game in four seasons at Louisville, where he teamed with his older brother, Scooter.

FACT FILE

Born: August 29, 1961
Height: 6′ 8″
Length of NBA career:
1983–93
Major teams:
Houston
Sacramento (joined 1988)
Dallas (joined 1990)
Chicago (joined 1992)
Records/Awards:
NBA Championship (1)
US Olympic Team (1980)

LEFT: RODNEY McCRAY'S EXCELLENT CAREER ENDED WITH A CHAMPIONSHIP RING AS A MEMBER OF THE CHICAGO BULLS.

DR. J'S LONGEST OPERATION

In the quiet of the New York Nets' dressing room after the long game, the Doctor, Julius Erving, was applying ice bags to his feet.

"I've never seen a game like this before," said Erving, "and nobody else ever did."

Dr. J, who performed hoop surgery on opponents in his day like no other man before him, had just completed his longest operation. The San Diego Conquistadors had outlasted the Nets, 176–166 in four overtimes for what was then the longest game (after the inception of the 24-second shot clock) in professional basketball history.

From a personal standpoint, the good Doctor's operation was a success on that Friday night, February 14, 1975. Erving scored a career-high 63 points for the Nets, but it wasn't enough in a game that took three hours and ten minutes to complete the 68 minutes of playing time.

The historic ABA contest, which took place at the International Sports Arena in San Diego, CA, drew a sparse crowd of 2,916, which was actually a decent fan turnout for the troubled San Diego franchise. Many of those fans, however, had left with the Nets ahead by five points with less than 45 seconds remaining in regulation time.

Those who stayed, however, witnessed a contest in which 72 personal fouls were committed, 128 rebounds were hauled down, and 342 points were scored. The combined 342 points remained a record until December 13, 1983, when the Detroit Pistons, led by Isiah Thomas' 47 points, squeaked past the Nuggets, 186–184, in a triple-overtime NBA game in Denver.

"It's disheartening to lose when you have put so much into it," said Erving, who played 66 of the 68 minutes, made 25 of 51 shots, and pulled down 23 of the Nets' 57 rebounds.

"I hope I'm never in one like this again," said Erving, pausing for a second before adding, "unless we win."

XAVIER MCDANIEL

FACT FILE

Born: June 4, 1963
Height: 6′ 7″
Length of NBA career:
 1985–95
 1996–present
Major teams:
 Seattle
 Phoenix (joined 1990)
 New York (joined 1991)
 Boston (joined 1992)
 New Jersey (joined 1996)
Records/Awards:
 NBA All-Star (1)

With his bald head, icy stares, and deadly turn-around jumper, Xavier McDaniel has been intimidating opponents for more than a decade.

The "X-Man," as McDaniel was called, after the comics character, was a shooting star and fierce rebounder at Wichita State and was selected by the Seattle SuperSonics in the first round of the 1985 NBA draft.

He earned a place on the 1986 All-Rookie team after averaging 17.1 points and 8.0 rebounds per game. The following season, McDaniel erupted for career-high averages in scoring and rebounding, tallying 23.0 points and 8.6 rebounds per contest.

A 6-foot-7-inch forward who loved to shoot the basketball in crunch time, McDaniel averaged 20 or more points in four straight seasons for the SuperSonics. He starred in Seattle until he was traded to Phoenix midway through the 1990–91 campaign.

The following year, McDaniel took his act to Broadway for one season with the New York Knicks, averaging 13.7 points and 5.6 rebounds per game. He spent the next three seasons coming off the bench in Boston to add firepower to a weak offensive attack. After a brief absence, the X-Man resurfaced in the 1996–97 season with the New Jersey Nets.

For his career, McDaniel has averaged 16.0 points and 6.2 rebounds per game, adding 17.0 points and 7.0 rebounds in fifty-one career playoff contests.

At Wichita State, McDaniel averaged 18.4 points per game over four seasons. In 1985, he became one of only three players in NCAA history to lead the nation in scoring (27.2) and rebounding (14.8) in the same season.

RIGHT: X MARKS THE SPOT. XAVIER MCDANIEL NOTCHES TWO POINTS AS A MEMBER OF THE NEW YORK KNICKS.

BOBBY McDERMOTT

A fiery guard with a tremendous shooting touch, Bobby McDermott starred for the NBL's Fort Wayne Pistons in the early 1940s. Before that, McDermott played for the last of the great Original Celtic teams and was the leading scorer in the ABL.

McDermott, a 5-foot-11-inch, two-handed shooter who quit Flushing High School in New York to pursue a career in professional basketball, helped Fort Wayne reach the NBL championship in 1942, where the Pistons lost to Oshkosh in three games. The following season McDermott and the Pistons made it back to the championship round, but lost again, this time to Sheboygan, in another three games.

Finally, in the 1943–44 season, McDermott and the Pistons broke through for the first of back-to-back championships. Fort Wayne defeated Sheboygan in three straight to win the 1944 championship, and, with McDermott leading the way with 20 points per contest, took the Redskins in five games to capture the 1945 title. After that season, McDermott was voted by league coaches as the greatest player in professional basketball history.

In the 1946–47 season, McDermott was traded to the Chicago Gears, which had on their roster a young center named George Mikan, the most celebrated player in college basketball history at that point in time.

Together, McDermott and Mikan helped the Pistons defeat the Rochester Royals in four games to win the 1947 championship. A dynasty seemed almost certain, but evaporated in the 1947–48 season when the Gears pulled out of the NBA.

McDermott was voted into the Hall of Fame by the NBA's Veterans Committee in 1988.

FACT FILE

Born: January 7, 1914
Height: 5′ 11″
Length of professional career: 1933–50
Major teams:
Brooklyn
Original Celtics
Fort Wayne
Chicago
Records/Awards:
Championships (2)

LEFT: AFTER THE 1945 SEASON, BOBBY McDERMOTT WAS VOTED BY LEAGUE COACHES AS THE GREATEST PLAYER IN PROFESSIONAL BASKETBALL HISTORY.

ANTONIO MCDYESS

FACT FILE

Born: September 7, 1974
Height: 6' 9"
Length of NBA career:
1995–present
Major team:
Denver

A 6-foot-9-inch power forward with a 42-inch vertical leap, Antonio McDyess, who wrecked defenses at Alabama, was the second pick overall in the 1995 NBA draft.

After just two seasons at Alabama, McDyess was selected in the draft by the Los Angeles Clippers, who then traded his draft rights to the Nuggets for forward Rodney Rogers and guard Brent Barry.

McDyess, a physical player who has a number of neat moves in the low post and has a soft, accurate release from 15 feet out, had a tremendous rookie season for the Nuggets. He earned a place on the All-Rookie team by averaging 13.4 points, 7.5 rebounds, and 1.0 assists in 76 games.

Filling in at the center position on occasion, McDyess logged in 2,280 minutes, using his tremendous leaping ability to block 114 shots.

Last season, McDyess' scoring average improved to 18.3 points per game. He also added 7.3 rebounds per game and 126 blocked shots.

"McDyess is a warrior," said Denver team president and general manager Bernie Bickerstaff. "He has the intensity going for rebounds, and the quickness to the ball of a Shawn Kemp."

At Alabama McDyess averaged 12.8 points and 9.3 rebounds in two seasons. In his sophomore year, he tallied averages of 13.9 points and 10.2 rebounds per contest.

RIGHT: ANTONIO MCDYESS, LETTING ONE FLY FROM THE CORNER, PUTS THE POWER IN POWER FORWARD.

GEORGE MCGINNIS

Along with the legendary Julius Erving, George McGinnis shared center stage as the ABA's top attraction in the early 1970s.

McGinnis, a strong 6-foot-8-inch forward who played with the finesse of a guard, left Indiana University after one season to join the Indiana Pacers of the ABA in 1971. He earned a place on the ABA's All-Rookie team by averaging 16.9 points and 9.1 rebounds per game in helping the Pacers capture the first of back-to-back ABA Championships.

The following season, McGinnis erupted for averages of 27.6 points and 12.4 boards per game, and was named the MVP of the playoffs.

In 1975, McGinnis scored a career-high 29.8 points—he led the league in scoring—and hauled down a hefty 14.2 rebounds per game. He was named co-winner of the ABA's MVP award, which he shared with Erving, who had a tremendous season for the New York Nets.

McGinnis joined Philadelphia of the NBA for the 1975–76 campaign and continued to be a dominant force in basketball, averaging 23 points and 12.5 rebounds in his first season with the 76ers.

For seven straight seasons from 1972 through 1979, McGinnis averaged 20 or more points per game. His last 20-point season came as a member of the Denver Nuggets in the 1978–79 season, when he scored 22.6 points per game.

Midway through the 1979–80 season, McGinnis, a six-time All-Star, was traded back to Indiana, which was now a part of the NBA. He finished his career with the Pacers in 1982, hanging up his sneakers with career ABA averages of 24.8 points and 12.7 rebounds. His career NBA averages rested at 17.2 points and 9.8 rebounds.

FACT FILE

Born: August 12, 1950
Height: 6′ 8″
Length of ABA career:
  1971–75
Length of NBA career:
  1975–82
Major teams:
  Indiana
  Philadelphia (joined 1975)
  Denver (joined 1978)
  Indiana (joined 1980)
Records/Awards:
  ABA All-Star (3)
  ABA co-Most Valuable
    Player (1)
  ABA Championship (2)
  NBA All-Star (3)

LEFT: IN 1975, GEORGE MCGINNIS SHARED THE ABA MOST VALUABLE PLAYER AWARD WITH JULIUS ERVING.

DICK McGUIRE

FACT FILE

Born: January 25, 1926
Height: 6′ 0″
Length of NBA career:
  1949–60
Major teams:
  New York Knicks
  Detroit (joined 1957)
Records/Awards:
  NBA All-Star (7)
  Hall of Fame (1993)

When Dick McGuire was elected to the NBA's Hall of Fame in 1993, he thought about his paltry, 11-year career scoring average of 8 points per game and said softly, "I might be the guy with the lowest scoring average in the whole place."

There was a reason why McGuire, a native New Yorker, didn't score very much. He loved to pass, and long before "point guard" became a part of basketball's vocabulary, McGuire was the prototypical, pass-first, shoot-only-if-absolutely necessary point guard.

"Tricky Dick," a name McGuire earned in his playing days by handling the basketball like a magician and often making blind, accurate passes to teammates, played his college basketball at St. John's before signing with the hometown New York Knicks in 1949.

A seven-time All-Star, McGuire played his first eight seasons with the Knicks before he was traded to Detroit in 1957, where he played the last three seasons of his career.

As a Knicks rookie in the 1949–50 season, McGuire averaged 8.6 points per game and set an NBA record with 386 assists, a 5.8 average. His career New-York-Knick total of 2,950 assists is third behind Mark Jackson's 3,237 assists and Walt Frazier's club record 4,791.

"Every coach Dick had," said the legendary point guard Bob Cousy, a childhood friend of McGuire's, "had to threaten his life to get him to shoot more often."

McGuire, who averaged a career-high 9.2 points per game for the Knicks in the 1951–52 season, finished his career with averages of 8.0 points and 5.7 assists per game, dishing out a total of 4,205 assists. His playmaking helped the Knicks into three consecutive NBA Finals, only to lose to The Rochester Royals and twice to George Mikan and the mighty Minneapolis Lakers.

RIGHT: DICK McGUIRE GOES TO THE BASKET HERE, BUT HIS SCORING HAD LITTLE TO DO WITH HIS HALL-OF-FAME ELECTION.

KEVIN McHALE

Perhaps no other big man in the history of the game possessed the kind of low-post moves that made Kevin McHale one of the all-time greats.

McHale, a 6-foot-10-inch forward center with long arms that helped him block 1,690 shots, rip down key offensive rebounds, and put back numerous clutch baskets throughout his career, helped the Boston Celtics win championships in 1981, 1984, and 1986.

Teaming with Robert Parish and Larry Bird to form one of the greatest front-line attacks in NBA history, McHale, with an arsenal of snaky spin moves and clever head fakes, was nearly unstoppable when being guarded one-on-one around the basket.

A seven-time All-Star and three-time All-Defensive First Team selection, McHale made immediate contributions as a rookie, earning a place on the 1981 All-Rookie team with averages of 10.0 points and 4.4 rebounds per contest.

For thirteen straight seasons, McHale averaged double digits in scoring. His best overall season was 1986–87, when he posted 26.1 points, 9.9 rebounds, and 2.6 assists per game.

Often used off the bench to spark Boston's offensive attack, McHale twice won the NBA's Sixth Man Award, pulling off that feat in 1984 and again in 1985.

The Hall of Fame-bound McHale averaged 17.9 points and 7.3 rebounds in a career spent entirely in Boston, adding 18.8 points and 7.4 boards in 169 career playoff contests.

At the University of Minnesota, McHale averaged 15.2 points and 8.5 rebounds in four seasons. He was selected by the Celtics in the first round of the 1980 NBA draft.

FACT FILE

Born: December 19, 1957
Height: 6' 10"
Length of NBA career:
1980–93
Major team:
Boston
Records/Awards:
NBA All-Defensive First Team (3)
NBA Sixth Man Award (2)
NBA All-Star (7)
NBA Championship (3)

LEFT: KEVIN McHALE SHOWS HOW TO BOX-OUT AN OPPONENT, BUT HE WILL FOREVER BE REMEMBERED FOR HIS SENSATIONAL, LOW-POST OFFENSIVE MOVES.

NATE MCMILLAN

FACT FILE

Born: August 3, 1964
Height: 6' 5"
Length of NBA career:
  1986–present
Major team:
  Seattle

Seattle's all-time assists and steals leader, Nate McMillan has been a valuable swingman for the SuperSonics since joining the franchise out of North Carolina State in 1986.

A defensive specialist, McMillan ended the 1996–97 season with 778 games played in a Seattle uniform, second only to "Downtown" Fred Brown, who played in 963 regular-season contests for Seattle from 1971–84.

Selected by Seattle in the second round of the 1986 NBA draft, the 6-foot-5-inch McMillan has been a super find. He averaged 5.3 points, 4.7 rebounds, and 8.2 assists as a rookie, tying a single-game record that season for most assists by a rookie, 25, on February 23, 1987, against the Los Angeles Clippers.

The following season, McMillan averaged a career-high 7.6 points per game for the Super-Sonics, filling in at either guard spot or the small forward position if needed.

A two-time All-Defensive Second Team selection, the versatile McMillan led the NBA with 2.96 steals per game in 1994. Through the 1996–97 season, he was Seattle's all-time assists leader with 4,838, and all-time steals leader with 1,530. Injuries limited him to a minor role in the 1996 championship series, which was won by the Chicago Bulls in six games.

During Seattle's 1996 playoff run, McMillan tied the single-game post-season record for most three-point field goals made without missing any, knocking down five three-pointers against the Houston Rockets on May 6, 1996.

Through his first eleven NBA seasons, all spent in Seattle, McMillan has averaged 6.0 points, 6.2 assists, and 4.1 rebounds per game. He has added 5.2 points, 3.6 rebounds, and 5.4 assists in 91 career playoff contests.

RIGHT: THE DEFENSIVE SPECIALIST NATE MCMILLAN HAS BEEN A CATALYST IN SEATTLE'S ATTACK.

GEORGE MIKAN

amed by the Associated Press as the "Greatest Player of the First Half a Century," George Mikan revolutionized the game of basketball.

The first true "Big Man" the sport had ever known, the 6-foot-10-inch, 240-pound Mikan was the College Player of the Year at DePaul in 1944 and the following season led the nation in scoring with 23.1 points per game.

By the time Mikan graduated from DePaul in 1946, he had swatted away so many shots that the NCAA had in 1944 introduced the rule prohibiting goaltending.

In the 1946–47 season, Mikan broke into the professional ranks with the Chicago Gears of the NBL. Using his height and weight advantage and his baby hook shots from either side of the basket, Mikan led the Gears to the league title. The next season, the Gears split up, and Mikan was shipped via a dispersal draft to the Minneapolis Lakers.

Teaming with frontcourt stars like Vern Mikkelsen and Jim Pollard, and backcourt talents like Slater Martin and Whitey Skoog, Mikan's presence in the Minneapolis lineup made the Lakers practically unbeatable.

Over the span of seven seasons, from the years 1947 through 1954, Minneapolis won the last World Tournament in Chicago (in 1947), plus an NBL title (in 1948), and the BAA Championship before the league's integration into the NBA (in 1949), and four of the first five NBA Championships (1950, '52, '53, and '54).

While Mikan's teams were racking up championships, he was earning scores of individual honors and awards. He led the league in scoring three times and in rebounding once. He was also voted to the 25th and 35th Anniversary All-Time NBA teams, played in the first four All-Star games, and was its Most Valuable Player in 1953.

In nine professional seasons, Mikan averaged 22.6 points per game, adding 23.5 points per game in ninety-one career playoff contests. His best scoring seasons came in 1950–51, when he averaged 28.4 points per game for the Lakers.

FACT FILE

Born: June 18, 1924
Height: 6' 10"
Length of NBL career:
  1946–48
Length of BAA career:
  1948–49
Length of NBA career:
  1949–54, 1955–56
Major teams:
  Chicago
  Minneapolis (joined 1947)
Records/Awards:
  NBL All-Star (2)
  NBL MVP (1)
  NBL Championship (2)
  BAA All-Star (1)
  BAA Championship (1)
  NBA All-Star (4)
  NBA Championship (4)
  All-NBA First Team (5)
  Hall of Fame (1959)

LEFT: BEFORE WILT CHAMBERLAIN ENTERED THE SCENE, GEORGE MIKAN, SEEN COACHING AT LEFT, WAS CONSIDERED BASKETBALL'S TRUE GOLIATH.

VERN MIKKELSEN

FACT FILE

Born: October 21, 1928
Height: 6' 7"
Length of NBA career:
  1949–59
Major team:
  Minneapolis
Records/Awards:
  NBA All-Star (6)
  NBA Championship (4)
  Hall of Fame (1995)

George Mikan and Jim Pollard had already won a championship with the Minneapolis Lakers before Vern Mikkelsen arrived on the scene in the 1949–50 season. After adding the 6-foot-7-inch forward to their lineup, the Lakers were the talk of the basketball world.

Mikkelsen, who played his college basketball at Hamline College in Minnesota, helped the Lakers win four championships during his ten-year stint with the team. The first championship for Mikkelsen came in his rookie season, when he averaged 11.6 points per game. He would go on to average double digits in scoring every season for the rest of his career.

A six-time All-Star, Mikkelsen helped Mikan and company capture three more championships in 1950, 1952, and 1953.

For his career, Mikkelsen averaged 14.4 points per contest, adding 13.4 points in 85 career playoff games. His best scoring seasons came in 1954–55, when he averaged a career-high 18.7 points per game, and 1957–58, when he scored 17.3 points per game.

A four-time All-NBA Second Team Selection, Mikkelsen holds the league's career record for most disqualifications with 127.

In four seasons at Hamline, Mikkelsen averaged 13.6 points per game early in his career. He led NCAA Division II with a .538 field-goal percentage in 1949.

RIGHT: AFTER ACQUIRING THE TALENTED VERN MIKKELSEN, THE MINNEAPOLIS LAKERS WERE THE TALK OF BASKETBALL.

EDDIE MILLER

ddie Miller was a star of one of the first great basketball teams, the Buffalo Germans. The Germans were organized in 1895 at the Buffalo "Y," which was located in a German-American neighborhood on the east side of the city, according to the *NBA Encyclopedia.*

Teaming with turn-of-the-century stars like Al Heerdt, Miller and the rest of the Germans began competing as amateurs when they were just fourteen years old.

The Germans, who played from 1895–1929, compiling an amazing 792–86 record during that time, also played against professional competition. They won 111 straight games before losing, 26–21 to a team from Herkimer, New York, managed by Frank Bledsoe.

Miller's Germans were not the only team from New York State traveling the basketball circuit in that era. The Troy Trojans of the early 1900s were also a competitive team, and are credited for inventing the bounce pass, as well as the so-called "baseball pass," a long pass thrown from one end of the court to the other, setting in motion the first fast break.

BELOW: EDDIE MILLER, RIGHT OF MIDDLE ROW, STARRED FOR THE BUFFALO GERMANS. THEY BEGAN AS AMATEURS, ALSO COMPETING AGAINST PROFESSIONAL TEAMS, WHEN THEY WERE JUST 14 YEARS OLD FROM 1895.

FACT FILE

Eddie Miller's Fact File is incomplete as very little information concerning professional basketball was documented around the turn of the century.

REGGIE MILLER

FACT FILE

Born: August 24, 1965
Height: 6′ 7″
Length of NBA career:
  1987–present
Major team:
  Indiana
Records/Awards:
  NBA All-Star (3)
  Olympic Gold Medal
  (1996)

One of the premier shooting guards in the NBA today, Reggie Miller is the cornerstone of the Indiana Pacers' franchise. Miller, a 6-foot-7-inch sharpshooter out of UCLA, has developed a reputation as one of the league's clutch bombers. He has connected on 100 three-pointers in an NBA-record eight straight seasons.

After averaging 17.2 points in four seasons at UCLA, Miller, a player who prefers to catch and shoot the ball rather than score off the dribble, was selected by Indiana in the first round of the 1987 NBA draft.

Through the first ten seasons of his career, Miller, Indiana's all-time leading scorer with 15,824 points, has proved his worth to the Pacers' fans.

As a rookie in 1987–88, Miller averaged 10.0 points per game, and has averaged double digits in scoring in each season thereafter. His best scoring campaign came in 1989–90, when he averaged 24.6 points per game.

A three-time All-Star and two-time All-NBA Third Team selection, Miller has averaged 19.8 points and 3.2 assists in ten seasons with Indiana, adding 24.7 points in forty-nine career playoff games.

A member of the 1996 gold-medal winning US Olympic basketball team, Miller holds the single-game playoff record for most three-point field goals made in one quarter, bagging 5 three-pointers in twelve minutes against the New York Knicks on June 1, 1994. Twice in his career, Miller has tied the single-game playoff record for most three-point field goals made in one half with 6.

Reggie's sister, Cheryl, was a member of the gold-medal winning 1984 US Olympic women's basketball team.

RIGHT: REGGIE MILLER IS THE PRIDE OF INDIANA, AND ONE OF THE PREMIER SHOOTERS IN THE GAME.

MIKE MITCHELL

When the San Antonio Spurs announced their All-Decade team in 1983, Mike Mitchell made the starting five, joining such outstanding players as George Gervin, James Silas, Mark Oldberding, and Artis Gilmore.

Mitchell, a 6-foot-7-inch forward, was a prolific scorer in ten NBA seasons split between Cleveland and San Antonio.

Selected by Cleveland out of Auburn in the 1978 NBA draft, Mitchell averaged 10.7 points per game in his rookie campaign. He would average double digits in scoring each season of his career.

Mitchell played his first three and a half years with Cleveland, averaging a career-high 24.5 points per contest for the Cavaliers in 1980–81, the only season he made the All-Star team.

Midway through the 1981–82 season, Mitchell joined forces with Gervin, one of the most prolific and exciting scorers in the history of the game. There was more than enough air in the basketball to satisfy both shooting stars.

Two years later, in the 1983–84 campaign, Mitchell posted a personal-best 23.3 points per game for San Antonio.

The following season, 1984–85, Mitchell led the Spurs in scoring, breaking a string of eight straight seasons in which Gervin had led the team in that department. That same season, both players reached major milestones.

Mitchell scored his 10,000th career point against his old teammates, the Cavaliers, on November 10, while Gervin chalked up his 25,000th point at Phoenix on February 22.

For his career, Mitchell averaged 19.8 points per game, adding 20.6 points in thirty-one career playoff contests.

FACT FILE

Born: January 1, 1956
Height: 6′ 7″
Length of NBA career:
1978–88
Major teams:
Cleveland
San Antonio (joined 1982)
Records/Awards:
NBA All-Star (1)

LEFT: MIKE MITCHELL DUCKING UNDER THE OUTSTRETCHED ARMS OF JULIUS ERVING.

CHAMPIONSHIP HOOPATHON

More than 20 years after the final buzzer sounded to end Game 5 of the NBA championship series, players from the Boston Celtics and Phoenix Suns are still trying to catch their breath.

On the night of June 4, 1976, at the Boston Garden, the Cinderella Suns and the mighty Celtics, tied two games apiece in the Finals, staged the first-ever three-overtime title game.

Before a crazed crowd of 15,320, the Celtics finally defeated the Suns, 128–126, but it was no easy task. The hoopathon took 3 hours and 8 minutes to play, leaving members of both teams physically exhausted, and a number of fans exchanging punches with referees, players, coaches, ushers, and fellow spectators.

In the opening minutes of the contest, Boston appeared headed for a rout. The Celtics jumped out to a 20-point lead, 32–12, as John Havlicek, Jo Jo White, and Dave Cowens controlled the boards, and the hometown crew shot sixty-one percent through the first period.

But just as they had done all season, the Suns stormed back. Phoenix patiently ran its offense, and by halftime, had trimmed a 22-point deficit to 16, trailiing 61–45 at the intermission. In the second half, a 19–7 spurt by the Suns trimmed Boston's lead to 68–64, and suddenly, the Celtics were looking beatable.

ABOVE: PAUL WESTPHAL, WHIRLING LEFT HERE AROUND THE NEW YORK KNICKS' EARL MONROE, WAS INSTRUMENTAL IN BOSTON'S THREE-OVERTIME VICTORY OVER PHOENIX IN GAME 5 OF THE 1976 NBA FINALS.

With five seconds left in the second overtime, Phoenix led 110–109. As time apparently expired, Havlicek buried a jumper that appeared to have given the Celtics a 111–110 victory. As hundreds of celebrating fans stormed onto the court, referee Richie Powers ruled that one second remained on the game clock.

When order was restored, Phoenix's Paul Westphal, an ex-Celtic, came up with a brainstorm. He suggested the Suns call timeout even though they had none remaining and a technical foul would be called. The Celtics might go up two points, but Phoenix would get the ball at midcourt, rather than under their own basket.

Westphal's strategy worked to perfection. After White made the free throw to put Boston up by two points, 112–110, Heard took the inbounds pass from Perry and launched a twenty-footer, which he swished, to send the game into a third overtime knotted at 112–112.

In the final overtime, with key players from both teams watching from the bench after fouling out, Boston survived, getting major bench help from Glenn McDonald, who had replaced Paul Silas.

After the game, Boston Coach Tom Heinsohn, a man who stood 6 feet 7 inches tall and weighed nearly 300 pounds, blacked out in the trainer's room, suffering from exhaustion. Phoenix guard Ricky Sobers, complained of feeling weak and dizzy. Richie Powers, a referee, got into a fist fight with one of the fans on his way to the dressing room.

"Can these go one more game?" a weary Silas wondered aloud. "Can I?"

It went one more game, and Boston won it to win the championship. But basketball history doesn't tell nearly as exciting a tale of Game 6 of the 1976 championship series as it does of Game 5, the most famous hoopathon of them all.

With nineteen seconds left in regulation and the Celtics now trailing by a single point, 95–94, Havlicek made one of two free throws to tie the score, then missed a follow-shot with .05 seconds left to send the game into the first extra session tied 95–95.

Boston forged ahead, 101–97 with 1:58 left in the first overtime, but Curtis Perry and Gar Heard brought the Suns back, sending the game into a second overtime session, which featured one of the most bizarre moments in the history of professional basketball.

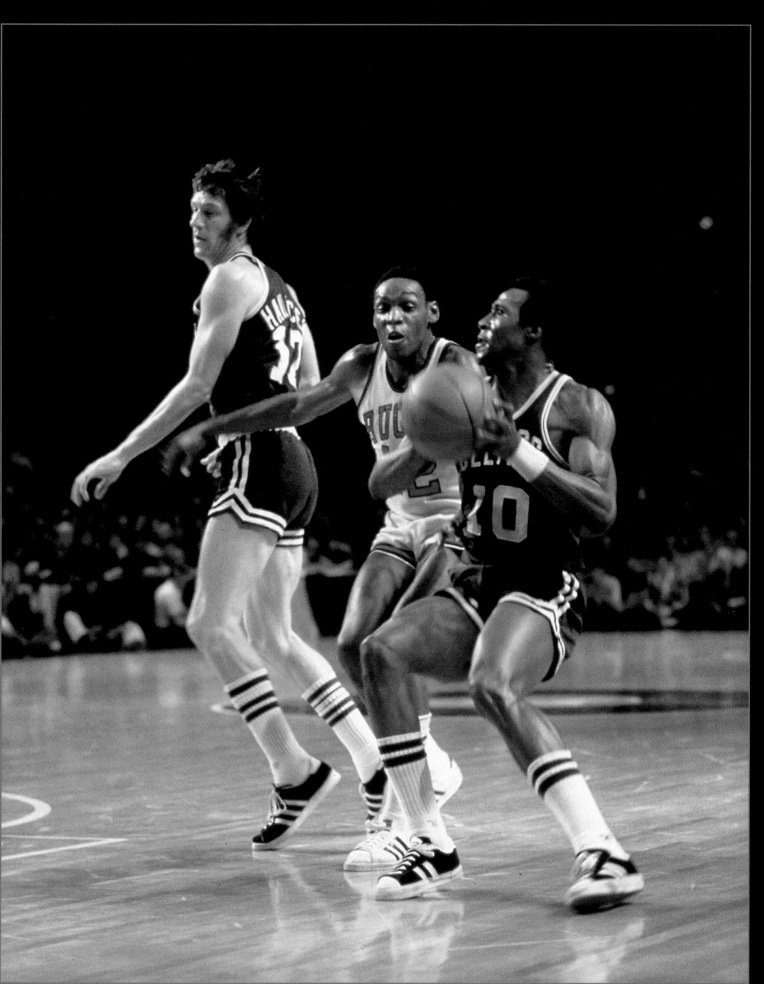

SIDNEY MONCRIEF

FACT FILE

Born: September 21, 1957
Height: 6′ 3″
Length of NBA career:
1979–89, 1990–91
Major teams:
Milwaukee
Atlanta (joined 1990)
Records/Awards:
NBA All-Star (5)
NBA Defensive Player of
the Year (2)
NBA All-Defensive First
Team (4)

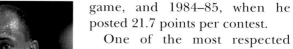

Slashing, diving, and driving his slender body through larger, more muscular opponents for eleven NBA seasons, Sidney Moncrief was one of the brightest stars ever to shine on a basketball court.

Moncrief, a 6-foot-3-inch guard out of Arkansas who scored around twenty or more points for the Milwaukee Bucks in four straight seasons from 1982–86, was more than just a one-dimensional player. He was also one of the best defenders ever to play the game.

Selected by the Bucks in the first round of the 1979 NBA draft, Moncrief averaged 12.4 points and 4.4 rebounds per game as a rookie, starting a streak of nine straight seasons in which he would continuously record double-digit averages in scoring.

A five-time All-Star, Moncrief enjoyed his best scoring seasons with the Bucks in 1982–83, when he averaged a career-high 22.5 points per game, and 1984–85, when he posted 21.7 points per contest.

One of the most respected defenders of his time, Moncrief was voted the NBA's Defensive Player of the Year in 1983 and 1984, and was voted onto the league's All-Defensive First Team four times in his career.

After ten seasons in Milwaukee, bad knees forced Moncrief into retirement. He stayed away from the game one year before making a one-season comeback with the Atlanta Hawks in 1990–91.

For his career, Moncrief averaged 15.6 points, 4.7 rebounds, and 3.6 assists. In 93 career post-season contests, he added 16.0 points, 5.0 rebounds, and 3.4 assists.

At Arkansas, Moncrief averaged 16.9 points, 8.3 rebounds, and 2.0 assists over four seasons. He led the NCAA Division I with a .665 field-goal percentage in 1976, connecting on 149 of 224 attempts from the field.

RIGHT: SIDNEY MONCRIEF, SLASHING TO THE HOOP AS ONLY HE COULD, WAS BRILLIANT AT BOTH ENDS OF THE FLOOR.

EARL MONROE

Earl "The Pearl." It was a name befitting a player who glittered on the basketball court for thirteen NBA seasons, spinning, whirling and dribbling the ball behind his back like a magician on the hardwood.

Monroe, who honed his pearly skills in the playgrounds of Philadelphia, had yet another nickname at Winston-Salem State, a predominantly African-American Division II college located deep in the heart of North Carolina tobacco country, where he set scores of individual records: Black Jesus.

A 6-foot-3-inch guard selected by the Baltimore Bullets in the first round of the 1967 NBA draft, Monroe earned Rookie of the Year honors in 1968 after posting averages of 24.3 points, 5.7 rebounds, and 4.3 assists per game.

After four seasons in Baltimore, Monroe, having contract problems, was traded to the New York Knicks, and, under the bright lights

on Broadway, the Pearl's legend grew larger than life.

In his first full season with the Knicks, 1972–73, Monroe's talents, combined with the skills of backcourt partner Walt Frazier and teammates like Willis Reed, Bill Bradley, and Dave DeBusschere, led New York to their second NBA title, a four-games-to-one thumping of the Los Angeles Lakers.

A four-time All-Star, Monroe averaged 18.8 points, 3.9 assists, and 3.0 rebounds in his career, adding 17.9 points, 3.2 assists, and 3.2 boards in 82 career playoff contests. His best scoring season was 1968–69, when he averaged 25.8 points per contest for the Bullets.

In his senior season at Winston-Salem State, 1967, Monroe set the NCAA Division II single-season record for most points, tallying 1,329. That same season, Monroe averaged a Division II-leading 41.5 points per contest en route to leading the tiny school to a championship.

FACT FILE

Born: November 21, 1944
Height: 6′ 3″
Length of NBA career:
 1967–80
Major teams:
 Baltimore
 New York (joined 1971)
Records/Awards:
 NBA Rookie of the Year
  (1968)
 NBA All-Star (4)
 NBA Championship (1)
 Hall of Fame (1989)

LEFT: EARL "THE PEARL" MONROE GLITTERED IN WASHINGTON BEFORE WINNING A CHAMPIONSHIP IN NEW YORK.

ALONZO MOURNING

FACT FILE

Born: February 8, 1970
Height: 6′ 10″
Length of NBA career:
 1992–present
Major teams:
 Charlotte
 Miami (joined 1995)
Records/Awards:
 NBA All-Star (4)

When Pat Riley and the Miami Heat went looking for a franchise center in 1995, they found their man in Alonzo Mourning, a 6-foot-10-inch pivotman who plays a tenacious brand of basketball at both ends of the floor.

Mourning, a shot-blocking demon from Georgetown, was selected by the Charlotte Hornets in the first round of the 1992 NBA draft. He earned a place on the 1993 All-Rookie team after averaging 21.0 points and 10.3 rebounds, and racking up a whopping 271 blocked shots.

Mourning, who played his first three seasons in Charlotte before he was traded to Miami early in the 1995–96 season, finished as the Hornets' all-time blocked shots leader with 684.

The biggest shot of Mourning's career came in the first round of the 1993 playoffs against Boston. With Charlotte trailing 103–102 and time winding down, Mourning took a quick inbounds pass from teammate Dell Curry along the left baseline, and with four-tenths of a second left in the contest, buried a 17-footer to give the Hornets a 104–103 victory, which wrapped up the series in four games.

A four-time All-Star, Mourning enjoyed his most productive season as a first-year member of the Heat under Coach Pat Riley. He averaged career-highs in all three major statistical categories: points (23.2), rebounds (10.4), and assists (2.3).

Through his first five NBA seasons, Mourning has averaged 21.4 points, 10.1 rebounds, and 1.4 assists per game, adding 20.0 points, 10.1 rebounds, and 1.4 assists in 33 career playoff games.

At Georgetown, Mourning averaged 16.7 points and 8.6 rebounds in four seasons. He led NCAA Division I in blocked shots with 169 in 1989, and 160 in 1992, finishing his sensational college career as the NCAA's all-time leader in blocked shots with 453.

RIGHT: A SHOT-BLOCKING DEMON, ALONZO MOURNING HAS FRANCHISE PLAYER WRITTEN ALL OVER HIM.

CHRIS MULLIN

Perhaps no honor said more about Chris Mullin's game than his selection to Dream Team I, arguably the greatest basketball team ever assembled.

Mullin, a 6-foot-7-inch swingman who grew up in New York, was a star for two seasons at Power Memorial High School in Manhattan, where Kareem Abdul-Jabbar had learned the basics of the game years before. After spending his last two schoolboy seasons at Xaverian in Brooklyn, Mullin was off to St. John's, where he teamed as a senior with future pros Mark Jackson, Walter Berry, Bill Wennington, and Shelton Jones to lead the Redmen to the 1985 NCAA Final Four. One season earlier, he helped the US Olympic basketball team, to a gold-medal victory.

The years of hard work paid off for Mullin, a gym rat who spent endless hours honing his skills throughout his youth, when he was selected by the Golden State Warriors in the first round of the 1985 NBA draft.

Playing in Coach Don Nelson's run-and-gun system, the sharp-shooting Mullin soon became one of the premier marksmen in the league. After averaging 14.0 points per game as a rookie, Mullin increased his scoring average in each of the next four seasons, topping at a career-high 26.5 points per game in the 1988–89 campaign.

A five-time All-Star, Mullin averaged double digits in scoring in each of his first twelve seasons in the league— all spent with Golden State.

During his peak years, Mullin averaged better than 20 points per game from 1987 through 1993. He led the league in minutes played in 1990–91 and again in 1991–92, the same year he was picked to join Michael Jordan, Larry Bird, Magic Johnson, and Charles Barkley on the US Olympic basketball team, securing his place in history as one of the NBA's all-time greats.

Through the 1996–97 season, Mullin has averaged 20.5 points, 4.0 assists, and 4.5 rebounds per game. Mullin, the Warriors' all-time leader in steals with 1,344, is now a member of the Indiana Pacers.

FACT FILE

Born: July 30, 1963
Height: 6' 7"
Length of NBA career:
1985–present
Major teams:
Golden State
Indiana (joined 1997)
Records/Awards:
NBA All-Star (5)
Olympic Gold Medals
(1984, 1992)

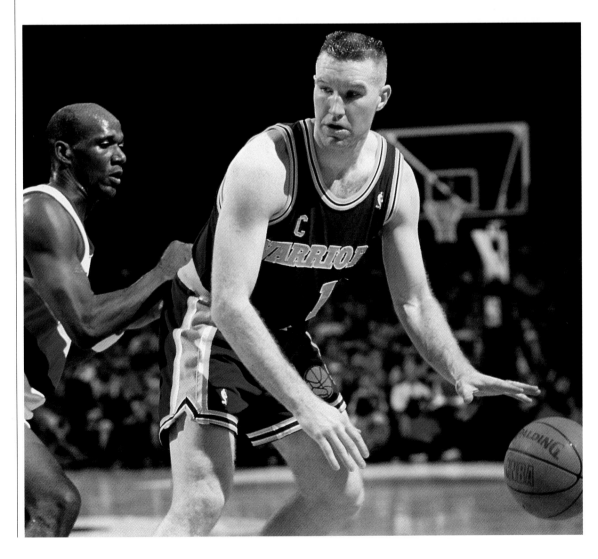

LEFT: GYM RAT CHRIS MULLIN'S HARD WORK EARNED HIM A ROSTER SPOT ON THE GREATEST BASKETBALL TEAM EVER ASSEMBLED.

GHEORGHE MURESAN

FACT FILE

Born: February 14, 1971
Height: 7′ 7″
Length of NBA career:
  1993–present
Major team:
  Washington
Records/Awards:
  NBA Most Improved
  Player (1996)

At 7-feet-7-inches in height, Gheorghe Muresan of the Washington Bullets is one of the few players in the NBA who looks down on Shaquille O'Neal.

Muresan, who learned the game of basketball while growing up in Romania, has improved drastically in each of his first four NBA seasons.

Selected by the Bullets in the second round of the 1993 NBA draft, Muresan needed more than a full season to find his rhythm on the basketball court, but eventually he established himself as a tough defensive presence and a major scoring threat.

"It took me a while to get used to the NBA game, but now I have no problem with it," said Muresan, just before entering his third season in the league. "Eventually, I would like to be among the top centers in the NBA."

From the looks of things, Muresan might be headed in that direction. As a rookie, he averaged just 5.6 points and 3.6 rebounds per game, adding 48 blocks. The following season, however, was a major breakthrough. He averaged 10.0 points and 6.7 rebounds per contest, while raising his shot-blocking total to 127.

In the 1995–96 campaign, Muresan moved closer toward his goal of being one of the league's elite centers when he posted career-highs in scoring (14.5), rebounding (9.6), and blocks (172). For his efforts, the Romanian giant was named the NBA's Most Improved Player. Muresan, who played his college ball at Cluj University in Romania, and played professionally in France for one season before joining the Bullets, averaged 10.6 points and 6.6 rebounds per game last season. He has averaged 10.6 points, 6.8 rebounds, and chalked up 443 blocks in his first three NBA seasons.

RIGHT: GENTLE GIANT GHEORGHE MURESAN HAS HIS SIGHTS SET NOT JUST ON THIS LOOSE BALL, BUT ON BECOMING ONE OF THE TOP CENTERS IN THE NBA.

CALVIN MURPHY

Pound for pound, inch for inch, Calvin Murphy may have been the best little man ever to play the game.

Murphy, a lightning-quick, 5-foot-9-inch, 165-pound guard out of Niagara College, scored 1,000 or more points in eleven straight seasons with the Rockets, who moved from San Diego to Houston for the 1971–72 season, Murphy's second season in the league. He finished fourth in the 1970–71 Rookie of the Year balloting after posting averages of 15.8 points, 4.0 assists, and 3.0 rebounds per game.

Along with Rick Barry, Murphy helped elevate free-throw accuracy to a new plateau. He still holds the single-season record for highest free-throw percentage, canning 206 of 215 free throws in 1980–81 for a .958 percentage. That same 1980–81 season, Murphy established a then-record streak of 78 consecutive free throws. In a thirteen-year career, all spent in a Rocket's uniform, Murphy posted averages of 17.9 points, 4.4 assists, and 2.1 rebounds per contest, adding 18.5 points, 4.2 assists, and 1.5 rebounds in fifty-one career playoff games. The closest he came to a championship ring was 1981, when the Rockets lost in the NBA Finals to Boston in six games.

At Niagara, Murphy averaged a remarkable 48.9 points with the Purple Eagles' freshman team. In the third game of his junior year, he made national headlines by lighting up Syracuse for 68 points—the third highest total ever against an NCAA Division I opponent.

"I never believed the people who said I was too short for the pros," Murphy once said. "I did it, I played in the championship round and I was recognized as one of the best in my business. And I left with something positive—those records. They'll be broken some day, but I've given somebody else a goal to shoot for."

FACT FILE

Born: May 9, 1948
Height: 5′ 9″
Length of NBA career:
  1970–83
Major teams:
  San Diego–Houston
Records/Awards:
  NBA All-Star (1)
  Hall of Fame (1992)

LEFT: IF EVER THERE WAS A ROCKET, IT WAS THE EXPLOSIVE CALVIN MURPHY.

DIKEMBE MUTOMBO

FACT FILE

Born: June 25, 1966
Height: 7′ 2″
Length of NBA career:
 1991–present
Major teams:
 Denver
 Atlanta (joined 1996)
Records/Awards:
 NBA All-Star (4)
 NBA Defensive Player of
 the Year (1995, 1997)

One of the most intimidating defensive players in the history of the NBA, Dikembe Mutombo set a record for most consecutive seasons leading the league in blocks, swatting his way to four straight crowns from 1993 through 1997.

Mutombo, a 7-foot-2-inch center out of Georgetown, was selected by the Denver Nuggets in the first round of the 1991 NBA draft. He made the 1992 All-Rookie squad after averaging a career-high 16.6 points per game, adding averages of 12.3 rebounds and 2.2 assists while blocking 210 shots.

The following season, Mutombo averaged 13.8 points, 13.0 rebounds, and 1.8 assists, increasing his blocked-shot total to 287. During his four seasons of shot-block dominance,

Mutombo chalked up 336, 321, 332 and 264 rejections, respectively.

A four-time All-Star, Mutombo led the NBA with 4.1 blocked shots per game in 1994, and again in 1995 en route to being named the league's Defensive Player of the Year. The following season, Mutombo topped all shot-blockers with 4.49 blocks per game.

Mutombo, who signed as a free agent after the 1995–96 season with the Atlanta Hawks, has averaged 13.0 points, 12.2 rebounds, and 1.6 assists through his first five NBA seasons, tallying 1,750 blocks. Last season, his first with Atlanta, Mutombo captured his second defensive player of the year award, averaging 11.6 rebounds per game while blocking 264 shots.

RIGHT: DEFENSIVE ENFORCER DIKEMBE MUTOMBO GOES TO WORK ON THE OFFENSIVE END OF THE FLOOR.

LARRY NANCE

The career shot-blocking leader among forwards with 2,027, Larry Nance was also a deadly outside shooter, a consistent scorer, rebounder, and great defender for thirteen NBA seasons.

Nance, a 6-foot-10-inch power forward from Clemson with incredible leaping ability, was selected by Phoenix in the first round of the 1981 NBA draft. In a limited role as a rookie, he averaged 6.6 points and 3.2 rebounds per game.

The following season, however, Nance received substantial minutes and began to display the all-around skills that would make him one of the most respected players in the league. He averaged 16.7 points, 8.7 rebounds, and 2.4 assists per game, adding 217 blocks.

One of the most memorable moments from Nance's career came in 1984, when he outdueled Julius Erving to win the Slam Dunk Competition with a whirling reverse, right-handed slam that highlighted his sheer strength and the mighty springs in his legs. Midway through the 1987–88 season, Nance was traded to the Cleveland Cavaliers.

A three-time All-Star and NBA All-Defensive First Team performer in 1989, Nance averaged 17.1 points, 8.0 rebounds, and 2.6 assists per game, adding 15.7 points, 7.9 rebounds and 2.4 assists in 68 career playoff contests. Nance's best scoring season was 1986–87, when he averaged 22.5 points per contest. He shares the NBA career All-Star game record for highest field-goal percentage, connecting on 15 of 24 field goal attempts for a .714 percentage.

FACT FILE

Born: February 12, 1959
Height: 6' 10"
Length of NBA career:
  1981–94
Major teams:
  Phoenix
  Cleveland (joined 1988)
Records/Awards:
  NBA All-Star (3)
  NBA All-Defensive First
    Team (1)

LEFT: LARRY NANCE WAS A DYNAMITE PERFORMER WHO ONCE OUTDUELED THE GREAT DOCTOR J IN A SLAM-DUNK CONTEST.

CALVIN NATT

FACT FILE

Born: January 8, 1957
Height: 6′ 6″
Length of NBA career:
  1979–90
Major teams:
  New Jersey
  Portland (joined 1980)
  Denver (joined 1984)
  San Antonio (joined 1989)
  Indiana (joined 1989)
Records/Awards:
  NBA All-Star (1)

A small forward who loved to throw his weight around on the basketball court, Calvin Natt was an NBA star for seven seasons before an injured left knee forced him out of the game.

Natt, a 6-foot-6-inch player who thrived on a physical, aggressive style of play, was selected by the New Jersey Nets out of Northeast Louisiana in the first round of the 1979 NBA draft. He split his first season between the Nets and Portland Trail Blazers, earning a place on the All-Rookie team by averaging 19.9 points per game, the first of seven straight seasons in which he would continuously make double-figure averages in scoring.

From 1980–84, Natt played in Portland. His best scoring season in a Trail Blazers' uniform came in 1982–83, when he averaged 20.4 points per contest. In 1984, Natt was traded by Portland to Denver and enjoyed the best campaign of his career, averaging 23.3 points per contest for the Nuggets while earning a spot on his only All-Star team.

"I'm an aggressive-type player," Natt once said. "I'm not a finesse type. I like to bang heads and throw my body around. I also try to be an all-around player and handle the ball as much as I shoot. Anybody can score a lot if they shoot a lot. I like to think I can get my points if I play defense and rebound."

For his complete NBA career, Natt averaged 17.2 points, 6.7 rebounds, and 2.1 assists, adding 18.4 points, 7.2 boards, and 2.4 assists in forty-five career playoff contests.

RIGHT: HE WAS A SMALL FORWARD, BUT CALVIN NATT LOVED TO MIX IT UP WITH OPPONENTS ON THE COURT.

DON NELSON

Bill Russell, who played with Don Nelson and coached him for three seasons, once called the 6-foot-6-inch forward "the epitome of what it means to be a Celtic."

Nelson, a cerebral player with a pretty outside shot, began his NBA career as the 1962 third round draft choice of the Chicago Zephyrs, who would eventually become the Washington Bullets.

After a poor rookie season with the Zephyrs and two quiet seasons with the Los Angeles Lakers, Nelson was placed on waivers. Just when he felt his career might be over, Celtic general manager and coach Red Auerbach invited Nelson to Boston for a tryout, making no promises.

Nelson not only made the team, he stayed in Boston for eleven seasons, helping the Celtics win five championship rings. During the 1974–75 season, at the age of thirty-four years, Nelson led the league in field goal percentage, bagging 423 of 785 field goal attempts for a .539 percentage.

For all he accomplished in Boston, Nelson is best remembered for sinking one of the most famous shots in league history on May 5, 1969, in Game 7 of the NBA Finals against the Lakers. With the game tied and time winding down, Nelson threw up a loose ball which hit the rim, bounced high off it, then somehow fell through the cords to give Boston a 108–106 victory.

Nelson, who averaged 21.1 points per game in three seasons at Iowa, averaged 10.3 points, 4.9 rebounds, and 1.4 assists per game in 14 NBA seasons, adding 10.5 points, 4.8 boards, and 1.4 assists in 150 career playoff games. After his playing days, he enjoyed a twenty-year career as an NBA coach and executive.

FACT FILE

Born: May 15, 1940
Height: 6′ 6″
Length of NBA career:
1962–76
Major teams:
Chicago
Los Angeles (joined 1963)
Boston (joined 1965)
Records/Awards:
NBA Championship (5)

LEFT: IN THE WORDS OF ONE TEAMMATE, DON NELSON WAS "THE EPITOME OF WHAT IT MEANS TO BE A CELTIC."

NORM NIXON

FACT FILE

Born: October 10, 1955
Height: 6′ 2″
Length of NBA career:
   1977–89
Major teams:
   Los Angeles Lakers
   San Diego–Los Angeles
      (joined 1983)
Records/Awards:
   NBA All-Star (3)
   NBA Championship (2)

Before Magic Johnson brought Showtime to Los Angeles in 1979, Norm Nixon was running the show for the Lakers. With Nixon and Johnson together in the backcourt, the Lakers won championships in 1980 and 1982.

An excellent passer, fine penetrator, and dependable shooter, the 6-foot-2-inch Nixon was selected out of Duquesne by the Lakers in the first round of the 1977 NBA draft. He won a place on the 1978 All-Rookie team after averaging 13.7 points, 6.8 assists, and 3.0 rebounds.

For nine straight seasons, the first six spent with the Lakers, Nixon averaged double digits in scoring. His best seasons were 1979–80, when he led the league with 3,226 minutes played and averaged 17.6 points per game, and 1981–82, when he again scored 17.6 points per contest. This was a career-high. A three-time

All-Star, Nixon was traded to the San Diego Clippers in 1983, and was hurt when the Lakers said goodbye. "I was initially very disappointed, very disturbed," Nixon said at the time.

Nixon played the last five seasons of his career with the Clippers, who relocated to Los Angeles in 1984. He split his last professional season with the Clippers and Scavolini Pesaro of the Italian League, where he averaged 12.4 points per game.

In ten NBA seasons—Nixon missed the entire 1987–88 campaign due to an achilles tendon injury—Nixon averaged 15.7 points, 8.3 assists, and 2.6 rebounds, adding 17.7 points, 8.0 assists, and 3.4 rebounds in 58 career playoff contests.

At Duquesne, Nixon averaged 17.4 points over four seasons, scoring a career-high 22.0 points per game in his senior season.

RIGHT: BEFORE MAGIC, NORM NIXON WAS ORCHESTRATING THE LOS ANGELES LAKERS' OFFENSE.

CHARLES OAKLEY

One day after the Knicks had finished practicing, a group of reporters chatted with then New York coach Pat Riley about Charles Oakley. "He's like a bull in a china shop," one reporter said to Riley. "Yeah," Riley answered. "I couldn't describe Oakley's style any better than that."

Ever since he arrived on the NBA scene with the Chicago Bulls out of little-known Virginia Union in 1985, the 6-foot-9-inch, 245-pound Oakley has indeed been a bull in a china shop, diving out of bounds for loose balls, taking hard charges, barreling into opponents on drives to the basket, or just playing his hard-nosed style of defense, which perks up the home crowd and usually frustrates the visitors. Oakley, who led the NCAA Division II with 17.3 rebounds per game in 1985, was selected by the Cleveland Cavaliers in the first round of the 1985 NBA draft, but his draft rights were traded from Cleveland to Chicago.

After averaging 9.6 points, 8.6 rebounds, and 1.7 assists in his first season with the Bulls,

Oakley earned a place on the 1986 All-Rookie Team.

The following season was Oakley's best-ever in Chicago as he posted 14.5 points, 13.1 rebounds, and 3.6 assists per contest. In 1988, Oakley was traded to the Knicks, where he joined forces with center Patrick Ewing to turn New York into an Eastern conference powerhouse.

His best scoring season in a Knick uniform was 1989–90, when he averaged 14.6 points per game. The lone All-Star appearance on Oakley's resume was made in 1994, while he was in the midst of putting together averages of 11.8 points and 11.8 rebounds. He was also named to the NBA's All-Defensive First Team that season, tallying a career-high 110 steals.

Through his first twelve NBA seasons, Oakley has posted averages of 11.0 points, 10.5 rebounds, and 2.4 assists, adding 11.2 points, 10.6 rebounds, and 2.0 assists in 119 career playoff games. At Virginia Union, Oakley averaged 20.3 points and 14.0 rebounds over four seasons.

FACT FILE

Born: December 18, 1963
Height: 6' 9"
Length of NBA career:
    1985–present
Major teams:
    Chicago
    New York (joined 1988)
Records/Awards:
    NBA All-Defensive First
    Team (1)
    NBA All-Star (1)

BELOW: PAT RILEY AGREED WITH ONE REPORTER'S DESCRIPTION OF CHARLES OAKLEY: "HE'S LIKE A BULL IN A CHINA SHOP," THE REPORTER SAID.

HAKEEM OLAJUWON

FACT FILE

Born: January 21, 1963
Height: 7′ 0″
Length of NBA career:
  1984–present
Major team:
  Houston
Records/Awards:
  NBA All-Star (12)
  NBA All-Defensive First
    Team (5)
  NBA Defensive Player of
    the Year (2)
  NBA Most Valuable Player
    (1994)
  NBA Championship (2)
  Olympic Gold Medal
    (1996)

Hakeem Olajuwon is regarded widely to be the best center in the NBA today, and one of the greatest in the league's history.

Olajuwon, a 7-foot pivotman who grew up playing soccer in his native Nigeria, is the complete package. He uses his quick and fancy footwork on the basketball court to help him rebound, block shots, and beat opponents to open spots on the floor, where he can hurt you with a thunderous dunk, a feathery outside shot, or a sneaky pass to an open teammate.

Defensively, there is no one better at his position. A five-time NBA All-Defensive First Team selection, Olajuwon was the league's Defensive Player of the Year in 1993 and 1994.

"Hakeem the Dream," as Olajuwon is called, led the Rockets to back-to-back championships in 1994 and 1995, winning the MVP award in both series.

Through the 1996–97 season, he was Houston's all-time leader in scoring (23,650 points), rebounding (11,739), steals (1,811), and blocked shots (3,363), which is also an NBA record.

Selected by the Rockets as the first pick overall out of the University of Houston in the 1984 NBA draft, Olajuwon made the 1985 All-Rookie team after averaging 20.6 points and 11.9 rebounds per game.

In each of his twelve seasons thereafter, Olajuwon has averaged no less than 20 points per game. His super skills and winning experience helped the United States capture an Olympic gold medal in 1996.

Olajuwon's best years were 1993–94, when he averaged 27.3 points and 11.9 rebounds per game en route to winning the league's MVP award, and 1994–95, when he scored a career-high 27.8 points and hauled down 10.8 rebounds per game.

In his first twelve seasons with the Rockets, Olajuwon, an All-Star in every one of them, has averaged 24.2 points and 12.0 rebounds per game, adding 27.3 points and 11.6 rebounds per game in 131 career playoff contests.

RIGHT: MANY BASKETBALL EXPERTS CONSIDER HAKEEM OLAJUWON TO BE THE GREATEST CENTER IN THE GAME TODAY.

SHAQUILLE O'NEAL

One of the most intimidating and talented presences in the NBA today, Shaquille O'Neal, the 7-foot-1-inch, 301-pound center of the Los Angeles Lakers, combines brute strength with an ever-improving arsenal of low-post moves to make him one of the NBA's marquee attractions.

"Shaq," as O'Neal is known around the basketball world, played his first three NBA seasons with the Orlando Magic, who selected him as the first pick overall in the 1992 draft.

After winning the 1993 NBA Rookie of the Year award with averages of 23.4 points, 13.9 rebounds, and a career-high 286 blocks, O'Neal averaged 29.3 points and 13.2 rebounds the following season.

With the powerful O'Neal and the super-talented guard Penny Hardaway providing a lethal one-two punch, Orlando seemed like a dynasty in the making but it never happened.

In the 1994–95 season, O'Neal led the league with a 29.3 average, spearheading a charge to the NBA Finals, where the Magic disappeared against Houston in four straight games. Through his first five NBA seasons, O'Neal averaged 27.0 points and 12.5 rebounds per game, adding 25.6 points and 11.2 boards in 45 career playoff contests. His only major weakness is at the free throw line, where he has made just 54 percent of his shots since joining the league.

After signing as a free agent with Los Angeles after the 1995–96 season, O'Neal left Orlando as the Magic's all-time leader in rebounding (3,691) and blocked shots (824).

An All-Star in each of his first five NBA seasons, O'Neal helped the US win an Olympic gold medal in 1996.

FACT FILE

Born: March 6, 1972
Height: 7′ 1″
Length of NBA career:
1992–present
Major teams:
Orlando
Los Angeles Lakers
(joined 1996)
Records/Awards:
NBA Rookie of the Year
(1993)
NBA All-Star (5)
Olympic Gold Medal
(1996)

LEFT: A MODERN-DAY WILT CHAMBERLAIN, SHAQUILLE O'NEAL OF THE LOS ANGELES LAKERS IS A ONE-MAN WRECKING CREW.

THE NBA'S GREATEST SCORING RACE

I t was simply the greatest scoring race in NBA history, and when the smoke cleared after Denver's David Thompson and San Antonio's George Gervin went gunning for that title on Sunday, April 9, 1978, Gervin was the shooter still standing.

On the final day of the 1977–78 regular-season, Thompson, a 6-foot-4-inch scoring machine out of North Carolina State who patented the "cradle-the-baby dunk" and also devastated opponents with his "windmill slams," had racked up 73 points in the Nuggets' 139–137 loss to the Detroit Pistons at the Cobo Arena.

Thompson's offensive explosion, the third-highest single-game point total in NBA history, lifted his scoring average to 27.15 points per game for the season.

The scoring championship seemed all but wrapped up as Gervin, whose Spurs would play the New Orleans Jazz at the Louisiana Superdome just seven hours later, needed 58 points to beat out Thompson for the title. The 6-foot-7-inch Gervin, who loved to score points off fancy, high-floating fingerrolls, seemed to have lost all hope at winning the scoring crown after he was held scoreless in the first three minutes of action against New Orleans.

Then suddenly, the Iceman, as Gervin was called, got hot. He bagged ten of the Spurs' next 13 points, finishing the first quarter with 20.

In the second quarter, Gervin, hungry for the title, exploded in record-breaking style. He netted 33 of San Antonio's 40 points in the period—an NBA record which still stands—breaking the mark, ironically, of 32 points in a single quarter set by Thompson only hours earlier.

In the second half, the Spurs kept feeding Gervin the ball, and with ten and a half minutes left in the third quarter, he buried a turnaround, ten-foot jumper which gave him 59 points, and brought the frenzied New Orleans crowd to its feet. Gervin would finish with 63 points on the evening, putting his scoring average at 27.22 points per game for the season, and taking the scoring crown away from Thompson in clutch, dramatic fashion. The Iceman would go on to capture three more scoring titles during his remarkable fourteen-year pro career.

"That was a phenomenal performance," then-San Antonio coach Doug Moe said at the time. "We were going to George exclusively and the Jazz were trying to stop him exclusively. It was something to watch. George could have scored 80 points the way he was going."

BILLY OWENS

FACT FILE

Born: May 1, 1969
Height: 6′ 9″
Length of NBA career:
 1991–present
Major teams:
 Golden State
 Miami (joined 1994)
 Sacramento (joined 1996)

A new breed of multi-talented NBA player, Billy Owens can score like a shooting guard, rebound like a power forward, or run the floor like a playmaker.

Owens, a 6-foot-9-inch swingman selected by the Sacramento Kings out of Syracuse in the first round of the 1991 NBA draft, was traded just before the start of his first season to the Golden State Warriors. He made the 1992 All-Rookie squad after averaging 14.3 points and 8.0 rebounds per game, helping the Warriors to an eleven-game turnaround and a 55–27 record, their best in sixteen years.

A knee injury limited Owens to just thirty-seven games the following season, but he bounced back in 1993–94 to average 15.0 points, 8.1 rebounds, and 4.1 assists per contest, joining Charles Barkley, Christian Laettner, David Robinson, and Scottie Pippen as the only players in the league to reach those plateaus. Just before the 1994–95 season, Owens was traded by Golden State to the Miami Heat. He fought off nagging injuries that season to average 14.3 points, 7.2 rebounds, and 3.5 assists. Midway through the 1995–96 season, Owens was traded by Miami to Sacramento, finishing the season with averages of 13.0 points, 6.6 rebounds, and 3.3 assists.

Last season, his first full campaign with Sacramento, Owens averaged 11.0 points and 5.9 rebounds per game.

Through his first six NBA seasons, Owens posted averages of 13.9 points, 7.2 rebounds, and 3.3 assists per game. He bettered those numbers in the post season, averaging 15.4 points, 8.1 rebounds, and 3.6 assists in eleven career playoff contests.

At Syracuse, Owens averaged 17.9 points and 8.8 rebounds in three seasons.

RIGHT: BILLY OWENS REPRESENTS A NEW BREED OF MULTI-TALENTED PLAYERS.

ROBERT PARISH

While Larry Bird, Kevin McHale, and Dennis Johnson got most of the headlines during Boston's glory years in the 1980s, Robert Parish, the 7-foot-1-inch workhorse center, who retired after last season, went out every night and gave the Celtics a much-needed lift on both ends of the floor, helping the fabled franchise win three championships during his fourteen-year stint with the club.

"He's the hub of the club," then teammate M. L. Carr said about Parish during the 1985 championship series against the Los Angeles Lakers. "He's where the defense starts. He directs traffic back there like Dave Cowens did, and he runs the court probably better than any other center in the league."

Parish, selected by the Golden State Warriors in the first round of the 1976 NBA draft, played four seasons with the Warriors before he was traded to Boston for the 1980–81 season. In his first season wearing a Celtic uniform, Parish averaged 18.9 points, 9.5 rebounds, and 1.8 assists per game, helping Bird and company capture the NBA title.

During the 1984 NBA Finals, in which Boston defeated the hated Los Angeles Lakers in seven games, Kareem Abdul-Jabbar out-scored Parish, averaging 26.6 points per game to 15.4, but Parish had more rebounds, 80 to 57, including more offensive rebounds, 30 to 23.

The "Chief," as Parish is called, holds the career record for most games played (1,611), most defensive rebounds (10,117), and shared the career record for most seasons played through the 1996–97 season.

He made averages in double digits for scoring during seventeen straight seasons from the 1977–78 campaign, his second with Golden State, through the 1993–94 season, his last with the Celtics.

A nine-time All-Star, Parish played with the Charlotte Hornets for two seasons before signing with the Chicago Bulls after 1995–96 for his record-breaking twenty-first NBA season. He went out in style, helping the Bulls win a championship last season.

Through his first 21 seasons, Parish averaged 14.5 points, 9.1 rebounds, and 1.4 assists, adding 15.3 points, 9.6 rebounds, and 1.3 assists in 184 career playoff games. He holds the career playoff record for most offensive rebounds with 571.

At Centenary College, Parish post averages of 21.6 points and 16.9 boards in four seasons.

FACT FILE

Born: August 30, 1953
Height: 7' 1"
Length of NBA career:
1976–1997
Major teams:
Golden State
Boston (joined 1980)
Charlotte (joined 1994)
Chicago (joined 1996)
Records/Awards:
NBA All-Star (9)
NBA Championship (4)

LEFT: ON THOSE GREAT BOSTON TEAMS OF THE 1980S, ROBERT PARISH WAS ALWAYS IN THE MIDDLE OF THE ACTION.

BILLY PAULTZ

FACT FILE

Born: July 30, 1948
Height: 6' 11"
Length of ABA career:
  1970–76
Length of NBA career:
  1976–85
Major teams:
  New York
  San Antonio (joined 1975)
  Houston (joined 1980)
  San Antonio (joined 1983)
  Atlanta (joined 1983)
  Utah (joined 1984)
Records/Awards:
  ABA All-Star (3)
  ABA Championship (1)

With the exception of Dolph Schayes, Billy Paultz made more consecutive playoff appearances than any other player in professional basketball history.

Paultz, a 6-foot-11-inch, 245-pound center from St. John's who answered to the nickname "Whopper," made his first playoff appearance as a rookie with the New York Nets of the ABA. Paultz spent his first five seasons with the Nets, averaging a career-high 16.7 points per game in 1972–73, and teaming with Julius Erving on the 1974 Nets to win the ABA championship.

After five playoff appearances with the Nets, Paultz, who moved with a bulky kind of stiffness but got the job done with hustle and heads-up play, made four straight post-season appearances with the San Antonio Spurs from 1975–79.

The post-season streak for Paultz continued in Houston, where he played for two and a half seasons, teaming with Moses Malone to help the Rockets into the 1981 Finals, where they lost to Boston in six games. With the Rockets in last place in the Western Conference late in the 1982–83 season, it seemed as if Paultz's post-season party would come to an end, but he was placed on waivers and picked up by playoff-bound San Antonio.

Paultz, who averaged 15.7 points per game in six ABA seasons, and 15.7 points per contest in nine NBA seasons, made playoff appearances in 1984 with Atlanta, and in 1985, his last year in the NBA, with the Utah Jazz.

A three-time All-Star, Paultz, who also advanced to post-season play with St. John's before entering the NBA, once described himself as a player.

"I have realized that I'm not the overpowering type center," said Paultz of his style of play. "I don't really know what my category is. I have always been the type of player that can do a little bit of everything. I add defensive stability, can shoot when I'm in position, set picks to get people free, and am smart enough to pick out the open man in double-team situations. I like to think I know the techniques of blocking out my man."

RIGHT: HUSTLE AND HEADS-UP PLAY WERE THE TRADEMARKS OF BILLY PAULTZ' GAME.

GARY PAYTON

The 1995–96 NBA leader in steals per game with a 2.85 average, Gary Payton has blossomed into one of the premier point guards in the NBA.

Payton, a 6-foot-4-inch lightning bolt out of Oregon State selected by Seattle in the first round of the 1990 NBA draft, teamed with Shawn Kemp to lead the Super-Sonics to the 1996 NBA Finals, where Chicago prevailed in six games.

A four-time All-Star who has developed into a consistent shooter, Payton's main strength is his defense. A four-time NBA All-Defensive First Team selection, the energetic Sonics playmaker was voted the league's Defensive Player of the Year in 1996, finishing with a league-high 231 steals. He also spent his summer in Atlanta helping the US Olympic basketball team earn a gold medal.

Payton, who averaged a career-high 21.8 points per game last season, fell just shy of making 200 steals, finishing with 197. Payton was named to the NBA's 1991 All-Rookie Second Team.

From there, Payton's scoring average increased in each of the next four seasons, topping at 20.6 points per contest in 1994–95. Through his first seven NBA seasons, all spent in Seattle, Payton has averaged 15.5 points, 6.5 assists, and 3.6 rebounds, racking up 1,309 steals. He has registered 16.1 points, 5.9 assists, and 4.0 rebounds in 74 post-season contests, and holds the single-game playoff record for most three-point field goal attempts in one half, connecting for 13 treys on May 4, 1996, against Houston.

FACT FILE

Born: July 23, 1968
Height: 6′ 4″
Length of NBA career:
1990–present
Major team:
Seattle
Records/Awards:
NBA Defensive Player of the Year (1996)
NBA All-Defensive First Team (4)
NBA All-Star (4)
Olympic Gold Medal (1996)

LEFT: GARY PAYTON HAS BLOSSOMED INTO ONE OF THE NBA'S GREAT POINT GUARDS.

JOHN PAXSON

FACT FILE

Born: September 29, 1960
Height: 6′ 2″
Length of NBA career:
  1983–94
Major teams:
  San Antonio
  Chicago (joined 1985)
Records/Awards:
  NBA Championship (3)

John Paxson, a clutch out-side shooter, was a key contributor to the three straight championships won by the Chicago Bulls from 1991–93.

A 6-foot-2-inch marksman out of Notre Dame, Paxson was often called upon to drain the big-money shots when higher-profiled team-mates like Michael Jordan and Scottie Pippen were being double-teamed—and more often than not, Paxson came through.

After breaking into the NBA slowly with the San Antonio Spurs in 1983, Paxson signed as a free agent with the Bulls in 1985. His best scoring season with the Bulls came in 1986–87, when he knocked down an average of 11.3 points per contest.

Paxson's finest moment in a Chicago uniform came on June 5, 1991, against the Los Angeles Lakers. With Chicago trailing in the series, one game to none, Paxson went wild from the field, setting an NBA Finals single-game record by connecting on all eight of his field goal attempts. Riding the strength of that effort, the Bulls tied the series at one game apiece with a 107–86 victory.

Chicago then reeled off three straight victories to get their dynasty run in full gear.

Retiring after nine seasons in Chicago, Paxson finished his NBA career with averages of 7.2 points, 3.6 assists, and 1.2 rebounds per game, adding 6.3 points, and 2.6 assists per game in 119 post-season contests.

The name Paxson is quite familiar in NBA circles. John's father, Jim Paxson, Sr, was a forward with the Minneapolis Lakers and Cincinnati Royals in the 1956–58 seasons, and his brother, Jim, was a guard with the Portland Trail Blazers and Boston Celtics between 1979 and 1990.

RIGHT: JOHN PAXSON WAS A KEY CONTRIBUTOR TO CHICAGO'S CHAMPION SUCCESS, ESPECIALLY ON JUNE 5, 1991.

SAM PERKINS

leepy-eyed Sam Perkins has had NBA defenses on the alert for the past thirteen seasons.

Perkins, who teamed with Michael Jordan and James Worthy on the 1982 North Carolina team which defeated Georgetown to win the NCAA Championship, was selected by the Dallas Mavericks in the first round of the 1984 NBA draft. He was named to the 1985 All-Rookie squad after averaging 11.0 points, 7.4 rebounds, and 1.6 assists per game. His best season with the Mavericks came in 1989–90, when he averaged 15.9 points and 7.5 rebounds per game.

A 6-foot-9-inch forward/center who has the ability to break a team's back with a long outside shot, Perkins spent his first six seasons with the Mavericks before signing as a free agent with the Los Angeles Lakers in 1990. He reached career-high scoring (16.5) and rebounding (8.8) totals with the Lakers in the 1991–92 season.

Midway through the 1992–93 campaign, Perkins was traded to Seattle, where he has helped create havoc in the paint. With Perkins in the fold, the SuperSonics reached the 1996 NBA Finals, but they were turned away by Michael Jordan and the Chicago Bulls in six games.

In each of his first thirteen NBA seasons, Perkins averaged double digits in scoring. For his career, Perkins has averaged 13.6 points and 6.7 rebounds per game, adding 13.9 points and 6.8 rebounds in 118 career playoff contests. At North Carolina, Perkins averaged 15.9 points and 8.6 rebounds over four seasons. He was a member of the gold-medal winning US Olympic basketball team.

FACT FILE

Born: June 14, 1961
Height: 6′ 9″
Length of NBA career:
　1984–present
Major teams:
　Dallas
　Los Angeles Lakers
　　(joined 1990)
　Seattle (joined 1993)
Records/Awards:
　US Olympic Gold Medal
　　(1984)

LEFT: SLEEPY-EYED SAM PERKINS (RIGHT), KEEPING CHICAGO'S LUC LONGLEY ON RED ALERT.

CHUCK PERSON

FACT FILE

Born: June 27, 1964
Height: 6' 8"
Length of NBA career:
 1986–present
Major teams:
 Indiana
 Minnesota (joined 1992)
 San Antonio (joined 1994)
Records/Awards:
 NBA Rookie of the Year
 (1987)

They call San Antonio's Chuck Person "The Rifleman" for a very good reason. He has been one of the NBA's most consistent and dangerous shooters since he was selected by the Indiana Pacers in the first round of the 1986 NBA draft.

Person, who averaged 18.3 points per game in four seasons at Auburn, was named the NBA's Rookie of the Year in 1987 after lighting up scoreboards for 18.8 points per contest, adding a career-high 8.3 rebounds per game.

The first six years of Person's career were spent in Indiana, with the highlight being the first round of the 1991 Eastern Conference Playoffs, Game 2, against the Boston Celtics.

With Boston ahead in that series, one game to none, Person, given the task of guarding the great Larry Bird, got the better of the Beantown legend, and the hometown fans didn't like it. In front of 14,890 screaming spectators at the Boston Garden, Person took Bird to school, scoring a season-high 39 points, including a playoff record seven three-point baskets, in leading the Pacers to a 130–118 victory. Boston eventually won the series in five hard-fought games, but Person was, and still is, a target of the Boston boo-birds whenever he steps onto the floor against the Celtics.

After his stint with Indiana, Person was traded to the Minnesota Timberwolves, where he spent two seasons before signing with the Spurs as a free agent in 1994. In each of his first ten seasons in the league, Person averaged double digits in scoring. Person's best scoring season was with Indiana in 1988–89, when he averaged 21.6 points per game. Through the 1995–96 campaign, Person averaged 16.4 points and 5.5 rebounds.

RIGHT: CHUCK PERSON HAD A MEMORABLE PLAYOFF SHOWDOWN AGAINST THE GREAT LARRY BIRD AND THE BOSTON CELTICS IN 1991.

GEOFF PETRIE

The first-ever selection of the Portland Trail Blazers in 1970, Geoff Petrie was well on his way to becoming one of the NBA's all-time greats when a knee injury in his sixth season forced him to retire.

Petrie, a 6-foot-4-inch, sharp-shooting swingman who helped Princeton win an Ivy League title in 1969, shared co-Rookie of the Year honors with Dave Cowens of the Boston Celtics in 1971. He averaged team highs in scoring (24.8)—the highest ever by a Portland rookie—and assists (4.8) per game that season, and also led the club with 463 free throws made.

By scoring a total of 2,031 points in his initial campaign, which was also the Trail Blazers' inaugural campaign, Petrie became one of just eight rookies in the NBA's history to surpass the 2,000-point plateau. A two-time All-Star who holds the Portland single-game scoring record with a total of 51 points (he did it twice in his career), Petrie put up healthy scoring totals for the next five seasons before he was forced to retire. His best scoring season was 1972–73, when he posted averages of 24.9 points per game.

In his six seasons with Portland, Petrie averaged 21.8 points per contest. His 9,732 career points ranks him fifth on the Trail Blazers' all-time scoring list, and his 2,057 assists places him third in that department.

Princeton's team captain as a senior in 1970, Petrie scored 1,321 points for the Tigers, earning consecutive All-East and All-Ivy League honors in his junior and senior seasons.

FACT FILE

Born: April 17, 1948
Height: 6′ 4″
Length of NBA career:
 1970–76
Major team:
 Portland
Records/Awards:
 NBA co-Rookie of the Year (1971)
 NBA All-Star (2)

LEFT: SHARP-SHOOTING SWINGMAN GEOFF PETRIE (LEFT), HAD A BLOCKBUSTER ROOKIE CAMPAIGN.

DRAZEN PETROVIC

FACT FILE

Born: October 22, 1964
Height: 6′ 5″
Length of NBA career:
 1989–93
Major teams:
 Portland
 New Jersey (joined 1991)

On June 7, 1993, Drazen Petrovic, then just twenty-eight years old and entering the prime of his athletic life, was killed in an automobile accident in Germany, sending shockwaves around the NBA and the rest of the basketball world.

Petrovic, a 6-foot-5-inch shooting guard from Yugoslavia who was starring for the New Jersey Nets at the time of his death, was selected by the Portland Trail Blazers in the third round of the 1986 NBA draft. After playing in Europe for three years, Petrovic joined the Trail Blazers for the 1989–90 season, averaging 7.6 points per contest as an NBA rookie.

Midway through the 1990–91 season, Petrovic was traded to New Jersey, and with the Nets, Petrovic became a star on the rise, averaging 10.2 points per game in his first season with the team, 20.6 in the 1991–92 season, and career-high 22.3 points in the 1992–93 season. At the time of his death, Petrovic was considered by many to be the best outside shooter in the game, and it seemed only a matter of time before he reached All-Star status.

He was among the league leaders in three-point accuracy in 1992–93, shooting at a .449 clip en route to an All-NBA Third-Team selection. In twenty-nine career playoff games, the man his teammates called "Petro" or "Draz" averaged 10.2 points per game.

Before joining the NBA, Petrovic, who averaged 15.4 points in four seasons in the league, was a member of the silver-medal winning Yugoslavian Olympic Basketball Team in 1988. In 1992, he won a silver medal with the Croatian Olympic Team.

"He was a good person and a great player," said Kenny Anderson, who teamed with Petrovic in the Nets' backcourt. "I just wish I could have said goodbye to him."

RIGHT: THE LATE, GREAT DRAZEN PETROVIC LAUNCHES A SHOT FROM DEEP IN THE CORNER.

BOB PETTIT

O n November 13, 1965, 31-year-old Bob Pettit of the St. Louis Hawks went up for an offensive rebound during a game at Cincinnati, gained control of the ball, and put it back into the basket to become the first player to score 20,000 points in a career.

"I wanted to be the first one," Pettit said after the game as celebrating teammates showered him with congratulations. "I'm proud to be the first to get 20,000 points. I've broken records before and I've been happy, but this record was the one I wanted."

A 6-foot-9-inch forward/center out of Louisiana State who played his entire eleven-year career with the Hawks—who moved from Milwaukee to St. Louis for the 1955–56 season—Pettit won just about every honor the NBA had to offer. After averaging 20.4 points, 13.8 rebounds, and 3.2 assists in his first season with the Hawks, Pettit was named the 1955 NBA Rookie of the Year.

The following season, Pettit won the first of two scoring championships and two Most Valued Player awards with a 25.7 average (adding a league-high 1,164 rebounds), and in just his third season, averaged 24.7 points per game in leading the Hawks to the first of five straight Western Division titles.

In Game 6 of the 1958 NBA Finals against the mighty Boston Celtics, Pettit exploded for a regulation game playoff record of 50 points, lifting the Hawks to a 110–109 series-clinching victory.

The following season, Pettit captured his second MVP award and his second scoring title, tallying a single-season scoring record with 2,105 points for a career-high, 29.2 points per game. One of the NBA's best ever offensive rebounders—he holds the Hawks' career rebounding record with 12,849—Pettit was selected for the All-Star team all eleven seasons and was voted the game's Most Valuable Player in 1956, 1958, and 1962, sharing the honor in 1959 with Elgin Baylor.

For his career, Pettit averaged 26.4 points, 16.2 rebounds, and 3.0 assists per game, adding 25.5 points, 14.8 rebounds, and 2.7 assists in eighty-eight career playoff contests. He was named to the league's 25th Anniversary All-Time Team in 1970, and 35th Anniversary All-Time team in 1980.

FACT FILE

Born: December 12, 1932
Height: 6′ 9″
Length of NBA career:
  1954–65
Major team:
  Milwaukee–St. Louis
Records/Awards:
  NBA Rookie of the Year
    (1955)
  NBA Most Valuable Player
    (2)
  NBA All-Star (11)
  NBA Championship (1)
  Hall of Fame (1970)

LEFT: BOB PETTIT SCORING TWO OF HIS 20,000-PLUS POINTS.

RICKY PIERCE

FACT FILE

Born: August 19, 1959
Height: 6′ 4″
Length of NBA career:
  1982–present
Major teams:
  Detroit
  San Diego (joined 1983)
  Milwaukee (joined 1984)
  Seattle (joined 1991)
  Golden State (joined
    1994)
  Indiana (joined 1995)
  Denver (joined 1996)
  Charlotte (joined 1997)
Records/Awards:
  NBA All-Star (1)
  NBA Sixth Man Award (2)

One of the NBA's most reliable veterans, Ricky Pierce has been providing major-league bench strength to a number of teams for the past fifteen seasons.

Pierce, a 6-foot-4-inch shooting guard out of Rice, is a two-time winner of the NBA's Sixth Man Award.

Selected by the Detroit Pistons in the first round of the 1982 NBA draft, Pierce played sparingly as a rookie in the Motor City, and was dealt to San Diego the following season, where he averaged 9.9 points per game.

After one season in San Diego, Pierce moved on to Milwaukee, and he wasn't playing there long before he gained a reputation as one of the league's most dangerous shooters.

In the 1986–87 season, Pierce's third year with the Bucks, he came off the bench to average 19.5 points, 2.2 assists, and 3.4 rebounds per game en route to winning his first Sixth Man award.

Three seasons later, Pierce averaged a career-high 23.0 points, 2.3 assists, and 2.8 rebounds per contest, making room on his trophy case for his second Sixth Man award.

For ten straight seasons from 1985 through 1995, which included stints with Seattle and Golden State, Pierce averaged double digits in scoring. He made his only All-Star appearance in 1990–91, averaging 20.5 points in a split season with Milwaukee and Seattle.

Through his first fifteen NBA seasons, Pierce has averaged 15.4 points per game, adding 14.9 points in 97 career playoff contests. He played for Indiana during the 1995–96 season before he was traded to Denver and then to Charlotte. At Rice, Pierce averaged 22.5 points in three seasons.

RIGHT: THE RELIABLE VETERAN RICKY PIERCE HAS PUT A CHARGE IN EVERY OFFENSE HE'S EVER PLAYED IN.

SCOTTIE PIPPEN

He might not even be the best player on his own team, but Scottie Pippen is certainly one of the greatest superstars in NBA history.

Pippen, a 6-foot-7-inch swingman out of Central Arkansas who excels in the open court and plays the game with a rare combination of power, speed, and finesse, has played his entire career in the long shadow of his legendary teammate, Michael Jordan. His individual accomplishments, however, shine brighter than the five championship rings he and Jordan helped the Bulls capture from 1991 through 1997.

By no means a supporting actor, Pippen has become a star in his own right since joining the Bulls in the 1987–88 season.

Since that time, Pippen has averaged double digits in scoring in nine straight seasons from 1988–97, was named to the NBA's All-Defensive First Team six times, and appeared in seven All-Star games.

Perhaps the most telling sign of Pippen's greatness is what he did for the Bulls while Jordan was away from the game for nearly two seasons trying to launch a baseball career.

Jordan was no longer taking the bows, or most of the crucial shots, for the entire 1993–94 season. That year Pippen went out and averaged career-highs in points (22.0) and rebounding, adding 5.6 assists per game and 211 steals.

Those efforts propelled the Bulls into the playoffs, where they lost to the Knicks in seven hard-fought games to decide the Eastern Conference semifinals.

The following year, Jordan would come out of retirement with just 17 regular-season games remaining, but before he came back, Pippen, who averaged 21.4 points, 8.1 rebounds, 5.2 assists, and a league-leading 232 steals, already had the Bulls primed for another playoff run.

"It's Scottie's team now," was one of the first comments made by Jordan upon his return to Chicago, confirming Pippen's ability.

Through his first ten NBA seasons, all spent with the Bulls, Pippen averaged 17.9 points, 6.9 rebounds, and 5.3 assists, adding 18.2 points, 7.7 rebounds, and 5.2 assists in 157 career playoff games.

He was also a member of Dream Team I, which won the gold medal for the US in the 1992 Olympics in Barcelona, Spain, and helped his country earn another gold medal in the 1996 Olympic Games in the USA.

FACT FILE

Born: September 25, 1965
Height: 6' 7"
Length of NBA career: 1987–present
Major team: Chicago
Records/Awards:
NBA All-Defensive First Team (6)
NBA All-Star (7)
NBA Championship (5)
Olympic Gold Medals (1992, 1996)

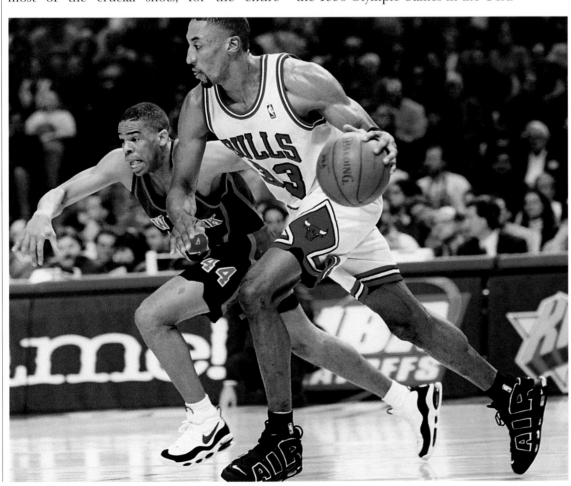

LEFT: WHEN MICHAEL JORDAN GAVE BASEBALL A TRY, THE CHICAGO BULLS BECAME SCOTTIE PIPPEN'S TEAM.

THE 1980 FINALS: A MAGICAL PERFORMANCE

Kareem Abdul-Jabbar was 3,000 miles away, nursing the left ankle he had sprained in the third period of the 108–103 victory in Game 5 of the 1980 NBA Championship Series, a victory which had put the Lakers ahead of the Philadelphia 76ers in the best-of-seven series, three games to two.

Desperately seeking a replacement for the injured Jabbar, Los Angeles Coach Paul Westhead turned to his heralded, 6-foot-9-inch rookie point guard, Magic Johnson.

When Johnson—who hadn't played center since his days at Everett High school in East Lansing, MI—strolled out to the center jump circle to meet Philadelphia's 7-foot-1-inch Caldwell Jones on that Friday night, May 16, the basketball world, and many of the Lakers themselves, looked on in stunned disbelief.

"I looked at Caldwell and realized he's 7-1 and he's got arms that make him around 9-5," Magic remembered. "So I decided to jump up and down quick, then work on the rest of my game."

The 76ers won the tip, but Johnson, backed up defensively by his 6-foot-11-inch teammate, Jim Chones, went to work on the rest of his game.

In the opening sequence, Johnson sneaked behind Philadelphia center Darryl Dawkins, tied him up, and forced a jump-ball. Seconds later, Johnson and two teammates trapped Dawkins, forcing him to travel.

Johnson's energy helped the Lakers race out to a 7—0 lead, and when Philadelphia cut the deficit to 7–4, Johnson went to work offensively. He fed Michael Cooper a scoring pass from the high post, and then, after hauling down a rebound, dribbled upcourt and buried a jumper from the foul line. He then drove past the legendary Julius Erving and connected on a bank shot.

When the Magic dust had cleared, Johnson had shocked the 76ers, and wowed the basketball world, with 42 points, 15 rebounds, 7 assists, and 3 steals. He made 14 of 23 shots from the field and hit all 14 of his free-throw attempts.

Thanks to Johnson, the Lakers won the game, 123–107, wrapping up their first NBA title since 1972.

"Magic?" a smiling Johnson said after the game. "Yeah, I guess the night was Magic."

KEVIN PORTER

FACT FILE

Born: April 17, 1950
Height: 5′ 11″
Length of NBA career:
  1972–83
Major teams:
  Baltimore–Capital–
    Washington
  Detroit (joined 1975)
  New Jersey (joined 1977)
  Detroit (joined 1978)
  Washington (joined 1979)

A point guard with great passing skills and a scorer's mentality, Kevin Porter, all 5-feet-11-inches of him, was an impact player for nine NBA seasons.

Porter, selected by Baltimore in the third round of the 1972 NBA draft, led the league in assists in 1975, 1978, 1979, and 1981.

In his rookie season with the Bullets, Porter averaged 6.6 points and 3.3 assists per game. The following season, Porter improved those averages to 14 points and 5.7 assists per contest. During the 1974–75 campaign, when the Bullets relocated to Washington. Here, Porter scored 11.6 points per game and won his first assists title, racking up 650 dishes for an 8.0 per game average.

On February 24, 1978, as a member of the New Jersey Nets, Porter set a single-game record for most assists, tallying 29 against the Houston Rockets on his way to his second assists crown.

One year later, as a member of the Detroit Pistons, he set the single-season record for assists with an amazing 1,099, wrapping up his third assists title with a 13.4 average.

Finishing his career where it had started, with the Bullets, Porter finished tops among 1981 league-leaders in assists with 734 for a 9.0 per game average.

Porter retired in 1983 with averages of 11.6 points and 8.0 assists per game, adding 11.0 points and 5.7 assists in thirty-three career playoff contests.

Prior to his NBA selection, at St. Francis College in Pennsylvania, Porter averaged 23.8 points per game over four seasons.

RIGHT: KEVIN PORTER, GOING AIRBORN WITH THE BASKETBALL HERE, HAD A SCORER'S MENTALITY.

TERRY PORTER

In ten seasons with Portland, Terry Porter helped the Trail Blazers make ten trips to the playoffs, including two appearances in the NBA Finals.

Porter, a 6-foot-3-inch, streaky-shooting point guard who signed as a free agent with the Minnesota Timberwolves in 1995, was selected by Portland in the first round of the 1985 NBA draft.

As a rookie in 1985–86, Porter, teaming in the Portland backcourt with Clyde Drexler, averaged 7.1 points and 2.5 assists per game.

The following season, Porter averaged 13.1 points per contest, starting a streak of eight consecutive seasons in which he would average double digits in scoring.

A two-time All-Star, Porter averaged 17.6 points per game, helping the Trail Blazers reach the NBA Finals in 1990, where that year they lost to the Detroit Pistons, four games to one.

Two years later, Porter, averaging 18.1 points per game, led another charge to the NBA Finals. This time, it was Chicago's turn to break Portland's heart, winning the title in six games.

Winner of the NBA's Citizenship Award in 1993, Porter left Portland as the Trail Blazers' all-time assists leader with a total of 5,319.

Through his first twelve NBA seasons, Porter averaged 13.7 points, 6.6 assists, and 3.3 rebounds. At Wisconsin-Stevens Point, Porter averaged 13.5 points, 3.8 assists, and 3.8 rebounds over four seasons.

Porter, who can still be an impact player in what is now the twilight of his career, averaged 6.9 points and 3.6 assists with Minnesota last season.

FACT FILE

Born: April 8, 1963
Height: 6′ 3″
Length of NBA career:
  1985–present
Major teams:
  Portland
  Minnesota (joined 1995)
Records/Awards:
  NBA All-Star (2)

LEFT: TERRY PORTER (RIGHT) AND THE PORTLAND TRAIL BLAZERS MADE TWO TRIPS TO THE NBA FINALS.

MARK PRICE

FACT FILE

Born: February 15, 1964
Height: 6' 0"
Length of NBA career:
1986–present
Major teams:
Cleveland
Washington (joined 1995)
Golden State (joined 1996)
Records/Awards:
NBA All-Star (4)

One of the great playmakers and clutch shooters in the game today, Mark Price led the usually undermanned Cleveland Cavaliers to seven playoff appearances from 1986–95. By the time he was traded to the Washington Bullets the following season, Price was Cleveland's all-time assists leader with 4,206 and all-time steals leader with 734.

A 6-foot point guard out of Georgia Tech, Price broke into the NBA with the Cavaliers in 1986, averaging 6.9 points and 3.0 assists in limited duty.

In his second season with the Cavaliers, Price, a deceivingly quick, slick ballhandler who always seems to get off a pass to a streaking teammate at precisely the right moment, emerged as an impact player. He averaged 16.0 points, 6.0 assists, and 2.3 rebounds per game, the first of eight straight seasons in which he would tally up double-digit averages in scoring.

A four-time All-Star, Price's best season was 1989–90, when he averaged 19.6 points, 9.1 assists, and 3.4 rebounds per contest for the Cavaliers. He showed the basketball world his great shooting skills by winning back-to-back Long Distance Shootout competitions in both 1993 and 1994.

An All-NBA First Team selection in 1993 after averaging 18.2 points and 8.0 assists per game, Price has amassed 15.8 points, 6.9 assists, and 2.6 rebounds per game in his career, and holds the career mark for highest free throw percentage, shooting at a .907 clip.

Price, who also holds the career playoff record for highest free-throw percentage, .944, has posted 17.4 points, 7.0 assists, and 2.6 rebounds in forty-seven career post-season games. Signed by the Golden State Warriors in 1996, Price returned from injury the previous season to average 11.3 points in 70 games.

RIGHT: MARK PRICE (RIGHT) IS AN EXCELLENT PLAYMAKER WITH THE ABILITY TO MAKE CLUTCH BASKETS.

KURT RAMBIS

With his thick, black, horn-rimmed eyeglasses and bulky frame, Kurt Rambis hardly seemed to fit the image of the colorful Los Angeles Lakers Showtime teams of the early 1980s.

Despite his appearance, the 6-foot-8-inch Rambis fitted in splendidly with the Lakers, helping Magic Johnson, Kareem Abdul-Jabbar, and the rest of his extremely talented teammates capture championships through the decade in 1982, 1985, 1987, and 1988.

Rambis may not have been the fastest runner, highest leaper, or best shooter on the Lakers' roster, but he gave Los Angeles enough physical presence to balance out their finesse, run-and-dunk attack.

After he was selected by the New York Knicks out of Santa Clara in the third round of the 1980 NBA draft, Rambis was cut by the Knicks and played briefly in Greece before signing with the Lakers as a free agent in 1981.

For seven seasons in Los Angeles, Rambis continued to repay Coach Pat Riley and the Lakers for never giving up on him, hustling for every loose ball, leaning on an opposing star player if necessary, even grabbing key offensive rebounds or putting back clutch baskets on occasion.

After stints in Charlotte, Phoenix, and Sacramento from 1988–93—he enjoyed his best overall season with the Hornets in 1988–89, averaging career-highs in points (11.1), rebounds (9.4), and assists (2.1)—Rambis returned to Los Angeles, where he spent the final two years of his career.

In fourteen NBA seasons, Rambis averaged 5.2 points and 5.6 rebounds per game, adding 5.2 points and 5.5 boards in a total of 139 career playoff contests.

At Santa Clara, Rambis averaged 16.0 points, 9.6 rebounds, and 1.8 assists per game.

FACT FILE

Born: February 25, 1958
Height: 6′ 8″
Length of NBA career:
1981–95
Major teams:
Los Angeles Lakers
Charlotte (joined 1988)
Phoenix (joined 1989)
Sacramento (joined 1992)
Los Angeles Lakers
(joined 1993)
Records/Awards:
NBA Championship (4)

LEFT: KURT RAMBIS LOOKED NOTHING LIKE SHOWTIME, BUT HIS PHYSICAL PRESENCE WAS MUCH-NEEDED IN THE LOS ANGELES LAKERS' LINEUP.

WILLIS REED

FACT FILE

Born: June 25, 1942
Height: 6′ 10″
Length of NBA career:
   1964–74
Major team:
   New York Knicks
Records/Awards:
   NBA Rookie of the Year
      (1965)
   NBA Most Valuable Player
      (1970)
   NBA All-Star (7)
   NBA All-Defensive First
      Team (1)
   NBA Championship (2)
   Hall of Fame (1981)

The first player in league history to win a regular-season Most Valuable Player award, NBA Championship, and an NBA Finals MVP trophy in the same year, 1970, Willis Reed was the heart and soul of the New York Knicks during their glory years of the late 1960s and early 1970s.

Reed, a 6-foot-10-inch center/forward whose passion for the game and desire to win helped him excel despite a pair of aching knees, was also the MVP of the 1973 Finals, leading New York to victory in five games over the Los Angeles Lakers.

A seven-time All-Star who averaged 20 or more points during five of his ten-year injury-shortened career, Reed became a legend in the NBA Finals of 1973. Just before Game 7 of that series, the Knicks' captain, who had missed the previous game with a serious hip injury, limped out onto the Madison Square Garden floor, pumping up the capacity crowd, and giving his New York teammates the inspiration they would need to defeat the Lakers in that deciding game.

Flipping in his long, left-handed jumpers from the top of the key, Reed, who was selected by the Knicks out of Grambling State in the second round of the 1964 NBA draft, was one of the finest shooting centers of his generation.

In his first season with the Knicks, Reed won the league's Rookie of the Year award after averaging 19.5 points, 14.7 rebounds, and 1.7 assists per game. His best scoring season as a Knick was 1969–70, when he averaged a career-high 21.7 points per contest. That same season, Reed was voted MVP of the All-Star game after scoring 21 points and hauling down eleven rebounds.

For his career, Reed averaged 18.7 points and 12.9 rebounds per game, adding 17.4 points and 10.3 boards in 78 career playoff games.

At Grambling State, Reed averaged 18.7 points per game, leading his team to the 1961 NAIA Championship as a freshman.

RIGHT: A SEVEN-TIME ALL-STAR, WILLIS REED HAD PERHAPS THE GREATEST SINGLE SEASON (1969–70) OF ANY PLAYER IN HISTORY.

GLEN RICE

Ever since he led Michigan to the national championship in 1989—averaging 30.7 points per game in that tournament and shattering Bill Bradley's record for most points in an NCAA tournament with 184—Glen Rice has been a shooting star on the rise.

Rice, a 6-foot-8-inch swingman who left Michigan as the Big 10's all-time leading scorer with 2,442 points, did not cool off one bit at the NBA level. He earned a place on the 1990 NBA All-Rookie Second Team with averages of 13.6 points, 4.6 rebounds, and 1.8 assists per game.

For eight straight seasons since joining the NBA, Rice averaged double digits in scoring. He posted a career-high 26.8 points per game last season, and in the 1994–95 campaign won the NBA's Long Distance Shootout contest.

After six seasons in Miami—he averaged 19.3 points per game during that span and was the team's all-time leading scorer with 9,248 points—Rice was traded to the Charlotte Hornets for the 1995–96 campaign.

The change of scenery did not affect Rice's long-distance game. He earned a spot on his first All-Star squad after averaging 19.7 points, 4.9 rebounds, and a career-high 2.9 assists per game, bagging 171 of 403 three-point shots for a .423 percentage.

Through his first eight seasons, Rice averaged 20.6 points, 4.8 rebounds, and 2.3 assists per game, adding 18.6 points, 5.2 boards, and 2.4 assists in eleven career playoff contests.

Rice, voted the NCAA Division I Tournament Most Outstanding Player in 1989, averaged 18.2 points and 6.4 rebounds over four seasons.

FACT FILE

Born: May 28, 1967
Height: 6′ 8″
Length of NBA career:
1989–present
Major teams:
Miami
Charlotte (joined 1995)
Records/Awards:
NBA All-Star (2)

LEFT: GLEN RICE'S SHOOTING STAR JUST KEEPS RISING.

POOH RICHARDSON

FACT FILE

Born: May 14, 1966
Height: 6' 1"
Length of NBA career:
  1989–present
Major teams:
  Minnesota
  Indiana (joined 1992)
  Los Angeles Clippers
    (joined 1994)

He has never been an All-Star, but Pooh Richardson has put up solid numbers since joining the NBA in 1989 with the Minnesota Timberwolves, who selected him that year in the first round of the draft.

Richardson, a 6-foot-1-inch point guard who played his college ball at UCLA, was a 1990 All-Rookie First Team selection after averaging 11.4 points, 6.8 assists, and 2.6 rebounds per game.

The following season, Richardson averaged career highs with 17.1 points and 9.0 assists per game. He averaged double digits in scoring in each of his first seven seasons in the league.

After three seasons in Minnesota—he was the Timberwolves' all-time assists leader with 1,973 and all-time steals leader with 383—Richardson was traded to Indiana. He averaged 10.2 points in two seasons with the Pacers before he was dealt again to the Los Angeles Clippers in 1994. He led the Clippers in assists-per-game with 7.9 in 1994–95, and again in 1995–96, dishing out 5.4 assists per contest.

A quality player who always seems to end up on poor teams, Richardson has averaged 12.1 points, 7.0 assists, and 3.0 rebounds per game in his career. In six career playoff games, Richardson has averaged 3.5 points, 4.3 assists, and 1.8 rebounds per game.

At UCLA, Richardson averaged 12.0 points, 6.8 assists, and 4.6 rebounds over four seasons, averaging a career-high 15.2 points per game as a senior in 1988–89.

RIGHT: HE WAS NEVER AN ALL-STAR, BUT POOH RICHARDSON HAS LOADS OF TALENT.

MITCH RICHMOND

From 1989–91, they were known in Golden State as "Run T.M.C." The T stood for Tim Hardaway, the C stood for Chris Mullin, and the M in the middle of that talented trio stood for Mitch Richmond.

A 6-foot-5-inch shooting guard capable of taking over any game when he gets hot, Richmond was the NBA's Rookie of the Year in 1989 after averaging 22.0 points, 5.9 rebounds, and 4.2 assists per game for the Warriors.

A remarkable shooter who can pass and play solid defense, Richmond has averaged 20 or more points per game in each of his first nine seasons in the league.

After three seasons in Golden State, Richmond was traded to Sacramento, where he has played ever since. His best scoring season was with Sacramento in 1996–97, when he scored 25. 9 points per contest.

Selected by Golden State out of Kansas State in the first round of the 1988 NBA draft, Richmond has averaged 23.1 points, 4.4 rebounds, and 3.9 assists per game in his career, tallying 21.2 points, 5.8 rebounds, and 3.3 assists in 21 career playoff contests.

An All-NBA Second Team selection in 1994, 1995, and 1997 with the Kings, Richmond was a member of the bronze-medal winning US Olympic team in 1988. He came back to help his country capture the gold medal in the 1996 Olympic Games.

From 1993–97, Richmond was named to the All-Star squad five straight times, and was named its MVP in 1995 when he scored 23 points in 22 minutes of action.

FACT FILE

Born: June 30, 1965
Height: 6' 5"
Length of NBA career:
  1988–present
Major teams:
  Golden State
  Sacramento (joined 1991)
Records/Awards:
  NBA Rookie of the Year
    (1989)
  NBA All-Star (5)
  Olympic Gold Medal
    (1996)

LEFT: MITCH RICHMOND PUT THE M IN "RUN TMC".

DOC RIVERS

FACT FILE

Born: October 13, 1961
Height: 6′ 4″
Length of NBA career:
 1983–1996
Major teams:
 Atlanta
 Los Angeles Clippers
 (joined 1991)
 New York (joined 1992)
 San Antonio (joined 1994)
Records/Awards:
 NBA All-Star (1)

One of the NBA's most respected veterans, Doc Rivers called it a career in 1996 after a superb thirteen seasons in the league.

Rivers, a 6-foot-4-inch floor general from Marquette, jump-started Atlanta's offense earlier in his career with explosive penetrations to the hoop.

As the years passed and Father Time began to chip away at his great athletic ability, Rivers was still an effective point guard capable of handling the ball in pressure situations or finding an open teammate with a timely pass.

Selected by the Hawks in the second round of the 1983 NBA draft, Rivers averaged 9.3 points, 3.9 assists, and 2.7 rebounds per game in his rookie season. He would spend his first eight seasons in Atlanta, scoring a career-high 15.2 points per game in 1990–91, his final season with the Hawks.

Atlanta's all-time assists leader with 3,866, Rivers was traded to the Los Angeles Clippers in 1991. He played in Los Angeles for one season before the Knicks brought him to New York in an effort to help them win a long-awaited championship.

With Rivers' competitive attitude and veteran savvy rubbing off on his Knick teammates, New York did indeed build a championship-caliber team. Unfortunately for Rivers, and for the Knicks, an injury limited him to just 19 games in the 1993–94 campaign. The Knicks did make it to the NBA Finals for the first time in 21 years, but lost the crown to the Houston Rockets in seven games.

For his career, Rivers, who finished up with San Antonio, averaged 10.9 points, 5.7 assists, and 3.0 rebounds per game, adding 11.4 points, 5.9 assists, and 3.3 boards per game in 81 career playoff contests. He shares the single-game playoff record for most assists in one half, chalking up 15 in 24 minutes against the Boston Celtics on May 16, 1988.

At Marquette, Rivers averaged 13.9 points, 4.6 assists, and 3.3 rebounds per game over four seasons.

RIGHT: DOC RIVERS IS ATLANTA'S ALL-TIME LEADER IN ASSISTS.

OSCAR ROBERTSON

Through the years, players have been noted for their outstanding individual gifts. Some had outstanding strength and speed, others had a great shooting touch, court savvy, stamina, aggressiveness, ball-handling, or fine rebounding skills.

The "Big O," Oscar Robertson, had them all.

Robertson, a 6-foot-5-inch guard who dominated the game offensively, won Rookie of the Year honors as a member of the Cincinnati Royals in 1961, posting hefty averages of 30.5 points, 10.1 rebounds, and a league-leading 9.7 assists per game.

In a ten-year career with the Royals, Robertson averaged 30 or more points six times. During that same span, Robertson led the league eight times in assists-per-game, and four times in free throws made.

In 1964, Robertson was named the league's MVP after averaging a career-high 31.4 points, 9.9 rebounds, and a league-best 11.0 assists per game. Ironically, Robertson did not break the 30-point plateau when he won his only scoring title in 1967–68, averaging 29.2 points per game.

"Oscar dominated the game offensively, much like Bill Russell did defensively," Boston's Red Auerbach once said. "As soon as he got his hands on the ball, there was no wasted motion. His jump shot was almost impossible to discourage anywhere around the key. He got up so high and took so little time to release the ball that no one man could consistently stop him."

For all his greatness and for everything he achieved on a personal level, Robertson's one frustration was never having won an NBA title. He realized that dream, however, when he was traded to the Milwaukee Bucks in the 1970–71 season, teaming with a youthful Kareem Abdul-Jabbar to lead the Bucks to a four-games-to-none sweep of the Baltimore Bullets in the 1971 NBA Finals.

A twelve-time All-Star—he was named MVP in three of those games—Robertson averaged 25.7 points, 9.5 assists, and 7.5 rebounds per game in his long and distinguished career, adding 22.2 points, 8.9 assists, and 6.7 boards in 86 career playoff contests. He was elected to the NBA's 35th Anniversary All-Time Team in 1980.

A standout at the University of Cincinnati, where he averaged 33.8 points and 15.2 rebounds per game in four seasons, Robertson was a member of the gold-medal winning US Olympic Basketball Team in 1960.

FACT FILE

Born: November 24, 1938
Height: 6' 5"
Length of NBA career:
1960–73
Major teams:
Cincinnati
Milwaukee (joined 1970)
Records/Awards:
NBA Rookie of the Year
(1961)
NBA Most Valuable Player
(1964)
NBA All-Star (12)
NBA Championship (1)
Olympic Gold Medal
(1960)
Hall of Fame (1979)

LEFT: THE "BIG O", OSCAR ROBERTSON, WAS A DOMINANT OFFENSIVE PRESENCE.

CLIFF ROBINSON

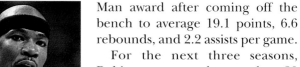

FACT FILE

Born: December 16, 1966
Height: 6′ 10″
Length of NBA career:
  1989–present
Major team:
  Portland
Records/Awards:
  NBA Sixth Man Award
  (1993)
  NBA All-Star (1)

Running the floor with his trademark headband, Cliff Robinson of the Portland Trail Blazers is one of professional basketball's smoothest-shooting big men.

Robinson, a 6-foot-10-inch player who can perform at either forward position, finished sixth league-wide in 1995–96 by making 178 three-pointers. Selected by Portland out of the University of Connecticut in the 1989 NBA draft, Robinson averaged 9.1 points and 3.8 rebounds in his rookie season.

The following season, Robinson averaged 11.7 and 4.3 rebounds per game, starting a string of seven straight seasons in which he would average double digits in scoring.

In 1992–93, Robinson won the league's Sixth Man award after coming off the bench to average 19.1 points, 6.6 rebounds, and 2.2 assists per game.

For the next three seasons, Robinson averaged more than 20 points per game, earning his only All-Star appearance in 1994 after scoring 20.1 points per contest, and topping out the following season at a career-high average of 21.3 points per game.

Through his first eight NBA seasons, all spent in Portland, Robinson has averaged 16.2 points, 5.2 rebounds, and 2.1 assists per game, adding 10.3 points, 4.4 rebounds, and 1.6 assists in 78 career post-season contests.

At Connecticut, Robinson averaged 15.3 points, 6.1 rebounds, and 1.2 assists per game over four seasons.

RIGHT: CLIFF ROBINSON RISES TO THE TASK AGAINST ORLANDO'S HORACE GRANT.

The only player to compete in three different Olympic Games, San Antonio's David Robinson is one of the most gifted and dominant centers ever to play the sport.

A 7-foot-1-inch pivotman from the Naval Academy with no major weaknesses on the basketball court, Robinson is perennially one of the league's top shot-blockers and rebounders.

A one-man wrecking crew since joining the NBA in 1989, Robinson has the ability to pop from the outside, but can play tough in the paint if he needs to. The only blemish on his phenomenal resume is the fact that he has failed to lead San Antonio to a championship.

"The Admiral" as Robinson is called, averaged 24.3 points, 12.0 rebounds, and 2.0 assists in his first season with the Spurs, earning 1990 Rookie of the Year honors.

In his first seven seasons with San Antonio, Robinson averaged 20 or more points per game. He posted a career high 29.8 points per contest in 1993–94, which gave him the league's scoring crown. The following season, Robinson posted averages of 27.6 points, 10.8 rebounds, and 2.9 assists per game en route to winning the MVP award.

An All-Star in seven of his eight NBA seasons and a four-time All-Defensive First Team selection, Robinson holds the career record for highest blocked shots per game average with 3.60 rejections per game. He led the league with 4.49 blocked shots per game in 1992, which helped him become the Defensive Player of the Year.

The Spurs' all-time leading rebounder with 6,614 and all-time blocked shots leader with 2,012, Robinson has averaged 25.5 points, 11.7 rebounds, and 3.1 assists per game through the 1996–97 season, adding 24.0 points, 11.8 boards, and 2.9 assists in 53 career playoff contests.

A model of consistency, Robinson registered 63 double-doubles in 1995–96, scoring at least 30 points 23 times to finish with a regular-season average of 25.0 points per game.

FACT FILE

Born: August 6, 1965
Height: 7' 1"
Length of NBA career:
1989–present
Major team:
San Antonio
Records/Awards:
NBA Rookie of the Year (1990)
NBA Defensive Player of the Year (1992)
NBA Most Valuable Player (1995)
NBA All-Defensive First Team (4)
NBA All-Star (7)
Olympic Gold Medals (1992, 1996)

LEFT: THE ADMIRAL, DAVID ROBINSON, GETS THE ATTENTION OF MOST OF HIS OPPONENTS.

THE ONE AND ONLY DREAM TEAM

Michael Jordan, the world's greatest basketball player; Larry Bird, a clutch, cerebral performer always one step ahead of the competition; Magic Johnson, an energetic floor leader without equal; Chris Mullin, a golden jumpshot; Karl Malone, physical and talented; Charles Barkley, a burning desire to win; Clyde Drexler, playing the game above the rim; Patrick Ewing, an intimidator in the paint; Scottie Pippen, an open-floor nightmare for opponents; David Robinson, a combination of agility, power, and grace; John Stockton, passer, shooter, sparkplug; and Christian Laettner, college hot-shot from Duke University.

Say hello to the greatest basketball team ever assembled. Twelve players who were brought together to represent the United States at the 1992 Summer Olympic Games in Barcelona, Spain. Say hello and "¡hola!" to the one and only Dream Team.

"I don't think that you'll see another team like this," said Chuck Daly, the head coach of the Dreamers. "This is a majestic team."

Daly spoke those words on the evening of August 8, 1992, shortly after the United States had crushed Croatia, 117–85, to capture the gold medal.

The Dream Team, sent to the 1992 Olympic Games because the rest of the world had caught up to the collegiate teams that previously represented the United States in international play, made a mockery of the competition, winning their slate of games by an average of 44 points, and raising questions around the global sports community as to whether or not the NBA's finest should have been sent off to basketball war in the first place.

"Americans can't make up their minds what they want," said Barkley, who led the Americans in scoring during Olympic play with an average of 18.0 points per game on 70 percent shooting. "They wanted us here and we're going to bring back the gold."

The Dream Team did indeed bring back the gold, but too many lopsided victories, like their 115–77 thrashing of Puerto Rico or their 127–76 wipeout of Lithuania, left little room for drama or emotion from the perspective of the average fan—or the average superstar.

"I've cried at home when I've seen Americans win close races," said Bird, whose Olympic highlight was a 19-point effort in a blowout of Germany. "I think you would've seen a lot more emotion up there if we hadn't won every game by 50 points." One Dream-Teamer, however, thought the world of some of the competition he had faced.

"Actually, the greatest basketball I've ever been involved in was in Monte Carlo," said Magic Johnson, referring, of course, to the Dream Team's intra-squad scrimmages.

GLENN ROBINSON

FACT FILE

Born: January 10, 1973
Height: 6′ 7″
Length of NBA career:
  1994–present
Major team:
  Milwaukee

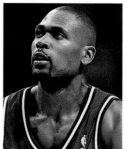

The first pick overall in the 1994 NBA draft, Glenn Robinson paid handsome dividends for the Milwaukee Bucks in his first three seasons.

Teaming on Milwaukee's front line with Vin Baker to form one of the marquee forward tandems in the league, the 6-foot-7-inch, 240-pound Robinson is a big man who can shoot the ball with accuracy and shake his defender off the dribble.

The "Big Dog," as Robinson is called, earned a spot on the NBA's 1995 All-Rookie First Team by averaging a career-high 21.9 points per game, adding 6.4 rebounds and 2.5 assists per contest. He made 636 of 1,410 field goal attempts for 45 percent. The following season, Robinson bounced back with similarly strong numbers. He averaged 20.2 points, 6.1 rebounds, and 3.6 assists per game, again shooting 45 percent from the field.

Through his first three NBA seasons, Robinson has registered 21.1 points, 6.3 rebounds, and 3.0 assists per game.

At Purdue, Robinson became one of the most celebrated players in college basketball history after averaging 27.5 points, 9.7 rebounds, and 1.9 assists per contest.

Robinson led the NCAA in his junior season with 30.3 points per contest. He decided to turn pro after being named the Sporting News College Player of the Year, as well as the winner of the Naismith and Wooden Awards.

RIGHT: THE "BIG DOG," DEFENDING HERE AGAINST CHICAGO'S SCOTTIE PIPPEN, HAS AVERAGED 20-PLUS POINTS IN HIS FIRST TWO NBA SEASONS.

DENNIS RODMAN

ennis Rodman is one of the most flamboyant, short-tempered players in the history of the league. He also happens to be one of the greatest rebounders in NBA history and a magnificent defensive player, and those skills have helped him earn four championship rings.

Rodman, a 6-foot-8-inch, 220-pound, north-south leaper out of southeast Oklahoma State, was selected by the Detroit Pistons in the second round of the 1986 NBA draft.

The "Worm," as Rodman is called, is a physical player and relentless hustler on the court, who sports various colored hairdos, tattoos, earrings, and an occasional dress. In other words, he fit in perfectly with the Bad-Boy Pistons, whose bruising style frustrated and intimidated opponents.

In 1988–89, just his third NBA season, Rodman tallied 9.0 points, 9.4 rebounds, and 1.2 assists per game, helping Detroit sweep the Los Angeles Lakers in four straight games to win the NBA Championship.

The following season, Rodman won the first of two NBA Defensive Player of the Year awards, adding averages of 8.8 points and 9.7 rebounds per game while helping the Pistons capture their second straight championship with a five-game victory over the Portland Trail

Blazers. For six seasons, from 1991 through 1997, Rodman led the NBA in rebounding averages, posting a career-high 18.7 boards per game for the Pistons in 1991–92. That amazing streak began in Detroit, was continued in San Antonio for two seasons, and kept alive in Chicago.

As a member of the Bulls, Rodman was instrumental in helping Michael Jordan and company defeat Seattle and Utah to win the last two NBA championships. His aggressive style often disrupted the flow of Seattle's offense, and diffused the greatness of Seattle's explosive power-forward, Shawn Kemp. In that series, Rodman tied an NBA Finals single-game record by hauling down 11 offensive rebounds on June 7, 1996.

A two-time All-Star and seven-time All-Defensive First Team Selection, Rodman has averaged 7.8 points, 1.7 assists, and 13.0 rebounds per game through the first eleven seasons of his career, adding 6.6 points, 1.1 assists, and 9.6 rebounds in 148 career playoff games. He has pulled down an amazing total of 10,324 rebounds.

Rodman showed his great talent for rebounding even before he entered the NBA. At Southeast Oklahoma State, he led the NAIA with 15.9 rebounds per game in 1985, and 17.8 rebounds per game the following season.

FACT FILE

Born: May 13, 1961
Height: 6′ 8″
Length of NBA career:
1986–present
Major teams:
Detroit
San Antonio (joined 1993)
Chicago (joined 1995)
Records/Awards:
NBA Defensive Player of the Year (1990, 1991)
NBA All-Defensive First Team (7)
NBA All-Star (2)
NBA Championship (4)

LEFT: THE OUTLANDISH AND CONTROVERSIAL DENNIS RODMAN ALSO HAPPENS TO BE A PHENOMENAL REBOUNDER.

BILL RUSSELL

FACT FILE

Born: February 12, 1934
Height: 6′ 10″
Length of NBA career:
  1956–69
Major team:
  Boston
Records/Awards:
  NBA All-Defensive First
    Team (1)
  NBA Most Valuable Player
    (1958, 1961, 1962,
    1963, 1965)
  NBA All-Star (12)
  NBA Championship (11)
  Olympic Gold Medal
    (1956)

Perhaps no one in the history of professional basketball placed a greater emphasis on defense than did Bill Russell, whose shot-blocking technique helped him earn the title of "Mr. Defense." After leading the University of San Francisco to a pair of championships and sixty straight victories, the 6-foot-10-inch, 220-pound Russell was the Celtics' top choice in the NBA draft of 1956.

Before his arrival in Boston, the Celtics had never won a championship, but Russell's intimidating defense, which often disrupted opposing offenses, changed all that. In his 13 seasons as a Celtic, including three as a player-coach, Boston won 11 championships.

Russell, who averaged double digits in scoring in every season except his last—he scored 9.9 points per game in 1968–69—won five rebounding titles during his career, reaching the peak of his rebounding greatness in 1963–64, when he hauled down an incredible 24.7 boards per game.

A five-time MVP and an All-Star in 12 of his thirteen seasons in a Celtic uniform, Russell, whose battles in the paint against Wilt Chamberlain is now the stuff of NBA legend, holds the single game record for most rebounds in one half, collecting 32 boards against Philadelphia on November 16, 1957.

Also a member of the gold-medal winning 1956 Olympic basketball team, Russell finished his career at Boston with averages of 15.1 points, 22.5 rebounds, and 4.3 assists per game.

In the playoffs, Russell turned up his act a notch, averaging 16.2 points, 24.9 rebounds, and 4.7 assists per contest. He holds the career playoff record for most rebounds (4,104), and the NBA Finals records for highest rebounds per-game-average (29.5), and highest rebounds per-game-average by a rookie (22.9).

For everything he ever achieved on a basketball court, Russell's greatest honor was bestowed upon him eleven years after he retired from the game. In 1980, he was declared the Greatest Player in the History of the NBA by the Professional Basketball Writers' Association of America. He was also voted onto the NBA's 25th Anniversary All-Time Team in 1970 and the 35th Anniversary All-Time Team in 1980.

At the University of San Francisco, Russell averaged 20.7 points and 20.3 rebounds per game in four seasons. He was named the NCAA Tournament Most Outstanding Player in 1955.

RIGHT: BILL RUSSELL, PERHAPS THE GREATEST DEFENSIVE PLAYER EVER, SNATCHES THIS REBOUND AGAINST THE NEW YORK KNICKS.

CAZZIE RUSSELL

When the New York Knicks won their first-ever world championship in 1970, Cazzie Russell was their invaluable sixth man.

Russell, a 6-foot-5-inch shooting guard from Michigan, was selected as the top overall pick by New York in the 1966 NBA draft.

Soon after he arrived in the Big Apple, the Knicks turned the slick-shooting Russell into a small forward, a position he would share with Bill Bradley.

In his first three seasons with the Knicks, Russell averaged 11.3 points, 16.9 points, and 18.3 points per game, respectively.

In his fourth season, 1969–70, Russell, who started over Bradley earlier in his career, came off the bench to back up the star from Princeton. Russell averaged 11.5 points per game that season, helping the Knicks get to the NBA Finals, where they disposed of the Los Angeles Lakers in a hard-fought seven-game series.

After spending his first five NBA seasons with the Knicks, Russell was traded to the Golden State Warriors in 1971 for Jerry Lucas, who would end up being a key contributor to the Knicks' 1973 championship squad. In his first season with the Warriors, Russell averaged a career-high 21.4 points per game. In a 12-year career that also included stints with the Los Angeles Lakers and Chicago Bulls, Russell averaged double digits in scoring ten times.

For his career, Russell averaged 15.1 points, 2.2 assists, and 3.7 rebounds per game, adding 11.8 points, 1.3 assists, and 3.0 rebounds in 72 career playoff contests.

FACT FILE

Born: June 7, 1944
Height: 6′ 5″
Length of NBA career:
1966–78
Major teams:
New York Knicks
Golden State (joined 1971)
Los Angeles (joined 1974)
Chicago (joined 1977)
Records/Awards:
NBA All-Star (1)
NBA Championship (1)

LEFT: CAZZIE RUSSELL WAS AN INVALUABLE SIXTH MAN IN NEW YORK'S LINEUP.

THOMAS "SATCH" SANDERS

FACT FILE

Born: November 8, 1938
Height: 6′ 6″
Length of NBA career:
  1960–73
Major team:
  Boston
Records/Awards:
  NBA Championship (8)

A strong defensive forward, Thomas "Satch" Sanders helped the Boston Celtics capture eight NBA Championships during his thirteen seasons in the league. Sanders, a 6-foot-6-inch cornerman out of New York University—where he helped the Violets to a surprising appearance in the 1960 NCAA semifinals—teamed in his prime with the legendary center Bill Russell and fellow-cornerman Tom Heinsohn to form one of the most lethal front lines in the history of the game.

After a rookie season in which he averaged just 5.3 points per game, Sanders' career took flight. The following season, he averaged 11.2 points per contest, starting a string of nine straight seasons in which he would average double digits in scoring.

In his sixth season with the Celtics, Sanders racked up an average of a career–high 12.6 points per contest, helping the Celtics that season to the NBA Finals, where Boston defeated Los Angeles in seven games.

Through his professional career, Sanders averaged 9.6 points and 6.3 rebounds per game, adding 8.8 points and 5.8 boards in 130 playoff contests. Those numbers suffered during the last three years of his career, when the Celtics faded from glory—at least for a while—and Sanders was reduced to a part-time player.

Although he was never voted onto an All-Star team, Sanders was a most valuable contributor in helping the Celtics create their dynasty.

RIGHT: THOMAS "SATCH" SANDERS (LEFT), SHOWING THE HUSTLE THAT HELPED THE BOSTON CELTICS CAPTURE EIGHT CHAMPIONSHIPS.

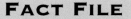

DOLPH SCHAYES

One of the top scorers in the early years of the NBA, Dolph Schayes led the Syracuse Nationals to the 1955 NBA title.

Schayes, a 6-foot-8-inch marksman out of New York University, was named the NBL's Rookie of the Year after averaging 12.8 points per contest in 1948–49, the last season of the NBL's existence.

The following season, Schayes and Syracuse joined the NBA and he became one of the league's early household names by averaging 16.8 points and 4.0 assists per contest. In his third season, 1951–52, Schayes raised his scoring to 17.0 points per game, and led the league with a 16.4 rebounds-per-game average.

In a career that would span sixteen years, Schayes averaged double digits in scoring fourteen straight seasons from the time he joined the Nationals. In a six-season period from 1955–61, he averaged better than 20 points per game, hitting a career-high 24.9 points per contest in 1957–58.

A twelve-time All-Star and six-time All-NBA First Team Selection, Schayes, whose son, Danny, has played in the NBA for the past sixteen seasons, finished his career in Philadelphia—the Nationals moved there for the 1963–64 season—with 19,247 regular-season points to his credit, and a one-time record 1,059 games played.

Overall, Schayes averaged 18.2 points per game throughout his brilliant career, posting 19.2 points per contest in 103 playoff games. He was voted onto the NBA's 25th Anniversary All-Time Team in 1970.

FACT FILE

Born: May 19, 1928
Height: 6′ 8″
Length of NBL career:
 1948–49
Length of NBA career:
 1949–64
Major team:
 Syracuse–Philadelphia
Records/Awards:
 NBL Rookie of the Year
  (1949)
 NBA All-Star (12)
 NBA Championship (1)
 Hall of Fame (1972)

LEFT: DOLPH SCHAYES, BACK IN HIS NYU DAYS, SPLITTING ST. LOUIS' DEFENSE.

DETLEF SCHREMPF

FACT FILE

Born: January 21, 1963
Height: 6′ 10″
Length of NBA career:
1985–present
Major teams:
Dallas
Indiana (joined 1989)
Seattle (joined 1993)
Records/Awards:
NBA All-Star (3)

Anyone who believes the myth that white men can't jump has never seen Detlef Schrempf play the game of basketball. Schrempf, a 6-foot-10-inch explosive forward who helped the Seattle SuperSonics reach the NBA Finals in 1996, was selected by the Dallas Mavericks out of the University of Washington during the first round of the 1985 NBA draft.

As a rookie with Dallas, Schrempf averaged just 6.2 points and 3.1 rebounds per game. He averaged 9.3 and 8.5 points, respectively, the next two seasons, but never really reached his potential with the Mavericks.

Midway through the 1989–90 campaign, Schrempf got his big break when he was traded to the Indiana Pacers, who brought him off the bench, where his smooth outside shooting, crisp passing, and explosive leaping ability added a much-needed spark to the offense.

In 1989–90, his first full season with the Pacers, Schrempf averaged 16.2 points per game. The following season, he won the first of back-to-back Sixth Man awards.

A three-time All-Star, Schrempf scored a career-high 19.2 points per game for Seattle in 1994–95.

Just before the start of the 1993 season, the championship-minded SuperSonics acquired the German-born Schrempf in a trade with the Pacers, and that move helped make Seattle one of the elite clubs in the Western Conference.

An All-NBA Third Team selection with Seattle in 1995, Schrempf has averaged 14.5 points, 6.3 rebounds, and 3.4 assists per game through the first twelve seasons of his career, adding 13.6 points, 5.0 boards, and 2.6 assists in 86 career playoff games. He was a member of the West German Olympic team in 1984, and the German Olympic team in 1992.

RIGHT: IF YOU BELIEVE THE MYTH THAT WHITE MEN CAN'T JUMP, YOU HAVEN'T SEEN DETLEF SCHREMPF PLAY THE GAME OF BASKETBALL.

DENNIS SCOTT

One of the scariest long-distance shooters in the NBA, Dennis Scott helped Shaquille O'Neal and Penny Hardaway transform the Orlando Magic into one of the strongest teams in the league.

Scott, a 6-foot-8-inch swingman out of Georgia Tech, helped shoot the Magic into the 1995 NBA Finals, where they were swept by the Houston Rockets in four straight games.

A first round pick of the Magic in the 1990 NBA draft, Scott earned a place on the league's 1991 All-Rookie team, tallying 15.7 points, 2.9 rebounds, and 1.6 assists per contest. He has averaged double digits in scoring in each of his first seven seasons, registering a career-high 19.9 points per game in the 1991–92 campaign.

The Sporting News College Player of the Year in 1990, when he averaged 27.7 points per contest in his third and final season at Georgia Tech, Scott has averaged 14.8 points, 3.1 rebounds, and 2.3 assists per game through the 1996–97 season, adding 12.2 points, 3.0 boards, and 1.9 assists in 41 career post-season games.

By the end of the 1995–96 campaign, Scott, who possesses incredible shooting range, had set the single-season record for most three-point field goals made with 267. He tied the single-game mark for most three-point field goals made, bagging 11 against Atlanta on April 18, 1996; and most trifectas made in one half, connecting on 7 shots from behind the three-point line in the same contest.

Scott, who averaged 21.4 points per contest in three seasons at Georgia Tech, once held the NBA's single-game playoff record for most three-point field goals attempted, launching 15 treys against Indiana on May 25, 1995.

FACT FILE

Born: September 5, 1968
Height: 6′ 8″
Length of NBA career:
  1990–present
Major team:
  Orlando

LEFT: GREAT SCOTT! THEY KNOW ALL ABOUT HIM IN ORLANDO.

BARNEY SEDRAN

FACT FILE

Barney Sedran's fact file is unknown. Very little information concerning professional basketball was documented around the turn of the century.

The man who once scored seventeen baskets in a game—without the benefit of a backboard—Barney Sedran was one of pro basketball's superstars. Sedran, a fiery, 5-foot-4-inch guard, led the Carbondale PA squad to thirty-five consecutive victories and a Tri-County League title during the 1914–15 season.

The season before, he had pulled off his seventeen-basket feat, hitting the bull's-eye from 25–30 feet away on a court with no backboards. Playing in an era when professional leagues folded on a weekly basis and athletes performed on a pay-for-a-day salary, Sedran was also a star for Utica of the New York State League. One of the great small men of his era, Sedran played with all the major Eastern Pro teams, including the great Fort Wayne "K of C" in the 1923–24 campaign. He finished his great playing career with the Cleveland Rosenblums from 1924–26 before going into coaching.

Sedran, elected to the Hall of Fame in 1962, played his college ball at CCNY in New York. He led the team in scoring for three seasons and was voted team captain in 1910.

In fifteen years of professional basketball, Sedran played on ten championship teams.

RIGHT: BORN IN THE NINETEENTH CENTURY, BARNEY SEDRAN WAS ONE OF PRO BASKETBALL'S EARLIEST SUPERSTARS.

BILL SHARMAN

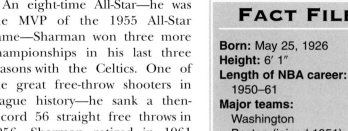

One of the greatest shooting guards and greatest free-throw shooters who ever lived, Bill Sharman was instrumental in helping the Boston Celtics capture four NBA championships.

Sharman, a fierce, 6-foot-1-inch competitor out of USC, broke into the NBA in the 1950–51 season with the Washington Capitols, averaging 12.2 points, 3.1 rebounds, and 1.3 assists per game as a rookie.

The following season, Sharman was traded to the Boston Celtics. When the great Bill Russell arrived in Beantown for the 1956–57 season, Sharman's life was made a lot easier, as defenses softened around him in order to drop back and pay more attention to Russell.

During Russell's rookie year, Sharman averaged 19.9 points per game en route to earning the first of his four championship rings.

An eight-time All-Star—he was the MVP of the 1955 All-Star game—Sharman won three more championships in his last three seasons with the Celtics. One of the great free-throw shooters in league history—he sank a then-record 56 straight free throws in 1956—Sharman retired in 1961 having shot an incredible 88 percent from the foul line over eleven NBA seasons.

For his career, Sharman, a four-time All-NBA First Team selection, averaged 17.8 points, 3.9 rebounds, and 3.0 assists per game, adding 18.5 points, 3.7 rebounds, and 2.6 assists in 78 career playoff contests.

Sharman, who holds the single-game All-Star record for most field goals attempted in one quarter, hoisting 12 shots in the 1960 classic, was selected to the NBA's 25th Anniversary All-Time Team in 1970.

FACT FILE

Born: May 25, 1926
Height: 6′ 1″
Length of NBA career:
    1950–61
Major teams:
    Washington
    Boston (joined 1951)
Records/Awards:
    NBA All-Star (8)
    NBA Championship (4)
    Hall of Fame (1975)

LEFT: BILL SHARMAN WAS A SUPERB SHOOTING GUARD AND EVEN BETTER FREE-THROW SHOOTER.

PURVIS SHORT

FACT FILE

Born: July 2, 1957
Height: 6′ 7″
Length of NBA career:
1978–90
Major teams:
Golden State
Houston (joined 1987)
New Jersey (joined 1989)

A high-scoring swingman who loved to run in the open floor, Purvis Short's great talents were hidden for years on poor NBA teams.

Short, a 6-foot-7-inch run-and-gunner out of Jackson State University, averaged double digits in scoring in ten of his thirteen NBA seasons, the first nine of which were spent with the Golden State Warriors.

After averaging 23.4 points per game in four seasons at Jackson State, Short scored 10.6 points per contest as a rookie with the Warriors in 1978–79, raising that total to 17.0 points per game the following season.

In four seasons from 1982–86, Short posted averages of more than 20 points per game, reaching a career-high 28.0 points per contest in the 1984–85 season. But while Short was lighting up scoreboards around the country, Golden State was losing basketball games.

Unfortunately for Short, the Warriors did not reach post-season play until his final season with the team in 1986–87.

Golden State advanced beyond the first round of the Western Conference Playoffs that season by defeating the Utah Jazz in five games, but were eliminated in the conference semifinals by the Los Angeles Lakers, four games to one.

After a glorious individual career at Golden State, Short was traded to the Houston Rockets, where he played for two seasons before signing with the New Jersey Nets as a free agent.

The brother of Eugene Short, a forward who played with the Seattle SuperSonics and New York Knicks in the 1975–76 season, Purvis Short averaged 17.3 points in his career, adding 10.4 points in just eighteen career playoff contests.

RIGHT: PURVIS SHORT LOVED TO RUN-AND-GUN.

JACK SIKMA

A hard-nosed center/forward with a great scoring touch around the basket, Jack Sikma helped the 1978–79 Seattle SuperSonics win their only NBA Championship.

Sikma, a rugged 7-foot, 250-pound competitor out of Illinois Wesleyan, was selected by Seattle in the first round of the 1977 NBA draft. He quickly gained recognition as an impact player after averaging 10.7 points, 8.3 rebounds, and 1.6 assists in his first season with the SuperSonics, earning a spot on the All-Rookie team.

The following season, Sikma, teaming with talents like Dennis Johnson and Gus Williams, put up 15.6 points, 12.4 rebounds, and 3.2 assists per game, giving Seattle the muscle it needed to reach the NBA Finals, where the SuperSonics defeated the Washington Bullets in five games.

In nine years with Seattle, Sikma was voted onto seven All-Star squads. His big, banner year was 1981–82, when he averaged his career-high in scoring (19.6) and rebounding (12.7).

Sikma also led the league that season with 815 defensive rebounds, earning a spot on the NBA's All-Defensive Second Team.

In 1986, Sikma was traded to the Milwaukee Bucks, where he spent the last five years of his professional career.

Sikma, who left Seattle as its all-time leading rebounder with 7,729 boards, averaged 15.6 points, 9.8 rebounds, and 3.2 assists in his career, posting 14.3 points, 9.3 rebounds, and 2.4 assists in 102 career playoff games.

FACT FILE

Born: November 14, 1955
Height: 7′ 0″
Length of NBA career:
1977–91
Major teams:
   Seattle
   Milwaukee (joined 1986)
Records/Awards:
   NBA All-Star (7)
   NBA Championship (1)

LEFT: THE RUGGED JACK SIGMA HELPED SEATTLE WIN ITS ONLY NBA CHAMPIONSHIP.

BULLING THEIR WAY INTO HISTORY

The 1996–97 Chicago Bulls, which finished 69–13 and won their fifth championship in the Michael Jordan era, were a great basketball team.

But arguably, the greatest team that ever lived was the 1995–96 Chicago Bulls, a team that lacked a true point guard, a team that lacked a dominant center. Those Bulls were an average foul-shooting team, and they had newly acquired Dennis Rodman, a famous rebounder with an infamous temper, capable of blowing his lid at any moment and blowing apart the chemistry of the Bulls, just as he had done in San Antonio the season before.

Despite these shortcomings, the Bulls were standing tall at season's end, having compiled a record 72 regular-season victories against 10 losses, breaking the mark of 69 regular-season wins set by the Los Angeles Lakers in the 1971–72 campaign.

Jordan, who won his eighth scoring title to break Wilt Chamberlain's record of seven (he added his ninth scoring crown last season), manned the backcourt with his super-talented teammate, Scottie Pippen and solid role players Ron Harper and Steve Kerr. The foul-shooting never really made a difference, and Rodman went about the business of continuing to be the best rebounder in the game. Bill Wennington, Luc Longley and James Edwards made a formidable three-headed center, and Toni Kukoc added tremendous scoring punch along the front line.

After their magnificent season, the Bulls took care of business in the playoffs, sweeping the Miami Heat in three Eastern Conference first round games, knocking off the New York Knicks in five semifinal contests, sweeping the Orlando Magic in four games to capture the Eastern Conference Championship, and finally, dumping Seattle in six games to win the NBA title.

Along the way, Jordan won a rare triple crown, winning the Most Valuable Player Award for the regular-season, All-Star Game and NBA Finals. Phil Jackson won Coach of the Year honors, team-owner Kerry Krause was voted Executive of the Year, Kukoc was named the league's top Sixth Man, and Rodman won his fifth straight rebounding title.

"I'm glad it's over with," said Jordan, speaking on behalf of most of his teammates, who had been pressured heavily by fans and media to achieve the victories record. "This was a long time coming. We didn't start out the season to win 70 games. We started out the season to win the championship. It's going to take some time for this to sink in. I feel in the future, when we look back, 70 wins will mean a lot."

BACK ROW:
JERRY KRAUSE, CLARENCE GAINES, JR., JOHN PAXSON, JIMMY RODGERS, JIM CLEAMONS, PHIL JACKSON, TEX WINTER, JIM STACK, AL VERMEIL, ERIK HELLAND

BELOW: A 72–10 REGULAR-SEASON RECORD STRONGLY
SUGGESTS THAT THE 1995–96 CHICAGO BULLS TEAM WAS THE
BEST EVER.

BELOW: A 72–10 REGULAR-SEASON RECORD STRONGLY
SUGGESTS THAT THE 1995–96 CHICAGO BULLS TEAM WAS THE
BEST EVER.

MIDDLE ROW:
JOHN LIGMANOWSKI, JUD BUECHLER,
JASON CAFFEY, JAMES EDWARDS,
BILL WENNINGTON, DICKEY SIMPKINS,
JACK HALEY, RANDY BROWN, CHIP SCHAEFER

FRONT ROW:
TONI KUKOC, LUC LONGLEY,
DENNIS RODMAN, MICHAEL JORDAN,
SCOTTIE PIPPEN, RON HARPER,
STEVE KERR

PAUL SILAS

FACT FILE

Born: July 12, 1943
Height: 6′ 7″
Length of NBA career:
  1964–80
Major teams:
  St. Louis–Atlanta
  Phoenix (joined 1969)
  Boston (joined 1972)
  Denver (joined 1976)
  Seattle (joined 1977)
Records/Awards:
  NBA All-Star (2)
  NBA All-Defensive First
    Team (2)
  NBA Championship (3)

A phenomenal rebounder, Paul Silas earned three NBA Championship rings in a sixteen-year career that spanned three decades.

After setting the NCAA Division I record for most rebounds in a three-year varsity career at Creighton with 1,751, Silas was selected by the St. Louis Hawks in the 1964 NBA draft.

The 6-foot-7-inch Silas, who played center and forward, spent five seasons with the Hawks, who moved from St. Louis to Atlanta for the 1968–69 season. His best year in a Hawks uniform was 1967–68, when he scored 13.4 points per game.

In 1969, Silas was traded to Phoenix, where he became a bona fide star, averaging double digits in scoring and rebounding in three seasons with the Suns.

In need of a rebounding force to bolster its front line, Boston traded for Silas shortly before the start of the 1972–73 season. In his first season with the Celtics, Silas responded with career highs in scoring (13.3) and rebounding (13.0).

The following season, Silas posted 11.5 points and 11.2 boards per game as the Celtics went on to win the NBA title, defeating Milwaukee in seven games.

Two seasons later, Silas, named to the NBA All-Defensive First Team for the second time in his career after 12.7 rebounds per game, helped Boston to another championship, knocking off Phoenix in six games.

A two-time All-Star, Silas helped the Seattle SuperSonics capture the only championship in their history, defeating the Washington Bullets in five games to win the 1979 title. Silas came off the bench that season to average 5.6 points and 7.0 rebounds per game.

After retiring in 1980, Silas left the game with averages of 9.4 points and 9.9 rebounds per contest, adding 6.9 points and 9.4 boards in 163 playoff contests.

RIGHT: PAUL SILAS WAS A TERROR BENEATH THE BOARDS.

JOE SMITH

In West Harlem, at the fabled Rucker League Tournament which brings together some of the most talented players in the country each summer for a three-week tournament, Joe Smith is called the "Emergency Man," as he makes a habit of coming to the rescue in the late, critical stages of basketball games.

A 6-foot-10-inch forward out of Maryland, Smith enjoyed a spectacular rookie season with the Golden State Warriors in 1995–96, earning a place on the NBA's All-Rookie squad by posting averages of 15.3 points and 8.7 rebounds per game.

Smith, who left Maryland after his sophomore season and was selected by Golden State as the first pick overall in the NBA draft of 1995, was a much-needed presence beneath the boards for the Golden State team, who have had their share of untimely injuries and bad luck in recent seasons.

In his initial season with the Warriors, Smith led all NBA rookies in rebounding and blocks, and led his teammates in double-digit scoring 67 times. Extremely versatile for a player his size, Smith also chalked up 134 blocks and 85 steals. Last season, Smith improved his scoring to 18.7 points per game, adding 8.5 rebounds per contest.

At Maryland, Smith averaged 20.2 points, 10.7 rebounds, and 1.0 assist per game over two seasons. He was named the 1995 Naismith Award winner, and that same year was also voted onto the Sporting News All-America Second Team.

FACT FILE

Born: July 26, 1975
Height: 6' 10"
Length of NBA career:
   1995–present
Major team:
   Golden State

LEFT: IN HARLEM, N.Y., THEY CALL JOE SMITH THE "EMERGENCY MAN."

KENNY SMITH

FACT FILE

Born: March 8, 1965
Height: 6′ 3″
Length of NBA career:
  1987–present
Major teams:
  Sacramento
  Atlanta (joined 1990)
  Houston (joined 1990)
  Detroit (joined 1996)
  Orlando (joined 1996)
  Denver (joined 1997)
Records/Awards:
  Championships (2)

One of many quality NBA point guards from New York City, Kenny Smith was a key contributor to Houston's back-to-back championships in 1994 and 1995. A 6-foot-3-inch rock-steady floor leader who can handle the ball under pressure or sink a big shot if the situation calls for it, Smith was selected by the Sacramento Kings out of North Carolina in the first round of the 1987 NBA draft.

Smith earned a spot on the 1988 All-Rookie team after averaging 13.8 points, 7.1 assists, and 2.3 rebounds per game with the Kings, starting a streak in which he would average double digits in scoring for eight straight seasons.

Smith followed his rookie performance with an extremely productive second season, tallying averages of 17.3 points, 7.7 assists, and 2.8 rebounds per game. Midway through the 1989–90 campaign, Smith was traded to Atlanta Hawks, finishing the year with 11.9 points per game.

The following season, Smith was traded to Houston and became a permanent fixture in the Rockets' backcourt, feeding key passes in the post to Hakeem Olajuwon, or stepping up to launch the big shot around the perimeter.

In his first season with the Rockets, Smith averaged a career-high 17.7 points per game. During the 1995 playoffs, Smith set a record for most three-point field goals made in one game, 7, and most three-point field goals made in one quarter, 5, against the Orlando Magic, who would lose the series to the Rockets in four straight games. Smith, who played for Detroit, Orlando and Denver last season, has career averages of 12.8 points, 5.5 assists, and 2.0 rebounds per game.

RIGHT: KENNY SMITH WAS A KEY FACTOR IN HELPING HOUSTON CAPTURE BACK-TO-BACK CHAMPIONSHIPS.

RANDY SMITH

A modern-day ironman, Randy Smith played in a record 976 straight games during his twelve NBA seasons.

Smith, a 6-foot-3-inch guard who was also a soccer All-American at Buffalo State College during the late 1960s, was selected by the Buffalo Braves in the seventh round of the NBA draft in 1971.

A longshot to make the pros, Smith latched on with Buffalo and became one of the shiniest stars in the league, averaging double digits in scoring in every season except his last.

Smith's best season in a Buffalo uniform was 1977–78, when he averaged a career-high 24.6 points per contest. He made the second of two All-Star appearances that season and was awarded the game's Most Valued Player,

scoring 27 points to lead the East to a 133–125 victory over the West.

After spending his first eight NBA seasons with the Buffalo franchise, which moved to San Diego in 1978, Smith was traded to Cleveland in 1980. He would play two seasons for the Cavaliers, one more with the New York Knicks, and split his final season, 1982–83, with San Diego and Atlanta.

For ten straight years from 1972–82, Smith suited up for each and every game on the 82-game schedule, a rarity in the rough-and-tumble world of modern pro sports.

After calling it quits in 1983, Smith left the game having averaged 16.7 points and 4.5 assists for his career, adding 17.5 points and 6.5 assists in twenty-four career playoff games.

FACT FILE

Born: December 12, 1948
Height: 6′ 3″
Length of NBA career:
  1971–83
Major teams:
  Buffalo–San Diego
  Cleveland (joined 1980)
  New York (joined 1981)
  San Diego (joined 1982)
  Atlanta (joined 1983)
Records/Awards:
  NBA All-Star (2)

LEFT: FOR AN ENTIRE DECADE, IRONMAN RANDY SMITH NEVER MISSED A GAME.

RIK SMITS

FACT FILE

Born: August 23, 1966
Height: 7' 4"
Length of NBA career:
  1988–present
Major team:
  Indiana

Over the years, Rik Smits, the 7-foot-4-inch "Dunking Dutchman" from Holland, has slowly become one of the elite centers in the NBA.

Smits, who played his college ball at Marist, was a raw talent when the Indiana Pacers selected him in the first round of the 1988 NBA draft.

A mobile player with a feathery shot and an increasing number of slick offensive moves in the low post, Smits earned a place on the 1989 All-Rookie team after averaging 11.7 points and 6.1 rebounds per game, and has been getting better with each passing season. Since he joined the league, Smits has averaged double digits in scoring, and in every season except for his first, the Pacers have made the playoffs.

The highlight of Smits' career came in Game 4 of the 1995 Eastern Conference Finals against the Orlando Magic. With 1.3 seconds left on the game clock and Indiana trailing 93–92, Smits took an inbounds pass near the foul line, wheeled, head-faked Orlando's Tree Rollins, and let loose a soft 16-footer over Rollins' fingertips that settled into the cords to give the Pacers an improbable 94–93 victory.

Although he has yet to make an All-Star team, Smits has certainly played like one. He has averaged 14.9 points, 6.2 rebounds, and 1.5 assists through the 1996–97 season, adding 16.6 points, 5 .9 rebounds, and 1.6 assists in 53 career playoff contests.

Smits' best scoring season was 1995–96, when he averaged 18.5 points per game.

At Marist, Smits put the tiny school on the college basketball map, averaging 18.2 points and 7.6 rebounds per game over four seasons.

RIGHT: RIK SMITS' MOBILITY AND SOFT-SHOOTING TOUCH MAKE HIM ONE OF THE PREMIER CENTERS IN THE NBA.

MOE SPAHN

The legendary City College Coach Nat Holman considered Moe Spahn to have been "the smartest player" he ever coached and among "the ten greatest to have played the game." A unanimous All-American candidate in 1932 and 1933 who helped City College build a remarkable 33–2 record during those two seasons, the 6-foot-1-inch Spahn went on to an even greater professional career.

Spahn, who broke into the professional ranks with the Brooklyn Visitations of the American Basketball League, led the ABL in free throws five straight seasons from 1934–38.

From 1934–42, Spahn also played for the New Britain Basketeers, the Original Celtics and the New Jersey Reds, winning a combined five championships during that span.

Spahn's first championship came in 1935 as a member of the Original Celtics. He helped the Celtics defeat their greatest rival of that era, the all-black Original Renaissance, 49–44, scoring 22 points to help seal the victory.

At the height of his career in 1938, Spahn captained the Jersey Reds to the World's Professional Championship. He led the charge despite a dislocated shoulder he injured just before the championship game. Spahn had his shoulder snapped back into place and taped his good shoulder as a decoy, setting new standards of leadership and courage for all future athletes to follow.

Spahn, who twice finished as the second-leading scorer in the ABL and was the league's runner-up as MVP from 1935–37, finally earned MVP honors after the 1937–38 season. For his heroic efforts, Spahn received the David Soden Trophy, emblematic of the best basketball player in the world.

FACT FILE

Born: May 3, 1912
Height: 6′ 1″
Length of professional career:
1933–40
Major teams:
Brooklyn Visitations (1933–34)
New Britain Basketeers (1934–35)
Original Celtics (1935–36)
Jersey Reds (1936–40)
Records/Awards:
ABL Most Valuable Player (1938)

LEFT: MOE SPAHN SET NEW STANDARDS OF LEADERSHIP AND COURAGE FOR ALL FUTURE ATHLETES TO FOLLOW.

LATRELL SPREWELL

FACT FILE

Born: September 8, 1970
Height: 6′ 5″
Length of NBA career:
  1992–present
Major team:
  Golden State
Records/Awards:
  NBA All-Star (3)

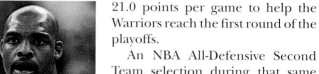

Many professional basketball experts feel that Golden State's Latrell Sprewell also has the potential to become the next Michael Jordan.

Sprewell, a 6-foot-5-inch shooting guard who can flat-out fly in the open court, was selected by the Warriors out of Alabama in the 1992 NBA draft. He is arguably the most athletically gifted off-guard in the league, and if he manages to lower his turnover rate in the coming seasons, he will certainly be mentioned in the same breath as Jordan.

A member of the NBA's 1993 All-Rookie Second Team, "Spree" as Sprewell is affectionately known, averaged 15.4 points, 3.5 rebounds, and 3.8 assists per game in his initial season. In 1993–94, Sprewell led the entire league in minutes played with 3,533, averaging

21.0 points per game to help the Warriors reach the first round of the playoffs.

An NBA All-Defensive Second Team selection during that same 1993–94 season—he racked up a career-high 180 steals—Sprewell made the first of back-to-back All-Star appearances.

In each of his first five NBA seasons, Sprewell averaged double digits in scoring, not an easy task when one considers he shares the floor with super-scorer Chris Mullin and the high-scoring Joe Smith.

Through the 1996–97 season, Sprewell has 20.0 points, 4.3 rebounds, and 4.6 assists, averaging 22.7 points, 7.0 assists, and 3.0 rebounds in just three career playoff contests.

At Alabama, Sprewell averaged 13.5 points, 5.1 rebounds, and 2.0 assists over two seasons.

RIGHT: LATRELL SPREWELL, GUARDING PORTLAND'S CLYDE DREXLER HERE, HAS MICHAEL JORDAN-LIKE POTENTIAL.

JERRY STACKHOUSE

Quick to the bucket, a reliable ballhandler, rock-solid defender, and super scorer, Jerry Stackhouse is one of the rising young stars on the NBA horizon.

Stackhouse, a 6-foot-6-inch swingman selected by Philadelphia out of North Carolina in the first round of the 1995 NBA draft, had a phenomenal first season with the 76ers, giving their fans reasons to smile after years of watching dreadful basketball.

While setting a Philadelphia mark for first-year minutes played with 2,701, Stackhouse earned a spot on the 1996 NBA All-Rookie team by averaging 19.2 points, 3.9 assists, and 3.7 rebounds per game.

His 1,384 points during the 1995–96 campaign set a franchise record for most points scored as a rookie. Stackhouse also tallied 79 blocks and 76 steals in 72 games.

Although his scoring average topped all other NBA rookies, he caught a bad break when he fractured a thumb late in the season.

Last season, Stackhouse returned from his injury to increase his scoring output to 20.7 points per game. He also increased his rebounding average to 4.2 per game while chalking up 93 steals.

In two seasons at North Carolina, Stackhouse averaged 15.7 points, 6.6 rebounds, and 2.3 assists per game. He was voted onto The Sporting News' All-America Second Team after his sophomore campaign in 1995.

FACT FILE

Born: November 5, 1974
Height: 6' 6"
Length of NBA career:
 1995–present
Major team:
 Philadelphia

BELOW: IS PHILADELPHIA'S BACKCOURT BIG ENOUGH FOR JERRY STACKHOUSE (BELOW) AND ALLEN IVERSON?

JOHN STOCKTON

FACT FILE

Born: March 26, 1962
Height: 6' 1"
Length of NBA career:
    1984–present
Major team:
    Utah
Records/Awards:
    NBA All-Star (9)
    Olympic Gold Medals
        (1992, 1996)

If you checked the NBA assists list every season from 1987 through 1996, you found John Stockton's name at the very top of it.

Stockton, a 6-foot-1-inch, super-cerebral, deceptively quick point guard, has been running the show for the Utah Jazz since he was selected out of little-known Gonzaga College in the first round of the 1984 NBA draft.

Working his pick-and-roll magic with team-mate Karl Malone for more than a decade, Stockton holds the career record for most years leading the league in assists (9), most assists overall (12,170), most steals (2,531), and highest assists-per-game average (11.5). Besides being a great assists and steals man, Stockton is also an underrated scorer, having averaged double digits in points in ten straight seasons from 1987 through 1997.

A nine-time All-Star—he and Malone were named coMVP's of the 1993 All-Star contest—

Stockton set the NBA's single-season record for highest assists-per-game average (14.5) in 1990, and for most assists (1,164) in 1991. He led the NBA in steals-per-game average twice, first in 1989 (3.21), and again in 1992 (2.98).

A member of Dream Team I, which won the Olympic gold medal at Barcelona, Spain, in 1992, and a member of the 1996 US Olympic gold-medal winning team, Stockton averaged 13.6 points, 11.5 rebounds, and 2.7 assists through his first 13 seasons with the Jazz, adding 14.4 points, 10.8 assists, and 3.3 re-bounds in 127 career playoff games.

Adding to his shiny resume, Stockton also holds the single-game playoff record for most assists in one quarter, tallying 11 against San Antonio on May 5, 1994, and shares the single-game playoff record for most assists, dishing out 24 against the Los Angeles Lakers on May 17, 1988.

RIGHT: JOHN STOCKTON, MASTER OF THE PICK-AND-ROLL, GOES AIRBORN FOR A LAYUP.

MAURICE STOKES

During a rebound scramble against the Minneapolis Lakers late in the 1957–58 season, Maurice Stokes of the Cincinnati Royals crashed to the floor and bumped his head. A few days later, Stokes, a 6-foot-7-inch, 235-pound forward, produced 12 points and 15 rebounds in a 100–83, playoff-opening loss to Detroit.

On the plane ride returning to Cincinnati, Stokes suddenly collapsed.

After being rushed to a hospital, Stokes was diagnosed as having post-traumatic encephalopathy: a paralysis and unconsciousness brought on by a swelling of the brain caused by bumping his head, presumably in that fall in the Laker game.

Eventually, Stokes regained consciousness, and though he could think and speak clearly, the illness left him paralyzed and bedridden.

In the years to follow, his Royals teammate, Jack Twyman, became Stokes's legal guardian, setting up benefit games and charity functions on his behalf to help raise money. Twelve years later, Maurice Stokes, just 36 years old, died of a heart attack relating to his illness. The basketball world was in shock.

"To me," said Kevin Loughery, a former NBA guard and longtime coach, "he will always be a legend." For certain, Stokes was well on his way to a legendary career in pro basketball, but it was only to last three seasons.

A standout player at St. Francis of Loretto College in Pennsylvania—he was the most valuable player of the 1955 National Invitation Tournament—Stokes was the NBA's rookie of the year with Rochester in 1956, averaging 16.8 points per game.

The following season, he averaged 15.6 points per contest, and in 1957–58, when the Royals moved from Rochester to Cincinnati, Stokes posted his career-high average of 16.9 points per contest.

A great rebounder with fluid moves who is often compared as a player to the great Elgin Baylor, Stokes was a Second-Team All-Star in each of those seasons.

FACT FILE

Born: June 17, 1933
Height: 6′ 7″
Length of NBA career:
1955–58
Major teams:
Rochester
Cincinnati
Records/Awards:
NBA Rookie of the Year
(1956)
NBA All-Star (3)

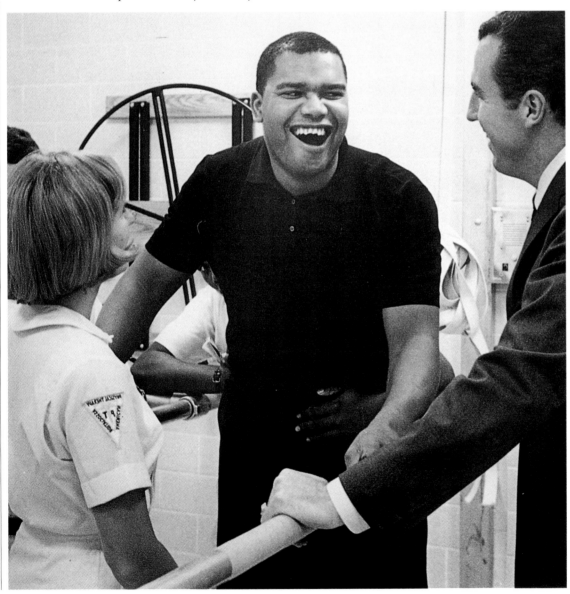

LEFT: MAURICE STOKES AT A HOSPITAL AFTER THE LIFE-THREATENING INJURY HE SUFFERED WHILE PLAYING BASKETBALL.

DAMON STOUDAMIRE

FACT FILE

Born: September 3, 1973
Height: 5′ 10″
Length of NBA career:
  1995–present
Major team:
  Toronto
Records/Awards:
  NBA Rookie of the Year
  (1996)

Astruggling expansion franchise, the Toronto Raptors didn't have much to brag about during the 1995–96 season—except, of course, Damon Stoudamire. A 5-foot-10-inch blur out of Arizona, Stoudamire won Rookie of the Year honors with a season Canadian basketball fans won't soon forget.

Playing in seventy games, Stoudamire averaged 19.0 points, 9.3 assists, and 4.0 rebounds per contest in his initial season with the Raptors. He led all rookies in steals (98), assists (653), minutes played (2,865), free-throw percentage (.797), and three-point marksmanship (39 percent). Selected by Toronto in the first round of the 1995 NBA draft, Stoudamire finished second in per-game-scoring average among rookies by 0.2 points, behind Philadelphia's Jerry Stackhouse (19.2). His 1,331 points and 653 assists lead the Toronto franchise.

To add to his incredible rookie campaign, Stoudamire also set the single-season record for most three-point field goals made by a first-year player, bagging 133 of 337 trifecta attempts. Last season, Stoudamire continued to dazzle, averaging 20.2 points, 8.8 assists, and 4.1 rebounds per game.

RIGHT: DAMON STOUDAMIRE IS A BLUR ON THE BASKETBALL COURT.

ROD STRICKLAND

When the media is rating the top point guards in the NBA, he is rarely mentioned, but just ask his peers who they think is one of the toughest playmakers in the league, and they'll point to Rod Strickland.

A 6-foot-3-inch ball-handling demon out of Depaul, Strickland was selected by his hometown New York Knicks in the first round of the 1988 NBA draft. A resourceful scorer with a get-to-the-hoop mentality, Strickland earned a spot on the 1989 All-Rookie Second squad after averaging 8.9 points, 3.9 assists, and 2.0 rebounds per game.

Midway through the following season, Strickland was traded to San Antonio. He finished with averages of 10.6 points, 5.7 assists, and 3.2 rebounds in that split year, starting a streak of eight straight seasons in which he averaged double digits in scoring.

After two and a half seasons in San Antonio, Strickland was traded to the Portland Trail Blazers, where he enjoyed the best years of his career. In his first season with the Trail Blazers, 1992–93, Strickland averaged 13.7 points, 7.2 assists, and 4.3 boards per game. He raised his average to 17.2 points per game the following season, and in the 1994–95 campaign averaged career-highs in points (18.9) and rebounds per game (5.0).

The 1995–96 season was also memorable for Strickland, as he averaged 18.7 points and a career-high 9.6 assists per contest.

Strickland, traded after the 1996 season to the Washington Bullets, where he averaged 17.2 points, 8.9 assists and 4.1 rebounds per game last season, averaged 14.6 points, 7.6 assists, and 3.9 rebounds per game through his first nine NBA seasons, adding 15.1 points, 8.4 assists, and 4.5 rebounds in 44 career playoff contests.

FACT FILE

Born: July 11, 1966
Height: 6' 3"
Length of NBA career:
1988–present
Major teams:
New York
San Antonio (joined 1990)
Portland (joined 1992)
Washington (joined 1996)

LEFT: THE MEDIA MAY NOT THINK SO, BUT ROD STRICKLAND'S PEERS WILL TELL YOU THAT HE IS ONE OF THE TOP PLAYMAKERS IN THE GAME.

STREET MOVES: NEW YORK'S PLAYGROUND LEGENDS

There are whompfs all night at Norfolk State. However, if you took away their passer, the Spartans would hear a lot less of that noise. The passer is Richard Kirkland, a 6-foot guard who weighs 150 pounds and may be the fastest man in college basketball."

Those were the very words written about Richard "Pee Wee" Kirkland in the January 8, 1968, edition of *Sports Illustrated*. Five months later, Kirkland was drafted by the Chicago Bulls.

But Kirkland, perhaps the most spectacular point guard in the history of New York City basketball, never played a minute in the National Basketball Association. A heated argument with the coach drove him back to the life he had known best—a gangster on the streets of East Harlem.

"The bitterness and pain comes not from what I didn't do," said Kirkland, an Al Capone with a crossover dribble who served ten years of jail time for tax evasion, "but how far I didn't go."

Along with Joe Hammond, his old backcourt partner from their legendary days in the Pro Rucker Tournament, Kirkland is now a spokesman for Nike, sharing tales of a haunted past with a new generation of children, urging them to stay off drugs and in school. The message is simple: this is how you play basketball, a game we always won, and this is how you deal with life, a game we once lost.

"Everything is timing," said Kirkland. "Twenty-five years ago, we were part of the problem. Twenty-five years later, we are part of the solution."

Twenty-five years later, children in the schoolyards of New York City still try to emulate their parents' favorite playground legends. For Hammond and Kirkland teamed up against other superstars like Julius Erving, Tiny Archibald, and Connie Hawkins at the fabled Rucker Tournament on 156th Street and 8th Avenue, a stage that brought together playground phenomenons, college all-Americans, and pro players.

We were the perfect example of what to be on the court, and the perfect example of what not to be off the court," said the 45-year-old Hammond, who spent six years behind bars for conspiracy to sell drugs, but is more famous for scoring 50 points on Dr. J in the 1970 Rucker championship game. "We wasted a God-given talent, and we can't let these kids do the same."

ROY TARPLEY

FACT FILE

Born: November 28, 1964
Height: 6′ 11″
Length of NBA career:
  1986–91, 1994–95
Major team:
  Dallas
Records/Awards:
  NBA Sixth Man Award
  (1988)

As talented on the court as he was troubled off it, Roy Tarpley played a total of six seasons in the NBA, his career constantly interrupted by injuries, as well as fines and suspensions for violating the league's substance-abuse policy.

Tarpley, a 6-foot-11-inch center/forward who was selected by the Dallas Mavericks in the first round of the 1986 NBA draft, earned a place for himself on the 1987 All-Rookie team after averaging 7.5 points and 7.1 rebounds per game.

The following season, Tarpley came off the bench to average 13.5 points and 11.8 rebounds per game en route to capturing the NBA's Sixth Man Award.

After injuries limited him to just 19 games in 1988–89 and 45 games in 1989–90, Tarpley was suspended by the NBA in 1991 after testing positive for drugs. Tarpley's long road back to the NBA began with Wichita Falls of the CBA and the Miami Tropics of the USBL during the 1991–92 season.

From 1992–94, Tarpley played his basketball in Greece and became one of the Greek League's top players. He averaged 22.2 points and 17.8 rebounds per contest for Aris Thessaloniki in 1992–93, and 19.6 points and 12.7 boards per game for Olympiakos SFP in 1993–94.

After he was reinstated by the NBA in 1994, Tarpley re-joined Dallas, and proved, after all he had been through, that he was still a quality NBA player, averaging 12.6 points and 8.2 rebounds in 55 games.

Unfortunately for Tarpley, he was again tossed out of the NBA in December of 1995, this time for using alcohol. That banishment was costly, as Tarpley's five-year, $23-million contract was nullified.

RIGHT: TALENTED AND TROUBLED WAS ROY TARPLEY.

REGGIE THEUS

Before Michael Jordan became a Bull, Reggie Theus was the main man in Chicago, a 6-foot-7-inch swingman who ran the floor hard and displayed one of the best shooting touches in the NBA.

Selected by Chicago out of the University of Nevada—Las Vegas in the first round of the NBA draft in 1978, Theus made an immediate impact with the Bulls, shooting his way onto the 1979 All-Rookie squad with an average of 16.3 points per game, adding averages of 5.2 assists and 2.8 rebounds.

A two-time All-Star, Theus's best season was 1982–83, his last full season with the Bulls, when he averaged 23.8 points, 5.9 assists, and 3.7 rebounds per game.

Midway through the following season, Theus was traded to the Kansas City Kings—which moved to Sacramento in 1985—and starred for the Kings for four seasons. He averaged 21.6 points per game for the Kings in 1987–88, marking the fourth time in his career that he had broken the 20-point scoring barrier in a season.

Theus, who spent his last three years with Atlanta, Orlando, and the New Jersey Nets, averaged 18.5 points, 6.3 assists, and 3.3 rebounds per game over his illustrious thirteen-year career. Playing on teams that rarely reached post-season play, Theus averaged 14.4 points, 5.7 assists, and 2.8 rebounds in seventeen career playoff games.

After his NBA playing days were over, Theus went to Italy and was a smashing success. He averaged 29.3 points, 5.4 assists, and 3.9 rebounds per game for Ranger Varese of the Italian League in 1991–92.

At UNLV, Theus averaged 12.9 points over three seasons.

FACT FILE

Born: October 13, 1957
Height: 6' 7"
Length of NBA career:
 1978–91
Major teams:
 Chicago
 Kansas City–Sacramento
 (joined 1984)
 Atlanta (joined 1988)
 Orlando (joined 1989)
 New Jersey (joined 1990)
Records/Awards:
 NBA All-Star (2)

LEFT: BEFORE A GUY NAMED JORDAN CAME ALONG, CHICAGO WAS REGGIE THEUS' TOWN.

ISIAH THOMAS

FACT FILE

Born: April 30, 1961
Height: 6′ 1″
Length of NBA career:
1981–94
Major team:
Detroit
Records/Awards:
NBA All-Star (12)
NBA Championship (2)

One of the most talented and scrappiest point guards ever to play on court in the NBA, Isiah Thomas was the driving force behind the Detroit Pistons' championship teams of 1989 and 1990.

Thomas, a 6-foot-1-inch ball-handling whiz out of Indiana, left defenders dizzy with a wicked cross-over dribble. He played his entire thirteen-year career in Detroit, making All-Star appearances in every season except his last.

With an incredible first step, Thomas could hurt a defense with an arsenal of offensive moves. He averaged double digits in scoring every season in the league, and from 1982–87, averaged better than 20 points per contest.

A clever and unselfish playmaker as well, Thomas averaged double digits in assists four straight seasons from 1984–87. He led the league with 13.9 assists per game in 1984–85.

A three-time All-NBA First Team selection, Thomas was voted Most Valuable Player of the 1990 NBA Finals, in which Detroit defeated Portland, four games to one.

Thomas, whose fiery style behind a wide smile led the charge of the Bad-Boy Pistons during their back-to-back championship seasons, was also the ringleader of the Detroit team which lost to Magic Johnson and the Los Angeles Lakers in seven games to decide the 1988 NBA championship. He set a Finals single-game record that season for most points in one quarter, scoring a total of 25 on June 19, 1988.

In a title rematch the following season, Thomas and the Pistons swept the Lakers in four straight games.

A member of the US Olympic Team in 1980, Thomas was named the NCAA Division I Tournament Most Outstanding Player en route to leading Indiana to the national title.

For his career, Thomas averaged 19.2 points, 9.3 assists, and 3.6 assists per game, adding 20.4 points, 8.9 rebounds, and 4.7 boards in 111 career playoff contests. He is the Pistons' all-time leading scorer with 18,822 points, all-time assists leader with 9,061, and all-time steals leader with 1,861.

RIGHT: THE HALL-OF-FAME BOUND ISIAH THOMAS HAD AN INCREDIBLE FIRST STEP.

DAVID THOMPSON

In his day, David Thompson was the best player in professional basketball west of Julius Erving. Thompson, an explosive 6-foot-4-inch swingman out of North Carolina State who led the Wolfpack to the 1974 NCAA championship, was the top overall pick in the 1976 NBA draft.

A tremendous leaper who loved to soar to the hoop, Thompson began his pro career with Denver of the ABA, averaging 26 points per game on his way to earning the ABA's Rookie of the Year award. His 26-point average marked the first of six straight years in which he would average better than 20 points per game in a season.

When the ABA and NBA merged for the 1976–77 campaign, Thompson became a star all over again in a new league, averaging 25.9 points per contest.

The following season, Thompson and San Antonio's George Gervin waged the greatest scoring race in NBA history. That scoring title, which produced two of the league's greatest offensive performances, was decided on April 9, 1978, the final day of the regular season.

Earlier in the day, Thompson thought he had locked up the title with a 73-point performance that left him at a career-best 27.15 points per game. But later that evening, Gervin piled up 63 points against the Utah Jazz, stealing the crown with 27.22 points per game.

After seven seasons in Denver, Thompson was traded to the Seattle SuperSonics, with whom he spent the last two years of his career.

When his playing days were over, Thompson left the game with an NBA average of 22.1 points per game, and an ABA average of 26.0.

A five-time All-Star, and the only Nugget to be named Most Valuable Player in both an ABA and NBA All-Star game, Thompson's No. 33 jersey hangs in the McNichols Arena rafters in Denver alongside the retired uniforms of Dan Issel (44) and Byron Beck (40).

FACT FILE

Born: July 13,1954
Height: 6′ 4″
Length of ABA career:
  1975–76
Length of NBA career:
  1976–84
Major teams:
  Denver
  Seattle (joined 1982)
Records/Awards:
  ABA Rookie of the Year
    (1976)
  ABA All-Star (1)
  NBA All-Star (4)
  Hall of Fame (1996)

LEFT: WEST OF JULIUS ERVING, DAVID THOMPSON (LEFT) WAS ONCE BASKETBALL'S TOP-FLIGHT ATTRACTION.

MYCHAL THOMPSON

FACT FILE

Born: January 30, 1955
Height: 6′ 10″
Length of NBA career:
  1979–90
Major teams:
  Portland
  San Antonio (joined 1986)
  Los Angeles (joined 1987)
Records/Awards:
  NBA Championship (2)

When Mychal Thompson was traded by San Antonio to the Los Angeles Lakers in 1987, it was the fulfillment of a lifelong dream.

"It's my face," Thompson said at the time. "It hurts because I've been smiling so much."

Thompson, a 6-foot-10-inch center who dreamed of playing for the Lakers when he starred at the University of Minnesota from 1974–78, saw his dream come true nine years later. It was also a dream come true for the Lakers, who went on to capture back-to-back NBA championships with Thompson in 1987 and 1988. Thompson played an integral role on both of those teams, averaging 11.4 points per game on the '87 squad, and 11.6 points per contest on the '88 squad.

The Lakers would have loved to have had Thompson on their roster a lot sooner, but by the time Los Angeles made its selection in the 1978 NBA draft, Thompson was long gone, scooped up on the very first pick by the Portland Trail Blazers.

In his initial season with the Trail Blazers, Thompson earned a place on the 1979 All-Rookie team, tallying up averages 14.7 points and 8.2 rebounds per game to go along with 134 blocked shots.

Thompson, who averaged double digits in scoring in ten of his eleven NBA seasons, spent the first seven years of his career in Portland. In his third season with the Trail Blazers, 1981–82, he averaged 20.8 points per game.

For his career, Thompson averaged 14.5 points and 7.7 rebounds per game, adding 11.8 points and 6.4 boards per game in 96 career playoff contests.

At Minnesota, Thompson posted collegiate averages of 20.8 points and 9.9 rebounds per game over four seasons.

RIGHT: MYCHAL THOMPSON'S DREAMS WERE REALIZED THE MOMENT HE PUT ON A LOS ANGELES LAKERS UNIFORM.

SEDALE THREATT

A pure scorer for fourteen NBA seasons, Sedale Threatt played sparingly with Houston last season, but appeared in all eighty-two games for the 1995–96 Los Angeles Lakers, finishing with only six more turnovers (74) than steals (68).

Threatt, a 6-foot-2-inch gunner out of West Virginia Tech, was a longshot selection by the Philadelphia 76ers in the sixth round (139th pick overall) of the 1983 NBA draft.

After playing just forty-five games in his initial NBA season with Philadelphia, Threatt played in all eighty-two games for the 76ers the following season, averaging 5.4 points per game. After coming off the bench in his first eight NBA seasons to help Philadelphia, Chicago, and Seattle, Threatt was traded to the Lakers in 1991 and became a starter.

In his first two seasons with the Lakers, Threatt averaged an identical 15.1 points per game, a career high in that department.

In his thirteenth season with the 1995–96 Lakers, Threatt filled in admirably for teammate Nick Van Exel after Van Exel was suspended for bumping an official.

Through the 1996–97 season, Threatt averaged 9.8 points and 3.8 assists per game in an NBA career that hardly seemed possible thirteen years earlier. He added 8.7 points, 3.6 assists, and 1.6 rebounds in 70 career playoff contests.

FACT FILE

Born: September 10, 1961
Height: 6′ 2″
Length of NBA career:
 1983–present
Major teams:
 Philadelphia
 Chicago (joined 1986)
 Seattle (joined 1988)
 Los Angeles (joined 1991)
 Houston (joined 1997)

LEFT: SEDALE THREATT OVERCAME LONG ODDS TO GET TO THE NBA LEVEL.

NATE THURMOND

FACT FILE

Born: July 25, 1941
Height: 6′ 11″
Length of NBA career:
  1963–77
Major teams:
  San Francisco–Golden
    State
  Chicago (joined 1974)
  Cleveland (joined 1975)
Records/Awards:
  NBA All-Defensive First
    Team (2)
  NBA All-Star (7)
  Hall of Fame (1984)

In an era of super-centers that included players like Wilt Chamberlain, Bill Russell, and later Kareem Abdul-Jabbar, Nate Thurmond, who began his 14-year NBA career with the San Francisco Warriors, was one of the very best.

Thurmond, a 6-foot-11-inch pivotman who also played forward, was an all-around talent who excelled at playing defense. In 1974, he became the first player in NBA history to get a quadruple double in one game, tallying 22 points, 14 rebounds, 13 assists, and 12 blocked shots.

An All-American at Bowling Green in 1963—he set the NCAA Tournament record for most rebounds (31) in one game—Thurmond earned a place on the NBA's 1964 All-Rookie team after averaging 7.0 points and 10.4 rebounds per game.

The following season, Thurmond set a record for most rebounds in one quarter, hauling down 18 boards against Baltimore on February 28, 1965. He averaged 16.5 points per game during that campaign, starting a streak of ten straight seasons in which he would average double digits in scoring.

A seven-time All-Star and two-time NBA All-Defensive First Team selection, Thurmond spent 11 of his 14 seasons with San Francisco, which was renamed Golden State for the 1971–72 season. His best season in a Warriors uniform was 1969–70, when he averaged 21.9 points, 17.7 rebounds, and 3.5 assists per game.

Golden State's all-time leading rebounder with 12,771, Thurmond was traded to Chicago in 1974. He split his last three seasons between the Bulls and the Cleveland Cavaliers.

For his career, Thurmond averaged 15.0 points, 15.0 rebounds, and 2.7 assists per game, adding 11.9 points, 13.6 boards, and 2.8 assists in 81 career playoff contests.

At Bowling Green, Thurmond averaged 17.8 points and 17.0 rebounds in four seasons.

RIGHT: NATE THURMOND DOING WHAT HE DID BEST—PLAYING STELLAR DEFENSE.

WAYMAN TISDALE

A grizzled NBA veteran, Wayman Tisdale became the league's fourteenth active player to register 5,000 rebounds and 12,000 points for his career last season.

A 6-foot-9-inch, 260-pound center/forward, Tisdale was selected by the Indiana Pacers in the first round of the 1985 NBA draft.

Tisdale, who has a smooth shooting touch from short range and doesn't mind throwing his weight around on the basketball court, had a super rookie season, averaging 14.7 points and 7.2 rebounds per game. He posted double-digit averages in scoring during each of his first eleven NBA seasons.

Midway through the 1988–89 campaign, Tisdale was traded to Sacramento, where he enjoyed the best seasons of his career.

In his first season with the Kings, Tisdale racked up a career-high average of 22.3 points per game, and followed that up later with 20 points and a career-high 7.7 rebounds per game during the 1990–91 campaign.

After five seasons in Sacramento, Tisdale signed as a free agent with the Phoenix Suns in 1994, coming off the bench for the Suns.

Through the 1996–97 season, Tisdale had racked up 12,878 points. He posted averages of 15.3 points, 6.1 rebounds, and 1.3 assists per game, adding 7.1 points, 2.6 rebounds, and 1.0 assists in 22 career playoff games.

Tisdale, who helped the 1984 US Olympic team capture a gold medal, averaged 25.6 points and 10.1 rebounds per game in three seasons at Oklahoma.

FACT FILE

Born: June 9, 1964
Height: 6' 9"
Length of NBA career:
 1985–present
Major teams:
 Indiana
 Sacramento (joined 1989)
 Phoenix (joined 1994)
Records/Awards:
 Olympic Gold Medal
 (1984)

LEFT: WAYMAN TISDALE'S CAREER STATS RANK WITH THE BEST AMONG ACTIVE PLAYERS.

RUDY TOMJANOVICH

FACT FILE

Born: November 24, 1948
Height: 6′ 8″
Length of NBA career:
  1970–81
Major team:
  San Diego–Houston
Records/Awards:
  NBA All-Star (5)

Perhaps better remembered for having his face shattered by a right-hand punch thrown by Kermit Washington of the Los Angeles Lakers on December 9, 1977, Rudy Tomjanovich was one of the best players in Houston Rocket history.

A 6-foot-8-inch forward out of Michigan with a nose for scoring, Tomjanovich was selected by the then-San Diego Rockets in the first round of the 1970 NBA draft.

As a rookie with the Rockets, "Rudy T" as Tomjanovich is called, averaged just 5.3 points and 4.9 rebounds per game in limited duty.

The following season, the Rockets moved to Houston, and Tomjanovich moved into the elite group of forwards, averaging 15.0 points and 11.8 rebounds per game. He started a streak in which he would post averages of double digits in scoring for ten straight seasons until he retired in 1981.

Tomjanovich, a five-time All-Star who scored 20 or more points per game four times in his career, enjoyed his best season in 1973–74, when he registered 24.5 points, 9.0 rebounds, and 3.1 assists per game.

The closest Tomjanovich came to winning an NBA championship was his last season, when the Rockets lost to Larry Bird and the Boston Celtics in six games to decide the 1981 Finals.

For his career, Tomjanovich averaged 17.4 points, 8.1 rebounds, and 2.0 assists per game, adding 13.8 points, 5.1 boards, and 1.6 assists per contest in 37 career playoff contests. In 1991, he rejoined the Rockets as their head coach, since leading them to a pair of championships.

At Michigan, Tomjanovich averaged 25.1 points and 14.4 rebounds over four seasons.

RIGHT: RUDY TOMJANOVICH (LEFT), LEAPS TO SWAT AWAY AN ATTEMPTED FIELD GOAL.

ANDREW TONEY

A n explosive scorer out of Southwestern Louisiana, Andrew Toney teamed with Maurice Cheeks to form the gold dust twin backcourt of the Philadelphia 76ers, which struck NBA championship gold in 1983.

The essence of Toney's game, a mix of power and grace, was to score on a few jump shots, lure opponents into playing tighter defense, and zip past them for easy layups.

Selected by Philadelphia in the first round of the 1980 NBA draft, the 6-foot-3-inch Toney improved his scoring average in each of his first four NBA seasons. As a rookie, he scored 12.9 points per game, increasing that total to 16.5 points the following season.

In his third season, Toney averaged 19.7 points per game in helping the 76ers sweep the Los Angeles Lakers in four straight games to win the NBA Championship. He returned the following season to post a career-high average of 20.4 points per contest.

"I envisioned Andrew as an explosive player from the first day of training camp," Philadelphia Coach Billy Cunningham said of Toney early in his career. "He has great vision. When he's passing the ball the way he is capable, he makes his teammates better players. Great players make their teammates better."

A two-time All-Star, Toney played eight seasons in the NBA, finishing his career with averages of 15.9 points, 4.1 assists, and 2.1 rebounds per game, adding 17.4 points, 4.4 assists, and 2.3 rebounds in seventy-two career playoff games.

At Southwestern Louisiana, Toney averaged 23.6 points in four seasons.

FACT FILE

Born: November 23, 1957
Height: 6′ 3″
Length of NBA career:
 1980–88
Major team:
 Philadelphia
Records/Awards:
 NBA All-Star (2)
 NBA Championship (1)

LEFT: ANDREW TONEY'S GAME WAS A MIXTURE OF POWER AND GRACE.

KELLY TRIPUCKA

FACT FILE

Born: February 16, 1959
Height: 6′ 6″
Length of NBA career:
 1981–91
Major teams:
 Detroit
 Utah (joined 1986)
 Charlotte (joined 1988)
Records/Awards:
 NBA All-Star (2)

A scoring machine out of Notre Dame and one of the most dangerous gunners ever, Kelly Tripucka had an explosive ten-year NBA career.

Selected by the Detroit Pistons in the first round of the 1981 NBA draft, Tripucka earned a place on the 1982 All-Rookie squad after scoring 21.6 points per game. The following season, 1982–83, the 6-foot-6-inch Tripucka averaged a career-high 26.5 points per contest.

A two-time All-Star, Tripucka played his first five seasons with Detroit—averaging 20 or more points in five of those seasons—before he was traded to Utah in 1986. Injuries limited Tripucka to just forty-nine games for Utah in 1987–88, and he managed just 7.5 points per contest. He was traded to Charlotte the following season and regained his super scoring touch. In eight of his ten NBA seasons, the last three spent with the Charlotte Hornets, Tripucka averaged double digits in scoring. His best season in a Charlotte uniform was 1988–89—the Hornets' inaugural campaign—when he scored 22.6 points per contest

When his NBA playing days were over, Tripucka went to France, where he averaged 15.4 points per game for Limoges of the French League in the 1991–92 season.

For his career, Tripucka averaged 17.2 points and 2.9 assists per game, adding 15.6 points and 2.2 assists in 25 career playoff contests.

At Notre Dame, Tripucka averaged 15.3 points over four seasons.

RIGHT: SCORING MACHINE KELLY TRIPUCKA LOOKS FOR A SPOT WHERE HE CAN LAUNCH YET ANOTHER SHOT.

JACK TWYMAN

One of the great shooting forwards of his era, Jack Twyman placed second among the league's leading scorers twice in his career, finishing behind NBA legends each time.

A 6-foot-6-inch forward with sloping shoulders, Twyman played his entire career with the Royals, who moved from Rochester to Cincinnati for the 1957–58 season. He averaged 25.8 points per game in 1958–59, finishing second that season to Bob Pettit of St. Louis. The following season, Twyman averaged a career-high 31.2 points, but Wilt Chamberlain won his first scoring title.

A product of the University of Cincinnati, Twyman was selected by Rochester in the second round of the 1955 NBA draft. He posted 14.4 points per game as a rookie and went on to average double digits in scoring in each of his 11 seasons in the league.

A six-time All-Star and two-time All-NBA Second Team selection. Twyman did finish first in the 1959–60 season with 598 free throws made. He also chalked up a single-game career high that season with a 59-point effort against the Minneapolis Lakers on January 15, 1960.

Twyman, who scored 15,840 points in 823 regular season games, averaged 19.2 points, 6.6 rebounds, and 2.3 assists in his career, adding 18.3 points, 7.5 boards, and 1.8 assists in 34 career playoff contests.

At Cincinnati, Twyman averaged 17.8 points and 13.8 rebounds over four seasons.

FACT FILE

Born: May 11, 1934
Height: 6′ 6″
Length of NBA career:
 1955–66
Major team:
 Rochester–Cincinnati
Records/Awards:
 NBA All-Star (6)
 Hall of Fame (1982)

LEFT: IN HIS QUEST FOR A SCORING CROWN, JACK TWYMAN TWICE FINISHED SECOND, LOSING OUT EACH TIME TO A LEGEND.

Spider and Worm, to (Nick)name just a few . . .

Theodore Edwards was dribbling—out of the sides of his mouth—when an older sister peeked into his crib and noticed that he was choking on his baby bottle. "She saw me choking and ran to call my mom," said Edwards. "I was turning blue. That's how I got my nickname."

Years later, Blue Edwards was dribbling himself rich in the NBA, a league filled with some of the most colorful and storied nicknames in the world.

Where else could you watch John "Spider" Sally and Dennis "Worm" Rodman crawl around the hardwood, or have Glenn "Doc" Rivers make a house call to cure your nasty case of the basketball blues?

Want the skinny on some of the league's more dubious dubs? Remember "Fat" Lever?

"When Lafayette Lever was a kid growing up in Tucson, Az, all the kids he played ball with looked at his first name and felt it was just too fat," said Roland LaVetter, Lever's coach at Pueblo High School, where Fat helped the Warriors waddle to back-to-back state championships in the late 1970s. "And that's what they started calling him—fat."

And just how did Chuck Connors Person become the "Rifleman?"

"My mom was a big fan of that old cowboy show, *The Rifleman*, which starred Chuck Connors," said Person. "She practically named me after him."

What about Vernell Eufaye "Bimbo" Coles? Did he get his nickname by teasing his afro to the moon and prancing around locker rooms in cheap lipstick and leather mini-skirts?

"Not exactly," said Coles. "I was just a few months old and a cousin decided to start calling me Bimbo. Over the years, the name just stuck."

Like Bimbo, Ronald Jerome "Popeye" Jones, who doesn't even like spinach, also had nothing to do with the creation of his own nickname.

"When I came home from the hospital, my brother David, who was two years old at the time, was watching that Popeye cartoon. My mother asked him what they were going to call me, and David looked at the television and said Popeye. My other brothers and sisters liked it and my mom liked it. And now, my mother doesn't even call me by my first name. Very few people do. You've got to like your nickname, because that is all anybody has ever called you."

But not every player was born with the god-given ability to acquire a nickname before ever having slapped his first backboard. Guys like Greg "Cadillac" Anderson had to log in some serious miles to earn his. He was nicknamed by teammates at the University of Houston, where he was famous for his long bicycle rides around campus.

"Everywhere I went, I took my bike, and people at school started joking, saying stuff like, 'Hey, Greg, I like your Cadillac,'" Anderson said. "And then it got to the point where even I wasn't riding my bike, people still called me Cadillac."

If Eric Augustus Floyd ever gets tired of hearing his nickname, he's got a legitimate excuse. How would you like to have run up and down the floor with some of the fastest athletes in the world during your career having to answer to the name "Sleepy."

"I got that name playing little league baseball," said Floyd. "I was playing second base and misplayed a ground ball, and some guy yelled out 'wake up, sleepy.'"

And if you think Chris Jackson suffered from an identity crisis when he changed his name to Mahmoud Abdul-Rauf for religious reasons, consider the unholy plight of Anthony "Spudd" Webb, whose nickname was changed just because he stopped growing.

Spudd, you see, is actually an abbreviated version of an earlier nickname—"Sputnik", which the little Webb earned by launching over much taller first and second graders while growing up in Dallas. But with every inch the Webb-man failed to grow, Spudd just became a natural fit. So one of the shortest players in NBA history was stuck with one of the league's shortest nicknames.

On the subject of nerves, just how did Pervis Ellison become "Never Nervous" Pervis.

Just think back to the 1986 NCAA championship contest which matched Ellison's underdog Louisville squad against the Blue Devils of Duke. Just a freshman who wasn't even worthy of a nickname, Ellison was cool as cucumber in that big game, scoring 25 points, hauling down 11 boards, and swatting away two shots to help the Cards calmly pull of the upset.

Karl "The Mailman" Malone didn't get his nickname pushing a cart through Salt Lake City in the rain, sleet, or sunshine during his off seasons. Malone, who always delivered on the basketball court for Louisiana Tech, was given his postmark by a sportswriter who covered the team there.

Of all the nicknames in the NBA, perhaps the most justified belongs to David Maurice "Admiral" Robinson of the Spurs, who played four seasons at Navy. And perhaps the most adorable belongs to Anfernee "Penny" Hardaway, whose grandmother, Louise, felt her little basketball star was just as pretty as a penny.

But the biggest salute of all goes out to Fat Lever's wife, Charlene, who managed to marry into a nickname.

"Charlene's nickname is Lean," said Coach LaVetter. "When she comes back to Tucson with her husband, everyone looks at them and says 'Hey, there go Fat and Lean.'"

BELOW: ERIC "SLEEPY" FLOYD, HERE BRINGING THE BALL
UPCOURT FOR THE NEW JERSEY NETS, IS ONE OF MANY NBA
STARS WITH COLORFUL NICKNAMES.

WES UNSELD

FACT FILE

Born: March 14, 1946
Height: 6′ 7″
Length of NBA career:
  1968–81
Major teams:
  Baltimore–Capital–
  Washington
Records/Awards:
  NBA Rookie of the Year
    (1969)
  NBA Most Valuable Player
    (1969)
  NBA All-Star (5)
  NBA Championship (1)
  Hall of Fame (1987)

Only the second player—the other was Wilt Chamberlain—in NBA history to win Rookie of the Year and Most Valuable Player honors in the same season, Wes Unseld of the Baltimore and Washington Bullets, is the franchise's all-time leading rebounder with a total of 13,769, and the all-time assists leader with 3,822.

A 6-foot-7-inch, 245-pound strongman out of Louisville who played center and forward, Unseld was voted MVP of the 1978 NBA Finals in which the Bullets squeezed by the Seattle SuperSonics in seven games.

Selected by Baltimore in the first round of the 1968 NBA draft, Unseld's phenomenal rookie campaign featured averages of 13.8 points and an amazing 18.2 rebounds per game. In his first five seasons with the Bullets, Unseld ripped down better than 15 rebounds per game. In the 1974–75 season, one year after the Bullets moved from Baltimore to Washington, Unseld topped the league with 14.8 boards per contest. In the 1975–76 campaign, he led the league with a .561 shooting percentage, connecting on 318 of 567 shots from the field.

A five-time All-Star, Unseld averaged 10.8 points, 14.0 rebounds, and 3.9 assists in his career, adding 10.6 points, 14.9 boards, and 3.8 assists in 119 career post-season contests. He later coached the Bullets from 1987–94.

At Louisville, Unseld averaged 20.6 points and 18.9 rebounds per game. As a freshman with the Cardinals, he raised eyebrows after tallying averages of 35.8 points and 23.6 rebounds per contest.

RIGHT: LOUISVILLE STRONGMAN WES UNSELD WAGES REBOUNDING WAR BENEATH THE BASKET.

DICK & TOM VAN ARSDALE

The 1965 NBA draft brought the league its first set of identical twins when the New York Knicks selected Dick Van Arsdale and the Detroit Pistons took his brother, Tom Van Arsdale.

Playing in the NBA for the identical number of years, 1965–77, the Van Arsdale brothers, both of whom starred at Indiana, had teammates, opponents, and fans around the country doing double-takes during the twelve seasons they played in the league.

After posting three straight double-digit scoring seasons for the Knicks, Dick Van Arsdale became the first player chosen by the Phoenix Suns in their 1968 expansion draft, and the first player to score a point for the franchise.

Dick Van Arsdale's best season was with Phoenix in 1970–71, when he averaged 21.9 points per game. From 1968–71, his first three seasons with the Suns, he averaged better than 20 points per game.

A three-time All-Star, Dick Van Arsdale averaged 16.4 points, 4.1 rebounds, and 3.3 assists in his career, adding 9.9 points, 2.4 rebounds, and 2.7 assists in thirty-four career playoff games.

Tom Van Arsdale—at 6-feet-5-inches he is half an inch taller than his brother—started his career with the Detroit Pistons and bounced around with four other teams before reuniting with Dick in Phoenix for the 1976–77 campaign, their last season of NBA ball.

Oddly enough, the best season of Tom Van Arsdale's career was the same as his twin brother's, 1970–71, when he registered an average 22.9 points per game.

A three-time All-Star like his brother, Tom Van Arsdale averaged 15.3 points, 4.2 rebounds, and 2.2 assists in his career. His teams never appeared in post-season play.

Co-winners of Indiana's Mr. Basketball Award as seniors in high school, the Van Arsdale's were also voted all-Big Ten guards at Indiana University.

"Once in a while, we'd go to class and take notes for each other," Dick Van Arsdale joked. "It all depended on who wanted to sleep later."

Twenty-two years after the Van Arsdales joined the NBA, the league got its second set of identical twins in Horace and Harvey Grant. Horace came along in 1987 as a first-round draft choice of the Chicago Bulls. A year later, the Washington Bullets used their first-round draft choice for Harvey, who was redshirted his freshman season at Clemson.

FACT FILE

Name: Dick Van Arsdale
Born: February 22, 1943
Height: 6' 4½"
Length of NBA career:
 1965–77
Major teams:
 New York Knicks
 Phoenix (joined 1968)
Records/Awards:
 NBA All-Star (3)

Name: Tom Van Arsdale
Born: February 22, 1943
Height: 6' 5"
Length of NBA career:
 1965–77
Major teams:
 Detroit
 Cincinnati (joined 1968)
 Kansas City (joined
  1972)
 Philadelphia (joined 1973)
 Atlanta (joined 1975)
 Phoenix (joined 1976)
Records/Awards:
 NBA All-Star (3)

LEFT: DICK VAN ARSDALE MOTORS TO THE BASKET FOR A LAYUP.

KIKI VANDEWEGHE

FACT FILE

Born: August 1, 1958
Height: 6′ 8″
Length of NBA career:
1980–93
Major teams:
Denver
Portland (joined 1984)
New York (joined 1989)
Los Angeles Clippers
(joined 1992)
Records/Awards:
NBA All-Star (2)

Staying healthy was always a bigger challenge for Kiki Vandeweghe than playing basketball, but the 6-foot-8-inch forward managed thirteen NBA seasons, and is considered one of the league's all-time great shooters.

After helping UCLA to the Final Four in 1980, Vandeweghe broke into the NBA with the Denver Nuggets, where he established himself as a shooter with great range who scored his points in big spurts. A two-time All-Star, Vandeweghe's best campaign in a Denver uniform was his last, 1983–84, when he averaged a career-high 29.4 points per contest.

After four seasons in Denver, Vandeweghe was traded to Portland, where he played four and a half years, keeping intact a streak of seven straight seasons in which he would average better than 20 points per game. As a member of the Trail Blazers during the 1986–87 season, Vandeweghe led the NBA with a .481 three-point field goal percentage, bagging 39 of 81 shots from behind the three-point stripe.

Midway through the 1988–89 season, Vandeweghe realized a lifelong dream when he was traded to the New York Knicks, following in the footsteps of his father, Ernie Vandeweghe, who played for the Knicks in the 1950s.

For his career, Vandeweghe averaged 19.7 points per game, adding 16.1 points in 68 career playoff contests. He averaged double digits in scoring in his first eleven seasons.

At UCLA, Vandeweghe averaged 12.2 points over four seasons, including a career-high 19.5 points per game as a senior.

RIGHT: KIKI VANDEWEGHE, DRIVING TO THE HOOP HERE, FOLLOWED HIS FATHER'S FOOTSTEPS INTO THE NBA.

NORM VAN LIER

Norm Van Lier's wife, Nancy, once said of her temperamental husband: "On the court he's very aggressive. He's always falling and diving after the basketball. It scares me. It's only basketball. He expects to win every game. He just doesn't listen. He's hard-headed."

Hard-headed indeed. Basketball historians will probably remember Van Lier more for his battles with opposing players, team owners and league officials than for his stellar playmaking abilities on the basketball court.

A three-time NBA All-Star, the 6-foot-2-inch Van Lier played ten seasons in the league with Cincinnati, Chicago and Milwaukee. A standout at St. Francis College in Pennsylvania, Van Lier broke in with Cincinnati in the 1969–70 season, averaging 9.5 points in 81 games.

The following season, Van Lier averaged a career-high 16 points per game with Cincinnati—his last full season as a member of the Royals—starting a streak of seven straight seasons in which he would average double figures in scoring.

For the next six and one-half seasons, Van Lier starred in Chicago, occasionally making headlines for all of the wrong reasons.

On March 27, 1975, in the midst of his best scoring season with the Bulls (15 points per game), Van Lier was called for three personal fouls in a game against the Houston Rockets. He was tossed out of the game and fined $1,000 for his behavior.

After stating that he would rather quit the game than pay the fine, several fans came forward and said they would pay the fine themselves, proving just how much they valued Van Lier's basketball contributions, and just how much of his antics they would put up with.

After spending the 1978–79 season with Milwaukee, the last season of his career, Van Lier left the game with an 11.8 regular-season scoring average, posting 13.9 points in 38 career playoff contests.

FACT FILE

Born: April 1, 1947
Height: 6′ 2″
Length of NBA career:
1969–79
Major teams:
Cincinnati
Chicago (joined 1972)
Milwaukee (joined 1978)

LEFT: NORM VAN LIER'S WIFE ONCE DESCRIBED THE TALENTED PLAYMAKER AS "HARD-HEADED."

CHET WALKER

FACT FILE

Born: February 22, 1940
Height: 6′ 7″
Length of NBA career:
  1962–75
Major teams:
  Syracuse–Philadelphia
  Chicago (joined 1969)
Records/Awards:
  NBA All-Star (7)
  NBA Championship (1)

The intended receiver in the "Havlicek stole the ball" playoff game between the Boston Celtics and Philadelphia 76ers—the decisive play of the 1965 Eastern Division Finals made famous by the rasping voice of Celtic announcer Johnny Most—Chet Walker received his share of glory in thirteen NBA seasons.

A silky, 6-foot-7-inch swingman from Bradley selected by the Syracuse Nationals in the second round of the 1962 NBA draft, Walker earned a place on the 1963 All-Rookie squad after averaging 12.3 points, 7.2 rebounds. and 1.1 assists per game.

Next season, Syracuse moved to Philadelphia and the team was renamed the 76ers. Walker, who averaged double digits in scoring in each of his thirteen NBA seasons, posted 17.3 points and a career-high 10.3 rebounds per game for the relocated franchise. A seven-time All-Star,

Walker's greatest season was 1966–67, when he averaged a career-high 19.3 points per game serving as a cornerman on one of the greatest teams in NBA history.

Teaming with stars like Wilt Chamberlain, Hal Greer, Luke Jackson, and Larry Costello, Walker and company knocked off the San Francisco Warriors in six games to win the 1967 NBA championship.

Shortly before the start of the 1969–70 season, Walker was traded to the Chicago Bulls. He played his last six seasons in Chicago, averaging better than 20 points per game in his first three seasons in the Windy City.

Walker, who held the Bulls' single-game record of 56 points until Michael Jordan came along and broke it, averaged 18.2 points, 7.1 rebounds, and 2.1 assists in his career, adding 18.2 points, 7.0 boards, and 2.0 assists in 105 career playoff contests.

RIGHT: CHET WALKER, BACKING IN FOR POSITION, AVERAGED DOUBLE-DIGITS IN SCORING IN EACH OF HIS THIRTEEN NBA SEASONS.

RASHEED WALLACE

Despite missing the final 15 games of his rookie season in 1995–96 with a fractured right thumb, Rasheed Wallace posted thumbs-up numbers with the Washington Bullets.

Wallace, a 6-foot-10-inch center/forward who was traded to the Portland Trail Blazers after his initial NBA campaign, made 51 starts in his lone season in Washington, finishing in double figures in 30 of those games.

For a player who would have only been a junior had he decided to stay at North Carolina instead of making himself eligible for the NBA draft after his sophomore season with the Tar Heels, Wallace adjusted quite well at the next level. In 65 games with Washington, Wallace earned a place on the NBA's All-Rookie Second Team after averaging 10.1 points, 4.7 rebounds, and 1.3 assists per game.

Last season, Wallace was traded to Portland, where he averaged a career-high 15.1 points per game.

In his two seasons at North Carolina, Wallace averaged 13.0 points and 7.4 rebounds. In his final season as a sophomore, he averaged 16.6 points and 8.2 boards en route to being named to The Sporting News' All-America first Team.

FACT FILE

Born: September 17, 1974
Height: 6' 10"
Length of NBA career:
  1995–present
Major teams:
  Washington
  Portland (joined 1996)

LEFT: RASHEED WALLACE HAS PROVEN THAT LEAVING COLLEGE EARLY, AT LEAST FOR HIM, WAS THE RIGHT THING TO DO.

BILL WALTON

Born: November 5, 1952
Height: 6′ 11″
Length of NBA career:
1974–88
Major teams:
Portland
San Diego–Los Angeles
Clippers (joined 1979)
Boston (joined 1985)
Records/Awards:
NBA Most Valuable Player
(1978)
NBA All-Defensive First
Team (2)
NBA Sixth Man Award
(1986)
NBA All-Star (2)
NBA Championship (2)
Hall of Fame (1993)

Once the NBA's preeminent center, a star whose rebounding and passing and defense set the standard for all other pivotmen during his prime, far too many injuries interrupted Bill Walton's fabulous professional career. A 6-foot-11-inch red-headed intimidator who led UCLA to back-to-back championships during 1972 and 1973, Walton was selected as first overall pick by the Portland Trail Blazers in the 1974 NBA draft.

A three-time Player of the Year at UCLA, Walton first encountered medical problems before the start of his rookie season. Having undergone surgery on his right knee for the removal of loose cartilage, Walton appeared in just 35 games as a rookie, posting solid averages of 12.8 points, 12.6 rebounds, and 4.8 assists per game.

In five seasons with the Trail Blazers, the often-injured Walton never played a full slate of games, but he was healthy enough to play sixty-five contests in 1976–77, guiding Portland to a six-game victory over Philadelphia in the NBA Finals. The MVP of that championship series, Walton led the league with 14.4 rebounds per game and was also tops with 3.25 blocked shots per contest.

The following season, Walton managed to play fifty-eight games, but he made the most of his 1,929 minutes, averaging a career-high 18.9 points, 13.2 rebounds, and 5.0 assists per game in capturing the league's MVP Award. After missing the entire 1978–79 campaign with the

Trail Blazers, Walton considered limping away from the game, but he signed as a free agent with the San Diego Clippers. He managed to play just fourteen games in his initial season with the Clippers, and then missed two more entire seasons.

Financially secure, it was Walton's love for the game that brought the two-time All-Star back to the Clippers for the 1982–83 campaign. He dressed for thirty-three games that year, fifty-five the next, and sixty-seven in 1984–85, the year when the Clippers moved from San Diego to Los Angeles.

The following season, Walton was traded to the Celtics, and the luck of the Irish smiled upon him.

He played in a career-high eighty games that season, helping Boston in a key reserve role capture the 1986 Championship in six games over the Houston Rockets. For his heroic efforts, Walton received the NBA's Sixth Man Award. Walton's comeback party didn't last long, however, as injuries forced him to miss all but ten games for the Celtics in 1986–87, as well as the entire 1987–88 campaign.

The aching legend finally called it quits after a career in which he averaged 13.3 points, 10.5 rebounds, and 3.4 assists in 468 games, adding 10.8 points, 9.1 rebounds, and 3.0 assists in forty-nine career playoff contests. He still holds the NBA Finals single-game record for most defensive rebounds, ripping down 20 boards against Philadelphia on June 3, 1977.

RIGHT: IF NOT FOR SERIOUS INJURIES, THERE'S NO TELLING JUST HOW GREAT THE GREAT BILL WALTON COULD HAVE BEEN.

BOBBY WANZER

A deft playmaker, dribbler, and ballhandler, Bobby Wanzer was a star in the backcourt for the Rochester Royals for ten seasons until his retirement in 1957. A terrific shooter who achieved All-American status at Seton Hall, Wanzer averaged 4.2 points per game as a rookie with Rochester in 1947–48.

The following season, Rochester left the NBL to join the NBA, and Wanzer more than doubled his scoring average in the new league, posting 10.2 points per contest and starting a streak of eight straight seasons in which the 6-footer would average double digits in scoring.

Wanzer, teaming with stars of his day like Arnie Risen and Bob Davies, helped Rochester capture the 1951 NBA Championship in seven games over the New York Knicks.

The following season, Wanzer averaged a career-high 15.7 points per game and set the free-throw record by making 377 of 417 shots from the charity stripe for a .904 percentage.

A five-time All-Star, Wanzer won the NBA's Most Valuable Player award in 1953, averaging 14.6 points, 3.6 assists, and 5.0 rebounds per contest.

For his career, Wanzer averaged 12.2 points, 3.2 assists, and 3.4 rebounds, adding 14.6 points, 3.5 assists, and 4.8 rebounds in 38 career playoff contests.

FACT FILE

Born: June 4, 1921
Height: 6′ 4″
Length of NBL career:
 1947–48
Length of NBA career:
 1948–57
Major team:
 Rochester
Records/Awards:
 NBA All-Star (5)
 NBA Most Valuable Player
 (1953)
 NBA Championship (1)
 Hall of Fame (1986)

LEFT: FOR TEN SEASONS, BOBBY WANZER WAS A DO-IT-ALL PLAYMAKER FOR THE ROCHESTER ROYALS.

ANTHONY "SPUD" WEBB

FACT FILE

Born: July 13, 1963
Height: 5′ 6″
Length of NBA career:
1985–present
Major teams:
Atlanta
Sacramento (joined 1991)
Atlanta (joined 1995)
Minnesota (joined 1996)

Tiny Spud Webb, who provided one of the most electric moments in NBA history when he soared high above the rim to win the 1986 Slam Dunk contest, has been rising above the odds ever since he broke into the big leagues with the Atlanta Hawks in 1985.

At 5 feet 6 inches, Webb was the floor-leading sparkplug of the Atlanta Hawks for six seasons. He averaged 7.8 points and 4.3 assists as a rookie in 1985–86, shocking hoop fans around the world that season by outdunking players more than a foot taller than himself, including Atlanta's 6-foot-8-inch Dominique Wilkins.

Webb, who first gained national attention as a lightning-quick playmaker at North Carolina State, saved his best for last in Atlanta, registering averages of 13.4 points, 5.6 assists, and 2.3 rebounds per game in 1990–91, his last season with the Hawks.

The following season, Webb was traded to Sacramento and, in his first season with the Kings, he averaged a career-high 16.0 points per game. He played four years in Sacramento, averaging double digits in scoring in every one of those seasons.

After averaging 7.1 points, 3.8 assists, and 1.3 rebounds in a split season with Atlanta and Minnesota in 1995–96, Webb became a free agent. Through his first eleven NBA seasons, he averaged 10.0 points, 5.4 assists, and 2.1 rebounds, adding 8.2 points, 5.1 assists, and 2.2 rebounds in thirty-nine career playoffs.

RIGHT: BELIEVE IT OR NOT, TINY SPUD WEBB HAS A NBA SLAM-DUNK TITLE UNDER HIS BELT.

JERRY WEST

he NBA logo, which is seen throughout the world, depicts the silhouette of a player dribbling a basketball in perfect form. The model for the perfect player is the legendary Los Angeles Laker shooting guard, Jerry West, one of the greatest performers in NBA history.

An All-Star in each of his 14 NBA seasons, the 6-foot-2-inch West was a phenomenal shooter who topped the Lakers in scoring seven times, averaging 30 or more points in four different seasons, including a career-high 31.3 points per game in 1965–66.

A ten-time All-NBA First Team Selection who was also voted onto the league's All-Defensive First Team on four occasions, West helped lead the Lakers to the 1972 NBA Championship.

Nicknamed "Mr. Clutch" for his ability to come through with the game on the line, West scored 25,192 points in his career, and was the all-time playoff leader in points (4,457) and assists (970) until Kareem Abdul-Jabbar and Magic Johnson, respectively, surpassed those totals. One of West's most famous playoff shots was a 60-foot bomb he hit at the buzzer to send Game 3 of the 1970 NBA Finals against the New York Knicks into overtime.

West, who became the oldest player in league history to average over 30 points per game in a season, scoring a league-high 31.2 points per contest in 1969–70 at the age of thirty-one years, retired with a career scoring average of 27.0 points, which was fourth-best in league history through the 1995–96 season.

A member of the 1960 gold-medal winning US Olympic basketball team after his senior season at West Virginia, West's sparkling NBA resume also boasts that he compiled a 40.6 scoring average during the 1965 playoffs (11 games), including an astounding 46.3 scoring average during a six-game series against the Baltimore Bullets.

In addition, West was the Most Valuable Player of the 1969 NBA Finals. He holds the career playoff record for most free throws made (1,213), the single-season record for most free throws made (840 in 1966), and was the MVP of the 1972 All-Star game.

With a playoff scoring average of 29.1 points per game, West is second-highest all-time in that category behind Michael Jordan (34.4). He was voted onto the NBA's 35th Anniversary All-Time Team in 1980.

FACT FILE

Born: May 28, 1938
Height: 6′ 2″
Length of NBA career:
1960–74
Major team:
Los Angeles Lakers
Records/Awards:
All-Defensive First Team (4)
NBA All-Star (14)
NBA Championship (1)
Olympic Gold Medal (1960)
Hall of Fame (1979)

LEFT: THE PHENOMENAL JERRY WEST, WHOSE PERFECT FORM HAS BECOME THE NBA LOGO, WAS AN ALL-STAR IN EACH OF HIS FOURTEEN NBA SEASONS.

PAUL WESTPHAL

FACT FILE

Born: November 30, 1950
Height: 6′ 4″
Length of NBA career:
 1972–84
Major teams:
 Boston
 Phoenix (joined 1975)
 Seattle (joined 1980)
 New York (joined 1982)
 Phoenix (joined 1983)
Records/Awards:
 NBA All-Star (5)
 NBA Championship (1)

After helping the Boston Celtics win the 1974 NBA Championship, Paul Westphal, a 6-foot-4-inch shooting guard, went on to Phoenix and became one of the league's top attractions.

Selected by Boston out of Southern Cal in the first round of the 1972 NBA draft, Westphal spent his first three seasons with the Celtics. During that span, he averaged 7.3 points per game as a role player, and in his last year in Beantown, he helped the fabled franchise knock off the Milwaukee Bucks in seven games to win the title.

Traded to Phoenix in 1975, Westphal averaged 20.5 points per contest, starting a streak of five straight seasons with the Suns in which he would average better than 20 points per game. In the 1977–78 season, Westphal poured in a career-high average of 25.2 points per contest. A five-time All-Star and three-time All-NBA First Team Selection, Westphal was traded to Seattle in 1980, and in his only campaign with the SuperSonics, registered averages of 16.7 points and 4.1 assists per game.

Westphal signed as a free agent with the New York Knicks during the 1980–81 season, but foot surgery limited him to just eighteen games. The following season, Westphal returned to Broadway with a vengeance, posting averages of 10.0 points and 2.5 assists per game en route to winning the NBA's Comeback Player of the Year award.

For his career, which ended in Phoenix, Westphal averaged 15.6 points, 4.4 assists, and 1.9 rebounds per game, adding 12.5 points, 3.3 assists, and 1.4 boards in a total of 107 career playoff contests.

RIGHT: WHEN PAUL WESTPHAL LEFT BEANTOWN FOR PHOENIX, HE BECAME A STAR.

JO JO WHITE

During his ten seasons in Boston, Jo Jo White sparked the Celtics' fast break and used his deadly jump shot, which he loved to launch from the top of the key, to help the Celtics capture NBA Championships in 1974 and 1976.

White, a 6-foot-3-inch guard from the University of Kansas selected by Boston in the first round of the 1969 NBA draft, earned a spot on the 1970 All-Rookie team after averaging 12.2 points per game, the first of ten straight seasons in which he would average double digits in scoring.

A seven-time All-Star and two-time All-NBA Second Team selection, White enjoyed a banner year in the 1971–72 season, recording career-high averages in points (23.1) and rebounds (5.6) per game.

In 1973–74, White averaged 18.1 points, 5.5 assists, and 4.3 rebounds per game, igniting the Celtics' run toward the championship, where they dumped Milwaukee in seven games.

Two years later, White, averaging 18.9 points per contest, had the Celtics on the move again. Boston met Phoenix in the championship round and defeated the Suns in six games. White, who had averaged 22.7 points in eighteen playoff games that season, was named the Finals MVP.

After spending the last two and a half years of his career with Golden State and Kansas City, White called it quits. He left the game having averaged 17.2 points, 4.9 assists, and 4.0 rebounds over 12 seasons, adding 21.5 points, 5.7 assists, and 4.5 boards in eighty career playoff games.

Seven years after his retirement, White attempted a basketball comeback with the Topeka Sizzlers of the CBA, but lasted only five games before giving up that dream.

FACT FILE

Born: November 16, 1946
Height: 6′ 3″
Length of NBA career:
1969–81
Major teams:
 Boston
 Golden State (joined
 1979)
 Kansas City (joined 1980)
Records/Awards:
 NBA All-Star (7)
 NBA Championship (2)
 Olympic Gold Medal
 (1968)

LEFT: JO JO WHITE, DRIBBLING LEFT, SPARKING YET ANOTHER BOSTON CELTIC FAST BREAK.

THAT'S ENTERTAINMENT

The play-by-play man, rapping to the hundreds of spectators who have gathered in the tiny park, is a cross between Marv Albert and Snoop Doggy Dog. The scorer's table, scoreboard, and microwave oven are all plugged into the same street light, filling the warm air with the sounds of basketball and music, and the smell of fresh popcorn.

The real electricity, however, comes from the players themselves, gifted athletes with nicknames straight out of the World Wrestling Federation: Black Widow, Afro Puffs, Predator, Long Fingers, the Handler, and of course, the Undertaker.

"Afro Puffs rises for a jump shot, but Long Fingers gets a piece of it," says the man behind the microphone, sending the crowd into a frenzy. "Here they come the other way. The Handler makes his way through traffic and feeds the Undertaker, who buries another one."

Welcome to the Entertainer's Basketball Classic in West Harlem, NY, a popular summertime tournament staged in Rucker Park at 156th Street and Eighth Avenue, across the street from the site of the old Polo Grounds, where project buildings cover the same earth that Willie Mays once did for the New York Giants.

"This tournament is and always has been the best place to get a run," said Richie Parker, who plays his college ball at Long Island University in Brooklyn, NY.

The Entertainment games bring together some of the top college and high school stars from near and far, as well as playground wizards eager to display their own magic. A spinoff of the fabled Rucker Tournament of the 1960s and '70s—which included pro players—the Entertainer's Classic remains a pastime each week for thousands of local residents, and a major hunting ground for scores of college recruiters.

In recent summers, the Entertainment games have included major NBA talents like Joe Smith of the Golden State Warriors, Allen Iverson of the Philadelphia 76ers, and Stephon Marbury of the Minnesota Timberwolves. Those stars mix company with other talented players on teams with names like Flavor Unit, Dogs of War, and X-Men.

"Everyone who plays has a nickname," said head announcer Duke "Tango" Mills. "Joe Smith, he shows up only in an emergency, so we call him 911."

Said the Black Widow, otherwise known as Al Evans: "Making fancy moves has always been the key to success in Rucker Park. Around here, people have always been used to classic entertainment."

BELOW: ALLEN IVERSON IS ANOTHER TALENT WHO HAS DROPPED IN ON THE RUCKER TOURNAMENT.

LENNY WILKENS

FACT FILE

Born: October 28, 1937
Height: 6′ 1″
Length of NBA career:
  1960–75
Major teams:
  St. Louis
  Seattle (joined (1968)
  Cleveland (joined 1972)
  Portland (joined 1974)
Records/Awards:
  NBA All-Star (9)
  Hall of Fame (1988)

A scrawny, 6-foot-1-inch point guard with a quick left-handed dribble and uncanny ability to create off the dribble, Lenny Wilkens was a solid, Hall-of-Fame playmaker for fifteen NBA seasons.

A first-round draft pick of the St. Louis Hawks out of Providence College in 1960, Wilkens averaged 11.7 points, 4.5 rebounds, and 2.8 assists as rookie, starting a phenomenal streak of fourteen seasons in which he would average double digits in scoring.

Noted for his one-handed set shots, his left-handed running hooks, and his ability to slither through traffic, Wilkens starred for the Hawks for eight seasons before he was traded to the Seattle SuperSonics in 1968.

A nine-time All-Star—he was the MVP of the 1971 All-Star contest—Wilkens averaged a career-high 22.4 points per game in the 1968–69 season, his first season with Seattle. In his second year with the SuperSonics, Wilkens, who was also a hard-nosed defensive player, was named as the team's player-coach, becoming the second African-American head coach in the NBA's history. (Bill Russell of the Boston Celtics was the first, in 1966.)

After four seasons in Seattle, the thirty-five year old Wilkens was dealt to Cleveland, and after two years with the Cavaliers, where he was strictly a player, he was off to Portland, spending one season as a player-coach before becoming a full-time coach.

In fifteen seasons overall, Wilkens finished with 17,772 points and 7,211 assists. He finished his brilliant NBA career with averages of 16.5 points, 6.7 assists, and 4.7 rebounds per game, adding 16.1 points, 5.8 assists, and 5.8 rebounds in sixty-four career playoff contests.

RIGHT: LENNY WILKENS ABOUT TO LET FLY ONE OF HIS PATENTED, LEFT-HANDED HOOK SHOTS.

JAMAAL WILKES

An integral member of the Los Angeles Laker dynasty teams of the 1980s, Jamaal Wilkes won four NBA championships in twelve seasons.

Wilkes, a 6-foot-6-inch swingman who won NCAA Championships at UCLA in 1972 and 1973, continued his winning ways at the next level.

Selected by Golden State in the first round of the 1974 NBA draft, Wilkes won the 1975 Rookie of the Year award with the Warriors, averaging 14.2 points, 8.1 rebounds, and 2.2 assists per game, adding 107 steals.

That same season, Wilkes teamed with the legendary Rick Barry to win the NBA Championship, dusting off the Washington Bullets in four straight games.

After three years in Golden State, "Silk," as the smooth-operating Wilkes was called in his playing days, signed as a free agent with the Lakers in 1977.

In eight seasons with the Lakers, Wilkes helped Magic Johnson, Kareem Abdul-Jabbar, and the rest of the Showtime crew win championships in 1980, 1982, and 1985, his last year at Los Angeles.

A three-time NBA All-Star and two-time All-Defensive Second Team selection, Wilkes enjoyed his best season in a Laker uniform in 1980–81, averaging a career-high 22.6 points per game. After playing just thirteen games with the Los Angeles Clippers in the 1985–86 season, Wilkes decided to retire.

He left the game with averages of 17.7 points, 6.1 rebounds, and 2.4 assists per game, adding 16.1 points, 6.3 boards, and 2.1 assists in 113 career playoff contests.

FACT FILE

Born: May 2, 1953
Height: 6′ 6″
Length of NBA career:
 1974–86
Major teams:
 Golden State
 Los Angeles Lakers
  (joined 1977)
 Los Angeles Clippers
  (joined 1985)
Records/Awards:
 NBA Rookie of the Year
  (1975)
 NBA All-Star (3)
 NBA Championship (4)

LEFT: JAMAAL WILKES' ALL-AROUND TALENTS EARNED HIM FOUR CHAMPIONSHIP RINGS.

DOMINIQUE WILKINS

FACT FILE

Born: January 12, 1960
Height: 6′ 8″
Length of NBA career:
  1982–95, 1996–present
Major teams:
  Atlanta
  Los Angeles Clippers
    (joined 1994)
  Boston (joined 1994)
  San Antonio (joined 1996)
Records/Awards:
  NBA All-Star (9)

A human highlight reel, Dominique Wilkins rejoined the NBA as a member of the San Antonio Spurs for the 1996–97 campaign after spending the previous season playing in Greece.

As a member of the Spurs last season, Wilkins averaged 18.2 points and 6.4 rebounds per game. Wilkins, a 6-foot-8-inch forward who uses his great leaping ability to explode to the rim, compiled 26,534 points through last season.

After three seasons at the University of Georgia, Wilkins broke into the NBA with the Atlanta Hawks, and, playing the game above the rim with grace and power, wasted little time in becoming one of the league's marquee attractions. He earned a place on the All-Rookie squad after averaging 17.5 points, 5.8 rebounds, and 1.6 assists per game.

A two-time winner of the NBA's Slam Dunk contest (1985 and 1990), Wilkins averaged double digits in scoring in each of his 14 seasons in the NBA. He cracked the 30-point plateau twice in his career, winning the scoring crown in 1985–86 after averaging 30.3 points per game. His career-high was 30.7 points per contest in 1987–88. A nine-time All-Star, Wilkins shined in Atlanta for 11½ seasons before he was traded to the Los Angeles Clippers midway through the 1993–94 campaign. The following season, Wilkins signed as an unrestricted free agent with the Boston Celtics, and played in Beantown for one season before taking his high-flying act to Greece.

The Atlanta Hawks franchise all-time leading scorer with 23,292 points and all-time steals leader with 1,245, Wilkins averaged 25.3 points, 6.8 rebounds, and 2.5 assists through the 1996–97 season. He has posted 25.8 points, 6.8 rebounds, and 2.6 assists through 55 career playoff games.

Wilkins, who holds the NBA's single-game record for most free throws without a miss, hitting 23 straight against Chicago on December 8, 1992, averaged 21.6 points per game in three seasons at Georgia.

RIGHT: DOMINIQUE WILKINS' POWERFUL AND FLUID GAME IS THE STUFF THAT HIGHLIGHT FILMS ARE MADE OF.

BUCK WILLIAMS

A super-talented workhorse since joining the NBA way back in the 1981–82 season, Buck Williams still remains an impact player.

Williams, a 6-foot-8-inch power forward out of Maryland with the ability to score and the willingness to fight for rebounds, was selected by the New Jersey Nets in the first round of the 1981 NBA draft.

A member of the 1980 US Olympic team which didn't compete for political reasons, Williams raised eyebrows around the NBA in his first season, averaging 15.5 points, 12.3 rebounds, and 1.3 assists per game en route to capturing the Rookie of the Year award.

The lone bright spot on some terrible New Jersey Net teams, Williams was a three-time All-Star with the downtrodden franchise. He posted double-digit scoring averages during each of his eight seasons with the Nets, and

kept that streak alive for three more seasons in Portland, where he was traded in 1989.

As a member of the Trail Blazers, Williams became a born-again basketball star. He was voted onto the NBA All-Defensive First Team in his first two years, helping Portland reach the NBA Finals in 1990 and again in 1992.

After seven successful seasons in Portland, Williams headed back East, signing as a free agent with the New York Knicks after the 1995–96 campaign.

Through his first sixteen NBA seasons, Williams produced averages of 13.1 points, 10.1 rebounds, and 1.3 assists per game, adding 11.4 points, 8.8 rebounds, and 1.1 assists per game in 105 career playoff contests. He remains New Jersey's all-time leading scorer with 10,440 points, and all-time leading rebounder with 7,576 boards.

FACT FILE

Born: March 8, 1960
Height: 6′ 8″
Length of NBA career:
   1981–present
Major teams:
   New Jersey
   Portland (joined 1989)
   New York (joined 1996)
Records/Awards:
   NBA Rookie of the Year
      (1982)
   NBA All-Star (3)
   NBA All-Defensive First
      Team (2)

LEFT: WHEREVER HE'S GONE, BUCK WILLIAMS HAS BEEN A MAJOR CONTRIBUTOR, ESPECIALLY IN THE REBOUNDING DEPARTMENT.

WALT WILLIAMS

FACT FILE

Born: April 16, 1970
Height: 6′ 8″
Length of NBA career:
1992–present
Major teams:
Sacramento
Miami (joined 1996)
Toronto (joined 1996)

Once asked who he thought was the best all-around player in the NBA, Scottie Pippen, a teammate of Michael Jordan's, paused for a second, and said softly, "Walt Williams."

A 6-foot-8-inch smooth scorer who can play shooting guard or small forward and has been steadily improving on defense, Williams was selected out of Maryland by the Sacramento Kings in the first round of the 1992 NBA draft.

Williams earned a place on the 1993 All-Rookie squad after averaging a career-high 17.0 points, along with 4.5 rebounds and 3.0 assists per game. He has posted double digits in each of his first four seasons in the league.

Midway through the 1995–96 campaign, Williams was traded to the Miami Heat. His stay was brief, as he signed as a free agent with Toronto last season, averaging 16.4 points, 5.0 rebounds, and 2.7 assists per game. One dismal note: Williams tied for the league lead with 11 disqualifications.

Through his first five NBA seasons, Williams has averaged 15.0 points, 4.5 rebounds, and 3.1 assists per game. He reached the playoffs only once, averaging 4.7 points and 4.0 rebounds in just three post-season contests with Miami.

At Maryland, Williams averaged 16.2 points, 4.6 rebounds, and 3.9 assists per game over four seasons. He had a tremendous senior year, averaging 26.8 points, 5.6 rebounds, and 3.6 assists per game en route to being voted onto the Sporting News' All-America First Team.

RIGHT: CHICAGO'S SCOTTIE PIPPEN THINKS THAT WALT WILLIAMS (LEFT) IS THE BEST ALL-AROUND PLAYER IN THE NBA.

JOHN WILLIAMSON

When 21-year-old rookie John Williamson joined the New York Nets of the ABA for the 1973–74 season, he was immediately thrust into a starting role—and produced like a quality veteran. In his first season with the Nets, Williamson, a muscular 6-foot-2-inch guard out of New Mexico State who could bury a shot from 15–20 feet, averaged 14.5 points per game—earning a spot on the league's All-Rookie squad—helping Julius Erving and company storm into the ABA Finals, where the Nets took care of Utah in five games.

Two years later, Williamson scored 16.2 points per contest and helped the Nets into the post-season, where they defeated Denver in six games to win the last ABA championship.

Midway through the 1976–77 season, the Nets, now part of the NBA, traded Williamson to the Indiana Pacers, but the favorite of Net fans would return to the franchise via a trade during the 1977–78 season, the year the Nets moved from New York to New Jersey.

During an outstanding eight-year career, which ended with the Washington Bullets, Williamson averaged 20.1 points per game as an NBA player, and 14.1 points per contest as an ABA performer. His best season was 1977–78, when he averaged 23.7 points per game in split duties with Indiana and New Jersey, one of three seasons in which he would crack the 20-point plateau.

In twenty-nine ABA playoff contests, Williamson racked up 15.4 points per contest. He added 21.5 points in just four career NBA playoff games.

FACT FILE

Born: November 10, 1952
Height: 6′ 2″
Length of ABA career:
1973–76
Length of NBA career:
1976–81
Major teams:
New York Nets
Indiana (joined 1977)
New Jersey Nets
(joined 1978)
Washington (joined 1980)
Records/Awards:
ABA Championship (2)

LEFT: JOHN WILLIAMSON (LEFT) TEAMED WITH JULIUS ERVING TO BRING TWO CHAMPIONSHIPS TO THE NEW YORK NETS OF THE ABA.

HARDWOOD HONCHOS: BASKETBALL'S GREATEST COACHES

"Winning isn't everything, it's the only thing."
VINCE LOMBARDI

I f winning is indeed the only thing, as the great Green Bay Packer football coach Vince Lombardi once suggested, then Lenny Wilkens is the greatest coach in NBA–ABA history. Through the 1996–97 campaign, Wilkens had won more regular-season games than any other sidelines-stroller, compiling a record of 1,070–876 for a .550 winning percentage.

"It's a nice achievement because it shows how far you've come," said Wilkens, who coached at Seattle (1969–72, 77–85), Portland (1974–76), and Cleveland (1986–93) before taking over the reins in Atlanta, where he is still adding victories to his resume. "It's also nice because it can be shared with all the people who've lent you a hand over the years."

Wilkens, who won his lone NBA championship as coach of the Seattle SuperSonics in 1979, is trailed on the all-time wins list by the legendary Boston Celtic Coach, Red Auerbach, who left the sidelines after chalking up a 938-479 mark for a .662 winning percentage. More impressively, Auerbach won nine NBA championships with the Celtics during a 20-year coaching career that stretched from 1946 through 1966. He was selected as the "Greatest Coach in the History of the NBA" by the Professional Basketball Writers' Association of America in 1980.

"Records are made to be broken, but this one lasted 28 years, which is an indication that breaking it was not an easy thing to do," said Auerbach, shortly after Wilkens surpassed him during the 1994–95 season in the lifetime victories department.

Through the 1996–97 campaign, the top-ten winning coaches, in terms of victories, included Dick Motta (935–1,017), Bill Fitch (927–1,041), Jack Ramsay (864–783), Pat Riley (859–360), Larry Brown (853–587), Don Nelson (851–629), Cotton Fitzsimmons (832–775), and Gene Shue (784–861).

If winning percentage makes the man, then Phil Jackson, who coached Michael Jordan and the Chicago Bulls to five NBA Championships, is tops in the history of the sport. Jackson had produced a regular-season mark of 483–173 for a whopping .736 winning percentage through 1996–97. He was followed closely by Pat Riley, who won four championships with the Los Angeles Lakers and had put together a regular-season mark of 859–360 for a .705 winning percentage.

ABOVE: IF SHEER VICTORIES IS HOW ONE MEASURES GREAT COACHING, THEN NO ONE IS BETTER THAN LENNY WILKENS.

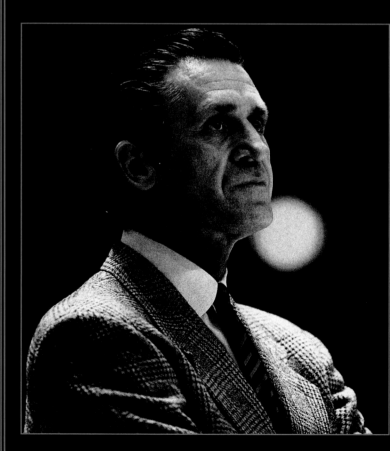

ABOVE: PAT RILEY, WHO DIRECTED LOS ANGELES' SHOWTIME ATTACK IN THE 1980S, IS WITHOUT QUESTION ONE OF THE VERY BEST COACHES.

BELOW: MANY BASKETBALL EXPERTS WOULD SAY THAT RED
AUERBACH, WHO LED THE BOSTON CELTICS TO NINE TITLES,
WAS THE GREATEST COACH IN HISTORY.

343

KEVIN WILLIS

FACT FILE

Born: September 6, 1962
Height: 7' 0"
Length of NBA career:
  1984–present
Major teams:
  Atlanta
  Miami (joined 1994)
  Golden State (joined 1996)
  Houston (joined 1996)
Records/Awards:
  NBA All-Star (1)

One of the hardest-working big men in the NBA today, Kevin Willis of the Houston Rockets is still going strong after a dozen years of battling in the paint.

Willis, a 7-foot forward/center from Michigan State who was selected by the Atlanta Hawks in the first round of the 1984 NBA draft, teamed with Dominique Wilkins for years to form one of the better frontline attacks in the game.

With his trademark semi-hook shot, which he releases while sweeping through the lane, and a dependable turnaround jumper from short range, Willis is an offensive threat. His best scoring season in an Atlanta uniform was 1993–94, when he averaged a career-high 19.1 points per game, picking up the scoring slack in the absence of Wilkins, who was traded that season to the Los Angeles Clippers.

Willis, who made his only All-Star appearance in 1992, the year he scored 18.3 points and ripped down an incredible 15.5 boards per game, is also one of the league's best rebounders, having hauled down better than ten boards per game in five seasons.

After ten and a half seasons with Atlanta—he missed the entire 1988–89 season because of an injury—Willis was traded to Miami. Midway through the 1995–96 campaign, he was traded to Golden State. He averaged 10.6 points per game that season, extending his streak of double-digit scoring seasons to ten.

Willis, who signed as a free agent with Houston after the 1995–96 campaign, has averaged 14.1 points and 9.7 rebounds through his first thirteen NBA seasons, adding 12.7 points and 8.0 rebounds in 65 career playoff contests.

RIGHT: MUSCULAR KEVIN WILLIS IS ONE OF THE HARDEST WORKING HOOPSTERS IN THE BUSINESS.

BRIAN WINTERS

A high-scoring guard for nine seasons in the NBA, Brian Winters was forced to cut short his stellar career at the age of thirty-one years because of recurring back injuries.

Winters, a 6-foot-4-inch marksman from the University of South Carolina, was selected by the Los Angeles Lakers in the first round of the 1974 NBA draft.

After earning a place on the NBA's 1975 All-Rookie team with averages of 11.7 points, 2.8 assists, and 2.0 rebounds per game, Winters was traded to the Milwaukee Bucks as part of a deal which brought Kareem Abdul-Jabbar to the Lakers. Winters, who averaged double

digits in scoring in each season of his career, became a star in his own right in Milwaukee, where he played for the duration of his career. He averaged 18.2 points per game in his first season with the Bucks, increasing that total to 19.3 the following season, and a career-high 19.9 points per game in the 1977–78 season.

A two-time All-Star with the Bucks, Winters averaged 16.2 points, 4.1 assists, and 1.8 rebounds per game in his career, adding 15.5 points, 4.6 assists, and 2.8 boards in forty-one career playoff contests.

At South Carolina, Winters averaged 13.2 points per game.

FACT FILE

Born: March 1, 1952
Height: 6′ 4″
Length of NBA career:
   1974–83
Major teams:
   Los Angeles
   Milwaukee (joined 1975)
Records/Awards:
   NBA All-Star (2)

LEFT: BRIAN WINTERS WAS A TWO-TIME ALL-STAR WITH THE MILWAUKEE BUCKS.

ORLANDO WOOLRIDGE

FACT FILE

Born: December 16, 1959
Height: 6′ 9″
Length of NBA career:
1981–94
Major teams:
Chicago
New Jersey (joined 1986)
Los Angeles Lakers
(joined 1988)
Denver (joined 1990)
Detroit (joined 1991)
Milwaukee (joined 1993)
Philadelphia (joined 1993)

A high-scoring forward out of Notre Dame, Orlando Woolridge continued tallying points for thirteen NBA seasons, lighting up scoreboards for seven different teams.

Selected by the Chicago Bulls in the first round of the 1981 NBA draft, the 6-foot-9-inch Woolridge went on to average double digits in scoring in eleven of his thirteen seasons.

As a rookie with the Bulls, Woolridge averaged 7.3 points and 3.0 rebounds per game. In the next three seasons, his scoring average rose dramatically: 16.5, 19.3, and 22.9 points, respectively.

After five seasons in Chicago, Woolridge signed as a free agent with the New Jersey Nets. He scored averages of 20.7 and 16.4 points per game in two seasons with the Nets before signing a free-agent deal with the Los Angeles Lakers.

In his first of two seasons in Los Angeles, Woolridge averaged 9.7 points per game, adding offensive spark off the bench in helping the Lakers reach the NBA Finals, where they were swept in four games by the Detroit Pistons.

Woolridge, who spent his last four NBA seasons with Denver, Detroit, Milwaukee, and Philadelphia, averaged 16.0 points, 4.3 rebounds, and 1.9 assists in his career, adding 11.9 points, 3.6 rebounds, and 1.2 assists in 36 career playoff contests.

At Notre Dame, Woolridge averaged 10.6 points per game over four seasons. He averaged 14.4 points per contest as a senior in 1981, earning a spot on The Sporting News' All-America Second Team.

RIGHT: ORLANDO WOOLRIDGE, DRIVING TO THE BASKET AS A MEMBER OF THE NEW JERSEY NETS, MADE SEVEN STOPS IN HIS NBA CAREER.

JAMES WORTHY

The standard by which great power forwards are measured, James Worthy played all twelve of his NBA seasons in a Los Angeles Laker uniform, helping the team win three championships during that span.

A 6-foot-9-inch talent who could run the floor like a gazelle or use his great body strength to dominate in the low post, Worthy was one of the prime-time entertainers during the Lakers' Showtime era, often finishing off fast breaks by soaring to the basket, holding the basketball high over his head, and jamming it through the cords as he swooped back down to earth.

Selected by the Lakers out of North Carolina as the top overall pick in the 1982 NBA draft, Worthy paid immediate dividends. He earned a place on the 1993 All-Rookie team after averaging 13.4 points and 5.2 rebounds per game, adding 91 steals. A seven-time All-Star, Worthy averaged double digits in scoring in each of his twelve seasons. He reached a career-high 21.4 points per game in the 1990–91 campaign.

Teaming with greats like Kareem Abdul-Jabbar and Magic Johnson, Worthy helped the Lakers capture NBA championships in 1985, 1987, and again in 1988, when he was voted MVP of the Finals.

A certain Hall-of-Famer, Worthy averaged 17.6 points, 5.1 rebounds, and 3.0 assists in his career, adding 21.1 points, 5.2 rebounds, and 3.2 assists in 143 career playoff contests.

At North Carolina, Worthy teamed with future pros Michael Jordan and Sam Perkins to help the Tar Heels capture the 1982 NCAA Championship. Worthy was voted the Most Outstanding Player of the NCAA Division I Tournament that season.

FACT FILE

Born: February 27, 1961
Height: 6′ 9″
Length of NBA career:
1982–94
Major teams:
Los Angeles Lakers
Records/Awards:
NBA All-Star (7)
NBA Championship (3)

LEFT: JAMES WORTHY WAS THE EPITOME OF WHAT IT MEANT TO BE A POWER FORWARD.

GEORGE YARDLEY

FACT FILE

Born: November 23, 1928
Height: 6′ 5″
Length of NBA career:
  1953–60
Length of ABL career:
  1961–62
Major teams:
  Fort Wayne-Detroit
  Syracuse (joined 1959)
Records/Awards:
  NBA All-Star (6)
  Hall of Fame (1996)

The first NBA player to score 2,000 points in a season, George Yardley was a high-jumping, high-scoring forward with the Fort Wayne-Detroit Pistons and the Syracuse Nationals during the 1950s.

Yardley, a 6-foot-5-inch shooting star out of Stanford, was selected by Fort Wayne in the first round of the 1950 NBA draft. After playing in an Amateur Athletic Union League during the 1950–51 season and spending the next two basketball seasons in the military, Yardley finally arrived in Fort Wayne for the 1953–54 season.

As a rookie with the Pistons, Yardley registered averages of 9.0 points, 6.5 rebounds, and 1.6 assists per game.

The following season, 1954–55, Yardley's scoring average nearly doubled to 17.3 points per contest, and his rebounding average jumped to 9.9 per game. Yardley's improved play helped the Pistons reach the NBA Finals, where they lost in seven games to Syracuse.

The seventh game of that series was decided by a single point, Syracuse holding on for a 92–91 victory.

A six-time All-Star who averaged double digits in scoring in six of his seven NBA seasons, Yardley exploded in 1957–58, the year the Pistons moved from Fort Wayne to Detroit. He became the first player in league history to score 2,000 points in a season (2,001), winning the scoring title with a career-high 27.8 points per game.

Midway through the 1958–59 campaign, Yardley was traded to Syracuse, where his NBA career ended in 1960. He left the league having averaged 19.2 points, 8.9 rebounds, and 1.7 assists per game in his career, adding 20.3 points, 9.9 rebounds, and 2.4 assists in forty-six playoff contests.

Yardley made a brief return to professional basketball in the 1961–62 season, joining the Los Angeles Jets of the ABL. In twenty-five games with the Jets, he averaged 19.3 points and 6.9 rebounds.

RIGHT: GEORGE YARDLEY SHOWING THE FORM THAT ENABLED HIM TO BECOME THE FIRST PLAYER TO SCORE 2,000 POINTS IN A SEASON.

MAX ZASLOFSKY

The first guard ever to lead the league in scoring, Max Zaslofsky began his ten-year career with the Chicago Stags of the BAA in 1946. A 6-foot-2-inch sharpshooter out of St. John's, Zaslofsky played four seasons with Chicago, which moved into the newly renamed NBA for the 1949–50 season.

An All-First Team selection three times in the BAA and once in the NBA, Zaslofsky averaged 14.4 points per game as a rookie. The following season, 1947–48, he captured the scoring title after averaging a career-high 21.0 points per contest. After four seasons in Chicago, Zaslofsky's name was drawn out of a hat by the New York Knicks in the Stags' dispersal draft of 1950. He teamed in the New York backcourt for three seasons with Knick great Dick McGuire, earning his only All-Star appearance in 1952 after averaging 14.1 points per game.

Zaslofsky, who spent the last three years of his career with Baltimore, Milwaukee, and Fort Wayne, left the game posting averages of 14.8 points and 2.0 assists per game, adding 14.3 points and 1.6 assists in sixty-three career playoff contests.

In one season at St. John's, 1945–46, Zaslofsky averaged 7.8 points per game. He missed the 1944–45 season due to military service.

FACT FILE

Born: December 7, 1925
Height: 6' 2"
Length of BAA career:
  1946–49
Length of NBA career:
  1949–56
Major teams:
  Chicago
  New York (joined 1950)
  Baltimore (joined 1953)
  Milwaukee (joined 1953)
  Fort Wayne (joined 1954)
Records/Awards:
  NBA All-Star (1)

LEFT: LONG BEFORE MICHAEL JORDAN WAS BORN, MAX ZASLOFSKY (FAR RIGHT) WAS THE FLASHY GUARD WHO WAS LEADING THE LEAGUE IN SCORING.

THE LANGUAGE OF BASKETBALL

Want to speak up on the basketball court? Here is a glossary of hoop terms and phrases to help you better understand the language of the game. (Warning: memorizing all of this hoop slang will do absolutely nothing to improve your game.)

ROCK	Basketball
PILL	Basketball
MY BAD	Sorry, my fault
HANDLE	Ability to dribble
STUCK	Blocked
FACIAL	Shot made despite in-your-face defense
SWISH	Nothing but net
BOARD	Rebound
BRICK	Heavy shot, no touch
UPS	Ability to leap high
BAD	Good
TERRIBLE	Very good
THREW IT	Dunked
RIPPED	Stolen
NICE	Style and grace
SOFT	Not physical enough
THE BOMB	Awesome
DISH	Pass the ball
ILL	Phenomenal
ILLIN'	Screwing up
WATER	Shot flows
RAIN	Shot falls from everywhere
CASH	Shot guaranteed to fall
SWING IT	Pass the ball around the perimeter
DOPE	Excellent
GARBAGE	Horrible game
NEXT	Waiting turn for next game
TRASH TALK	Sarcastic comments aimed at getting under your opponent's skin
TREY	Three-point shot
PROPS	Respect
MONEY	On target
SHAKE AND BAKE	Lose a defender by making incredible moves
PIN	Stop the ball by holding it against the backboard
BLEW THE SPOT	Played like a star
YOU STINK	You stink

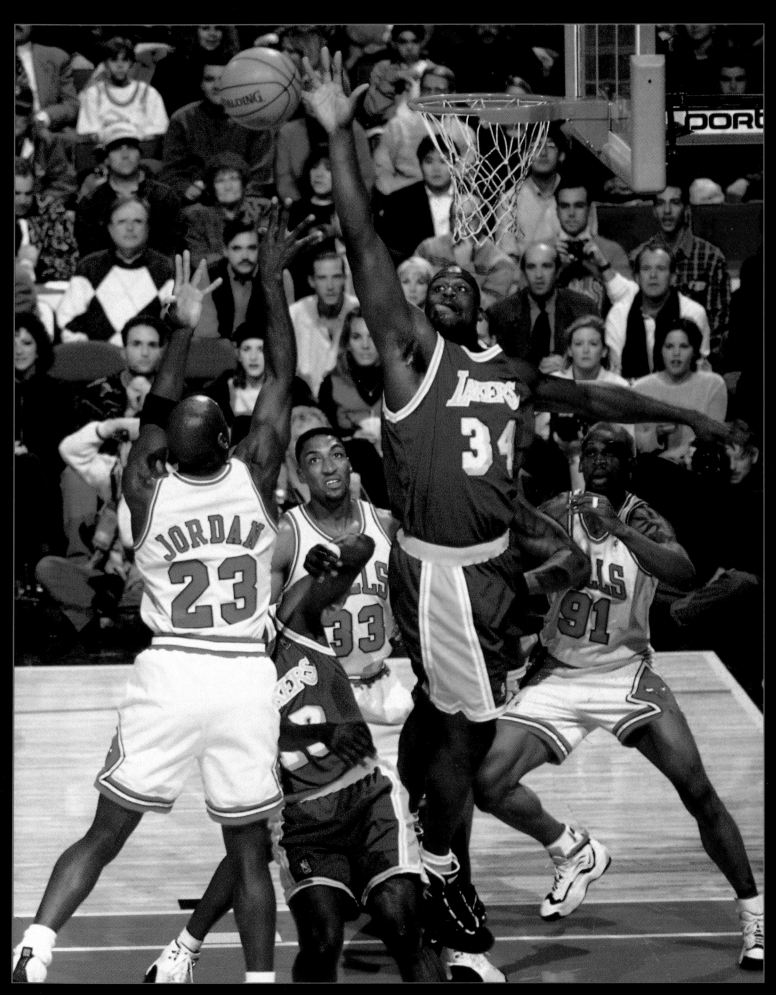

THE PLAYERS

ABDUL-JABBAR, KAREEM 10
ADAMS, MICHAEL 11
ADAMS, ALVAN 12
AGUIRRE, MARK 13
AINGE, DANNY 14
ANDERSON, KENNY 15
ANDERSON, NICK 18
ARCHIBALD, TINY 19
ARIZIN, PAUL 20
ARMSTRONG, BJ 21
BARKLEY, CHARLES 22
BARNES, JIM 'BAD NEWS' 23
BARNES, MARVIN 24
BARNETT, DICK 25
BARRY, BRENT 26
BARRY, RICK 27
BAYLOR, ELGIN 28
BEATY, ZELMO 29
BELLAMY, WALT 32
BIANCHI, AL 33
BIBBY, HENRY 34
BING, DAVE 35
BIRD, LARRY 36
BIRDSONG, OTIS 37
BLACKMAN, ROLANDO 38
BLAYLOCK, MOOKIE 39
BOGUES, MUGGSY 40
BOONE, RON 41
BOYKOFF, HARRY 42
BRADLEY, BILL 43
BRIAN, FRANK 46
BRIDGES, BILL 47
BROWN, 'DOWNTOWN' FRED 48
BRYANT, KOBE 49
CAMBY, MARCUS 50
CARR, ANTOINE 51
CARR, AUSTIN 52
CARTWRIGHT, BILL 53
CASSELL, SAM 54
CERVI, AL 55
CHAMBERLAIN, WILT 56
CHAMBERS, TOM 57
CHANEY, DON 60
CHEEKS, MAURICE 61
CLARK, ARCHIE 62
CLIFTON, NAT SWEETWATER 63
COLEMAN, DERRICK 64
COLLINS, DOUG 65
COOPER, CHARLES 'TARZAN' 66
COOPER, MICHAEL 67
COUSY, BOB 68
COWENS, DAVE 69
CUMMINGS, TERRY 70
CUNNINGHAM, BILLY 71
CURRY, DELL 72
DALLMAR, HOWIE 73
DAMPIER, LOUIE 76

DANDRIDGE, BOB 77
DANIELS, MEL 78
DANTLEY, ADRIAN 79
DAVIES, BOB 80
DAVIS, BRAD 81
DAVIS, JOHNNY 82
DAVIS, WALTER 83
DAWKINS, DARRYL 84
DAWKINS, JOHNNY 85
DEBUSSCHERE, DAVE 86
DIVAC, VLADE 87
DREW, JOHN 90
DREW, LARRY 91
DREXLER, CLYDE 92
DUMARS, JOE 93
ELIE, MARIO 94
ELLIOTT, SEAN 95
ELLIS, DALE 96
EMBRY, WAYNE 97
ENGLISH, ALEX 98
ERVING, JULIUS 99
EWING, PATRICK 100
FINLEY, MICHAEL 101
FLEMING, VERN 104
FLOYD, ERIC 'SLEEPY' 105
FORD, CHRIS 106
FOUST, LARRY 107
FRAZIER, WALT 108
FREE, WORLD B. 109
FULKS, JOE 110
GALLATIN, HARRY 111
GARNETT, KEVIN 112
GERVIN, GEORGE 113
GILMORE, ARTIS 114
GOODRICH, GAIL 115
GRANT, HORACE 116
GREEN, AC 117
GREER, HAL 120
GRIFFITH, DARRELL 121
GRUNFELD, ERNIE 122
GUERIN, RICHIE 123
HAGAN, CLIFF 124
HARDAWAY, ANFERNEE 125
HARDAWAY, TIM 126
HARPER, DEREK 127
HARPER, RON 128
HASKINS, CLEM 129
HAVLICEK, JOHN 130
HAWKINS, CONNIE 131
HAYES, ELVIN 134
HAYWOOD, SPENCER 135
HEERDT, AL 136
HEINSOHN, TOM 137
HENDERSON, GERALD 138
HILL, GRANT 139
HODGES, CRAIG 140
HOLZMAN, RED 141
HORNACEK, JEFF 142
HORRY, ROBERT 143
HOUSTON, ALLAN 144

HUBBARD, PHIL 145
ISAACS, JOHN 146
ISSEL, DAN 147
IVERSON, ALLEN 150
JACKSON, JIM 151
JACKSON, LUKE 152
JACKSON, MARK 153
JACKSON, PHIL 154
JOHNSON, DENNIS 155
JOHNSON, EARVIN 'MAGIC' 156
JOHNSON, EDDIE 157
JOHNSON JR, EDDIE 158
JOHNSON, GUS 159
JOHNSON, JOHN 160
JOHNSON, KEVIN 161
JOHNSON, LARRY 164
JOHNSON, MARQUES 165
JOHNSON, VINNIE 166
JOHNSTON, NEIL 167
JONES, BOBBY 168
JONES, CALDWELL 169
JONES, DONTAE 170
JONES, JAMES 171
JONES, KC 172
JONES, LARRY 173
JONES, SAM 174
JONES, STEPHEN 175
JORDAN, MICHAEL 176
KEMP, SHAWN 177
KERR, STEVE 180
KERSEY, JEROME 181
KIDD, JASON 182
KING, ALBERT 183
KING, BERNARD 184
KITTLES, KERRY 185
KUPCHAK, MITCH 186
LAIMBEER, BILL 187
LANIER, BOB 188
LAPCHICK, JOE 189
LEVER, FAT 190
LEWIS, FREDERICK L 191
LISTER, ALTON 194
LONG, JOHN 195
LONGLEY, LUC 196
LOSCUTOFF, JIM 197
LOUGHERY, KEVIN 198
LOVE, BOB 199
LOVELLETTE, CLYDE 200
LUCAS, JERRY RAY 201
LUCAS, JOHN 202
LUCAS, MAURICE 203
MACAULEY, EASY ED 204
MAHORN, RICK 205
MAJERLE, DAN 206
MALONE, JEFF 207
MALONE, KARL 210
MALONE, MOSES 211
MANNING, DANNY 212
MARAVICH, PISTOL PETE 213
MARBURY, STEPHON 214

MARTIN, SLATER 215
MAXWELL, CEDRIC 216
MAXWELL, VERNON 217
McADOO, BOB 218
McCRAY, RODNEY 219
McDANIEL, XAVIER 222
McDERMOTT, BOBBY 223
McDYESS, ANTONIO 224
McGINNIS, GEORGE 225
McGUIRE, DICK 226
McHALE, KEVIN 227
McMILLAN, NATE 228
MIKAN, GEORGE 229
MIKKELSEN, VERN 230
MILLER, EDDIE 231
MILLER, REGGIE 232
MITCHELL, MICHAEL 233
MONCRIEF, SIDNEY 236
MONROE, EARL 237
MOURNING, ALONZO 238
MULLIN, CHRIS 239
MURESAN, GEORGHE 240
MURPHY, CALVIN 241
MUTOMBO, DIKEMBE 242
NANCE, LARRY 243
NATT, CALVIN 244
NELSON, DON 245
NIXON, NORM 246
OAKLEY, CHARLES 247
OLAJUWON, HAKEEM 248
O'NEAL, SHAQUILLE 249
OWENS, BILLY 252
PARISH, ROBERT 253
PAULTZ, BILLY 254
PAYTON, GARY 255
PAXSON, JIM 256
PERKINS, SAM 257
PERSON, CHUCK 258
PETRIE, GEOFF 259
PETROVIC, DRAZEN 260
PETTIT, BOB 261
PIERCE, RICKY 262
PIPPEN, SCOTTIE 263
PORTER, KEVIN 266
PORTER, TERRY 267
PRICE, MARK 268
RAMBIS, KURT 269
REED, WILLIS 270
RICE, GLEN 271
RICHARDSON, POOH 272
RICHMOND, MITCH 273
RIVERS, DOC 274
ROBERTSON, OSCAR 275
ROBINSON, CLIFF 276
ROBINSON, DAVID 277
ROBINSON, GLENN 280
RODMAN, DENNIS 281
RUSSELL, BILL 282
RUSSELL, CAZZIE 283
SANDERS, TOM 'SATCH' 284

SCHAYES, DOLPH 285
SCHREMPF, DETLEF 286
SCOTT, DENNIS 287
SEDRAN, BARNEY 288
SHARMAN, BILL 289
SHORT, PURVIS 290
SIKMA, JACK 291
SILAS, PAUL 294
SMITH, JOE 295
SMITH, KENNY 296
SMITH, RANDY 297
SMITS, RIK 298
SPAHN, MOE 299
SPREWELL, LATRELL 300
STACKHOUSE, JERRY 301
STOCKTON, JOHN 302
STOKES, MAURICE 303
STOUDAMIRE, DAMON 304
STRICKLAND, ROD 305
TARPLEY, ROY 308
THEUS, REGGIE 309
THOMAS, ISIAH 310
THOMPSON, DAVID 311
THOMPSON, MYCHAL 312
THREATT, SEDALE 313
THURMOND, NATE 314
TISDALE, WAYMAN 315
TOMJANOVICH, RUDY 316
TONEY, ANDREW 317
TRIPUCKA, KELLY 318
TWYMAN, JACK 319
UNSELD, WES 322
VAN ARSDALE, DICK 323
VAN ARSDALE, TOM 323
VANDEWEGHE, KIKI 324
VAN LIER, NORM 325
WALKER, CHET 326
WALLACE, RASHEED 327
WALTON, BILL 328
WANZER, BOBBY 329
WEBB, SPUD 330
WEST, JERRY 331
WESTPHAL, PAUL 332
WHITE, JO JO 333
WILKENS, LENNY 336
WILKES, JAMAAL 337
WILKINS, DOMINIQUE 338
WILLIAMS, BUCK 339
WILLIAMS, WALT 340
WILLIAMSON, JOHN 341
WILLIS, KEVIN 344
WINTERS, BRIAN 345
WOOLRIDGE, ORLANDO 346
WORTHY, JAMES 347
YARDLEY, GEORGE 348
ZASLOFSKY, MAX 349

PICTURE CREDITS

The images in this book have been supplied by the author and by the organizations listed below. -

- ARCHIVE PHOTOS of 530 West 25th Street, New York, NY 10001-5518, USA

- ALLSPORT UK, 3 Greenlea Park, Prince George's Road, London SW19 2JD, England, UK

-THE JAMES NAISMITH MEMORIAL HALL OF FAME, 1150 West Columbus Avenue, Springfield, Massachusetts, MA 01101-0179, USA

- NBA PHOTO LIBRARY, NBA Properties Inc., 450 Harmon Meadow Boulevard, Secaucus 07094, USA

The author would like to thank colleagues at Bowling Green University, St John's University, Louisiana State University, Stanford University, The University of Toledo, Madison Square Garden, the Indiana Pacers, the Chicago Bulls, the Detroit Pistons, the Washington Bullets and the Syracuse Post Standard. While every effort has been made to ensure this listing is correct, both the publisher and the author apologize for any credit omissions.

Page 249 Brian Bahr; pages 203, 219, 240, 309, 318 Bill Baptist; pages 72, 150, 185 Al Bello; pages 172, 269, 313, 351 Andrew D. Bernstein; pages 9, 19, 70, 108,

194, 222, 237, 285 Nathaniel S. Butler; pages 82, 106, 154, 194 Louis Capozzola; page 82 Chris Covatta; pages 61, 113, 165, 169, 194, 209, 218, 236, 337 Jim Cummins; page 87 Jon D. Cuban; pages 26, 37, 61, 79, 83, 90, 109, 114, 121, 135, 147, 168, 169, 183, 195, 202, 236, 260, 281, 308, 309, 310, 311, 312, 316, 317, 346 Scott Cunningham; pages 2, 6, 8, 12, 18, 21, 22, 39, 40, 53, 54, 64, 85, 93, 94, 100, 101, 104, 105, 117, 139, 142, 143, 144, 161, 164, 176, 196, 212, 228, 238, 242, 247, 248, 253, 257, 263, 268, 274, 280, 281, 296, 302, 303, 304, 315, 327, 330, 332, 336, 338, 340, 350 Jonathan Daniel; pages 96, 239, 267 Steve Diapola; page 70 Gary Dineen; pages 87, 99, 151, 273, 324 Brian Drake; pages 14, 181, 198, 267,

328 Stephen Dunn; pages 10, 36, 57, 64, 95, 207, 227, 242, 339 Tim Defrisco; pages 92, 295, 334 Sam Forencich; pages 157, 177, 255, 345 Barry Gossage; pages 12, 51, 72, 142, 210, 214, 227, 255, 286, 300, 305 Otto Greule; pages 166, 181, 187, 256, 310 Jim Gund; page 249 Elsa Hasch; pages 26, 50, 131, 176, 177 Andy Hayt; page 327 David Hernandez; page 138 John C. Hillary; pages 49, 185, 202, 252 Jed Jacobsohn; page 92 Glenn James; page 66 Naum Kashdan; pages 120, 179, 282 George Kalinsky; pages 115, 132, 133 Neil Leifer; page 272 Tod Marchan; pages 11, 113, 297, 347 Ronald C. Modra; page 199 Layne Murdoch; pages 19, 69, 165, 251, 253, 283, 341 Anthony Neste; page 13 J. Patronite; pages 150, 170, 180,

214, 247, 263, 305 Doug Pensinger; page 264, 265 Mike Powell; pages 11, 60, 69, 106, 130, 188, 201, 216, 234, 235, 241, 245, 270, 284, 332, 333 Dick Raphael; pages 25, 29, 35, 62, 67, 86, 108, 114, 131, 135, 154, 168, 188, 201, 241, 289, 314, 316, 322, 336, 337 Wen Roberts; page 346 Jon Soohoo; pages 224, 245 Harry Scull; pages 207, 262, 302 Tom Smart; page 170 Jamie Squire; page 328 Rick Stewart; pages 36, 99, 243, 296, 324 Damian Strohmeyer; page 295 Noren Trotman; pages 134, 184, 266 Jerry Wachter; page 334 Scott Wachter.